Contents at a Glance

Part VII: Sales   *243*

Part VIII: Globalization   *333*

Table of Contents

Part II Research and Development

Part III Human Resources

Part IV Production and Operations Management

Part V Information Management

Part VI Marketing

16 COORDINATING BRAND RECOGNITION 235

Part VII Sales

17 SALES FORCE AUTOMATION 245

Part VIII Globalization

About the Authors

About the Author

Lead Author

Joseph Lowery has been writing about computers and new technology since 1981. He is the author of *Buying Online for Dummies*, the technical editor for *Selling Online for Dummies*, a reviewer for *Wired* magazine, and a contributing editor to the online consumer electronics magazine, *Gadgetboy*. He is the author of the *Dreamweaver Bible* and the *Ten Minute Guide to Internet Explorer 4.0*. Joe has contributed to the *Special Edition Using Microsoft Word 97, Bestseller Edition* and *Microsoft Office 97 Small Business Edition 6-in-1* books.

In addition to teaching people how to use computers through his books, Joe also trains individuals, classes, and corporations how to get the most out of their Office 97 applications. He has taught advanced Word skills to other trainers going for certification as well as secretaries looking for the inside techniques that will land them their next promotion. Joe has helped corporate accountants speed up their work with Excel macros and salesmen output quarterly presentations with PowerPoint. Recently, Joe developed an automated billing system for a video rental company that used Access, Excel, and Word and a publish-to-the-Web database for an online store. He specializes in real-world solutions for real-world problems by using the full complement of Office 97 programs and any third-party software that eases the workload.

Joe is currently Webmaster for the MCP Office 97 Resource Center as well as other sites for a variety of clients, including a managed health care organization, a stock market research firm, and a bar. Joe and his wife, the dancer/choreographer Debra Wanner, have a daughter, Margot who hogs the computer.

Contributing Authors

Cliff Allen has more than 20 years' experience in the marketing and sales of technology products, and was an early user of the Internet. After a career in radio and television, he worked for computer companies before starting his own marketing communications that focuses on helping companies use the Web to build relationships with customers. His enthusiasm for the Internet began in 1989 when his firm was one of the first marketing communications companies to help businesses grow and prosper using the Internet. In addition to writing articles about the Internet for various magazines, Cliff is co-author of two books about applying one-to-one Web marketing principles: the *Web Catalog CookBook* and the *Internet World Guide to One-to-One Web Marketing*. He speaks at national conferences about using the Web to build relationships and conducts workshops for corporate executives looking to use the Web to increase awareness and sales.

Johnny Jackson is an IT professional experienced in web programming, electronic commerce, and cryptography. He specializes in building virtual storefronts, online catalogs, and secure payment systems. He is currently helping a number of private clients to develop secure, online commercial applications. He is also employed as a full-time web programmer with Macmillan Publishing's online division. Johnny currently resides in Indianapolis, Indiana, with his wife Heather, and two daughters, Amber and Alexis. If you have questions for Johnny about secure online transactions or electronic commerce in general, he can be reached at johnny@newguitar.com. (No spam, please!)

Kevin Kloss is a Project Manager for Macmillan Digital Publishing. He was a contributing author for *Upgrading PC's Illustrated*, *Platinum Edition Using Windows 95*, and developed more than a dozen books on Windows NT/95, Visual Basic, and networking. In a previous position with Quality Systems, Inc., Kevin worked as a technical consultant for the company's specialized Management Information Systems (MIS). Kevin has a B.S. from Eastern Michigan University, and currently lives in Carmel, Indiana, with his wife Michelle.

Marcia Layton Turner has had an avid online presence for many years, serving as a Start-Up Consultant with CompuServe's International Entrepreneurs forum in the early 90s, then as a Start-Up Coach with iVillage's About Work Web site, and as a content provider to Macmillan's Online Resource Center. As a result, she has secured tens of thousands of dollars of business, has earned national publicity, and has met many interesting people around the world. A non-fiction author, Ms. Layton's book, *Successful Fine Art Marketing* (The Consultant Press, Ltd.) was published in December 1993. She also co-authored the *Complete Idiot's Guide to Starting Your Own Business*, which has sold more than 100,000 copies and is in its second edition. Her latest work, the *Complete Idiot's Guide to Terrific Business Writing* was released in July 1996. Ms. Layton received an M.B.A. from the University of Michigan Business School and a B.A. with Honors from Wellesley College.

Dedication

To Debra, who was born on the same day as W. B. Yeats, Christo, Basil Rathbone, Ally Sheedy, and Paul Lynde. Because you have the best of their qualities, as well as your own style and my heart, this book is for you.

Acknowledgements

You may not normally think of writing as a social act, but it is. Imagine being part of a team of people you've never met who are all working together to achieve your goals. That's writing today—and I'm happy to report that my team for *Netrepreneur: The Dimensions of Transferring Your Business Model to the Internet* never blinked, even under some knuckle-whitening (not to mention hair-whitening) conditions. Thanks to Karen Reinisch and Don Essig of MCP for getting me in the cockpit and strapping me down before this particular rocket launched. Another team member, Anne Martinez, contributed very insightful suggestions during her technical edit and her work is much appreciated. I'd especially like to express my gratitude to Noelle Gasco for her unswerving dedication to the heart of the book; without you, Noelle, this book would be far, far less and I'm extremely grateful for your encouragement and your courage.

Other team members responded with amazing work under fearsome deadlines. I'd like to thank contributors Marcia Layton, Cliff Allen, Johnny Jackson, and Kevin Kloss for all their hard work. The next round is on me, everyone—actually, that should probably be the next couple of rounds given the tremendous effort that everyone put in. Thanks again.

Finally, I'd like to thank all the business men and women who took precious moments out of their work-crazed days to assist me. Chief among them are Lisa Donlan of EFAP New York and Jean-Christophe Muyl of C3i, Inc. who not only offered core material during the book's development but also graciously opened up their address books and contact managers to me. May all your ventures be fully capitalized and your benefactors, silent.

Introduction

Getting Up to Speed

The standard manufacturing joke is, "You can have it soon, right, or cheap—pick any two." Enabling an Internet strategy, as described throughout this book, brings all three elusive goals within reach: expedience, quality, and value.

- When I asked an expert in Sales Force Automation what he thought the Internet meant to business in general, he had one word for me: speed. Every aspect of business touched by the Internet—or any of its variations, such as an intranet or extranet—enables companies to act much faster. It doesn't matter if you're talking about market research, product design, sales and marketing, fulfillment, or expansion, the enhanced communication quickens every process.

- What's the cornerstone of Total Quality Management? Quality in every element of the enterprise. A fully realized Internet/intranet strategy enables the flow of information from all segments of a business. Most importantly, an integrated Internet system can give managers and all employees ownership of their respective divisions and responsibilities.

- Intranets have proven time and again to be one of the most cost-effective investments a company can make. An intranet solves the problems it was brought online for—and then goes on bringing more cost benefits to an organization, across the board. What can you call a technology that typically offers a return on investment topping 1000% other than a "no-brainer?"

Many books on the World Wide Web focus on its marketing and selling potential. After all, you've got a global marketplace that just opened up—that's pretty hard to ignore. However, what many enterprises miss are the implications offered by a worldwide network. *Netrepreneur: The Dimensions of Transferring Your Business Model to the Internet* addresses all of those implications and shows you how to best exploit the advantages and avoid the pitfalls.

What is a Netrepreneur? A Netrepreneur is a businessman first and a technologist second. A Netrepreneur recognizes the potential for raising the bottom line hidden deep within the worldwide network called the Internet. A Netrepreneur sees the needs throughout the enterprise and completes that need with the best from developing technologies. A Netrepreneur uses Internet/intranet strategies to gain a global advantage.

How This Book Is Organized

I've structured this book the same way you've structured your business. Each of the key components of an enterprise are represented in their own part. Within each part, you'll find chapters highlighting the significant advantages that an Internet/intranet strategy can bring. Throughout the book, case studies are used to demonstrate how other organizations have integrated the technology to gain a competitive edge.

Part I: The Business of the Internet

When you're first investigating a major new direction for your organization you need to know three things: what are the advantages, what are the risks, and what does it cost? Part 1 supplies the necessary information for you to gauge the worth of implementing an Internet/intranet strategy. Chapter 3, "Technology Investment," details the various expenditure areas for integrating an intranet into a typical mid-sized business.

Part II: Research and Development

The Internet isn't called the Information Superhighway for nothing. Whether you're researching marketing demographics, conducting an electronic survey, or seeking competitive intelligence to out-maneuver a competitor, the Internet is a treasure-trove of information—and Part II explains how best to unearth that treasure. You'll also find case studies that describe how other companies have used the Internet and their intranets especially to share data across the enterprise.

Part III: Human Resources

It's been said that a corporation's greatest resource is its employees. The Internet can make that statement much more than an annual report truism—fully Web-savvy personnel bring a much enhanced productivity to your organization. This part covers using the Internet to educate your employees (even if you're educating them about the Internet itself) as well as tapping into the global job-bank that has emerged.

Part IV: Production and Operations Management

Before the wide-spread adoption of the Internet, the hope of applying just in time methodology across the enterprise was remote at best. Part IV covers just in time strategies all along the supply chain on through the distribution chain. A special section is devoted to demonstrating how bringing legacy electronic data interchange (EDI) into the Internet age can benefit your organization. The final chapter in this part covers the growing trend of outsourcing logistics and how the Internet can keep this option cost effective and manageable.

Part V: Information Management

Information Technology (IT) departments are among the fastest growing sectors of the modern enterprise. Part V shows, with case study after case study, how IT forms the heart of an Internet/intranet strategy. Of particular note are business-to-business extranets, which extend the power of the internal intranet to a corporation's partners. You'll also see how various organizations have taken the additional step of opening extranet to their customer base.

Part VI: Marketing

The Internet is a marketer's dream: a new medium available to a worldwide audience, 24 hours a day, year around. In addition to covering the ins-and-outs of online marketing—through Web sites, banner ads, email, and other venues—Part VI investigates techniques for handling the voluminous amount of direct response. Along with these new medium comes new methods for increasing the value of your company's brands; these methods and more are covered in the final chapter in this part.

Part VII: Sales

While selling products through your Web site can impact significantly on almost any company's bottom line, electronic commerce can mean so much more. Sales Force Automation (SFA) can be a major force in centralizing an organization's Internet efforts as well as increasing the profit margin. Part VII opens with an in-depth look at the present and future possibilities for SFA. After exploring all you'll need to know to direct your company's online sales effort, the part concludes with a look at new business models that have emerged through the Internet—many of which could open another revenue stream for your company.

Part VIII: Globalization

If there's any part of the Web that gets a growing company's juices flowing, it's the "worldwide" aspect. Part VIII looks at the advantages opened up for global business-to-business partnerships as well as the techniques necessary for expanding into international markets. This part concludes with a look at how an Internet/intranet strategy can be beneficial to your expansion efforts, whether you're interested in merging or acquiring other companies.

Elements of This Book

Throughout the book, you'll notice some terms that may be new to you are italicized, such as *intranet*. While these terms are explained in context of their use, you'll find a fuller explanation of them in the Glossary. Other special elements include the Case Studies, which have a brief business profile of the organizations examined and the FAQs, which are designed to answer those Frequently Asked Questions that can crop up so often. Finally, the Appendix is a compilation of Web site resources of special interest to the net-centric CEO. Each Web site is described with an Internet address for easy viewing.

PART

I

The Business of the Internet

Advantages of the Cutting Edge

- Improving internal communication

- Working with your suppliers and vendors

- Reaching out to old and new customers

- Broadening your market share

Wired for Business with the Internet

A business is made up of many separate parts: administration, production, sales, marketing, and so on. For a business to survive, much less thrive, it must connect internally as well as with outside entities—suppliers, distributors, wholesalers, retailers, and finally, customers. Throughout history, businesses have made increasingly more efficient connections between their internal organization and these external entities. From the earliest sea-going trade routes to the latest satellite communication, each era brings a better way to transact business.

Overall, the Internet is the most efficient business communication medium in existence today—not because it's the fastest mode of communication, but because it's the fullest, offering the capacity for a complete exchange of information from all parties involved.

FAQ: What's the difference between the Internet and the Web?
Technically, the Internet preceded the World Wide Web by several years. Originally the Internet was a text-document-only medium, and the Web first brought images online and later, multimedia. However, the two terms are used interchangeably today.

To some, making a business and Internet connection means putting up a Web site—or at most, an online storefront. Although these are beneficial and, in some cases, extremely lucrative, a Web site is only one aspect of an all-encompassing Internet strategy.

SEE ALSO

➤ *To learn more about establishing a Web site, see page 245.*

➤ *For the inside scoop on selling online, see page 287.*

If your business is not taking full advantage of the Internet, you're history. A few compelling examples demonstrate its importance:

- In six months of operation, Boeing Co. sold over $25 million in airplane parts to its established vendor base—through the Internet.

- Covering both retail and business-to-business, computer manufacturer Dell pulls in over $3 million in orders per day from its Web site.

- Web-based bookseller Amazon.com reports that 55% of its sales are to repeat customers.

- In addition to raking in over $250 million in its first year of operation, Cisco Connection Online, a major manufacturer of networking equipment, saved another $250 million in product literature distribution and staff time.

- Columbia Healthcare/HCA Healthcare Corp. screens cold calls from vendors through the Web by having medical supply houses prequalify through an online form.

- Independent truckers can log on to Volvo Trucks North America's Web site and customize and purchase a $120,000 Volvo cab online.

If your competitors have not taken full advantage of the Internet, you can bet it's only a matter of time. What makes the Internet so strategically vital is the degree and type of communication it makes possible—internally, business-to-business, and with your customer base.

Internal Communication

The Internet can centralize your communication system regardless of how far flung your operations may be. Three key areas where the Internet can benefit your company's internal communication are

- Messaging
- Administration
- Publishing

Messaging

Email is often considered the killer application for both *intranet* and Internet use. Email can be reviewed more quickly than voice-mail, sent to multiple parties, and forwarded and incorporated easily into other documents. Moreover, email can act as a courier for the transportation of other documents—and even other media. But messaging isn't just about email. Messaging is the ability to share information to a select set of people, whether it's one person or a hundred thousand people.

FAQ: What's the difference between the Internet and an intranet?
The Internet is the large public communication network that links computers around the world. An intranet is a company network that enables access out to the Internet—and sometimes access in.

Case Study: BC Telecom
BC TELECOM is Canada's second-largest telecommunications company, with approximately 2.5 million customer access lines. The company's net earnings for 1997 were $286.7 million. BC TELECOM is listed as BCT on the Toronto, Montreal, and Vancouver stock exchanges and maintains a Web site at www.bctel.com.

BC Telecom, whose home page on the Web is shown in Figure 1.1, deployed a state-of-the-art intranet and messaging infrastructure to replace its aging mainframe system with its separate applications for email, calendaring, and human resources. The company is highly diverse, and its new messaging system manages over 60 internal *newsgroups* accessed by about 5,000 people. The newsgroups provide an ongoing discussion that can answer frequently asked questions.

BC Telecom uses a *certificate server* to authenticate users from within the intranet and to allow outside callers access through the Internet. Employees can check their email no matter where they might be. The certificate server can also handle *encrypting* sensitive email and emailed documents.

Like many intranets, BC Telecom standardizes on a particular browser for all its users' systems or *clients*. Most browsers maintain a common look-and-feel for the different messaging applications, which saves considerable expense in information technology training.

Administration

Any office needs to keep in constant touch with all its employees. The advent of the intranet has opened up a hotline of communication. Now, for instance, instead of Human Resources distributing memo after unread memo, the information can be published once on the company intranet and accessed as needed. More importantly, updates can be handled by altering a single source, rather than republishing and redistributing to the entire organization.

Figure 1.1   BC Telecom integrates email with other messaging services to solidify the internal communication.

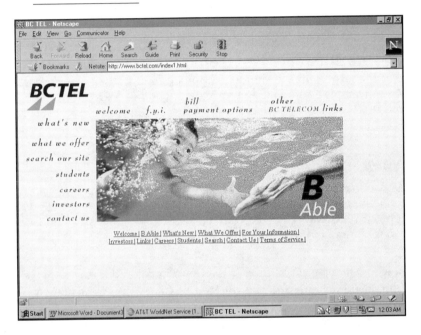

Case Study: AT&T

AT&T is the world's leading voice and data communications company, serving more than 90 million customers, including consumers, businesses, and government. With annual revenues of more than $51 billion, AT&T provides services to more than 250 countries and territories around the world.

AT&T uses the Internet to connect its global intranet system and communicate with its 300,000 plus employees. AT&T's system includes the following innovative features:

- To facilitate the various business units working together with multiple budgets and expense transfers, AT&T has instituted a universal currency system that uses "digital cash." This intranet e-commerce system enables AT&T to stay decentralized while eliminating the overhead expense that usually accompanies decentralized billing systems.

- Ordering office supplies is a necessary but time-consuming chore. AT&T has adapted its global procurement organization with a Web interface to its internal ordering systems so that employees can order supplies online—and check for stockroom availability, as well.

- The first component of AT&T's intranet was an internal contacts database with employee phone numbers, addresses, titles, and business units. With the browser-based interface, users can find contacts up and down the organizational ladder by pointing and clicking.

As you might suspect, AT&T has invested heavily, financially and corporately, in the Internet. And the investment is paying off. AT&T uses the Internet to access, work with, and distribute information throughout its vast organization.

Publishing

It's one thing to give your employees around-the-clock access to corporate documents; it's quite another to give them the power to publish key departmental information on their own. Empowering employees in this manner helps keep the most current information available to everyone from a centralized source. Ideas are shared across divisional or even international lines; staffs can easily adapt existing documents to be Web ready; and both time and money are saved on distributing publications throughout the enterprise.

Case Study: Ciba-Geigy
Ciba-Geigy AG is a leading worldwide pharmaceutical and chemical company that provides products and services for health care, agriculture, and industry. The company is headquartered in Basel, Switzerland and maintains a Web site at www.ciba.com.

Ciba-Geigy needed to find a way to coordinate communication among its 80,000 employees in 50 countries. Faxes and email placed the burden on the staff to take on additional duties, such as filing and sorting; still, employees were unsure whether the information was the most current available. The answer was the centralized source made possible by the Internet.

FAQ: How difficult is publishing on the Internet?
The basic language of the Internet and intranet alike is HTML, which, although relatively easy to learn, is not a required skill for basic Web publishing. The latest word processing software offers a Save As HTML feature whereby any document can be stored on the Web. More complex documents can be built from answers supplied on a form and then submitted for processing and publication. Bottom line: although it's not a no-brainer, it's not difficult to put up basic text. However, establishing an entire site requires much more skill, both in design and programming.

As new product information emerges from the development labs, it can be published direct-ly to the internal Web for dissemination to the sales and marketing departments. The cen-tralized information source also helped Ciba-Geigy leverage its international connections because employees in different countries could share problems and solutions at the press of a "publish" button.

Business-to-Business Communication

No business is an island. Without suppliers and distributors, you can't leverage your growth potential into something real. The Internet opens a whole new channel of communication between your business and your business partners. An intranet that has been extended to include a company's business associates is referred to as an *extranet*.

Whenever a company opens its internal affairs to outside eyes, security has to be addressed. Modern Internet technology lets you set the level that various external companies can reach in your information infrastructure. Generally, the more information that can be shared be-tween business partners, the faster both can complete their transactions. Opening up your extranet can effectively remove layers of middlemen.

SEE ALSO

➤ *To find out more about what it takes to protect your Internet connection, see page 17.*

Case Study: The Boeing Company
With assets in 1997 of $45.8 billion and a recent merger with McDonnell Douglas, the Boeing Company is well positioned to serve three principal aerospace markets—com-mercial, military, and space. The company has an extensive global reach with customers in 145 countries and operations in 27 U.S. states. Worldwide, Boeing and its subsidiaries employ more than 238,000 people.

The Boeing Co., whose home page on the Web is shown in Figure 1.2, maintains an inven-tory of 410,000 parts for a wide range of airplanes. Airline and aviation repair shops require a speedy delivery for ordered equipment. Boeing has implemented an extranet to facilitate the straightforward purchasing of repair parts. Valued customers are registered and given a password to gain entry into the Boeing extranet.

Using the extranet, customers can check inventory during the ordering process to avoid back orders. After a part is requested, it's removed from inventory and shipment is guaran-teed within 24 hours. Customers are emailed a separate confirmation of the order and the tracking information. The extranet allows ordering around the clock with no additional staffing requirements. Because the Boeing goods are of a known and respected quality, no personal inspection is necessary, and the availability and price quoting are handled without middlemen.

Figure 1.2   The Boeing Company lets customers order repair parts directly through its extranet.

Customer Communication

One method of building brand loyalty is to establish ongoing communication with your customers. The Internet can give your customers a central information source that can be easily updated and maintained by your office. In addition, online customers can receive special sales bulletins directly in their email inbox. By opening up the information flow with product information and related value-added data, a business can broaden a customer's comfort level and reinforce the bonds between itself and its customer base.

Sales information, in exhaustive detail, can be posted on an online storefront for easy customer access. Customer support can also be directed largely through the Internet. Moreover, online ordering allows customers to circumvent lengthy back-order delays, while simultaneously informing management of requested, but unavailable, items.

SEE ALSO

➤ *To see how your company can cut down on back orders, see page 108.*

Case Study: KinderCare Learning Centers

KinderCare Learning Centers is the largest preschool and child-care company in the United States. As of 1997, the company operates more than 1,150 child-care centers in 38 states and the United Kingdom; it has more than 23,000 employees, and enrolls approximately 126,000 children.

In addition to product-specific information, the Internet allows a company to attach a wide variety of value-added information and services to its Web site, thus becoming an identifiable resource in the minds of its customers. KinderCare Learning Centers, for example, a chain of child-care centers in the U.S. and the United Kingdom, offers parents a central resource for parenting information, as well as links to child-oriented activities. In addition, the KinderCare Web site allows parents to search for the nearest center—and even provides them with directions and a map. KinderCare plans to expand its Web site to include center-specific information such as staff profiles, education, experience, and accreditation data.

Technology improves customer communication

Customer communication can even take advantage of cutting-edge technologies. A rival child-care facility offers the "baby-cam," which allows parents, after entering a password to keep out prying eyes, to remotely view their children at the center through the Internet. The picture is updated every 15 seconds and made available on the Web.

Expanding the Customer Base

What would you say to a store that is open 24 hours a day, 365 days a year, is available to almost any customer on the planet, and requires only minimum staffing? Storefronts on the World Wide Web offer all these advantages and more. The Web gives companies a global opportunity to attract—and sell to—customers.

Internet access is approaching a truly worldwide reach with all manner of consumers coming online. Fears of e-commerce security are going by the wayside as more customers buy products over the Internet without incident. A wider range of payment options—from traditional credit cards and checking accounts to digital cash solutions—is now available. Products targeted to a narrow market don't have to be placed in a mall to assure enough traffic because the world is your new marketplace.

SEE ALSO

➤ *To find out more about the various Internet payment options, see page 313.*

The Internet doesn't just bring a world of potential new customers to your storefront, it can also enhance brand loyalty and redouble marketing efforts for your offline products as well. The Internet can help your business-customer relations in three primary ways:

- Reaching new customers

- Retaining prior customers

- Upselling and cross-selling current customers

Reaching New Customers

Expanding the customer base likens any business to a shark—it's got to keep moving or it dies. Selling online gives your company an opportunity to broaden your base without regard for geographic or even temporal boundaries. And if your business is a small one, customer expansion is extremely important. One method is to run an online store and use some of the marketing bullets in your Internet arsenal, such as marketing surveys and direct contact with established customers through email.

One small business, Dog Toys of West Chester, Pennsylvania, found that it can enhance both its direct sales and its retailer connections through an online store. Dog Toys, with its specialty market of toys for pets, would have a hard time making a go of it in a traditional storefront. Selling online opens up the possibility of an almost limitless customer base—Dog Toys reports selling to clients in Germany and Singapore. Furthermore, the high-rent, high-maintenance storefront required by a mall in a major traffic area is neatly side-stepped with the virtual store.

Dog Toys finds more new customers by developing toys requested in online surveys. By partnering with high-traffic, related sites, Dog Toys can conduct valuable market research in exchange for product. In addition, email gives the company an easy method for responding to product queries. As any salesperson can tell you, after you establish a rapport with a potential buyer, you're one step closer to a sell. Prompt email responses can have a definite impact on increased sales.

Retaining Prior Customers

The only thing worse than not getting any new customers is losing the ones you already have. All businesses must devote resources to preventing the erosion of their customer base. A complete Internet strategy can make your company leaner and more competitive, thus providing basic customer incentives such as innovative products and lower prices. In addition, the Internet can help you earn your current customers' brand loyalty. One tactic is to simplify the ordering process.

At present, online ordering involves filling out a series of forms with customer information, such as shipping address and credit card information. Savvy online stores, such as bookseller Amazon.com, maintain an account for each online customer that stores the vital information on its secure server. To access the account, a user name and password are required. (Should a different shipping address be desired, Amazon.com requires the credit card information be re-entered, further protecting the customer.) With policies such as these, it's no wonder that Amazon has a 55% return customer rate.

The Internet can also be used to provide a feedback mechanism for current customers. Ford's Web site gives the customer access to a high-level executive, the Group Vice-President of Marketing, Sales & Service, to foster the sense of responsiveness and community. In addition to binding the customer closer to the company, direct response is valuable information in and of itself.

Companies with technical products use the Internet to provide another route for customer support. Computer products, both hardware and software, are ideal for multi-tiered support systems. Microsoft, for example, has a searchable knowledge base in which business partners, consultants, and end users can find solutions to existing problems—or report new ones. The company's Web site also has a trouble-shooting "wizard" to help diagnose specific system difficulties. In addition, Microsoft uses the Web to market its premium support opportunities in which response time is tied to the charge—the more the customer pays, the more quickly the problem is solved.

Upselling and Cross-selling

As any salesperson worth his or her salt knows, after you've got your foot in the door, it's time to see what other products the customer is interested in. The Internet offers several innovative methods for creating the upselling opportunity, far beyond the "Want fries with that?" approach.

As online customers make purchases, their buying habits begin to leave a trail for companies to follow. Certain e-commerce software can tailor upsell offers to take advantage of both the customer's desires and the company's needs. If, for example, a customer just bought a new pair of brown shoes, the vendor could offer a shoe-polish kit at a special low price while the customer is still online. I once placed an order for a radio-controlled UFO from Hammacher-Schlemmer's online store, only to be offered a deal on extra helium tanks as I completed the checkout form.

Moreover, additional product selling doesn't have to be so directly linked. Cross-selling can be much more subtle—and effective. The major search engines, such as Yahoo! and Excite, attempt to offer context-sensitive advertising. Put in an entry for "scanner" and you might get a banner ad for a new Xerox product that promises to do more with your scanner. Or you can click the Amazon.com link to look for books based on your search request.

Microsoft recently purchased Firefly, whose *intelligent agent* technology recommends other products that customers might like based on their current orders. Firefly and similar technologies are very effective in online music and book stores, where the customer is likely to be open to trying something similar but unfamiliar. It's also possible to apply the technology to unrelated products based on consumer buying habits.

FAQ: How does Recommending Software work?

Firefly uses a technology it refers to as Automated Collaborative Filtering. Sites employing the Firefly system make recommendations to customers based on what other people with similar tastes buy. If, for example, you purchase a book by the latest, top-of-the-charts mystery author, Firefly searches its database for other people who bought the same book. Then it examines what else they bought; if Firefly finds a significant overlap with many people buying the same book, that book is offered to you.

Bottom Line

Netscape commissioned a study on an intranet's return on investment from the International Data Corporation (IDC). Whereas most financial managers look for a return of 20 percent or better on technology investments, the IDC study found that the typical company achieved a return of 1,000 percent or better—one company's return reached an astounding 1,766 percent!

The other significant find was the short *payback period*. The payback period is the time it takes for the project to return enough money to cover the investment. IDC found the payback period for a fully integrated intranet project to range from six to twelve weeks, indicating that an intranet project carries an extremely low risk of not recovering the investment.

Where do the savings come from? Overall, three main areas are considered:

- *Training*. Because Internet/intranet applications rely on one central interface—the browser—to handle all applications, training time (and costs) are significantly reduced; fewer outside trainers and less class time are needed.

- *Productivity*. Centralizing information increases productivity across the board. Multiplying even a small fraction of the time saved per employee results in significant savings.

- *Communication Costs* . The implementation of many intranets leads to the wholesale slashing of costly publications, such as newsletters, employee manuals, and directories. Additional savings are derived from using email to transmit messages almost instantly around the world, in contrast to reproducing and overnighting documents.

To better understand how an intranet project can impact on a company's bottom line, let's take a look at a typical return-on-investment (ROI) worksheet. The worksheet shown in Table 1.1 is taken from the IDC intranet study and details return-on-investment information for Booz, Allen & Hamilton, Inc., an international management and technology consulting firm.

The return on investment for Booz Allen was typical of the study: 1,389 percent with a payback period of .19 years (about 12 business weeks). Most of Booz Allen's savings came from the elimination of fax, overnight deliveries, and telephone calls ($130,000), and the centralizing of information leading to a significant savings in a consultant's time to find and access accurate employee information ($6,969,600).

Table 1.1 ROI Worksheet for Booz, Allen & Hamilton Intranet Project

Annual Savings	Base	Year 1	Year 2	Year 3
Personnel Savings	$0	$6,969,600	$6,969,600	$6,969,600
Savings in Communications	$0	$130,000	$130,000	$130,000
Total Savings Per Period	$0	$7,099,600	$7,099,600	$7,099,600

Depreciation Schedule	Initial	Year 1	Year 2	Year 3
Software	$61,818	$0	$0	$0
Network Upgrades	$29,091	$0	$0	$0
Hardware	$218,182	$43,636	$43,636	$43,636
Total Per Period	**$309,091**	**$43,636**	**$43,636**	**$43,636**

Expensed Costs	Initial	Year 1	Year 2	Year 3
Maintenance	$0	$30,909	$30,909	$30,909
Personnel	$670,000	$783,636	$783,636	$783,636
Consulting	$30,000	$0	$0	$0
Training	$29,212	$29,212	$0	$0
Total Per Period	**$729,212**	**$843,757**	**$814,545**	**$814,545**

Annual Savings	Base	Year 1	Year 2	Year 3
Basic Financial Assumptions				
All Federal and State Taxes	50%			
Discount Rate	15%			
Depreciation - Straight Line (Years)	5			
Net Cash Flows	**Initial**	**Year 1**	**Year 2**	**Year 3**
Total Benefits		$7,099,600	$7,099,600	$7,099,600
Less Total Costs	$1,038,302	$843,757	$814,545	$814,545
Less Depreciation		$43,636	$43,636	$43,636
Net Profit Before Tax	$1,038,302	$6,212,207	$6,241,418	$6,241,418
Net Profit After Tax	$519,151	$3,106,103	$3,120,709	$3,120,709
Add Depreciation		$43,636	$43,636	$43,636
Net Cash Flow After Taxes	($519,151)	$3,149,740	$3,164,345	$3,164,345
Financial Analysis	**Results**	**Year 1**	**Year 2**	**Year 3**
Annual ROI		528%	988%	1,389%
3-Year ROI	1,389%			
Payback (Years)	0.19			
3-Year IRR	605%			
3-Year NPV	$6,693,061			

Risk Assessment

- Avoiding perils on the Information Superhighway

- Coordinating a security policy

- Basic components of Internet security

- Assuring remote security

The Dangers of Putting Your Business Online

By far, the biggest risk your company faces regarding the Internet is *not* fully using it. However, inherent dangers are involved in working closely with the Internet—and carefully defined solutions as well.

Why are hazards associated with the Internet? Whether you have a complete online storefront on the World Wide Web that hooks into your central database for inventory control, or whether you just allow your salespeople to dial in to the intranet for updates, you're allowing outside access to your company's internal network. That access, if not carefully controlled, can turn into a nightmare.

Although the vast majority of visitors to your Web site are innocent browsers and, hopefully, shoppers, a few aren't so innocent. The intent of malice runs the gamut:

- Some interlopers break into your network for the thrill of it and content themselves with a "look, but don't touch" tour.

Hackers show off for the world
Hackers looking for personal attention can alter your Web site's home page. The Fox Television Network's Web site was "hacked" in December, 1997, and its home page was replaced with the message, "Sorry Scully I can't give you my heart cause it belongs to the beautiful, wonderful Heike and NOTHING can change it!" The Fox logo was replaced with one incorporating the initials of the hacker's group—ADM.

- Certain hackers use their skills to show off; they prefer to alter files on your Web site to publicly show their prowess in an Information Age form of graffiti.

- Unauthorized users can invade the network and attempt to modify or crash the system.

- Vital company information can be stolen by cyber criminals—either by direct download or by eavesdropping on the Internet traffic—with the intent to use information, such as customers' credit card numbers, for direct profit or to sell to the highest bidder.

Unfortunately, not all attacks—of any level—come from outside the organization. A study of 300 Australian companies by accounting firm Deloitte Touch Tohmatsu found that 37 percent of companies had experienced some form of computer security compromise in 1997, and of those, 90 percent of the companies surveyed had traced the source of a security breach to someone within the organization. However, 60 percent of the companies also experienced attacks from external sources.

The first step in protecting your company from attacks, whether internal or external, is to develop a security policy.

Developing a Security Policy

Although many Internet security solutions are available, the tools and methods of the cyber criminal evolve quickly. To maintain a pertinent focus on the dangers, an enterprisewide security policy is vital.

An established security policy is useful on many fronts because

- It establishes the boundaries and defines for your Webmaster and other members of your Information Technology team what constitutes a violation.

- It raises the consciousness of all employees regarding Internet security.

- It serves as a list of requirements against which technical solutions can be judged.

- It creates a legal foundation for prosecution if a violation is detected.

An Internet security policy revolves around three key areas: access, authentication, and protection. *Access* determines who can retrieve what information and what they can do with it. Your network administrator can set permissions for areas, directories, and individual files on your computer system. These permissions determine whether a file is inaccessible, read-only, or editable—you can also give (or deny) permission to create files. Permissions can be given to individuals, groups of employees, or companywide. The internal newsletter should not be accessible to the general public, for example, but should be able to be read by all employees and editable only by members of the Information Services department. Your security policy should cover both the granting of access and its revocation.

Authentication is one of the thorniest issues of Internet security. The very nature of the Internet—one computer communicating with another computer—allows the identity of the user to be concealed. Authentication procedures are designed to make sure you know with whom you're dealing. Various high-end technical solutions for authenticating users have been developed, including digital certificates and smart cards, both of which are covered later in this chapter. Passwords are perhaps the simplest authentication method but, because they are easily transferred or even guessed, they are the weakest link in the security chain.

Finally, the security policy should cover what protective measures are to be implemented. Most of the protective strategies are centered on *encryption*, or the process of encoding the information to protect it from prying eyes. The protection level governs many facets of network use, including

- Login protocols for both remote and local users

- Procedures for monitoring the system for possible break-ins

- Procedures for responding to system security violations

Inviting a trespasser in

One of the most effective methods for discovering your security weaknesses is to hire an Internet security consultant to break into your network. This type of security check can alert you to undetected gaps before your system is breached by a *real* intruder.

Protecting Your Company in the Public Sector

In a meeting at the San Francisco Airport in May of 1997, an undercover FBI agent handed over $260,000 to a man who called himself "Smak." Smak passed the agent a computer disk and told him how to break the code on it. The agent inserted the disk into his laptop and verified several of the 100,000 credit card accounts it contained. Then he arrested Smak, who now faces up to 15 years in prison and a half-million dollars in fines.

How did Smak do it? He claims he got the information by hacking into various company databases and extracting the personal information, including credit card numbers, addresses, and passwords.

Is it worth doing business on the Internet where the possibility for such widespread theft exists? The short answer is "yes." However, companies that don't establish and follow a rigorous security policy are leaving their front door open for cyber criminals such as Smak.

Much of this book examines how your business can maximize its potential by using the Internet. The balance of this chapter describes some of the methods and tools available for you to protect that business. The primary tools to assure that your business is secure are

- Firewalls

- Encryption

- Digital signatures

- Digital certificates

Firewalls

In aeronautics, a firewall is a bulkhead of fire-resistant material placed between the engine of an aircraft and the rest of the structure to limit damage resulting from an engine fire. In computers, a *firewall* is a computer, router, or other communications device that protects a business's internal network from the external network that is the Internet.

The primary goal of a firewall is to allow authorized access to the Internet for email and Web searches while keeping unauthorized intruders out. Firewalls can also be used as an access control measure that allows only certain people within the organization access to the Internet. Likewise, firewalls can control the access of outsiders within the organization.

Two firewall configurations are the most common. The first places the *Web server* (the computer that actually connects the internal network to the Internet) inside the firewall, as shown in Figure 2.1. This strengthens the internal network but limits accessibility to the Internet, both in terms of speed and *bandwidth* (the amount of traffic that can travel the network at the same time), because the firewall acts as a bottleneck—slowing traffic down considerably.

Figure 2.1 Placing the Web server behind a firewall makes it far more difficult for intruders to penetrate your internal network.

The second type of firewall structure is known as the "sacrificial lamb" configuration. As shown in Figure 2.2, the Web server is placed outside the firewall, which, although making the server vulnerable, completely isolates the internal network. The key here is not to include any sensitive information on the Web server and keep all your valuable company data behind the firewall.

Generally, the sacrificial lamb configuration is a better option for enhanced security. Expenses associated with the two approaches have no appreciable difference. However, you do have to keep a close eye on the Web server to make sure no wolves have risen to the bait.

Figure 2.2 With the sacrificial lamb configuration, the Web server is placed outside the firewall.

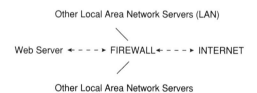

Case study: NetDaemons Associates
NetDaemons Associates is a Boston based computer consulting firm with annual revenue of $1.5 million. Its Web site is located at www.nda.com.

Although a firewall might seem to be the obvious choice for a first line of defense, sometimes even the obvious is ignored until it's too late. NetDaemons Associates, a computer network consulting firm, was contacted in February, 1995, by an Internet service provider (ISP) and accused of breaking into several Web sites the ISP hosted. Shocked and disbelieving, CEO Jennifer Lawton and Chief Technical Officer Christopher Caldwell investigated and discovered, much to their horror, that their own system had been hacked.

It took six months of investigation—including cooperation with the Secret Service—before the perpetrators could be apprehended. A band of eight hackers were responsible for breaking into various systems such as NetDaemon's, and using those systems to launch their attacks. The information, primarily credit card numbers and cellular phone IDs, were sold on the open market of hacker bulletin boards.

At the point of the computer break-in, NetDaemon Associates had been using only freely available software, which, when run monthly, made a cursory check for intrusions. Responding to the crises, NetDaemon installed a firewall to protect its system. The firewall was put in place before the hackers were caught, and it repulsed several attempts by the cyber thieves to re-enter NetDaemon's site. Aside from the blow to its core business, and the time and resources required to restore its clients' faith in them, NetDaemon regards the amount of downtime to be the most serious loss.

Encryption

Although a firewall is the primary method for controlling access, *encryption* is the main way information is protected as it travels through the Internet. Because of the way that the Internet works—with data traveling from one computer to another over various routes and sub-systems—it's possible for a talented hacker to grab bits of information (called packets) through a technique called sniffing. If the information is unprotected (and easily read), such as credit card numbers used for ordering online, the hacker can easily use the data. If, however, the packet is encrypted, the hacker's task is much more difficult.

Today's cryptography technology is based on what is known as *public-key encryption*, although it should more properly be referred to as "public-key, private-key." A pair of software "keys"—really a code that looks like a series of random numbers and letters—is used to pass secure information back and forth on the Internet. The public key is available to anyone who wants to send you a secure message and the other, the private key, is stored in your browser or security software.

1. An associate decides to send some sensitive information to you through your secure email program.

2. In addition to your email address, the associate's program also stores your public key, which is used to encode the message.

3. Should the message be intercepted, it will be scrambled and unreadable to anyone but you.

4. When you receive the message, the software on your computer uses your private key to decode the information. Only your private key can unlock the data.

Public key encryption is the underlying technology used to secure Web server transactions for electronic commerce. Developed by Netscape, the implementation is known as SSL, short for Secure Socket Layering, and has proven very effective against computer theft.

The toughest key

The strength of the encryption is measured in the amount of data that make up the key or the "bit" size. When SSL first began, 40-bit keys were thought to be adequate; unfortunately, researchers found a way to crack the code using a loose network of computers. At the present time, Internet browser users in the U.S. can upgrade the SSL included to use 128-bit public key encryption. However, the U.S. government considers encryption technology vital to national security and forbids the export of it outside the U.S. From a global business perspective, information should be routed through the most secure node first.

Digital Signatures

A second, distinct advantage to the concept of public key encryption is that it addresses the other major issue of Internet security—authentication. Just as only your private key can decode a message scrambled with your public key, the reverse is also true. When you send an encoded message, only the code identified as your public key can unlock it—thus proving that the message had to have come from you. It is, in fact, considered a *digital signature*.

Digital Certificates

While the digital signature implies your identity, the *digital certificate* states it. Digital certificates are another major reason why the Web is now "open for business." Digital certificates are issued by trusted third parties whose business it is to make sure you're who you say you are. VeriSign, Inc. is one of the primary issuers of digital certificates. Currently, digital certificates are used in business-to-business transactions; however, the new Secure Electronic Transaction (SET) standard relies on them for all electronic commerce.

Digital certificates for businesses are not issued lightly. A company must complete the information with verifiable business information, such as a Federal Tax ID and a Dun and Bradstreet reference. After the third party issues a digital certificate, it also generates a public key for the organization. The digital certificate is installed on the Web server over a secure connection.

Given enough time, any code devised by humans can be cracked by humans. So digital certificates, and their underlying public key encryption method, are dated and need to be renewed periodically. Whenever the certificate is renewed, a new code is generated and any hackers attempting to break into the system have to start all over again.

Access can be controlled through the use of certificates. Web servers or firewalls may be configured to grant access only to people with particular certificates; similarly, user systems can be configured to accept information only from Web servers that present certain certificates, which cuts down on possible computer virus contamination.

Managing Mobile Security

If your company's sales force and managers were always seated at their desks, behind the firewall, Internet security would be a lot simpler. True, your bottom line would fall through the floor, but you would have a secure system. Naturally, the real world demands that your company and its representatives be constantly on the move—and able to connect to the home office for up-to-the-minute information and support. In recent years, a whole new class of devices has emerged to handle the issue of mobile security. Smart cards and hardware tokens allow users to carry their digital certificates with them.

A *smart card* is basically a card with a magnetic stripe and an embedded microchip. Smart cards are positioned to play a major role in our electronic future, as everything from a digital cash "wallet" to a personal medical records resource. At the present time, smart cards are being used as an authentication device for remote users to log in to a secure network.

A *hardware token* provides a more flexible approach to the problem of remote authentication. A token is commonly a handheld device such as the one shown in Figure 2.3 from ActivCard. A token works with dynamic one-time passwords, in contrast to the more familiar static or re-used password. A dynamic password is generated by the hardware token based on the time and the specific token ID. When communication is established with the Web server, the dynamic password is checked against an internal database.

One key advantage to tokens is that they are software configurable. This allows for rapid deployment among large organizations; moreover, particular tokens can be easily frozen or disabled.

Both smart cards and hardware tokens use *two-factor user authentication*. Two-factor user authentication means that entry is authorized only if both of the following are confirmed:

- *Something you have.* A physical device such as a smart card or hardware token

- *Something you know.* Such as a personal identification number

Some companies are working with a third possibility, *something you are*, also known as biometrics. A biometric is a physical attribute unique to each person, such as iris patterns, retinal scans, or fingerprints.

Figure 2.3   A hardware token authenticates remote users and allows them secured access to sensitive information.

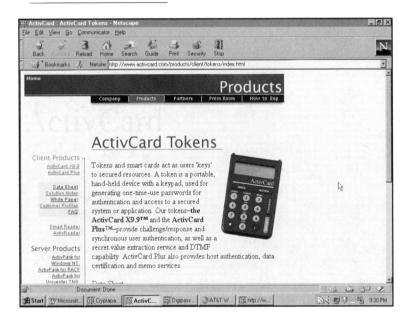

3

Technology Investment

- Costs of implementing an Internet strategy
- Detailing total cost of ownership
- Upgrading legacy systems

From Bottom Line to Top of the Line

After you've been convinced of the benefits of integrating your business into the Internet and apprised of the risks, what's left to discuss? The costs. Establishing a complete Internet strategy is neither simple nor inexpensive. However, as discussed in Chapter 1, "Advantages of the Cutting Edge," the return on investment more than justifies the cost.

And just what are those costs? The answer to that question begs several other questions:

- **What's the existing infrastructure?** Pop the hood of any business and there's no telling what computer system you're likely to find. Many older corporations are still reliant on mainframe technology that, although excellent at storing vast amounts of data, requires experts to retrieve useable information. Other companies are primed with a series of local area networks that is only waiting for a gateway to the Internet to connect them. The older the existing system, the higher your migration costs are going to be.

- **What are your goals?** As you'll see throughout this book, the Internet can impact your business in many different areas. Are you looking to shorten R&D cycles? Do you want to automate your sales force? Are you trying to cut enterprisewide costs? Do you need to expand your customer base? Are you intent on opening up another revenue stream? If your answer is, "Yes, all of the above," you need to take a hard look at the next question.

- **What are your priorities?** In December, 1995, Bill Gates announced to the world that Microsoft saw the Internet as the future, and the company rushed to embrace it—at all costs. If your organization doesn't have billions to spend on an almost overnight change of direction, it's prudent to prioritize your goals. Attempting to retool too much of the enterprise at one time can lead to duplication of efforts and skyrocketing costs—as well as overburdened employees.

Your employees feature prominently in any cost analysis. In a real sense, you must also regard them as part of the existing infrastructure and align their goals and priorities with those of the organization. Much of the savings engendered by fully utilizing the Internet for your business comes from increased productivity.

The decision about which tools to purchase is also employee-oriented. Centralizing on a particular software package can cut training and enhance efficiency. The depth of your corporation's involvement throughout the organization is also important.

Case Study: The Amdahl Corporation

The Amdahl Corporation is a supplier of complete enterprise computing solutions, meeting the critical information needs of organizations such as British Gas Technology and the New York Stock Exchange.

Consider the example of the Amdahl Corporation. To facilitate its enhanced reliance on its intranet, Amdahl first developed a Web council that consisted of managers and employees from across the corporation. The Web council's purpose was to advance the use of the intranet as an information dissemination device. They created a usage document and style guide that provided training and support. The Web council's cross-organizational collaborative nature promoted the best practices while avoiding bureaucratic stumbling blocks.

Responsibility and involvement were spread throughout the company by arranging for each division to assign an individual to manage that portion of the corporate Web. In the larger business units, the individuals gave way to Web minicouncils—thus involving more employees in content creation and information sharing.

Amdahl extended the intranet's import by beginning the WOW Club for senior management and their secretaries. The WOW Club's primary goal was to teach the value of the intranet on a one-on-one basis for these upper-management decision makers. One group of employees neglected in Amdahl's WOW Club was middle management. Getting the middle managers up to speed on the technology while raising their comfort level would have furfilitated the planning and implementation of the corporate Internet initiative.

This chapter explores both the set costs of hardware, software, and communication costs, as well as the indirect expenses such as those resulting from the downtime of an unreliable system.

Total Cost of Ownership

To truly evaluate the technology investment, you must understand the *total cost of ownership* (*TCO*). The TCO involves both direct costs—such as hardware, personnel, and communication costs and indirect costs—such as downtime and end user learning time.

Direct costs primarily are those budgeted to Information Services (IS). These include hardware, software, management labor, operations labor, and development and communication fees. Before determining the TCO for any given project, it's often necessary to reassess IS assets (such as the true number of systems and their condition), and the expenditure of labor. The clearer the picture of your baseline, the more accurate the forecast will be.

Indirect costs are generally not tracked by most IS departments, but they can have a sobering effect. When an organization cuts the IS budget line in areas such as training and help desk support, the end users take the burden on themselves—taking productive work time to "figure it out," or relying on peer support. Another major indirect cost area is downtime. When a network crashes, all work comes to a sudden and inglorious end. Not only are support personnel taken from their regular maintenance duties, but the staff takes a productivity hit across the board. Again, a bit of research for your particular organization can help quantify both the end-user support and the downtime indirect costs.

It's impossible to lay out a one-size-fits-all plan for establishing an Internet strategy— too many variables exist within the current state of the company and its future goals. The following section outlines typical (and some not-so-typical) expense areas that an organization might encounter.

To bring this overview out of the ether and offer a real-world context, each section contains a table of typical costs for a medium-size corporation with 3,000 users spread over four different locations and 75 percent of systems outdated. Standard industry rates are used throughout to give you an idea of the capital expenditure involved.

Before we delve into the details, look at Figure 3.1, which shows an overall perspective of how the costs break down.

Hardware & Software

Hardware and software costs are the annual capital expenditures associated with both desktop (PC) and network hardware and the accompanying software. The cost of purchasing new systems and upgrading existing ones is included in this category. Hardware considered as assets include PCs, laptops, servers, peripherals, hubs, bridges, routers, switches, printers, scanners, and even the network wiring.

Figure 3.1   The ongoing management of an Internet/intranet is the greatest expense in the Total Cost of Ownership.

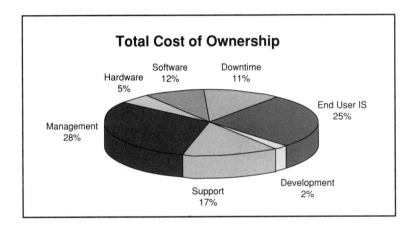

Within this category, several annual expenditures should be included. Among these are the upgrading of memory and storage (hard drives) necessary for desktop systems to keep up with increasing application requirements. You could also add annual capital expediters for computer peripherals, such as CD-ROMs, scanners, and printer memory. In addition, a budget line-item for spares could be allocated to prevent debilitating downtime for individual machine problems, as shown in Table 3.1.

Table 3.1   Hardware Upgrade Costs

	Units	Cost/Unit	Total Cost
Computer replacements	480	$1,500	$720,000
Servers with infrastructure	10	$5,000	$50,000
Processor upgrades	0	$250	$0
Memory upgrades (in 8MB units)	480	$75	$36,000
Storage upgrades (in 1GB units)	0	$200	$0
er	0	$0	$0
l **Hardware Upgrades**			**$806,000**

The network side of the equation also must be addressed annually. Upgrading and updating network hardware items, such as network cabling and network cards, and adding ports to routers to handle system expansion must all be expensed.

As shown in Table 3.2, upgrading software is an expensive process—albeit a necessary one. Not only is the software expensive, but the training costs (detailed under the Support category) add up quickly. Several types of software must be covered:

- *Operating system software.* Many firms still use older technology, such as Windows 3.1, which is not as Internet friendly as more recent systems, such as Windows 95, NT, or 98. Our example hypothesizes just such a firm.

- *Application software.* Word processors, databases, spreadsheets, financial, accounting, manufacturing, CAD/CAM, presentation, contact management, vertical applications, and other business software are included. Generally, a standard set of application software (such as Office 97) is installed enterprisewide, and a variety of professional software that's more expensive, but used by far fewer personnel, is added.

- *Connectivity software.* Additional communication software, which is used to connect users and to enable sharing of information across the network, is essential to an Internet strategy. Such software includes messaging and remote connectivity software.

Table 3.2 Software Upgrade Costs

	Units	Cost/Unit	Total Cost
Desktop Software			
Operating system	2,400	$101	$242,400
Standard application software	2,250	$388	$873,000
Professional level Application software	750	$466	$349,500
Subtotal - Desktop Software			**$1,464,900**
Server Software			
Operating system	10	$500	$5,000
Connectivity software	10	$1,000	$10,000
Subtotal - Server Software			**$15,000**
Total Software Upgrades			**$1,479,900**

Management

To achieve a front office running on all cylinders, you need a well-tuned back-office engine. An Internet infrastructure requires constant supervision by a diverse group of top-notch professionals. Network managers, user administrators, and data storage managers head up the three key areas needed in an Internet-oriented organization (see Table 3.3). The three areas are:

- *Network Management.* Network managers are the engineers who build, maintain, and police a company's information highways. In addition to basic operations and maintenance, network managers must be attuned to the entire system's growth needs and performance capabilities. System support at both the Tier III (troubleshooting and repair) and Tier II (in-depth solutions or on-site correction) is network personnel's responsibility. Network personnel must also handle the day-to-day tasks of adding or removing users from the system.

- *Systems Management.* The systems management team is the end-user connection. Responsible for evaluating and recommending desktop systems, systems management also handles the installation and management of application, security, and anti-virus software. Expect systems management to turn in a fairly hefty bill, particularly during a technical rollout period.

- *Storage Management.* You'll know that your company is serious about using the Internet to its fullest when it begins to emphasize information management. Storage management is vital because, to be useable, information must be archived and backed up, but still accessible. If the figures your sales force needs to close a big deal are sealed in a cardboard box in a warehouse in the middle of Montana, the game's over. Storage-management personnel handles desktop and server storage issues as well as disaster planning and, hopefully, recovery.

Table 3.3 Management Costs

	Annual Labor Total (hrs)	Annual Cost Total
Network Management		
Troubleshooting and repair (Tier III support)	3,900	$112,515
Traffic management and planning	8,580	$247,533
Performance tuning	8,400	$242,340
User administration (changes to users)	17,850	$514,973

	Annual Labor Total (hrs)	Annual Cost Total
Operating system support	2,730	$78,761
Maintenance labor	5,580	$160,983
Tier II support labor	6,990	$201,662
Total	**54,030**	**$1,558,767**
Systems Management		
Systems research and planning	1,530	$44,141
Evaluation and purchase	2,730	$78,761
Software licensing and distribution	39,600	$1,142,460[sr]
Asset management	2,010	$57,989
Application management	9,060	$261,381
Security and virus protection	3,480	$100,398
Hardware configuration/ re-configuration	11,670	$336,680[sr]
Hardware Installation	6,990	$201,662
Total	**77,070**	**$2,223,472**
Storage Management		
Disk and file management	12,270	$353,990
Storage capacity planning	480	$13,848
Data access management	5,220	$150,597
Backup and archiving	2,370	$68,375
Disaster planning and recovery	1,440	$41,544
Repository management	450	$12,983
Total	**22,230**	**$641,337**

Support

The more technologically dependent an office becomes, the stronger the need for a complete and ongoing support system. Across-the-board training is required to get the machine working, and an accessible help desk structure is necessary to keep the wheels greased.

Although support costs can certainly add up, one of the major benefits of a browser-based Internet/intranet system is that many functions are now combined into one interface. Using a single interface for many different tasks drastically lowers training costs because far fewer separate applications need to be covered, and it also eases the help desk burden because of the simpler operation.

Support can be broken into three main budgets: the help desk, operations labor, and operations fees, as shown in Table 3.4. Annual help desk costs are calculated by multiplying the total number of calls per year by the average duration of the call and the hourly rate for the help desk staff.

Operations labor, in addition to expected administrative costs, must take into account two important time-based factors: casual learning for the Information Technology staff and end-user training time. Your IT staff will pick up much of their working knowledge for handling the network and end-user applications outside of formal training programs, and that time should be budgeted as part of the TCO. Likewise, the time the end-users spend in training classes —and not "on the job"—should be included.

Operation fees generally include maintenance and support contracts, travel, and training. Of these, business travel initially takes the biggest chunk, but it can be expected to drop by 70 percent after the rollout is complete.

Table 3.4 Support Costs

	Annual Labor Total (hrs)	Annual Cost Total
Help Desk (Tier I & II support)		
Avg. number of calls per month per asset	3.2	
Avg. duration of each call (minutes)	18.0	
Help desk staff burdened salary ($/hr)	$14.42	
Total costs per asset		$166.12
Total person hours	34,560	
Total costs		$498,355
Operations Labor		
IS Administrative Assistant	5,160	$148,866
Management	5,580	$160,983
Casual learning (IT)	12,180	$175,636
Vendor management	7,230	$208,586

	Annual Labor Total (hrs)	Annual Cost Total
Training course development	2,160	$41,537
IS training (delivery and time)	11,520	$221,530
End-User training (delivery)	3,600	$69,228
End-User training (time)	14,400	$207,648
Travel time	7,320	$211,182
Purchasing	3,840	$55,373
Total	**72,990**	**$1,500,569**
Operations Fees		
Maintenance contracts		$174,000
Support contracts		$150,000
Training course/certification fees		$150,000
Travel		$306,000
Purchasing		$0
Total		**$780,000**
Total Support		**$2,778,924**

Development

Implementing an Internet strategy is not all plug-and-play. A moderate amount of resources must be devoted to developing the applications necessary to bond the general existing systems to the Internet/intranet structure. Beyond design and development, both testing and documentation of these solutions must be budgeted, as shown in Table 3.5.

One set of factors that cannot be generically forecast is the development costs associated with business-specific applications. Mission critical business applications must be assessed separately for each enterprise.

Table 3.5 Development Costs

	Annual Labor Total (hrs)	Annual Cost Total
Development Labor		
Design and development	16,410	$315,564

continues

Table 3.5 Continued

	Annual Labor Total (hrs)	Annual Cost Total
Testing	1,140	$21,922
Documentation	570	$10,961
Total	18,120	$348,447

Communication Costs

Communications costs is the budget line item closest to being labeled "Internet-only." The total fees shown in Table 3.6 are the annual expenses for lease lines, online access fees, remote access services, and Web hosting fees. The fees are assessed on a client-server basis, so the more users involved, the higher the budget item.

Table 3.6 Communication Costs

	Annual Cost Total
Communications Fees	$720,000

End User Information Systems Costs

The End User Information Systems (IS) Costs, although indirect, can be attributed directly to human nature. Put a group of people in the same office in front of some new technology—complete with an accessible help desk— and folks are still going to try to figure it out first or ask one another for help. Although you can't eliminate this factor, an Internet strategy can help minimize it by disseminating information broadly and making FAQs (Frequently Asked Questions) centrally available.

The more ambitious end users will attempt to automate their workload by developing solutions for repetitive tasks. This time is accounted for in the end-user scripting and development line item. Table 3.7 shows the costs calculated from a user survey at a midsized company.

Table 3.7 End User IS Costs

	Annual Labor Total (hrs)	Annual Cost Total
Peer and self support	143,040	$2,544,682
Casual learning (end user)	58,740	$1,044,985

	Annual Labor Total (hrs)	Annual Cost Total
End user scripting and development	21,600	$384,264
Total	223,380	$3,973,931

Downtime

Downtime (and the cost resulting from it) can be categorized in two ways: planned and unplanned. Although both result in a loss of productivity, unplanned downtime is far more costly, as shown in Table 3.8. Planned downtime, like system maintenance, is generally scheduled to impact fewer personnel. Unplanned downtime, such as a system crash, typically happens at the worst possible time—right before a contract is due or an order must be filled. Downtime does not have to be systemwide, however, to be debilitating. A single user waiting for a callback from the help desk can also impact productivity.

Table 3.8 Downtime Costs

Downtime	Annual Cost Total
Planned Downtime	
Monthly planned downtime hours	2.1
Users affected by each planned downtime event	26%
Labor rate	$17.79
Total annual productivity losses	$349,680
Unplanned Downtime	
Monthly unplanned downtime hours per desktop	5.7
Users affected by each planned downtime event	37%
Labor rate	$17.79
Total annual productivity losses	$1,350,688
Total Downtime Annual Cost	**$1,700,368**

PART II

Research and Development

4

Online Market Research

- Assessing the online market
- Uncovering secondary research
- Conducting an online focus group
- Taking electronic surveys

Online Demographics

Market research demands communication between a cross section of consumers and the researcher. The broader the pool of consumers, the more flexible—and valid—the market study. The Internet offers both direct and indirect methods to facilitate your organization's market research program:

- *Secondary Research.* The Internet is not just a mountain of information; it's an entire mountain range. The vast stores of data, both raw and professionally organized by such companies as Dow Jones and LEXIS-NEXIS, are easily accessed from any point around the world.

- *Focus Groups.* Firsthand market research has traditionally been gathered through the use of in-person focus groups. The Internet opens the possibility of another type of focus group—one that banishes geographic restraints.

- *Electronic Surveys.* For gathering strictly quantitative data, surveys have long been the primary tool. In addition to in-person, telephone, and mail-in surveys, the rise of the Internet adds two new tools to the market researcher's arsenal: the email and the on-line, Web-based surveys.

A fair amount of online market research is already in place. The Council of American Survey Research Organizations surveyed 300 executives of Fortune 2000 companies in the Fall of 1997 and found that 81 percent of surveyed corporate executives anticipate conducting the same amount of online research—or more—in the next five years. The same study showed that 87 percent found Web surveying to be somewhat or very useful.

Online market research firms

One of the leading providers of online market research data is @plan (www.webplan.net). @plan maintains a consumer database built from a random representative survey of 40,000 active adult users of the Internet. Some of @plan's clients include Wired Digital, Microsoft, Anderson Lembke, Onsale.com, and Autoweb.com.

Market research can be handled in-house or out-sourced to a specialist. Many market research firms have an online component, and a number of companies have made online market research their primary focus. A strong market-in-market research software has also emerged, leveraged on the possibility of online data collection.

Because of the enhanced communication made possible by email and the Internet, market research generally can be conducted in a shorter time span. Moreover, Web market research tends to be less expensive than traditional methods, primarily because of the lower communication costs, especially when applied to large samples.

Naturally, online market research isn't for everyone or every product. You can access a more diverse sample group and still take advantage of the Internet's communication structure. However, if you're looking for a direct sample, you have to take into account the demographics of the online responder.

Assessing a Community of Trendsetters

As a group, Internet users tend to be trend leaders and early adopters—which makes online market research ideal for certain types of companies, such as those in consumer electronics. Companies look to early adopters to pay a premium to be the first on the block to have the latest innovation and to influence others in the market.

A January 1988 survey by WebCensus—a Web site specializing in the demographics and usage of the Internet (www.webcensus.com)—paints a clear picture of the typical Internet user, the *Netizen*.

- *Well-educated.* 56 percent are educated beyond high school, and 16 percent attended some graduate school.

- *Male, but not exclusively.* Although the Internet is currently predominately male (61 percent), a higher rate of women are online today (39 percent) than in previous years. (Another study, by Lou Harris, saw the mix even more balanced with 54 percent male and 46 percent female online.)

Female Internet use on the rise
An earlier, 1995 survey found that the Internet was primarily a male domain; 77 percent of the total online population was male.

- *Income is spread across the board.* The Web survey revealed that income held to a standard bell distribution curve, with an average income of $50,000. A high rate of unemployment (14 percent) also was present, probably attributable to the responses by the young (36 percent).

- *Racially balanced.* A poll conducted by Lou Harris and Baruch College found that the Internet population is divided racially in about the same proportions as the U.S.: whites—37 percent, African Americans—30 percent, and Hispanics—27 percent.

- *Media savvy.* Contrary to popular belief, a new media form doesn't necessarily take market share away from other traditional media, such as print or television. Of those surveyed, 58 percent report that their hours per week on the Internet (6.5 on average) are in addition to those spent on other media.

Secondary Research

The Internet began as a tool for research scientists in various universities across the country—and later, around the world—to share data. That tradition of access to information remains strong today; it's axiomatic that you can find out almost anything through the Internet. Although it has yet to replace the corporate library, the Internet offers one of the most powerful research facilities available.

Information gathering for market research, referred to as *secondary research*, is efficiently handled through the Internet. Researchers can seek out the raw data by delving into the various search engines, or they can utilize any of the professional research firms now available online.

Researching via the Internet

The glory of the Internet is that you can find out almost anything online. Unfortunately, because so much information is available, searching the Internet has become an art in itself. The success of *search engines* is indicative of the power—and the frustration—of finding information online.

Search engines enable you or your planning and development team to gather a wide range of data, either through a direct search or through a series of categories. If you were planning to market a new soft drink in Thailand, for example, you could attack the problem head-on by entering "soft drink" and "Thailand" as your search criteria in any number of the public search engines. Or you could "drill down" the various categories by approaching the subject through the geographical area first, then exploring the cultural topics. Yahoo! is one of the best-known search engines that makes extensive use of categories, as shown in Figure 4.1.

Figure 4.1   Yahoo!'s categorization simplifies searching out a variety of information on a single topic, such as a country.

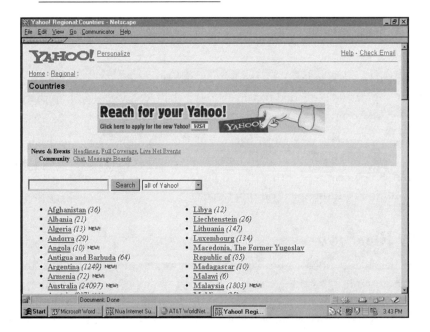

Search engines are one of the earliest areas on the Web to make a return on their investment, and there are many from which to choose. Each search engine has its own flavor and can be used for different purposes. Table 4.1 gives you a breakdown of the most popular search engines.

Table 4.1 Search Engines on the Internet

Name	URL	Description
AltaVista	altavista.digital.com	One of the widest-ranging and oldest search engines, AltaVista enables you to restrict your search to various parts of the Internet or to specific languages.
Excite	www.excite.com	Excite's key search feature is the small flag next to each returned result that asks, "More like this?" Selecting that option efficiently narrows your search.
HotBot	www.hotbot.com	Started by *Wired* magazine, HotBot enables you to limit your search to the proper category (such as News, Business, and People) and then add additional filters to further refine your search.
Infoseek	www.infoseek.com	Although Infoseek is useful for simple phrase or category searches, one of its strengths is the capability to search daily news services such as *Business Wire*, the *New York Times*, and CNN.
Yahoo!	www.yahoo.com	Yahoo! is the category (and sub-category) king. This search engine is very effective for approaching a market research project from the outside in.

Using meta-search engines

An effective alternative to using a single search engine is to use one of the *meta-search engines*. A meta-search engine takes your query and submits it to several search engines simultaneously. The results are then compiled and presented together. One such tool is Meta-Crawler (www.metacrawler.com).

Accessing Research Firms Online

Information is big business on the Internet, and it's only going to get bigger. Professional data vendors such as LEXIS-NEXIS, Dow Jones, and Dialog provide access to corporate quality reports on virtually any topic imaginable—for a price.

It's one thing to say that you can find almost any bit of information on the Internet (if you're willing to dig for it), it's quite another to see the actual statistics of what's available. Consider the following stats from the LEXIS-NEXIS Web site (`www.lexisnexis.com`), shown in Figure 4.2:

- Over 1.3 billion documents are accessible.

- Each week, approximately 9.5 million additional documents are added.

- More than 7,000 databases are used to categorize the information.

- Access is available to over 18,000 business, news, and legal sources.

Figure 4.2   LEXIS-NEXIS is a primary source for legal and business information.

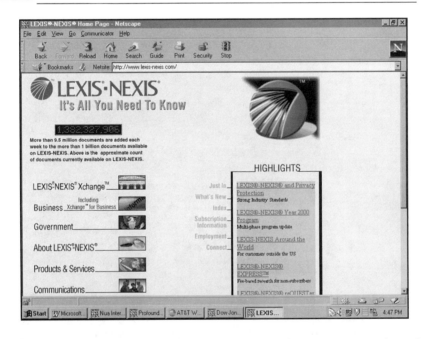

Most information resources are subscription-based and allow an unlimited number of searches per month. Rather than entering a single phrase in a search engine text box or sifting through a number of categories, most queries are form-based and allow a fairly sophisticated set of criteria to be posed. As Figure 4.3 shows, a primary topic and a secondary topic can be specified, and the search can be restricted to a research source, such as new stories, for a specific time period.

Figure 4.3 LEXIS-NEXIS' reQUESTer feature is representative of many professional databases.

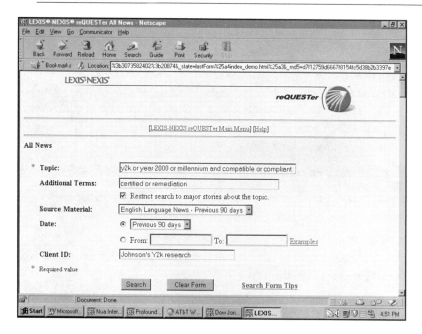

Dialog is another excellent source for business information. Dialog's (www.dialog.com) combined databases are said to be more than 50 times the size of those generally available over the World Wide Web. However, size doesn't matter if you can't hit the target market. Dialog allows searches limited to subjects such as company intelligence, chemistry, products and markets, intellectual property, biomedicine and pharmaceuticals, and engineering and technology. Dialog recently merged with Knight-Ridder Information and now offers over 1,000 U.S. and Canadian newspapers and news sources, and over 20,000 scientific journals and conference proceedings.

You don't always have to hunt for information. Recently, several of the professional information resources have begun to offer *notification services*. A notification service sends you an email message whenever a new report that matches your previous search criteria is filed. Notification services are a great way to keep ahead of the curve when it comes to market intelligence.

Conducting an Online Focus Group

Focus groups have long been used in market research efforts to gather both quantitative and qualitative information. In a traditional focus group, a diverse collection of individuals reflecting the target market are gathered in a room and exposed to the product, marketing campaign, or described service. The group is hosted by a professional moderator and is often observed, either in real-time through hidden video cameras or later through recordings and transcripts. The close observation allows the client to judge both what the group says and how they act.

The Internet opens the concept of the focus group to a world of possibilities. The main difference between a traditional and an online focus group is that instead of meeting in a regular room, the online focus group meets in a *virtual* room. This virtual meeting place, also called a *chat room*, removes all geographical boundaries and enables a focus group to incorporate consumers from around the country or around the world.

How does an online focus group work? Here's a step-by-step description of the process.

1. Potential participants (either pre-selected or volunteer) initially fill out a questionnaire, which is used to screen candidates for each focus group.

2. Selected candidates (about 8-10) are contacted via email and asked to log in to a particular Web site on a specific day at a specific time. Each candidate is given a password for entry into the chat room.

3. Before the session begins, the market research firm and the client devise a discussion outline with specific questions targeted toward the product.

4. At the time of the session, after all the participants have logged in, the moderator begins the presentation. Graphics, sounds or jingles, video, and other multimedia elements can be incorporated with text for evaluation and testing. Participants can be asked to interact with a presentation and their responses can be captured for further evaluation.

5. Throughout the session, participants reply anonymously to queries from the moderator.

6. The client can observe the entire session in real-time and is free to communicate with the moderator privately to follow a particular direction.

7. At the end of the session (1-2 hours), the participants log off; the transcript of the entire session is soon made available and transmitted to the client via email.

Traditional focus groups typically are dominated by one or two individuals—this is not the case with online focus groups, in which participants enjoy complete anonymity and their privacy is guaranteed. Because people can engage in an online focus group from their own homes or offices, their responses tend to be more natural and less guarded.

Case Study: Times Newspapers Ltd.
Times Newspapers Ltd. have published the London *Times* and the *Sunday Times* in the U.K. for over 200 years. Their Web site at `www.the-times.co.uk` is freely accessible; however, you must register first.

A market research firm, Cyber Dialogue (`www.cyberdialogue.com`), conducted a series of four online focus groups for the London *Times* to gauge the effectiveness of its Web site and gather data for a redesign of the site. Each virtual meeting took one hour and involved domestic and international participants.

The goals of the focus group were to understand the online market better, get reactions to the current site design, evaluate registration, and determine what would make the visitor return again and again. After the $10,000, two-week project, the Web site was redesigned and proven successful in attracting and keeping customers; it also subsequently won an award for being the "Best Web Site in the U.K."

Electronic Surveys

Surveys are the workhorses of market research. Telephone surveys, mail-in surveys, "stop 'em in the supermarket" surveys—they all beg just a moment of the consumer's time. The Internet has brought two new versions of the traditional survey form to the forefront of online market research: email and Web-based surveys.

Electronic surveys tend to be more time and cost efficient than traditional surveys. King, Brown and Partners, a full service market research firm based in San Francisco, reports that the Internet routinely gathers 3,000 respondents in a little more than a week, whereas a typical telephone survey would require 6-8 weeks for the same degree of response.

Email Surveys

An email survey is similar to a mail-in survey only in that the respondents are answering the questions in their own time. Emailed surveys are less costly to produce and distribute; they are easier to modify and tailor to particular market segments; and they are far less likely to be intercepted or lost "in the mail."

Generally, Email surveys can be completed in 30 days or less. After the company and the research firm have agreed upon the questionnaire, a list of email addresses is secured. The list can come either from the company or from a general pool of Internet respondents. If the addresses come from the company, response rate is greatly improved if the company notifies the respondents of the survey in advance, assuring them of confidentiality and asking for their support.

Privacy on the Internet

Privacy is a real hot-button on the Internet today. Make sure that your email survey assures your respondents that their addresses will not be sold or used for any other purpose. Most market research companies provide only survey results that are summarized and anonymous.

Email surveys can use multiple choice questions, short-answer fill-in-the-blank or open-ended comments, as shown in Figure 4.4. After the questionnaires are emailed, the responses tend to come back quickly—often almost immediately. Online market research firm Analysis.Net (www.analysis.net) routinely sends reminder letters to non-responders after a few days to improve the response rate. The data collection process takes about 10 days.

Figure 4.4   Email surveys offer quick turnaround time and significantly lower costs than traditional mail-in surveys.

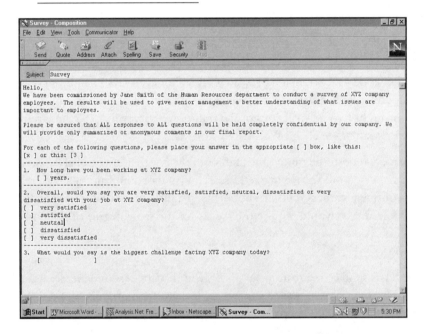

Web-based Surveys

A *Web-based survey* takes special advantage of the best of the Internet.

- *Browser-oriented.* A Web-based survey uses the Internet form structure that enables respondents to access it online via their browsers.

- *Full graphics support.* Surveys on the Web can use all the graphic and multimedia tools available to Web pages.

- *Database connectivity.* After the survey is completed, the respondent clicks a button and the data is automatically added to a database for further processing.

- *Accessible globally.* Because the survey is posted on a Web site, it can be reached from anywhere in the country or the world.

One of the most vexing problems facing market researchers is selecting a truly random sample. Web-based surveys can use a technique known as *pop-ups* to invite, at random, Web site visitors to participate in a survey. Figure 4.5 shows one version of the pop-up as used by SurveySite, an online market research firm based in Toronto. During a recent evaluation for Canadian Tire, SurveySite installed the pop-up software on the Canadian Tire Web site for 5 days and gathered 4,800 responses. These responses contained massive amounts of data on demographics, user interaction, visitor satisfaction, and usage rates.

Figure 4.5 Pop-ups such as this one from SurveySite can be used to attract a random sampling for a market research survey.

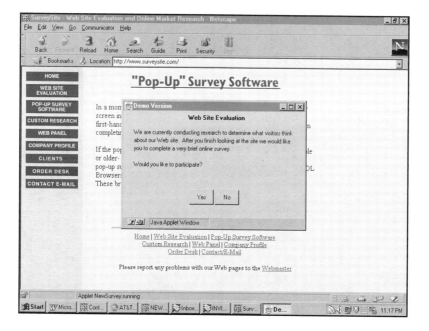

The Discovery Channel uncovered two additional benefits to their series of Web-based surveys conducted by King, Brown & Partners. In addition to a rapid turnaround time and lower costs (all survey responses were immediately downloaded to a back-end database, and tabulation was finished in 24 hours), information culled from the Web-based survey was deemed to be more accurate because the respondents were reacting to an immediate exposure of a product. Moreover, because all respondents were databased with an email contact address, follow-up studies could be handled with ease.

CHAPTER 5

Managing Business Intelligence

- Getting the competitive edge

- Mining the Internet

- Tracking your competitors

- Pushing competitive information to the desktop

Competitive Analysis

A large part of product development is understanding the competition. Existing and potential competitors should be identified—and targeted. The more you know about a competing product and the competitor itself, the better your company can develop and market your product.

The Internet is a boon to the field of competitive analysis. Public databases, government filings, and even your competitor's Web site are valuable resources for information gathering. What kind of information is available? A few examples were gathered by Competitive Analysis Technologies, a research firm specializing in the Energy field:

- By tracking import/export records, one company was able to identify a competitor's overseas supply source—and then bought out the supplier.

- Three previously unknown competitors were disclosed to one company through a search of the online Freedom of Information Act.

- A competitor was getting great press by inviting in an outside watchdog group. Research of the corporate records revealed that both organizations were run by the same company.

- By uncovering a pricing schedule for a competing product, one company was able to raise its rates by 10% without losing a customer.

In addition to uncovering information about your rivals, competitive analysis has two other profound implications. First, through a Web site and full-text press releases, you can gather a complete picture of how your competitors view their businesses. Second, by more fully understanding the type of information that is accessible, you'll know what your competitors can find out about your business.

Michael E. Porter, Professor of Business Administration at Harvard Business School and author of *Competitive Strategy: Techniques for Analyzing Industries and Competitors*, points out, in an interview with *CIO* magazine (October 1, 1995):

> As companies emerge from the last decade, many have been preoccupied with operational effectiveness—restructuring, reengineering, and improving efficiencies. These improvements are a necessity in today's competition, but they alone are not enough. They are approaching a point of diminishing returns. If companies are going to sustain competitive advantage, they can't do it by being more efficient at running the business. They have to have a distinctive way of competing.

The Internet offers several routes to gathering the business intelligence that can enhance this "distinctive way of competing."

- *Through Web sites.* The Web site of a business rival can yield an amazing amount of information.
- *Through government sources.* Governments around the world, and especially in the U.S. and Canada, have embraced the Internet as a massive distribution network—and routinely post valuable information online.
- *Through private research firms.* Organizations such as LEXIS-NEXIS and Dialog offer comprehensive methods for tracking a competitor's actions.
- *Through subscription services.* Using the latest *push technology*, you can be notified of any number of competitive factors.

Internet Accessible Information

Executives surveyed about their use of the Internet often give one of three answers: to check email, to check the market, and to check on their competitors. Web sites can give an instant snapshot of a competitor's goals, strengths, and alliances. I'm constantly amazed at just how much information is made publicly available—information that, with a bit of analysis, can be turned into a competitive advantage.

Although much of the information found on a competitor's Web site is available otherwise, the Internet offers one key edge—speed. Not only can the data be collected much more efficiently, but the essential elements can be uncovered in a fraction of the time. If you wanted to find a competitor's quarterly earnings for last year, for example, you could send for the annual report—and get your answer in about three or four weeks. Or you could find the information on your competitor's Web site by reading over the electronic version of its annual report, complete with hyperlinks that take you right to the needed info. Many public companies publish their entire annual reports to the Web in the Investor Relations area where they can be downloaded at no cost.

Complete documents on the Web

Many annual reports and other multiple page documents are archived and posted on the Web in a compressed form called Portable Document Format (PDF). Developed by Adobe, PDF files can be downloaded to your system or read online by using the freely available Adobe Reader (www.adobe.com).

In addition to the specific information available on a competitor's Web site, you'll also gain insights into the company's self-perception. Is it promoting one area of the business over another? Has it completely missed the boat in one arena? Many Web sites offer a company profile that details not only its corporate structure—a digital organizational chart, if you will—but also the company's goals for the next phase of business.

A company's public relations department tends to be diligent about posting its press releases. Many sites archive past press releases, which can outline business alliances, promotions, and new directions.

A company's press releases are also a good source for uncovering its key clients. After you've identified the clients, you can visit their Web sites and use the information to better determine their needs. The more information you have, the better you (or your sales force) can tailor a pitch for their business.

Another method you can use to discover a competitor's direction or weaknesses is to find which positions it wants to fill. Many corporate Web sites have a Human Resources section that lists the current openings. Posting employment opportunities over the Internet has become a common occurrence, and it's possible to search the major job boards on the Web for a competitor's name. Moreover, many newspapers routinely place classified advertisements online; you can search a competitor's home town newspaper electronically to see if it is expanding in a particular field. This is especially notable if you're aware that your competitor currently has no employees in a particular field.

SEE ALSO

➤ *For more detailed information on searching the Web for employment information, go to page 89.*

Mining Government Sources

Governments have seen the future of information management and it's called the Internet. By placing its ever-growing storehouse of data online, governments make it far more accessible without incurring substantial labor costs. Government regulations and forms were the first to come online, and now many governmental bodies are posting the filings online as well. Competitive analysis just found a friend with a wealth of information.

Although not all governments are as comprehensively represented on the Internet as the U.S. federal government, more are going online everyday. Most states and larger municipalities have begun filing online reports, as well as many larger counties. The Canadian and Australian governments are pro-active on the Internet, and many European countries are not far behind. The European Community movement is expected to accelerate this trend.

If your competitor is a public company, the Securities and Exchange Commission should be your first stop for investigative research. All public companies are required to make periodic filings covering virtually every aspect of their businesses. Moreover, since 1996 these filings have been posted to EDGAR (see Figure 5.1), the SEC's Electronic Data Gathering, Analysis, and Retrieval system, and are available over the Internet. Such filings are posted to the Internet just 24 hours after being received by the SEC. Table 5.1 details the forms accessible through EDGAR.

Figure 5.1 EDGAR, the SEC's Electronic Data Gathering, Analysis, and Retrieval system, is online at www.sec.gov.

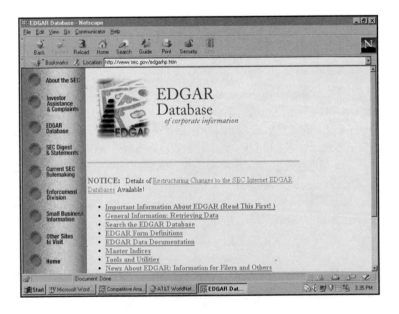

Table 5.1   SEC Documents Available

Form	Description
10-K	The official annual report with sections required by the SEC. This covers the state of the business, all properties, legal proceedings, financial data, and more. Filed annually.
20-F	Annual report for foreign corporations, similar to the 10-K. Filed annually.
10-Q	Required quarterly report with financial analysis and discussion. Submitted quarterly.
8-K	Any unscheduled material event or corporate change of importance.
13-D	Reports fiscal actions by anyone owning more than 5% of the company stock. This form can be used to report insider trading by the company's officers and senior management.
14D-1	Filed by the bidder in the event of a tender offer.
14D-9	Company's answer to the tender offer.
13-G	Annual filing by any owners of 5% or more stock.

It's not mandatory to post all filings to EDGAR. Forms 3, 4, and 5 (security ownership and transaction reports filed by corporate insiders); Form 144 (notice of proposed sale of securities); and Form 13F (reports filed by institutional investment managers showing equity holdings by accounts under their management) may be filed on EDGAR at the option of the filer. However, since 1966, companies have routinely filed their SEC requirements through EDGAR and for most, it remains the easiest way to comply.

Through Occupational Safety and Health Administration (OSHA) reports, you can find out not only if your competitors have any outstanding violations in their factories, but also the physical size of the plant and the number of employees. The Environmental Protection Agency and the Department of Transportation can also provide extensive information.

Many state and county offices make filed permits available at low or no cost. These permits can detail construction information as well as air, water, and solid waste permits to determine your competitor's manufacturing processes and capabilities. Similar permits are often filed on the local level, although most cities do not have open access to these records through the Internet.

Private Research Firms

Information not immediately accessible to the public through a government Internet connection can most likely be found through one or more of the numerous research firms online. Dun & Bradstreet, Dialog, TRW, and CDB Infotek all maintain extensive databases on public and private companies.

Looking for basic knowledge on a privately held company? Check out Dialog's IAC (Information Access Company) Company Intelligence with over 140,000 private and public U.S. companies in its database, as well as 30,000 international companies. Reports on domestic companies, as shown in Figure 5.2, include immediate and ultimate parent companies, number of employees, and sales revenue. In addition, abstracts of the 10 most-recent news references on each company are available, as found in over 5,000 journals, magazines, and newspapers indexed by IAC. Where available, full coverage is noted.

Figure 5.2   A sample report from IAC Company Intelligence—one of 450 databases that can be found at Dialog (www.dialog.com).

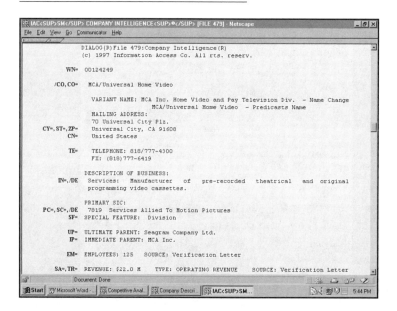

The import/export arena can provide meaningful insights for any international business. One resource, PIERS (Port Import/Export Reporting System) is maintained by The Journal of Commerce and is also reachable through Dialog. PIERS covers all imports and exports transported via ship. Details from a PIERS query include:

- Date of shipment
- U.S. based importer/exporter
- U.S. port, city/state
- Foreign port, city/country
- Product description
- Product weight and number of units

Another database, Trade Intelligence, from Trade Reporting and Data Exchange, Inc. also has port information and adds both the consignee and the "notify party" with addresses for each. In addition, Trade Intelligence can track Mexican imports and exports by air, ship, rail, or truck down to the shipper's tax ID.

A good, central source for checking your competitor's legal entanglements is CDB Infotek (www.cdb.com). Through CDB Infotek's Probe service, you can search hundreds of nation-wide, regional, and local databases for information on civil and criminal court filings, bank-ruptcies, tax liens, judgments, and more. CDB also offers a database of corporate/limited partnership records to determine the legal name and current status of a corporation or limit-ed partnership, as well as a database on fictitious business/assumed name filings, which provides names, addresses, filings, and ownership information. You can use CDB to search Uniform Commercial Code (UCC) Filings to determine the existence of secured debts, to determine who is on record for the debt, and to verify that a security interest has been per-fected through a state level UCC filing.

When it comes to getting the financial skinny, Dun & Bradstreet is second to none. D&B's online presence (www.dnb.com) offers up-to-the-moment information on more than one million leading public and private companies. D&B recently went live with its Million Dol-lar Database over the Internet. As a subscribing member, you can instantly find a wealth of company data, as shown in Figure 5.3, including a company's total employees, total sales, its bank, accountant, corporate officers, and even the officers' biographies.

Figure 5.3   Get detailed financial reports from Dun & Bradstreet's online Million Dollar Data-base service.

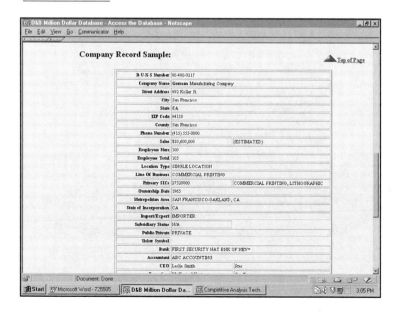

Interested in a competing company's future product direction? Visit Trademarkscan (www.trademarkscan.com) to look up a competitor's trademarks and service marks, including graphics, in 13 countries. You can even find the date of the company's first sale and the date of registration.

Receiving Intelligence on a Daily Basis

It's one thing to scour the vast resources of the Internet for business intelligence—it's quite another to have it routinely delivered to your desktop. In computing circles, the normal type of Web browsing is referred to as client pull, in which the persons investigating Web sites are the clients. In recent years, a slightly different technology, known cir as server push, has come to the forefront. Push technology, also referred to as narrow casting, was first popularized by the program PointCast, which replaced the screen saver with valuable business, weather, and other information that is continually updated. With server push, you don't have to go online and seek out the information, it's delivered to your desktop on a regular schedule, or whenever an update occurs.

PointCast (www.pointcast.com) is excellent for maintaining a close eye on an entire industry or for monitoring specific companies. As shown in Figure 5.4, you can get detailed information, such as a running market ticker or a chart overview.

Figure 5.4 Receive continually updated market information through PointCast's screen saver.

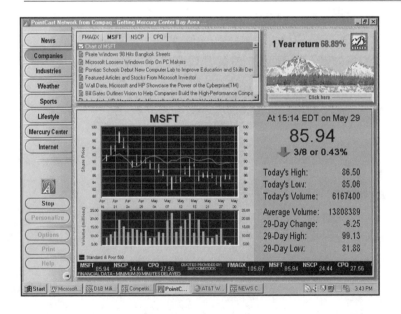

The success of PointCast prodded the manufacturers of both major browsers to add push technology to their features list. Microsoft's Internet Explorer uses Active Channels to enable Web sites to push content onto the desktop at scheduled intervals; Netscape refers to its entry as Netcaster. Both do essentially the same thing by enabling Web sites to offer a server push alternative to normal client pull services. If your competitors have Active Channels on their Web sites, you can be notified of any posted changes as they happen.

Many Web sites also feature email notification services. Specify an interest in a specific product or service, and the company will obligingly send you an electronic bulletin with the current news. Services also collect published business intelligence from around the world and submit it to you or your company on a routine basis. Inquisit (`www.inquisit.com`) is one such organization; it offers a corporatewide solution called Enterprise Inquisit. With Enterprise Inquisit, business intelligence is collected from wire services, such as Reuters, Associated Press (AP), and United Press International (UPI), from daily newspapers from hundreds of cities on every continent, and from a large selection of business journals and trade magazines. Then, depending on the configuration requested—summaries or full stories—the research can be posted directly to your company's intranet for enterprisewide dispersal. You can also specify that the report go to separate intranet pages or mailing lists for smaller groups of employees. Individual needs can also be addressed with Inquisit's Personal Agents, which can deliver email summaries on either a regular or an as-needed basis.

6

Team Product Development

- Creating with an online team
- Meetings in cyberspace
- Using virtual offices
- Implementing change orders online

Online Team Building

Although the definition of a team—a group of individuals working toward a common goal—doesn't explicitly say so, teams traditionally work together in the same place and at the same time. However, face-to-face meetings are no longer the only—or optimum—method in which teams can communicate and collaborate. In today's global economy, a product development team could easily be spread across the nation or the world. Advancements in the online world have made virtual team-building not only possible, but practical.

With online teams communicating over the Internet and intranet, your product development team can:

- Facilitate internal communications on specific topics and issues across geographical and temporal boundaries.
- Put forth ideas and solicit opinions in place of, or prior to, face-to-face meetings.
- Solicit comments and suggestions on draft documents from interested parties within the team and outside the team.
- Bolster creativity by providing a level platform for contributing ideas and suggestions.

Online team communication also has the benefit of being documented instantly, even with the most informal methods, such as email. The more sophisticated *groupware* software can automatically store notes and information in a database so that it can be more easily retrieved.

FAQ: What's groupware?

Groupware is software that is designed to enhance team collaboration through messaging, conferencing, and calendaring applications. Lotus Notes and its Web extension, Domino, are probably the best known systems in the groupware category.

Although an online team emphasis may seem to make the most sense when the members are spread out geographically, online team members housed within the same office also benefit. Meetings are often perceived as tremendous time-wasters, and in a hectic workplace, they're often difficult to schedule. Online communication to team members can keep in-person meetings to a minimum and make them more productive when they occur.

Each stage of team product development—innovating, designing, and refining—can benefit from an online strategy.

Innovating with a Virtual Team

After market research has pointed in the general direction for new product development, how does your team conceive of that "killer app" destined to sweep the marketplace? How do you find the innovation that will help you maintain, or even increase, market share with the next generation of your product?

An online strategy can benefit the creative process in many ways. Individual ideas can be sent to a publicly accessible "suggestion box" database, where team members can read and comment on the proposals. Scheduled brainstorming sessions can take place in a moderated cyberspace chat room with remotely located members sharing their thoughts and ideas.

Concept Mapping in a Virtual Meeting

One of the most engaging developmental techniques, concept mapping, is now possible online. Since the advancement of conferencing software, such as Microsoft's NetMeeting and Netscape's Conference, groups can brainstorm remotely by using the *whiteboard* or application-sharing features. An online whiteboard allows information drawn or typed onto a screen to be viewed by all participants, as if everyone was in the same conference room. Moreover, the whiteboard drawings, as shown in Figure 6.1, can be highlighted, modified, or added to by anyone in the session—or the creator can "lock" the drawing to prevent any alterations.

Figure 6.1 Use conferencing software such as Microsoft's NetMeeting to brainstorm new product development.

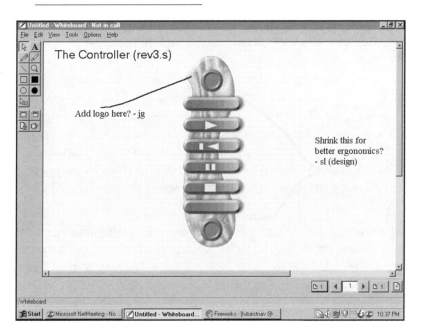

Application sharing takes the whiteboard concept one step further. Each member logged on to the virtual meeting can view the data onscreen—from spreadsheets to computer-aided design to a brainstorming software. You can even allow others to collaborate using the application, whether or not they have the software installed. Even information copied from a report can instantly be shared with others.

File and application sharing

Although you can share any application with Internet conferencing programs such as NetMeeting, you'll need to post them to a central location or send the final files to other team members so they can have copies. Application sharing doesn't automatically allow others to save your source files.

Working with Advisory Councils Online

Just as it's possible to conduct online focus groups to get consumer reaction to a new product or marketing direction, you can use the Internet to find out what your customers really want. The Internet is great for bringing advisory boards together to interact with your in-house team. Product advisors can be used either on a continual or an as-needed basis.

Case Study: Burton Snowboards, Inc.

Burton Snowboards dominates the industry with a 45 percent market share selling more than 100,000 snowboards a year. Burton's corporate headquarters are in Burlington, Vermont, with additional offices in Urawa, Japan, and Innsbruck, Austria.

Certain industries are more market driven than others. Burton Snowboarding is a leader in a field of more than 250 competitors, and to stay on top, it has to deliver what the customer wants. Rather than pursue its previous, expensive, and time-consuming course of flying its advisors to a central location for a brainstorming session, Burton now uses the Internet to communicate with professional and selected amateur riders. By posting specifications and designs for new snowboards to a special Web site, members of Burton's advisory council can review the material, no matter where they are, and respond thoughtfully with no particular time pressure.

Burton takes the concept one step further by sponsoring a mobile computing center in the Demo Days trailer right on the ski slopes. Amateur riders can try out a state-of-the-art snowboard in development and offer their feedback in an electronic format. Responses from the market are immediately available to the development team.

Case Study: Macromedia, Inc.

Macromedia, Inc. (www.macromedia.com) is a public company that specializes in multimedia authoring tools for both CD-ROM and Internet production. It reported an annual revenue of $107,365,000 for 1997.

Another example of using an outside advisory council comes from Macromedia, Inc. As developers of graphic multimedia creation software, such as Director and Freehand, they noticed that most of their customer base were also creating Web sites. Furthermore, very few were using the available WYSIWYG (what you see is what you get) software, preferring to write the code by hand. Macromedia set up an advisory council made up of premier Web site designers and contractors who, in a series of online and in-person meetings, began to outline their objections to the current software. From these early discussions, the overall structure of a Web authoring tool, later named Dreamweaver, emerged.

Throughout the yearlong software development process, the advisory council was routinely consulted. Using an Internet email method called a *listserv*, the advisory council was able to respond to each new stage in the product's development. A listserv allows everyone on the list to receive email from everyone else on the list. The advisory council was anything but a rubber-stamp committee. According to Steve Shannon, Product Manager for Dreamweaver, "On several occasions, entire feature categories were tossed aside as we bounced back to the drawing board."

The advisory council strategy proved to be very successful. Since its release, Dreamweaver has won award after award in its category. Most critics praise the program as being one that truly responds to the user's needs. Dreamweaver is among the best-selling Web authoring tools on the market today.

Establishing an Electronic Corporate Memory

No product stands alone. Each introduction of a new product takes place only after many development hours. The Internet makes it possible to shorten developmental time by creating a central data depository that can be drawn upon with each revision of the product. Typically, products go through various testing phases in numerous departments across the enterprise. The more the results of these tests can be documented and stored in a retrievable manner, the shorter the cycle for future products.

Take the example of Ford Australia. Faced with a four-year production cycle that involved team participation from design, assembly, supply, and finance and marketing departments, the company needed to find a way to pull together information from previously produced cars. Before developing an intranet strategy, the managers took part in numerous meetings and had to amass information from different networks and different computing platforms. Information was so hard to find it wasn't even looked for—and so test programs were often re-invented, from scratch.

With an intranet strategy in place, all documents are standardized and maintained in a central repository. Each design team has immediate access to the most current data. Particular cars or vehicular subsystems can be evaluated in light of previous projects. Furthermore, test programs build on the knowledge base of prior work, and management can more easily follow a project's progress. Finally, many of the forms and much of the data can be modified for reuse for the next product development program.

Online Project Management

The more multifaceted the project, the more difficult it is to manage. Project management software goes a long way toward putting all the factors and variables in a cohesive format, whereas in real life, altering one deadline affects others. Although one person may be ultimately responsible for the entire project, with an Internet management strategy, all valued team members can get the project status information they need—and move forward.

Depending on the sophistication of the particular project management software, you can

- View the schedule for yourself or other members of the team in a day-to-day, weekly, or monthly mode. The schedule can include everything from conference calls to out-of-town travel.

- Enter to-do lists and sort them by priority.

- Mark tasks as done, percentage completed, or overdue.

- Access a Gantt planner to show the project outline for the entire team over any specified time frame.

- Schedule appointments, phone calls, tasks, and work requests for yourself, others, or
the entire team. These appointments and tasks are emailed to the other team members
so that they can be acknowledged or declined. Responses are routed back to the
scheduler. Some intelligent agent software will even allow the team leader to automatically schedule a meeting with the team, through their systems.

Case Study: Waterhouse Securities

Waterhouse Securities is the nation's third-largest discount brokerage firm. Based in
New Jersey, Waterhouse services one million clients through its 125 branch offices and
over the Internet.

Some companies, such as Waterhouse Securities, are faced with a perpetual turnaround for
new products. Because of the nature of its business, Waterhouse Securities must send out
monthly customer statements, which require a high degree of maintenance. Both in-house
and outside programmers are used to develop custom charts and new products. Scheduling
is paramount for all their work. Prior to using a project manager program, information was
scattered far and wide, and a great deal of time was wasted establishing the status of various
aspects of the project.

Now the central scheduling program keeps track of what's done and what's lagging. Resources can be shifted or projects delayed, if necessary. The software handles additions of
contractors as extra labor by tracking their accessibility on the Gantt chart, as well as the to-
do lists. The bottom line—a more efficient, better product built with better communication
all around.

Using Virtual Offices

Teams can't exist with once-a-week meetings, whether the meetings are online or off. Much
of the teamwork that needs to take place happens in between official meeting times. Team
members need to consult a specific set of documents, update a design, or post an F.Y.I.
notice. One solution that goes beyond chat rooms and teleconferencing is the virtual office.

A virtual office can be set up for any configuration of in-house personnel, clients, or potential clients; however, it is very effective when used in a team situation. Imagine creating a

special office dedicated to one project and accessible only by team members on that project. Only materials—documents, spreadsheets, reports, or designs—pertinent to the project are located in the online area. Online meetings can be scheduled as needed and held within the virtual office, offering the full range of conferencing technology.

Setting up a typical virtual office is straightforward and offers some insight into the possibilities for the online team. The following example uses Instant!TeamRoom software from Lotus; however, most virtual offices are established in a similar fashion.

1. After you've started the virtual office software, select the **Administration** button.

2. Enter the team members as new users in the group, specifying each one as either a participant or an administrator, as shown in Figure 6.2. All you need is a name and an email address.

Figure 6.2 A virtual office is accessible only to team members, but it can be reached from anywhere on the Internet.

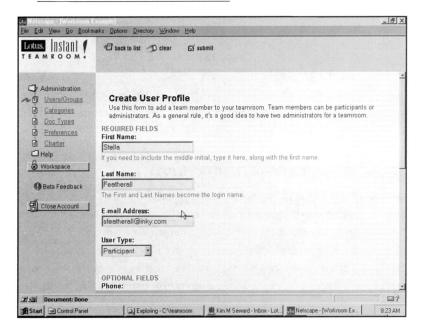

You can also set up numerous groups within the overall team by defining them within the Administration area.

3. Next, define the categories for the various documents that will be accessible in the virtual office. This is analogous to establishing the filing system.

4. Documents can also be given a particular type. Example types are

- *Action*. For documents that require completion by a specific date.

- *Discussion*. Documents to be read and commented on by team members.

- *Reference*. For pertinent but not time-critical documents.

Each team can define document types necessary for its organization.

5. Next, set the default invitation message that will be sent to every team member you included. Invitation messages will also automatically contain the address of the virtual office and a system-derived password.

You can customize the invitation message for each user through the user profile.

6. Define the default welcome message that everyone sees when logging in to the virtual office. The welcome message can be updated at any point to describe any new material or information for team members.

7. When you finish with the setup aspect of the virtual office, you can leave the administration area and return to the workspace at the click of an onscreen button.

After team members are in the virtual office, they can search for documents by title, author, date posted, or category. As shown in Figure 6.3, you can specify who—the entire group, a subgroup, or particular individuals—can read each document. Comments to documents are grouped under the document itself to make it easy to follow the flow of "conversation."

Mission Critical Change Management

No product is sprung fully-formed from a designer or engineer's head. Designs are refined time and again, incorporating the latest feedback from marketing, supplies, finance, and other departments. After an engineering team or other division agrees to make a modification, implementing the change can be an administrative headache, especially in larger organizations where concurrent engineering teams may be working on the same project. In such mission-critical change-management situations, an Internet strategy can decidedly cut time and expenses.

Case Study: Daimler Benz Commercial Vehicles

Daimler Benz Commercial Vehicles' business spans 42 countries, with manufacturing taking place across the world—from Germany to South America, and Spain to India. Daimler Benz recently merged with the Chrysler Corporation.

Figure 6.3 You can set the permissions for each document to determine who can read which documents in the virtual office.

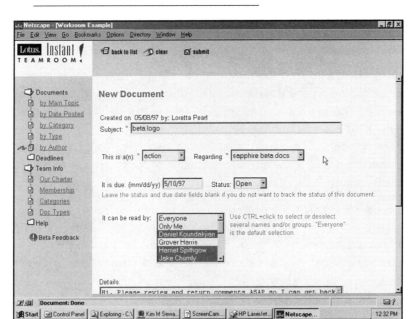

Design changes can come fast and furious in an automotive company. Alterations are constantly made to improve the product, cut costs, meet regulations, and address the changing needs of customers. Daimler Benz Commercial Vehicles realized the vital necessity of implementing changes effectively, and developed an Internet/intranet strategy to drastically reduce the time it takes to follow through on a design request.

Requests for changes come from a variety of sources, each with valid, and often urgent, requirements. In some cases, design and production can be improved by new technology; in other cases, costs can be brought down by the inclusion of newly-available components or processes. Quality problems need to be addressed, as do changing safety and environmental regulations. Suggestions also come regularly from customers, suppliers, and employees. And customers make special requests, such as unusual versions and additional functionality.

Daimler Benz Commercial Vehicles was ready to address issues such as concurrent engineering and delegation of the decision-making process. Managers complained that, under the old system, after requests were put on paper and submitted, it was difficult to track them. The company needed a more efficient change-management process for its commercial vehicles' products.

The company found the efficiency it needed in groupware using Lotus Notes technology, and it implemented a change-management support system. Since its inception in 1996, the implementation has shown a 60% reduction in the time taken to process modification requests. Because it was taking, on average, more than a hundred days to complete a change, this was clearly a significant improvement.

When making a case for a product modification, the full spectrum of information can come into play: text, spreadsheets, and design information such as sketches, drawings, and photographs. Sophisticated groupware such as Lotus Notes can handle all these formats with ease. Because Daimler Benz manufacturing was spread all over the world, and design teams often used different servers on their networks, a replication system was established. Material that needed to be shared was sent across the network daily so that every engineer could have the most current information.

After a change has been implemented, all the accompanying reports are archived. This archive can then be used as a basis for decisions on similar requests, further reducing the time spent on the process enterprisewide. More than 1,300 Daimler Benz employees, on a variety of engineering and design teams, have access to this type of mission-critical data, and change orders happen far more efficiently than in the past.

PART **III**

Human Resources

7

Training Through Distance Learning

- Running local presentations

- Working with streaming media

- Combining telephony and the Web

- Facilitating corporate communications

- Teaching resellers over the Web

- Attending an online classroom

- Remote testing on the Web

Better Training Through Technology

Scenario #1:

Your company has several-hundred dealerships in numerous countries around the world. Each dealership employs from 5 to 35 salespeople who need to be brought up to speed on your latest product line. What do you do?

Scenario #2:

Your business is expanding every quarter. The new employees need to be indoctrinated into your company's mindset, as outlined by your CEO, and taught how best to use the recently completed intranet infrastructure. What do you do?

Scenario #3:

You've just introduced a new product that your on-the-road sales force needs to under-stand—and it's six months until the next sales conference. There's no time, and certainly no budget, to bring everyone in for an in-person introduction. What do you do?

Increasingly, corporations are turning to distance learning solutions, particularly those involving the Internet or the corporate intranet. Although useful, the video conferencing solutions that emerged in the late 1980s have also proven to be expensive, both in required equipment and scheduling of personnel. The more recent Web-based instruction methods have the benefits of needing a smaller investment in hardware and offering greater flexibility when it comes to available training times.

Today's desktop systems are capable of handling an impressive degree of multimedia technology—CD-ROMs, digital video and audio, even virtual reality. However, it's not the playback of the information that's the primary factor in deciding which format to use, it's the timeliness of the content that makes the Internet so important. Web-based training allows time-sensitive information to be distributed, or *narrowcast,* to all the right people at a far lower cost than traditional broadcasting.

Not all types of training are right for distance learning. According to Philip McCrea, Vice-President of Training Services Group of C3i, Inc., a company specializing in online training for sales force automation, three key questions to ask yourself when determining whether a situation is right for distance learning are

- Is what you're teaching wholly new to the participants? If so, it might not be appropriate for distance learning. Online training works better where the application being taught is similar to a familiar one.

- What's the degree of technological competency in the target group? The more proficient the students are, the quicker they'll be able to adapt to the new teaching methods.

- Is the subject matter modular? It's difficult to maintain an online training session for long periods of time—90 minutes is optimum. If the topic can be broken into smaller pieces, the online learning can accrue over a series of lessons.

The Internet can act as a delivery system for your training lessons, which enables your employees to download the instructional material from a central source. Complete demonstrations or lessons can then be played back on the user's machine whenever desired. Because all the information is stored on the user's system, this is called a local presentation.

Recent advances have also made remote broadcasting over the Internet possible through a technology known as *streaming media.* Streaming audio and video are being used increasingly to disseminate both live and previously recorded presentations. The following sections describe what's possible with local presentations and streaming media; a section also describes a method for combining technologies for the best results.

Local Presentations

Initially, multimedia content—digital audio, video, or interactive slide-shows—needed to be downloaded over the Internet before it could be viewed. This method of transferring content to a local system before reviewing it is still useful for many types of corporate training, such as employee orientation or product familiarization. The key benefits of a local presentation are

- Playback and interaction are immediate, after the files are transferred.

- The multimedia content can be updated at a single source, eliminating all duplication and most distribution costs.

- The instructional material can be reviewed by the user repeatedly, without further use of the Internet.

The single largest drawback to using local presentations delivered over the Web as a distance learning tool can be summed up in two words: file size. The more media-rich the instructional content is, the larger the file—the larger the file, the longer the download. Depending on the type of Internet connection that the user has, this might be a factor; a local area network connection to a T1 line offers optimum connection speeds, but a dial-up modem line is at the lowest end of the spectrum. If the download takes too long, the user might be hesitant to begin the transfer process in a normally busy day. On the other hand, most modern desktop systems can handle more than one task at a time, so the user could conceivably perform other computing chores while downloading the presentation.

Because of the file size issue, techniques have been developed to compress the files. One of the leaders in the field, Macromedia, extended its multimedia compression capability called Shockwave to its courseware program, Authorware. In addition to incorporating digital audio, video, or high-resolution photographs, Authorware offers a complete interactive capability. It's been estimated that people retain 10% of what they see, 15% of what they see and hear, and 85% of what they see, hear, and interact with. Figure 7.1 shows a screen from an Authorware instructional program devised for the Dialog Corporation, an information resource company.

Case Study: Honeywell Inc.

Honeywell is the world's leading supplier of avionics systems for commercial, military, and space markets. Honeywell technology has been on board every manned U.S. space flight since Mercury, and it is on nearly every commercial aircraft flying today.

Figure 7.1 Courseware such as this one written using Authorware can be accessed by the user on an as-needed basis.

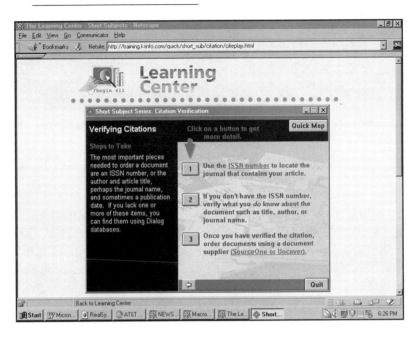

In order to help aviation personnel experience real-life radar scenarios while sitting at a desk, Honeywell developed an Airborne Radar Management Simulator program using Authorware. Through interaction with the simulator and its accompanying tutorial, trainees learn the basics of airborne weather radar, the effects of antennae size on radar, and storm types and resulting weather patterns—all without incurring the high cost either of actual flight training or leasing an industry simulator.

The Airborne Radar Management Simulator, shown in Figure 7.2, has demonstrated dramatic results in decreasing the cost of training pilots on Honeywell's radar systems. In fact, the simulator has attracted the attention of major airlines and other companies that operate fleets of planes, such as DHL Worldwide Express.

Many local presentations use a slide-show metaphor, where screen after screen of information is presented to the user. Microsoft's NetShow is an excellent program for incorporating this type of presentation, primarily because of the capability to use PowerPoint files. The recently released NetShow server software can integrate PowerPoint presentations with audio and video. NetShow can also handle a degree of interactivity that enables multiple choice questions leading to a number of responses.

Figure 7.2   Distance learning can handle training on highly sophisticated applications, such as this in-air radar simulator.

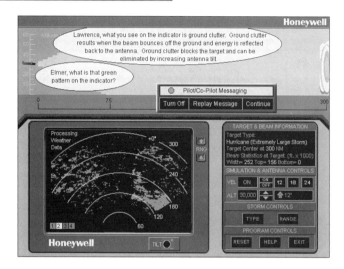

Many programs, NetShow included, can handle a variety of formats, including local presentations and streaming audio and video, as described in the following section.

Streaming Audio and Video

The problems associated with the large size of multimedia files prompted the streaming media solutions pioneered by RealNetworks. *Streaming media* is audio, video, animation, or text that begins playing shortly after the download is begun. The file continues to stream and play until it is finished.

FAQ: What's the hardware investment for streaming media?
Streaming media requires special network server software, but it doesn't necessarily require additional hardware. If, however, your organization places a great emphasis on streaming video and—to a lesser degree—streaming audio, you may need to beef up the intranet infrastructure with additional servers and networking to achieve the necessary bandwidth.

Streaming media makes live real-time broadcasts over the Web possible. Although the quality of both video and audio is not the best, it is improving by leaps and bounds with each new release. As of this writing, RealNetworks is now previewing its latest version, referred to as G2, which vastly improves the quality over even the slowest connection. Moreover, G2 adds the capability to download multiple streams of content simultaneously, opening the range of possibilities even further. In short order, you can expect to see training applications with streaming video, a slide-show presentation, and real-time chat—all on the same desktop system.

Case Study: Lucent Technologies, Inc.

Focused on worldwide communications, Lucent Technologies has offices and distributors in over 90 countries around the world. It reported revenue of $26.4 billion in fiscal year 1997.

Lucent Technologies is a big believer in streaming media. According to Bob Yurkovic, Manager of the Information Solutions Group, Lucent uses streaming media such as RealAudio to enhance its corporate communications and add depth to regular text announcements. Lucent also maintains an online library of audio archives of important industry speeches. Prior to the availability of digital-audio files, these archives were distributed via tape cassette. Now Lucent has found that using a central Web source has cut distribution costs and centralized the management of the archives. Lucent is also experimenting with daily 10-minute updates delivered via streaming audio over the Web. This access allows executives to listen to the important news of the day over Lucent's private intranet network.

Two special digital video methods

Apple has developed a multimedia format called QuickTime VR, which offers several unique possibilities. With QuickTime, you can make panoramic movies that allow a 360° view of a location—perfect for showing an environment. QuickTime also enables you to make movies that allow the viewer to see 3D images of an object, even as the object spins around. For more about QuickTime, visit the Apple Web site at quicktime.apple.com.

Teleconferencing with the Web

One of the complaints about computer-based or Web-based instruction is the lack of a human touch. Many employees pick up needed tasks more quickly if they have access to a trainer who can guide them over the trouble spots. Classroom training is an obvious, but expensive, alternative. Not only are in-person trainers costly, but so is the time taken away from the regular workday. Figure 7.3 illustrates comparative costs between classroom training and distance learning.

Another training route combines the visual interactiveness of the Web with the responsiveness of a personal trainer, but using teleconferencing technology to keep costs low. One company, C3i, Inc., a leader in sales force automation instruction, specializes in this technique called remote-based training (RBT). With RBT, all the travel and entertainment expenses associated with an in-person training session are avoided. This technique works very well with teaching new applications or enhancements to existing applications that normally would require a half-day or less of training.

Figure 7.3   The largest single cost for classroom training is physically bringing all your students together. Distance learning completely eliminates that expense.

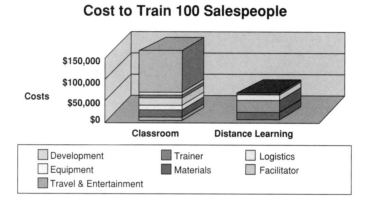

One-to-Many Training

Remote-based training generally takes one of two approaches: one-to-many or one-to-one. In a one-to-many scenario, the application or visual aids are posted to the Web. Before the session begins, each participant goes online and either downloads the necessary material or accesses the private Web site through a supplied password. At an appointed time, a conference call is arranged with the trainer and each of the students—for optimum impact, the virtual class size is kept to 6-8 participants. The trainer proceeds through a lesson plan, answering individual questions along the way. Participants can be either in a computer-center classroom or stationed at their own work areas.

A case from C3i's files illustrates the one-to-many remote-based training technique. A large financial services consumer company needed to migrate 200 of its sales people from an in-house contact management system to a customized version of Act. Because the sales force was composed of computing beginners and more savvy software users, C3i set up two training tracks. The RBT took place over a two-week period in the company's computer centers, and each class lasted 90 minutes. Whereas traditional classroom training for the same procedure would be budgeted at approximately $175,000, this remote-based training came in at just over $30,000.

One-to-One Training

The one-to-one RBT sessions, as devised by C3i, are especially effective when an on-the-road sales force is involved. Rather than spending a day of effective selling in a classroom, the training can be handled over the phone and the Web at the salesperson's discretion. Scheduled training times are established in advance and confined to a one- or two-week period. In one RBT situation, C3i was asked to train 200 sales representatives on an enhancement to its central sales force automation application. The training had to be accomplished in two weeks, in time for the national sales meeting.

The enhancement was disbursed through *electronic software distribution* over the Web, and the one-to-one RBT took place over a week's time. Although follow-up calls were available, 93% of the training was completed during the first call. Feedback from the sales representatives was overwhelmingly positive and indicated that the training was ideal for this type of situation. They especially appreciated that they could receive person-to-person training without taking time away from selling. The one-to-one RBT was effective from a cost analysis as well; final expenses for the remote-based training were 73% less than an equivalent in-person training.

Corporate Communications

Corporate training, in the overall sense, is never a one-time deal. The spirit, as well as the specifics, of the organization are communicated daily through everything from new employee orientations to important policy speeches by the CEO. Distance learning techniques are directly applicable to this broad range of corporate communiqués.

Employee Orientation

As the enterprise grows, so grows the amount of information each employee needs to function properly. Some companies are taking the high-technology road to employee orientation, and finding that the message is more consistently delivered with greater impact and at lower cost.

Case Study: Sybase Inc.
Sybase, Inc. is a leader in database solutions, data access, and data movement products, with its development tools such as Oracle. The company reported a total revenue of $903,937,000 for 1997.

Sybase is one company that recognizes the value of keeping its employees up to speed on both the overall market and the company's specific goals. To this end, Sybase uses Real-Video to distribute its employee orientation videos. The video, available on the intranet, covers information about the company, its products, and the benefits and responsibilities of its employees. By making the orientation available on demand, Sybase has found that the speed and efficiency of new-hire training has been vastly improved.

Case Study: Attachmate Corporation

For more than 16 years, Attachmate has been a leading provider of connectivity software, enabling PC users to safely and securely access mission-critical information located on hosts. Attachmate has 10 million customers worldwide and offices in 30 countries.

An intranet is a wonderful tool for gathering, storing, and retrieving information—as long as your employees can find their way around it. Attachmate has developed an intranet tour for new employees using RealNetwork's RealAudio Synchronized Multimedia. A pre-recorded, digitized narration explains the company's intranet areas while displaying the current content. This degree of timeliness is not possible in a video tour that has been previously recorded. The intranet tour begins in the Human Resources Web page for overall information about employee benefits and corporate policies. Next, the current company information page is displayed with an up-to-date organizational chart, office listing, and other pertinent data. All along, the narration describes the intranet page in general terms while the current page is shown.

Conveying Company Strategy

Sharing the vision of a corporation's leaders with the rest of the company has become a more obtainable reality thanks to intranet-based information. The more spread out an enterprise is, the more difficult it is to make corporate announcements across the board. The multimedia aspects of distance learning bring a whole new level of portability for the message and understanding for the employees.

Case Study: General Electric

General Electric (GE) is one of the world's largest diversified companies. GE operates in more than 100 countries around the world, including 250 manufacturing plants in 26 nations. GE employs 239,000 people worldwide, including 155,000 in the United States. Revenues in 1997 topped $90 billion.

General Electric was looking for a way to make its quarterly teleconference hosted by its CEO accessible to all employees. By teaming up with RealNetworks, GE's Information Services group was able to multicast the two-hour discussion to 2,400 employees in more than 100 locations. The formerly one-way teleconference became a live digital-video broadcast across GE's existing global network, with question and answer capabilities and immediate archiving for future playback.

Case Study: MCI Telecommunications, Inc.

MCI is one of the world's largest telecommunications companies, with 1997 revenue of $19.7 billion. Headquartered in Washington, D.C., MCI has 60,000 employees in more than 300 cities around the globe.

MCI broadened the concept of corporate communications by establishing its Virtual Forum series. Not only are corporate leaders able to deliver their strategic planning messages, but experts within the company can pass on key information. Previous intranet multicasts have included such topics as Enterprise Security as well as a motivational speaker forum. With a single forum going out to almost 1,500 digital video streams, MCI estimates that an equivalent employee meeting would have cost $550,000 in travel costs alone.

Just-in-Time Training

Educating resellers about your products is a particularly difficult problem. Only the most motivated resellers can wade through the tonnage of product literature that lands on their desks month after month. To properly train your resellers, your product information has to be compelling, concise, and engaging. Sales representatives need to know the key product advantages as well as the product's functionality. In today's fast-moving market with its ever-shortened product cycles, information can't be canned—the training has to be just-in-time.

Case Study: AT&T Wireless Services

AT&T Wireless Services, Inc., is a wholly owned subsidiary of AT&T Corporation and the leading provider of wireless communications services in the United States, which include wireless telephone, messaging, wireless data transmission, and aviation communications. Revenue for the first quarter of 1998 was listed as $1.11 billion.

A division of AT&T, AT&T Wireless Services (then known as the Global Information Systems division) found that it could deliver just-in-time training to its major resellers through an intranet-based desktop video conferencing system. The desktop video system enabled interactivity between the trainers and the resellers, and it provided the compelling focus needed to convey product information.

At the time, AT&T Wireless was introducing a new product called MessageFlash—software that could send a message from a personal computer to a pager. To test its just-in-time training techniques, AT&T Wireless arranged to train representatives from Inacom Corporation, a major U.S. reseller, at five sites around the country. To reinforce the training, each representative was given a pager that could be addressed during the training session.

An AT&T moderator, marketing personnel, and presenters spoke with the Inacom sites from Dayton, Ohio, and product experts contributed specialized knowledge from their base in South Carolina. After the moderator established the expectations of the trainees regarding content and technical issues, marketing information was presented by the marketing experts in Dayton, with pre-arranged questions asked of the sites every 10 to 15 minutes regarding issues they faced. Training points were summarized at regular intervals, and each location was polled for involvement.

Then MessageFlash was demonstrated. Reseller representatives were shown how to activate the pager, and then viewed the actions performed on the PC at Dayton that initiated the call. After a few minutes, the message appeared on the pager at the site, with each site receiving a unique message. A marketing videotape that included product testimonials was played over the desktop video system, and a final wrap-up ensued.

Again, the key cost savings came from travel for the AT&T personnel and the resellers. The inclusion of various experts in marketing and product design allowed a wider range of issues to be addressed than if only a well-prepped trainer had been involved. Moreover, because the various sites were interconnected, each group of resellers benefited from hearing the issues raised by their counterparts around the country.

The evolution of the Internet/intranet as a multimedia, interactive information delivery system has made just-in-time training a very real option.

Virtual Classrooms

Distance learning has many advocates in academic circles. The promise of a university open 24 hours a day, 7 days a week has prompted numerous campuses to offer online courses, both for auditing purposes and for academic credit. The techniques pioneered by such online universities have been adapted by industry to suit the constant training needs of a corporation.

One company in the vanguard of creating virtual classrooms is Centra Software, Inc. (www.centra.com), makers of Symposium. Symposium combines live training—accomplished with audio streaming technology—with interactive discussion over the Internet or a company's intranet. The incorporation of leader-led training with multimedia elements gives Symposium an edge many corporations have found compelling. The software interface, shown in Figure 7.4, gives trainees a chance to interact fully.

Figure 7.4 Distance learning software such as Symposium can handle large classroom situations.

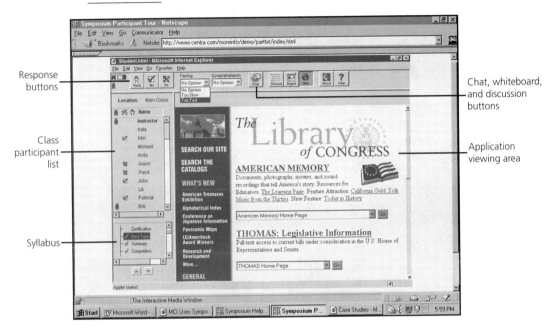

- Students can ask to be heard by symbolically raising their hands through the click of a button.

- At a glance, you can see who says they understand a point and who does not with Symposium's Yes/No buttons.

- Trainees can use virtual break-out rooms to form smaller, special interest groups for more detailed discussions.

- Multiway audio allows the trainer to "pass the microphone" so students can make their points or ask questions for all to hear.

- Application sharing and whiteboards are available to further enhance the point-to-point communication.

- Students can offer immediate feedback to the instructor regarding the speed of the presentation (too fast or too slow) or the degree of comprehension (clear or confusing).

Symposium is a powerful, distance learning software. In a recent test, MCI Systemhouse, MCI's global information technology company, used the software to work with a class of 50 students scattered across the U.S. and Canada. Participants felt that the session closely paralleled a live classroom situation. Moreover, some elements were deemed to be improvements. The text chat feature offers the ability to send the instructor a private message, for example, and the pacing and comprehension options enable the student to anonymously provide feedback.

Online Testing

With online learning comes online testing. Many of the distance learning solutions offer some form of evaluation. Forms on the Internet allow the standard methods of testing: fill-in-the-blank, multiple choice, and essay. It's even possible to have your students attach a previously written paper for submission.

One of the key advantages of online testing designed for multiple choice selections, and to a lesser extent, fill-in-the-blank, is that instant evaluation is possible. After a test has been completed, the online student clicks the submit button and the program evaluates the student's answers against the administrator-programmed solutions. The test results can be instantly sent to the administrator or provided to the student for feedback. Furthermore, the current student's test results can be compared to those of other students and incorporated into a report generated for the administrator.

In addition to the usual Internet advantages of having the capability to be administered anywhere in the world at any time, online testing has another advantage—the tests can be timed. From the time the students figuratively "pick up their pencils" until the end of the test, an ongoing timer can be running—and if desired, displayed for the student.

One company that handles online testing is Virtual Learning Technologies (`www.vlearning.com`). Its Prove-It software can be administered over the Web or on a company's intranet. Much of Prove-It's existing tests are geared to evaluating a job applicant's skill level in particular areas and computer applications. A company can opt to make one or many tests available. Applicants are given a user name and a password. The tests are multiple choice, as shown in Figure 7.5.

After the student has completed the test, he or she is free to go back over the questions and make any corrections. To complete the test, the student clicks the Submit button at the bottom of the test. After the Submit button is selected, the test results are evaluated and sent to the administrator. A sample administrator test report is shown in Figure 7.6. The student may receive feedback. On the sample test that I took, I was told which questions I got wrong, the correct answers, and the percentage of incorrect answers I had submitted. The student feedback can be as detailed as the administrator desires.

Figure 7.5 Online tests allow you to evaluate any student from anywhere via the Internet.

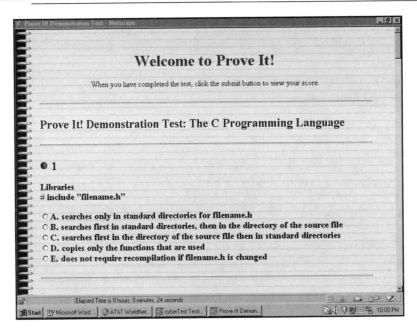

Figure 7.6 The test administrator receives a full report from an online test by email, minutes after the student completes the test.

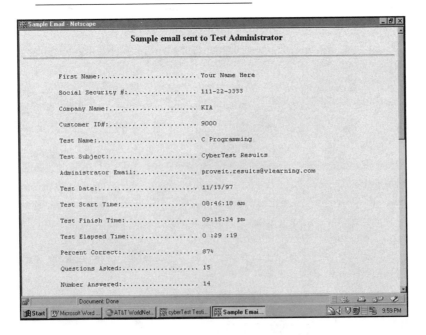

8

Accessing the World Wide Job Bank

- Extolling the virtues of your company online

- Placing want ads on the Web

- Using résumé databases

- Automatic employee searches

Using the Web to Publicize Job Openings

The Internet of today is known primarily as a marketing vehicle. The key function of a Web site is to provide information to help the company market its products and services. Therefore, you will find elaborate descriptions of a company's history, customer base, products and services, rates, and ordering information. Enticing customers is a company's main objective, in most cases.

However, companies making full use of their Web sites understand that it is capable of much more than marketing and sales. Yes, it is a marketing tool, but attracting customers is but one role. Attracting employees, suppliers, or business partners are additional—and equally important—roles.

Most companies have viewed the Internet solely as a means of disseminating information, but in fact, it can also offer two-way communications capabilities. Email links and online forms are great ways of soliciting feedback from customers, suppliers, employees, and potential employees. Such tools also enhance the efficiency of your organization, providing a central point of contact.

The Internet is an efficient and effective employment tool because of its convenience. By centralizing information on the Web site—such as company marketing materials, a listing of job openings, and online communications tools—job applicants can quickly and easily submit their résumés for consideration and companies can quickly and easily find the most qualified candidates for open positions.

Finding Qualified Employees Online

Finding qualified employees is becoming increasingly difficult these days. From Fortune 500 corporations to startup high-tech ventures to nonprofit agencies, virtually every type of organization is struggling with how to find and keep talented employees.

Whether the reason is tied to the improving economy, the graying of the workforce, or the shift from an industrial to a service economy, it's irrelevant. The fact is (as established in a study by Virginia Polytechnic Institute and State University and the Information Technology Association of America) that 346,000 Information Technology (IT) positions are currently vacant in the three core IT occupational clusters—129,000 in 5,874 IT companies and 217,000 in 97,733 non-IT corporations with more than 100 employees.

The lack of skilled and experienced workers is evident in almost every industry. And competition for the best and brightest is fierce.

Companies that continue to rely on traditional forms of announcing job openings will find it more difficult, time-consuming, and costly to reach potential employees. They will be at a significant competitive disadvantage to companies that are willing to test new recruiting tools. The Internet is one such tool that is already proving valuable to understaffed companies and job seekers alike.

Job applicants seem to have already recognized the potential of the Internet. Scanning online job banks has become a routine activity for many individuals, in addition to publicly posting résumés. But companies still unfamiliar with the Internet's capabilities have yet to make it part of their recruitment activities; those already familiar have a distinct advantage.

A few of the advantages of using the Internet to identify potential employees include:

- *Speed*. Traditional advertisements in a local or national newspaper can lead to waiting days or weeks for a response from interested applicants. Job offerings posted on the Internet can generate responses in hours, or even less.

- *Cost*. Reaching a regional or national audience can be accomplished extremely cost-effectively through online postings and job listings on popular career databases. How cost effective? Quite often, they are free.

- *Flexibility.* The scope of your candidate search can be expanded or narrowed as needed, varying factors such as location, salary, and title in order to identify more or fewer prospects.

- *Efficiency.* Using the built-in capabilities of the Internet also reduces the amount of involvement your human resource department needs to have. Instead of getting bogged down in low-level administrative activities such as placing ads, responding to initial inquiries, and sorting résumés, your human resource manager can focus on more strategic issues. Inexpensive search agents and automatic response mechanisms can do the rest.

FAQ: What is an Internet search agent?

Unlike a search engine that waits for you to enter criteria, a *search agent* is a computer program that automatically—and continually—sifts through mounds of online data in search of information you've requested. If you want to identify potential job candidates for an engineering manager slot you have open, for example, you can use a search agent to quickly and routinely scan new résumés on various Web sites. When a résumé appears that matches the criteria you've set, the search agent automatically alerts you. You'll find out more about search agents later in this chapter.

Developing a Candidate Profile

Two primary sources of job candidates are on the Web—your company's Web site and public databases, which we'll discuss shortly. To make the most of both sources, however, you'll want to first develop a clear profile of the types of job applicants you want to consider. The broader your definition of a qualified applicant, the more mail you'll find in your already-stuffed electronic mailbox. Conversely, the more defined your profile, the more efficient and effective your search will be.

In developing a candidate profile, you may want to consider using one or more of the following criteria:

- Job title

- Years of experience

- Years of industry-specific experience

- Educational level or degrees achieved

- Salary requirements

- Industry certifications, such as CPA or APR

- Budget amounts managed

- Supervisory experience

- Years in last position, or with last employer

- Specific functional experiences, such as repairing certain types of equipment or writing specific types of documents

After you've prepared a candidate profile, you're ready to begin the hunt. And the easiest place to start is also the closest—your own company's Web site.

Luring Candidates to Work for You

Many organizations have discovered that some of the best job prospects are people who visit their company's Web site. Someone who takes the time to scope you out online has already demonstrated some level of interest just by being there.

Promoting from Within—Online

Companies generally post openings internally first. Traditionally, this posting goes up on a central bulletin board or in a company newsletter. However, with an intranet, job postings can be reach the entire organization through the HR Web page. As with other publications on the intranet, you save both printing and distribution time and effort.

Why people initially came to your site doesn't matter. Perhaps they stopped in to review the company's financial statements, to learn about your newest product announcement, or to find a dealer close to home. Again, it doesn't matter. What matters is how you're going to use this opportunity to make them potential employment prospects. Now is your opportunity to capitalize on their presence and excite them into considering employment with your organization.

Many companies have set aside a separate "Job Opportunities" section on their Web site, where prospective employees can view current openings. This is really just the tip of the iceberg in terms of what can be done to entice visitors to become job applicants. Individuals often go to these areas because they're exploring what's available in the job market, not necessarily because the job is available with your company.

What you have now is a prime opportunity to "sell" visitors on your organization. You've given them a solid overview of what the job entails; now tell them more about the company as a whole. What makes your company unique? Fun? Challenging? What is it about your business that makes people want to work there? That's what you need to convey to your Web visitors.

Salary, work hours, benefits, and opportunities for advancement are only part of the picture for most applicants. In addition, they need to understand the corporate culture at your organization, as well as the company's mission, priorities, client base, future direction, and values.

Although an employer would like to think so, employees don't make job decisions based on the company alone. The quality of life, the cost of living, the educational opportunities, the climate—all these are factors which enter into consideration. Many companies spend as much room on their Web site describing the environment—both work and general living—as they do the specific position.

Using the Internet, you can convey this information in a number of ways. You can write about it, creating separate pages on the Web site to discuss each of these areas. You can include audio clips from managers, employees, and clients describing their view of the organization. Video clips and photos are a great way to give a tour of a facility, show the company's product portfolio, or communicate the important service work the company does.

Your goal should be to inform and excite every visitor who enters your "Job Opportunities" area. Not only will you expand your pool of potential employees, but you'll improve your selection process. With more information in hand at the start, potential employees can do a better job of self-selecting and de-selecting. That is, with a clear picture of what your company does and is, you'll receive fewer applications from individuals who don't fit your corporate culture. In the end, you'll hear from better qualified, better informed applicants.

Case Study: Oracle Corporation

Oracle Corp. (Nasdaq: ORCL) is the world's leading supplier of software for information management, and the world's second-largest software company. With annual revenues exceeding $6 billion, Oracle offers its database, tools and applications products, along with related consulting, education, and support services, in more than 140 countries around the world.

Oracle's Web site is a prime example of how to use the Internet to attract employees. Its job-related pages are contained in an area called Oracle University, which gives the company an opportunity to cover all aspects of its corporate life. Because Oracle has one West Coast location—outside of San Francisco—and two East Coast locations—Nashua, New Hampshire and Waltham, Massachusetts—the Web site extolls the virtues of all three so-called campuses. A multimedia presentation offered in QuickTime format combines digital video and audio to make the company pitch.

Oracle University offers a tour of each campus, the fitness center, the neighborhoods, and even the company café. In addition to physical locales, Oracle plays up its links to the community with information on its volunteer program. The site offers extensive information on

Oracle's continuing education opportunities—guaranteed to be a factor in any up-and-coming potential employee looking for advancement possibilities.

In the center of all this is an extensive job listing page. Each job listing, as shown in Figure 8.1, offers the title, work area, department, office location, and the required degrees—as well as other prerequisites and responsibilities. When prospective employees respond by email, they can reference this job description and attach their résumés.

Figure 8.1   Oracle maintains an extensive list of available jobs on its Web site as part of its Oracle University campus.

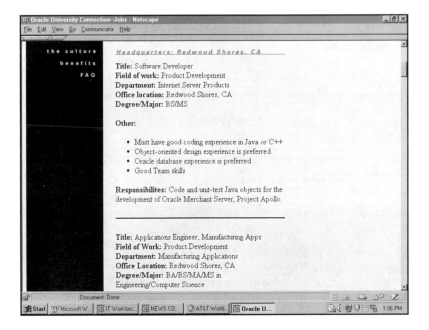

Working with Newsgroups

Elsewhere in this book, private newsgroups are discussed as offering terrific opportunities for team interaction. However, public newsgroups are extensively used to market job opportunities as well. Briefly, a *newsgroup* is an ongoing open discussion where anyone on the Internet can post a message or a response to a previously posted message.

Free Money! Free Money!
Perhaps the biggest annoyance in the newsgroups is the constant barrage of junk postings of "get-rich-quick" schemes. These can be readily identified with their blaring message headers offering everything for free. Most groups advise that you don't even justify their existence with a response.

Newsgroups are maintained on very specific subjects in a format such as, "alt.medical.sales.jobs.offered." The easiest way to locate a jobs newsgroup is to use your newsreader to search for the "job" keyword. The jobs listed tend to fall into one of three categories: industry, location, or company. The newsgroup listing displayed in Figure 8.2, for example, is from the bionet.jobs group, which specializes in the biology industry.

Figure 8.2 Newsgroups are a good source to find very technically savvy individuals interested in specific industries or topics.

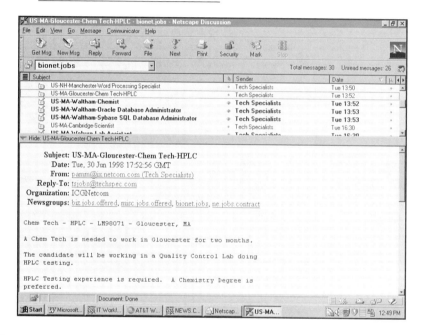

Setting Up a Career Page

To expand and enhance the purpose of your company's Web site, begin by establishing a career section or page. In this area, site visitors should be able to read, watch, or listen to information about your company and the type of people it seeks to hire.

FAQ: What is a bookmark?

When you bookmark a site, you are actually asking the computer to note where it is so that you can return easily. By choosing a simple command on your Internet browser, such as **Add Bookmark** or **Add Favorite**, you can capture the Web address of a particular site and save it on your hard drive. The more you use the Internet, the more book-marks—or Favorites—you'll collect.

Your career page should list current job openings and cutoff dates for applications. Both internal and external candidates should be able to submit their applications through the site. Keeping this list constantly updated will give visitors a reason to come back regularly, or even to bookmark the site.

Instructions regarding your company's application process, timeline for consideration, and hiring practices should also be prominent in this area. The more information you provide about the criteria being used to evaluate candidates—the turnaround time on résumés and potential for future consideration—the more you will improve the image of your company in the applicants' eyes. Because information is power, the more power you give applicants over their job search process, the more positively they will feel about your organization. Finally, the more information you can supply on the Web, the less time Human Resources will spend answering the same questions in person.

Links Create Opportunities

A useful feature unique to the Internet is the capability to establish links to other sites. That is, you can refer people who visit your career page to related sites simply at the click of an onscreen button. Instead of having to repeat the same information that appears elsewhere, you can just request a link to that site. Although you don't really need the other organization's permission to link your page to theirs, it's a good idea to notify them. Often the company will respond with a reciprocal link, sending traffic your way, as well.

In an employee search, links can help increase the number of visitors to your corporate Web site, as well as the number of applications you receive.

Links could be established between any of the following types of organizations:

- College and university placement offices
- High schools
- Professional and trade organizations
- Clients
- Suppliers
- Nonprofit organizations
- Related-industry career Web sites
- Recruitment firms

Look for organizations where a percentage of the members or constituents would be desirable employees. Encouraging Web traffic from those types of organizations is likely to increase job applications from its members.

You don't always have to offer reciprocal links, but if you do, keep in mind that you are offering to place a button on your site leading visitors to their site. If, for any reason, you would not want to encourage visits to another organization's Web site, they are not a strong link prospect for you.

Think of a link as a partnership between two sites; both organizations must benefit from the linkage in order for it to make sense.

Extend Newspaper Ads

Just as Web links are an opportunity for partnerships, employment searches create new partnering relationships as well.

Take newspaper advertising, for example. In late 1995, six major newspapers and their publishing parents partnered to create an online career management site that would supplement newspaper "Help Wanted" advertisements. Named CareerPath.com, this new site, shown in Figure 8.3, enables job seekers and employers to search for a match. All "Help Wanted" ads printed in participating daily papers across the country are loaded into the CareerPath database for perusal by visitors. In addition, visitors can submit a résumé to the Résumé Connection for potential review by employers.

If your company uses print advertising as a means of identifying potential employees, be sure to investigate whether you are entitled to be listed on any supplementary Web sites. Having your ad posted online increases the readership tremendously at little or no additional cost. That's where partnering makes sense.

Public Databases Extend Your Reach

A final, but extremely important, avenue for alerting potential employees to job openings is the online public database. Accessible by anyone with Internet access, job banks are a boon to job seekers, especially individuals looking beyond their immediate area.

Publicizing job openings via job databases incrementally increases the number of potential candidates who will see them.

Some of the more popular career and employment Web sites are

- www.careerpath.com
- www.monster.com

- www.careermosaic.com

- www.bestjobsusa.com

- www.careers.org

- www.espan.com

- www.helpwanted.com

On each site you'll find an employer section where you can learn the process for posting job opportunities online.

Figure 8.3   CareerPath enables you to explore hundreds of newspaper job listings at a time, using your own search criteria.

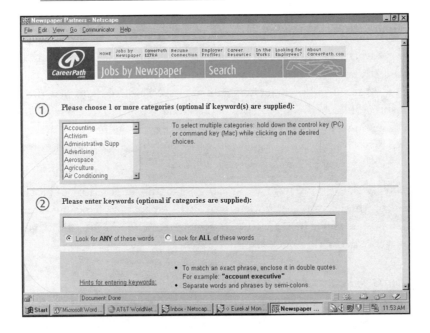

The Mechanics of Job Hunting Online

Job hunters need to know specific online techniques, the same as they must know the etiquette of applying for work offline. Unfortunately, no standard method has emerged to date that can be implemented across the board. The following sections take a look at several of the more automated solutions.

Online Job Applications

Traditionally, potential employees were asked to submit a résumé and cover letter, or to complete a printed job application before they could be considered for any job openings at a company. To receive a job application, a candidate needed to either call, write, or visit the company. Then, after completion, the application had to be sent back for review. The process could take days or weeks.

By placing an online job application on a company's Web site, the organization makes applying for a job more convenient and less time-consuming. Responses to applicants can also be achieved more quickly, simply by sending a return email message.

Case Study: Microsoft

Microsoft is an $11.4 billion computer software company employing more than 25,000 workers worldwide. Microsoft products include operating systems for personal computers, server applications, business and consumer productivity applications, and interactive media programs.

To make it easy for potential job applicants to be considered for openings, Microsoft has included a "Résumé Builder" on its site. By clicking **Résumé Builder**, shown in Figure 8.4, at `www.microsoft.com/isapi/jobs/mshridc/sub2.idc`, potential employees can craft a combination job application and résumé that can be immediately submitted to the company for review. The advantage to Microsoft is increased applications, and to applicants, faster consideration and response.

Online Job Orders

In addition to receiving applications more efficiently via the Internet, businesses can also request staffing help online. Job requests, or orders, can be completed and submitted on a company's Web site, allowing action to be taken immediately to fill an opening.

Case Study: Sullivan's Staffing

Sullivan's Staffing (`www.awod.com/sullivans/`) is a South Carolina-based provider of personnel services. From temporary placement to contract staffing to employee leasing, Sullivan's Staffing provides companies in South Carolina and Georgia with qualified personnel.

To provide its customers with yet another way of reaching the company, Sullivan's has added an online job order form to its Web site, shown in Figure 8.5. Companies in need of additional staffing can complete the form and submit it online. After Sullivan's receives the form, it compares the position requirements to its database of available personnel. Résumés that match the job description can then be emailed or faxed to the requesting organization.

Figure 8.4 Microsoft uses Résumé Builder to provide a front end for its job solicitations, which stores all submitted information into a database for easy retrieval.

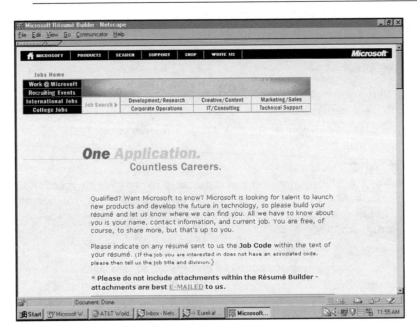

Not only do online order forms save time; they also save money. Instead of receiving multiple résumés by fax, which eats paper and toner, résumés can be reviewed online first. Only those to be seriously considered are printed.

Searching Résumé Database Centers

Although announcing available jobs is an important means of attracting interest from potential employees, evaluating résumés already posted is an equally valuable activity.

On most career databases, such as those listed earlier, along with information regarding the specific type of position they seek. These résumé databases provide employers with a built-in list of potential employees, complete with credentials and background information, in one central location.

College and university alumni Web sites may also prove fruitful when you're recruiting experienced professionals. Many educational institutions provide career support both to existing students and alumni through online résumé databases accessible by potential employers. Check with local colleges and universities, as well as national institutions with a reputation in the functional area you're working in, to see whether they offer an online résumé database. Use the keywords "university" and "placement" with any search engine to get a sense of what's out there. One such link led me to the State University of New York at Stony Brook's Web site, where the possibilities for on-campus recruiting, Internet recruiting, and other forums are detailed (see Figure 8.6).

Figure 8.5   Agencies such as Sullivan's Staffing offer online job order forms for easy employer access.

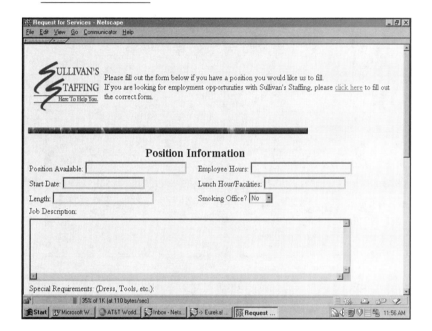

Not only are such searches efficient, they can save time and money. Although some sites require a small fee from employers, the fee is typically less than what a newspaper advertisement would cost. For companies desperate to fill a key opening, online résumé databases can be an excellent starting point.

Using Search Agents

A one-time search of a résumé database can provide potential candidates for an existing job opening, but routinely searching the same databases can become time-consuming and laborious. This is probably why search agents were developed.

The largest career databases have introduced search agents as a means of providing ongoing search capabilities, even when you're offline. After entering criteria regarding the type of job candidates you'd like to evaluate, a search agent makes you aware of any new résumés that are submitted matching the criteria you have set.

Figure 8.6 The placement offices of many universities sponsor Web pages, such as this one from SUNY Stony Brook, to encourage campus recruitment.

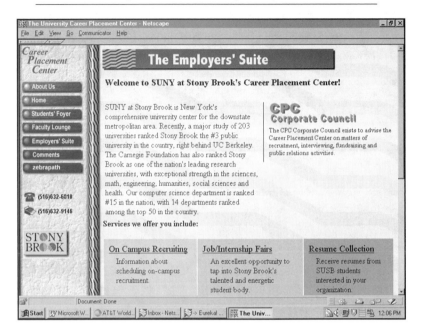

As job openings change or the company's hiring needs change, the search criteria can also be changed.

The Monster Board, shown in Figure 8.7, is a leader in the use of search agents, both on behalf of job seekers and employers. By creating a character called "Swoop," the company helps visitors understand the benefit of such a service. Through the use of such agents, the Monster Board gives job seekers a reason to frequently visit the site; whenever Swoop sends a message that a job has been posted that may be of interest, job seekers head back to the Monster Board.

Competitive Intelligence at Its Best

Keep in mind that every advantage has its corresponding disadvantage, and the Web is no different. In providing prospective employees a complete picture of your organization via the Internet, you're also educating your competitors.

Every job listing, every financial report, every description of salaries and benefits offered by your company becomes available to anyone who visits your site. Your company information quickly becomes competitive intelligence. Unfortunately, the Internet cannot yet distinguish between a true job seeker and a resourceful competitor trying to gain an edge. So be mindful as you post information online for potential employees that it will also be seen by the competition. This doesn't necessarily mean you should limit the scope of information you provide, just that you need to evaluate whether you really want such details to be public.

Figure 8.7 Monster Board, one of the largest Internet job sites, offers many services for employers and employees.

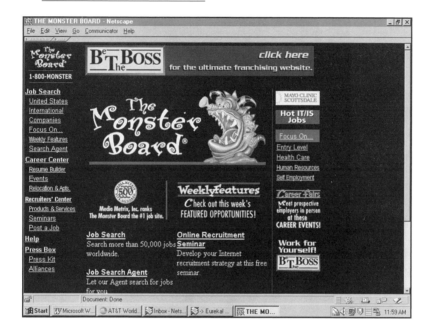

Despite this fact, speed, flexibility, and cost-effectiveness make the Internet an excellent resource for companies in need of quality employees.

PART IV

Production and Operations Management

Building Just In Time Systems

- Just in Time and online

- Minimizing back orders

- Handling inventory Just in Time

- Coordinating with suppliers

- Achieving Just in Time goals with EDI

Just In Time Benefits

I once consulted with a jewelry wholesaler who specialized in creating and importing Mexican silver. His business was perpetually close to extinction even though the orders were steady. The problem was inventory—he had too much of it. The stockroom represented several hundred thousand dollars of merchandise necessary for filling orders in a timely fashion.

To get his business on a more even keel, we instituted a series of Just in Time inventory management strategies. Inventory was computerized and tracked from order to receipt. Trade show orders were placed the next day, instead of a week later. Tighter quality control was instituted during the design and creation stages. Results? A lower inventory investment, a more robust cash flow, and minimum back orders.

Just in Time (JIT) techniques have come into their own with the enhanced communication possibilities brought by the Internet. This chapter examines online JIT strategies all the way down the supply chain from the reseller to the parts and components supplier. The chapter also covers the Electronic Data Interchange (EDI) initiative, which provided a major boost to Just in Time techniques by enabling trading partners to automate the ordering process.

Reducing Back Orders

Managing inventory is a tricky balance. You need to have enough goods in stock to handle customer orders as soon as they are placed, however, overstock and you find yourself inventory-rich, but cash poor. The problem is compounded when you continue receiving orders for goods that are not on-hand. Placing back orders can mean that your customers become frustrated with the delay in shipment while you have other merchandise sitting on the shelf.

One JIT strategy is to tackle the problem at the point of sale. Studies have shown that when customers know that the goods they have requested must be back ordered, the majority choose another in-stock item. Moreover, if the customer is informed up front of the delay and decides to place the back order anyway, the frustration level is drastically reduced. Finally, the reseller can keep informed of which items are so hot that they are being requested despite their back order status, and react accordingly.

This technique can be put into operation with any sales force that can connect to a central inventory database. Whether your salespeople are taking telephone orders or are on-the-road, a fully implemented Internet/intranet strategy can give them the feedback they need to offer the customer so that he can make an informed choice. A close connection between orders and inventory enables management to order new products on an as-needed basis and hold inventory to its lowest sustainable level.

Online resellers have a key advantage in back order control. Most virtual storefronts use some variation of an order form for customers to enter their requests. Although many of the current resellers simply accept the order without further processing, the savvier stores check the submitted order against in-stock inventory, and then inform the customer of any back orders. The more sophisticated stores even tell the customer when the product is expected.

Case study: Hammacher Schlemmer, Inc.

Founded in New York City in 1848, Hammacher Schlemmer has become the preeminent catalog source for the unusual and the essential. Their online storefront offers a full range of goods and they also have "offline" stores in New York, Chicago, and Beverly Hills.

Hammacher Schlemmer, best known for their catalog of exotic goods, has integrated their online storefront with their backroom inventory. Any customer placing an order at www.hammacher.com sees exactly the quantity, size, color and style of each item requested and whether it's in stock or not. Moreover, if the item is expected in two weeks, the customer gets that information as well. All this information is passed to the customer before the order is finalized and when the option to continue shopping is but a mouse click away as shown in Figure 9.1.

Figure 9.1 Online resellers such as Hammacher Schlemmer tell their customers whether an item is available without a personal sales agent.

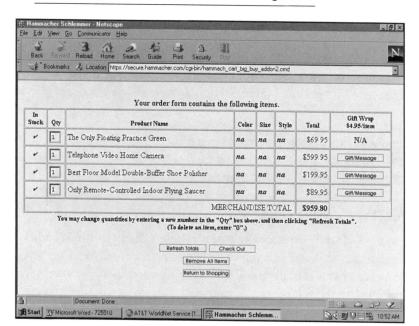

When a customer places an order for an in-stock item, the item is temporarily removed from inventory until the order is finalized and the credit card charge or other payment is approved. Certain types of online stores that must contend with a high-volume of sales for a limited quantity of goods, such as ticket agencies, hold the order for a set period of time, that is, three minutes. This enables a rapid turnover of merchandise that's in great demand.

Inventory Management

The goal of Just in Time inventory management is to keep the parts, supplies, or goods in your warehouse for the shortest amount of time. The enhanced connectivity made possible by the Internet can help manage inventory with:

- *Better tracking methods.* Today's technology enables you to follow the goods from the minute they are shipped in until the minute they're shipped out and arrive at their destination. The biggest sin in any JIT strategy is losing sight of your inventory.

- *Reacting more swiftly to demand.* By carefully monitoring demand increases (and decreases), you can better inform your suppliers of your needs. Ideally, you need to forge a close relationship with your trading partners, one that you can cement with the connectivity available through your intranet or extranet.

- *Planning for contingencies.* What if you're building television sets and your picture tube supplier went belly up? Do you have a backup plan to handle the supply problems? The global Internet lets you establish the connections today that you might need tomorrow.

- *Cashing out surplus inventory.* After you've identified merchandise that's no longer moving, your next problem is how to free up the capital that the excess inventory represents. The Internet offers a number of creative solutions including a direct-to-market online auction.

With the help of the Just in Time inventory strategies outlined in this section you can dramatically reduce your overhead and keep your inventory's stay in the warehouse as brief as possible.

Working the Wireless Warehouse

To achieve the fullest Just in Time advantages, it's not enough to record your incoming and outgoing shipments, even if you're computerizing the records. In fact, it's not even enough to know where each item is kept in your warehouse. To reap the most benefits, you have to wire your warehouse to the rest of your business. By using your intranet to communicate between the order-takers and the order-fillers, you'll cut waste, hasten delivery, and enhance customer satisfaction.

Warehouse technology has reached the wireless age. With the appropriate equipment, each forklift can be online and each stock person can enter information directly into the primary database through bar code readers and other tools. Moreover, the data connection doesn't have to be one way. Stock room managers can be alerted to orders already placed for incoming merchandise so that the goods won't have to be put on the shelf and then immediately taken off again.

Case Study: Quill Corporation

Founded in 1956 and headquartered in Lincolnshire, Illinois, Quill Corporation employs approximately 1,200 people nationwide. Quill is best known as one of the largest mail-order office supply companies.

Faced with filling over 15,000 office supply orders every day, Quill's warehouse has to be running at peak efficiency to give the company its needed edge. To keep its competitive lead, Quill put its warehouse services under the microscope. Although already relatively modern with bar-coding, automated conveyers, and a central computing system to handle its 750,000 customers, the survey turned up a telling weak spot. Upon mapping out the entire route that inventory must take, Quill found that the complete receiving, checking, and storing processes took up to 85 steps. The major stumbling block was the continued reliance on traditional "write it down" methods of recording information and then transferring the info to the computer system.

To supplement their existing technology, Quill brought in Integrated Warehousing Solutions (www.iws-irms.com), a software development firm that specializes in inventory management. Together, the decision was made to put more computing power on the warehouse floor itself and to link it to the existing systems. This meant supplementing the existing mainframe with a local area network that put terminals in the warehouse office and—using mobile radio-frequency terminals—on the forklifts themselves.

With enhanced inventory management software, incoming shipment information is put into the system right from the loading dock. Moreover, instead of waiting for the entire truckload to be sorted and stocked, each pallet of merchandise is bar-coded and deemed ready for order fulfillment. This gives Quill a much faster turnaround in all phases of shipping and receiving.

Perhaps the biggest innovation is the front-line to backroom connection. As shipments come in, the inventory management system checks to see if there are standing orders. If so, the terminals on the forklifts carrying the merchandise receive a message directing them to the same-day shipping area. By bypassing the warehouse storage phase, responsiveness to customer orders has improved noticeably. All in all, Quill's productivity has jumped 50 percent in the warehouse. Furthermore, the warehouse manager reports that the payback for the technology improvements was less than 7 months.

End of Life Cycle Programs

Let's say you've got all your suppliers for your primary product on a Just in Time schedule and the entire enterprise is so keenly honed that there's little room for error. Suddenly there's a glitch on the horizon: The manufacturers of a key component for your product announce that they are phasing out its production. You're now faced with the unpleasant choice of making a lifetime purchase of the remaining stock (and housing it somewhere) or finding an alternative and possibly retooling your system.

Neither of these alternatives is especially attractive. Buying out an entire product stock can be extraordinarily expensive, which is only part of the ongoing expense of warehousing the materials. Changing product design to accommodate an alternative component can not only cost money to retool, but you could also lose product functionality and eventually customer support.

The global connection of the Internet is your best resource for finding and securing contingency parts. Certain companies, such as General Materials Management (GMM), run end-of-life programs designed to work with such circumstances. In their case, GMM uses their global resources to locate and purchase the end-of-life product—they'll also handle the warehousing and Just in Time inventory management for you. Although their services aren't free, if you're working with a product that depends on particular components, it could be a far more cost expedient method than any of the alternatives.

Reducing Surpluses with a Liquidator

In inventory, too much is never a good thing. Excess inventory is money sitting high up on a shelf, out of reach. One of the primary goals of any Just in Time strategy is to reduce surplus inventory as much as possible. Depending on what exactly the excess inventory is, the Internet opens the door to a couple of methods for getting the most value from your stockroom.

If your excess inventory is primarily OEM (Original Equipment Manufacturer) components or parts necessary for further manufacturing, you could work with any number of consolidators over the Internet. Generally, the process involved takes the following steps:

1. You send the liquidator a list of items in your excess inventory.

   Where possible, it's best to use *Electronic Data Interchange* (EDI) protocols, described later in this chapter, over the Internet to avoid rekeying of data.

2. The liquidator assesses the inventory and then proceeds to classify the material in one of three categories:

   • High demand

   • Marketable

   • No resale value

3. The items in the first two categories are then delivered to the liquidator and put up for resale. Items with no resale value are liable to be scrapped by the company.

4. Liquidators can work on a percentage or on a flat fee basis. Merchandise is marketed through the Internet on industry Web sites and by email to prospective buyers.

Moving Merchandise through an Online Auction

Recently, the Internet has opened up a new avenue for disposing of surplus inventory: *online auctions*. Online auctions enable anyone connected to the Internet to bid for your goods whether you have one item or a truckload. Several companies that sell online have established their own separate online auction Web sites to handle surpluses. For example,

MicroWarehouse, one of the larger computer and electronics resellers has opened WebAuction.com (`www.webauction.com`), shown in Figure 9.2, to move merchandise that's otherwise stagnant.

Figure 9.2   WebAuction.com is the online auction arm of a major electronics reseller.

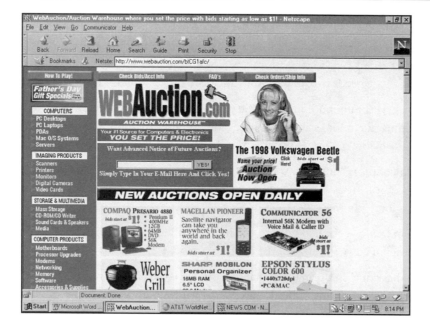

Let's take a tour of a sample auction so you can get a sense of how it works (and the added benefits your organization can gather):

1. To participate in the auction, each Web visitor must register. To register, a user must enter his billing, shipping, credit card information, and a username and password.

   Registration enables you to collect the names of people interested in your products for further marketing. The credit card information is taken up front because each bid is considered an intent to purchase. Although the user's credit card is not charged until the merchandise is shipped, it does make billing a snap.

The popularity of online auctions
Online auctions are one of the hottest on-going events on the Web. Studies estimate that online auctions could top $1 billion in sales in the next five years.

2. After the user is registered he is free to roam the Web site looking for bargains. When something is found, the user selects the **Bid Now** button and enters his username and password.

   Even if the user is unsuccessful in his bid, you can collect data on what he is interested in—even the amount of money he would be willing to spend. Such intelligence is invaluable in additional market research.

3. The user is then taken to a *bidding agent* screen. The bidding agent is a software program that enters bids for the user according to the user-selected guidelines. All the bidding agent needs to know is how much the user is willing to spend.

   All bids have a minimum opening bid and a set increment. Given these two factors, the bidding agent looks at the current bid and raises the bid by the increment if that amount is below the user's maximum bid.

4. Bidding continues until the auction is over. Auctions are set for a particular length of time, occasionally as short as one hour but sometimes—for more specialized merchandise—as long as a week.

5. The item being auctioned goes to the highest bidder, if there has been no additional bid in the final five minutes of the auction period.

   If a bid has come in during the final five minutes, the clock is reset. The bidding is not complete until a full five minutes has passed without any additional bidding.

6. After the auction is over and the merchandise ready to ship, the user's credit card is billed.

   Because the account has been set up, it's very easy for customers to return again and again to bid, and they never have to enter their user information again.

If you're clearing out a fair amount of surplus inventory, you can also auction off the goods in bulk, online. This type of auction is called a Dutch auction and the bidding rules are a little different. In a Dutch auction, the seller states the quantity of the item for sale and the lowest acceptable bid. Bidders can go for one or all of the lot. If a user submits the highest bid and the full quantity, everything goes to that user. However, if the bidder submitted the highest bid and only wants a portion of the lot, the next lowest bidder gets the balance of the lot (or whatever the quantity requested). The twist to a Dutch auction is that the lowest successful bid becomes the selling prices for the entire lot. So, if you were selling 1,000 units and got one bid for 999 of them at $100 and one bid for one of them at $80, the entire lot would go for $80 each. Although this may not seem like such a good deal for the seller, keep in mind that a lowest acceptable bid was specified and, using this method, all the merchandise is sold. If you're looking to move out some excess inventory, an online Dutch auction is worth investigating.

JIT Supplies

Getting your supplies right when you need them is what Just in Time techniques are all about. Get them too early and you have warehousing issues to address; get them too late and your shipping schedule is impacted. A fully engaged Internet strategy can help you gather your materials just before you're ready to assemble them.

The more closely you can monitor the orders that come in for your product, the more tightly you can gauge your JIT schedule. In an ideal industry, you know exactly what you'll need to produce far ahead of time, and you can schedule your suppliers accordingly. However today's competitive environment is anything but ideal. If an order comes in out of the blue, you've got to fill it—or you can bet your bottom dollar your competitor will. To protect oneself from such last-minute deals, the tendency is to overstock supplies, however, that can tie up a great deal of capital.

It's much better to establish a Just in Time relationship with your vendors and to program in a series of triggers within your ordering system. These triggers could fire off automatic communications to your vendors depending on the orders received. The format of the communications depends on the type of electronic relationship between your company and your suppliers. The faster the turn-around desired, the tighter the integration needs to be—intranet to intranet access is not uncommon.

Just in Time part supply techniques can even be applied on the assembly line. Delta Motor Company, a South African car manufacturer, uses a computer system that monitors each automobile as it is being assembled. After every tenth vehicle passes the midway point, the Delta Motor Company system fires off a number of faxes—via the internal fax modem—to JIT suppliers to advise them of the component needs for the ten particular models being assembled.

Occasionally your regular suppliers run dry and you need to switch to outside sources. In this case, the Internet can be a major boon. Part suppliers in almost every field are opening up shop on the Internet: electronic, medical, agricultural, and automotive to name a few. Most have full input/output setups established on the Web that enable you to do most, if not all, of the following:

- *Search their database.* Having an online parts database available can give you the quickest results. Most parts databases work by enabling you to input a part number, manufacturer, or description. Some of the more sophisticated search engines allow you to combine features and, for example, look for a specific part from one or more manufacturers in a particular price range.

- *Download a regularly published list.* I've seen numerous instances of a supplier putting a list of available goods online in a compressed or zipped format. One supplier, General Components (www.gencom.com), publishes a zipped file with the available inventory in three different formats: text, spreadsheet, and database.

FAQ: What's a zipped file?
Zip refers to a popular compression utility that figuratively squeezes the air out of files, makes them more compact for transmitting over the Internet and enables you to combine several files in one packet. To view the material contained within a zipped file, you need a program capable of decompresses or unzipping the file. Two popular choices are WinZip and PKZip. They are widely available on the Internet, or you can go to one of the creators of the zip format at www.pkware.com.

- *Submit a requirement.* To meet the specific needs of a company, many supply houses such as General Components let you submit a form outlining exactly the parts you're looking for. The submission can be handled in one of two ways. First, you can send an email to the contact listed on the Web site, describing your requirements in a general letter. Or, second, you can use the supplied form similar to the one shown in Figure 9.3. If at all possible, it's better to use a form because this can often lead to faster results. The form data is entered into a database and can be searched far more easily. Moreover, if a requested part is not on-hand presently, the database system can be set up to alert you (via email) when the part or parts become available.

- *Upload a parts list.* Although this option will not help you locate a needed part, it will help you to get a little money out of your excess inventory. If your company has unused parts sitting around taking up warehouse space, you can send or *upload* a list of all the material to many parts supply companies for their disposal. How much on the dollar you receive for your goods depends pretty much on the demand for the material.

Electronic Data Interchange

Arranging for your parts, supplies, and orders to arrive just in time is at the heart of a worldwide electronic commerce initiative called Electronic Data Interchange or EDI. EDI has been around since the mid-80s but has recently gained favor as worldwide connections began to flower through the Internet. Often considered to be the advent of "paperless trading," EDI is formally defined as "the interchange of structured data according to agreed message standards between computer systems, by electronic means." Breaking that definition down can help to make it more understandable:

- "Structured data" refers to a clear format for presenting information such as an invoice or an order form.

- "Message standards" takes the structured data concept one step further and puts all the information in a format agreed upon, and subscribed to, by the participants also known as trading partners.

- "Electronic means" is what gives EDI its power and speed of communication. Originally, and still in use by many companies, the electronic means developed were special computer networks called VANS, short for *Value-Added Networks*. Today, EDI can be carried out through the Web and over the Internet as well as over a VAN.

Figure 9.3 Specify the parts you need by filling out an online form such as this one from General Components.

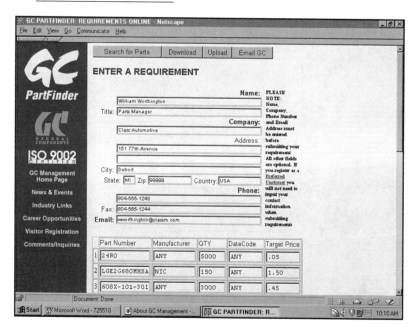

EDI is much more than enhanced email however. The concept behind EDI is to automate the processes involved as much as possible. So instead of an order being received via email and then input manually into the system by the recipient, the EDI-based order is automatically inserted into the datastream of the receiving company.

EDI in Manufacturing

Furthermore, EDI cuts down—way down—on clerical input errors and the associated costs. This type of order taking also impacts significantly on the number of personnel required for order-taking and even accounting.

EDI can have a ripple effect on JIT strategies in a well-connected company and its trading partners. Let's hypothesize that Company B gets an order for 1,000 widgets from Company A via EDI. Each widget contains 10 frizzballs, supplied by Company C. When Company B gets the order from Company A, it triggers a further order for 10,000 frizzballs from Company B to its supplier, Company C. When Company C receives the EDI order from Company B, that order triggers an order to Companies D, E, and F for the raw materials needed by Company C to make the requested items. Because EDI transactions can also contain financial transfers, that is, payments to accounts, the money, as well as the order, trickles down from Company A to Companies B–F. Figure 9.4 illustrates the flow from one company to another.

Figure 9.4 Companies that have instituted EDI procedures with their suppliers—and their suppliers' suppliers—can automate the part ordering process.

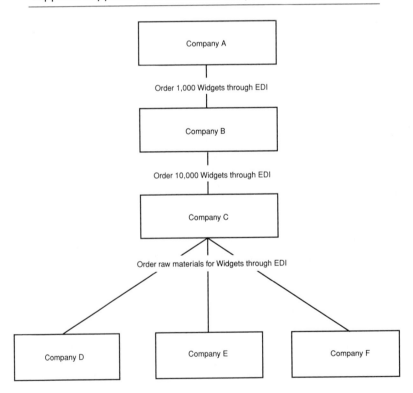

EDI isn't restricted to affecting orders and invoicing either—it can assist with speeding up the shipping department as well. For example, an EDI order sent from one company in England to another in California can trigger pick lists to be generated and available when the day shift walks in the door.

The primary connector between trading partners involved in EDI has been the Value-Added Networks. Each VAN is based in a specific industry; there are VANs for banking, the automotive industry, electronics, and retail, among others. As EDI grew it became necessary to enable interconnection between the different VANs. Today, the Internet is used as well as the specific VANs.

What does a VAN do? Basically, a VAN provides a secure messaging environment with audit control. Typically, a company using a VAN does not send the order or invoice information directly to its trading partner; instead the message goes to the trading partner in care of the VAN. Connection to the VAN is over a secured network through password control. Moreover, messages sent from one trading partner to another are not accepted unless the VAN is aware that both partners have agreed to the service. Each message is checked for the mandatory EDI elements in the particular form.

Just as valuable as the secure messaging capabilities of a VAN are its audit control features. If there is any dispute whether an invoice or a payment was sent—and received—the VAN's auditing features can clear up the discrepancy.

Because all EDI transactions require the information passed to be in a specific format, an entire breed of software known as EDI translation software has arisen. Generally the function of the EDI translation package is to present an industry-specific user interface from which:

- EDI standard communications can be encoded and sent.

- Received EDI information can be decoded and filed.

- Reports can be derived and routed to the appropriate management personnel.

Certain EDI translation software can make use of the security advances of the Internet to bypass the VANs, but still retain all its benefits. Using secure servers, information can be validated (assured of using the proper format), encrypted (coded to prevent unauthorized viewing) and authenticated (making sure that each trading partner is who they are claiming to be).

Case Study: Tallent Engineering

Tallent supplies chassis parts to automobile manufacturers across Europe, including customers such as Nissan Manufacturing UK Ltd., and Ford Belgium. Tallent employs approximately 700 people and is a wholly owned subsidiary of the Thyssen Group.

Tallent moved into using EDI to comply with requirements set out by the automotive OEMs. However, rather than opt for the basic EDI sending and receiving of communication, the company has moved toward a complete system integration. Finished goods are supplied to all plants according to their Just in Time requirements, which are transmitted daily. This constant flow of communication has enabled Tallent to keep their inventory to the lowest level possible, holding a mere eight hours of production.

EDI in Retail

If Just in Time strategies through EDI in manufacturing is a no-brainer, the retail side of the picture might need some justification. EDI isn't completely work free—it requires some training of personnel, a bigger overhead for computerization and some additional work on the vendor side to enable merchandise to go from the shipping dock to the selling floor. However, for even a mid-sized retailer, the benefits can be substantial.

Retailers have to handle a constant parade of purchase orders and invoices. Without EDI, purchase orders are filled out, printed and mailed. With EDI, POs are just filled out. There are no additional mailing delays or costs; POs are received the same day they are sent. Many purchase orders now include retail prices so that a vendor's ticketing program can have the necessary information to pre-ticket the goods.

Invoices are an even bigger headache. Each invoice received from a different supplier is in its own format and the information must be entered by hand into your own accounting system. Naturally, data entry mistakes are incurred, compounding the problem. With EDI, all invoices are received electronically and immediately transferred into your system. Only those with errors from the supplier-side (mismatching quantities or invoice numbers) are flagged and must be attended to by an employee. Moreover, payment terms can be set for each supplier and payments are issued automatically and electronically through EDI.

However, the biggest savings from retail EDI come from automation of the distribution. EDI software can generate bar code labels for each carton that detail the contents as well as its final destination. If the retail operation is sufficiently large to use distribution centers to multiple stores, this automation is a major benefit. Without an EDI system in place each carton must be checked manually against the orders in the system. Then the goods are carted to a location in the warehouse to await disbursement.

However, with an EDI-based system, the process is far more streamlined. As the cartons are unloaded from the incoming truck and roll down the conveyor belt, the bar code label is scanned. The received goods indicated on the carton are checked off against POs and the carton is routed directly to a truck going to the specified store. Days or even weeks of warehouse storage are eliminated. Aside from the EDI component, it is necessary for your vendors to make the merchandise ready for the showroom or selling floor, which generally means pre-ticketing the items and/or placing them on hangers.

To create such floor-ready merchandise, the manufacturer must initially assign a Universal Pricing Code (UPC). Because the UPC includes all the necessary product information such as style, size, and color, an EDI transaction can draw from an electronic catalog. The retail buyer's EDI system uses the same UPC codes as the manufacturer, which transfer automatically whenever a particular item is ordered. This enables retail outlets to track sales and, as a further enhancement to Just in Time techniques, automatically order replenishments when a preset minimum stock number is reached.

Case Study: Levi Strauss & Co.

Levi Strauss & Co. was founded in 1866 and has become the world's foremost maker of jeans and casual wear. A privately held company, Levi Strauss currently has 39 branch offices around the world and a central corporate Web site (www.levistrauss.com).

By following the EDI/Just in Time chain all the way through to the retailer, Levi Strauss has cut the workload for both parties. Instead of relying on the individual stores to run their own inventory and replenishment systems—or spending sales personnel time checking up on reorders—Levi Strauss can automatically send needed goods to EDI enabled stores. Each store first agrees to minimum and maximum levels for the various product lines. Then as data is accumulated through bar code reading of sales over the week, the EDI program checks current stock levels against the minimums. If indicated, an order is automatically placed through EDI and the goods are shipped out.

The benefits are clear:

- The retailers benefit because they get their shelves restocked of the items that sell without having to do the analysis themselves.

- The customers benefit because more of what's in demand is available.

- Levi Strauss benefits because they get a clearer picture of what's selling as well as a constant flow of product without using valuable sales time. Additionally, sales volume increased more than 10 percent in the early stages of the program for each participating store.

CHAPTER 10

Enabling Direct Distribution

- Consolidating your internal systems
- Communicating with shippers online
- Distributing documents and software electronically
- Disbursing goods from a cybershop
- Coordinating imports/exports on the Web

Cybercharging Your Distribution Network

You can hone your just-in-time development cycles as sharply as you want, but if you don't get the product on the store shelves or in the customer's hands in a timely manner, the game is lost. Distribution is a crucial phase in all commerce, and one that can be greatly enhanced through Internet and intranet techniques.

The basis of all distribution is communication and coordination: Package A needs to be in warehouse B by date C. Today's Internet/intranet systems offer distinct advantages over traditional communication methods. In addition to being virtually instantaneous, email messages can also be automatically generated to keep shipping managers or customers informed as to anticipated delivery dates. Coordinating shipping schedules with consolidators, custom brokers, trucking, rail, sea, and air cargo companies is far simpler—and far more auditable—through the computer networks now operational. In fact, one of the very first extranets was developed by FedEx to ease the tracking problems associated with shipping.

Direct distribution of goods from reseller to customer has been revolutionized through the online stores. Many online businesses have based their reputation—and their bottom line—on the shorter distribution cycles made possible by the Internet. Moreover, the types of deliveries now available have started whole new categories of businesses, including electronic software and information distribution.

Perhaps the biggest benefit that Internet strategies have brought the distribution phase of business is cost effectiveness. Previously, only the largest companies could handle their own distribution; however, the more centralized communication structure of the Internet brings distribution into a range obtainable by far more companies.

Enhancing In-house Systems

Want to improve your back-office performance in fulfillment and distribution? Give your front office as much information as you can. The more fully integrated a company's overall system, the smoother the entire operation runs. When an order taker can see what's currently in stock as well as the shipping schedules, goods can be routed faster and more efficiently.

An ideal in-house distribution network has only a few steps on the surface, but much happening in the background.

1. The customer places an order.

   Whether the order is placed over the Internet or one of the more traditional channels—fax or telephone sales—the order taker checks the products requested against available inventory. If the product is not in stock, the customer is informed as soon as possible. Should the customer be online, that information can be handled in real-time. If the requested product has been discontinued, a substitute product can be suggested.

   If the product is currently on backorder, the customer should be told when delivery is anticipated and given the option to order a substitute product. Product availability can also be tied to current shipping schedules—and such information can also be available to the order takers.

   If the delivery of the product moves the item inventory below the minimum level, a re-order of the merchandise is automatically generated. Anticipated delivery dates of the new stock are entered into the system.

2. The order is filled.

   The pick list that was generated based on the order contains identification information (SKU number, model, style, color, and quantity) as well as storage location information. If the order requires an additional shipment before being fulfilled, the pick list is generated on the day of the anticipated delivery. The incoming delivery can be routed directly to a holding area, or even to the waiting truck—without being restocked first.

3. The order is shipped.

   Tracking information goes into the system, attached either directly to the order or with an identifying number. The customer's account is billed and the information is entered automatically in Accounts Receivable. If desired, a confirmation of the product shipping, with the tracking information, is generated and sent to the customer.

A fully implemented intranet strategy can automate the vast majority of the back-office steps outlined here. Depending on the sophistication of your warehousing system, even much of the order filling and distribution can be affected.

Working with Shipping Agents

Tracking merchandise after it has left the plant or warehouse has become an important part of every company's overall distribution plan. Whether the goods were sent by overnight delivery or slow boat, "Well, we sent it," just doesn't cut it in today's competitive marketplace. Luckily, the shipping companies have responded to this need with a wide range of Internet solutions that open the channel of communication between businesses and their shippers.

An amazing amount of data to assist you in your logistics planning is now available over the Web. No matter how your company ships its goods around the globe, you can get the details over the Internet:

- *By rail.* Whether you need to send your merchandise via rail or through an intermodal service using both road and rail, you can find available resources on the Internet. Certain sites, such as Blue Thunder (`www.blue-thunder.com`), enable you to submit shipping forms over the Internet, as well as track or trace shipments already in transit.

Centralized Tracking on the Web
The Tracking Web (`www.geocities.com/Eureka/7292/trakengl.htm`) lists 13 major tracking sites (FedEx to Austrian Airlines), and links to the world's airports' cargo connections.

- *By air.* More than 100 air cargo services are available on the Web. Depending on the site, you can check real-time schedules and flight availability, as shown in Figure 10.1, for literally anywhere in the world. Other services enable you to track shipments with information such as the total number of pieces, the weight, when it was picked up, and when it was delivered.

Figure 10.1 Need to find out when that shipment is hitting Cairo? Check the Web!

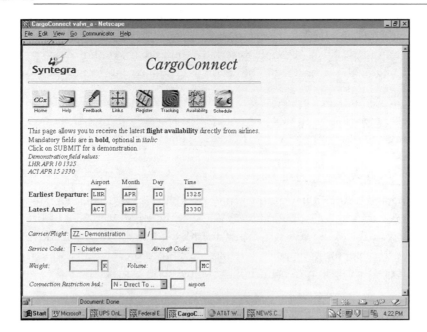

- *By sea*. You can search the Web by shipping lane, departure port, arrival port, or carrier for sailing schedules, container tracking or even weather conditions affecting deliveries. A good starting point is the Electronic Shipping Guide on the Web (`www.shipguide.com`). Many Web sites contain import/export forms and information, as well.

- *By truck*. Of all the transportation services, trucking has taken to the Web wholeheartedly. Web sites, such as those run by Roadway (`www.roadway.com`), enable clients to check the en route status of their shipments—or even the status of a cargo loss and damage claim. Many truckers have begun taking laptops with cellular modems on their hauls to keep in touch with the home office and to check directions and weather conditions.

FedEx was one of the first companies to see the added value that an extranet could bring its customers and its business. By opening up its tracking system to the world at large through the Internet, FedEx was able to save money by reducing the number of telephone operators who previously provided the information, while simultaneously providing their customers with a printable record. The other major shipping companies swiftly followed suit, and now you can get tracking information from UPS, Airborne Express, DHL, and many others—right over the Web.

UPS is one shipping company that has totally embraced the electronic way of doing business. By offering a range of Internet-related services, UPS makes it possible for every organization—from the smallest to the largest—to automate their shipping to a remarkable degree. One new program, UPS OnLine Host Access, integrates the UPS tracking system with a company's own computer system for all-electronic labeling and rapid response to tracking requests. Additional features include:

- Detailed management reports

- Point-and-click address books

- Entry validation to make sure the proper type of data is entered in the electronic forms

- The ability to track multiple packages with one query

- Easy look-up of domestic and U.S. origin international shipments

This service, and others like it from competing shipping companies, are being used by online stores to extend their shipping capabilities and make it easy for customers to determine their own shipping arrangements.

Distribution in the Online Age

The Web has opened up entirely new distribution—and revenue—channels. Entrepreneurs are using the Internet to distribute all manner of digital goods. Information for specialized markets appears to be a definite growth industry.

Information Distribution

Some companies have questioned whether users would pay for access on what is largely a free source of information. The most widely known example is the online *Wall Street Journal* (www.wsj.com), which began offering paid subscription access in August, 1996. As of this writing, over 200,000 subscribers have deemed it worthy of the $49 annual fee ($29 for paper subscribers). In this case, the "distribution" is simply one of publishing directly to a single Web site, and the subscribers enter the site whenever they like. Current editions of other newspapers, such as the *Washington Post*, are available for free online, but charge a fee for access to their archives.

Other information services, such as Lexis-Nexis, also open their research databases to subscribers. However, many also send the data requested via email as part of a notification service.

SEE ALSO

➤ *For more information about online research firms, see page 46.*

SEE ALSO

➤ *For more about notification services, see page 60.*

A significant advantage to Internet information delivery is the cost. After it is developed, the report or other subject matter can be stored on a system accessible to anyone through the Internet at no direct cost to the vendor. Although expenses are attributable to the overall maintenance of the Web site, it costs the company nothing to serve the information to the customer.

But what if your business depends on distributing more than just an email notice or report? Documents can be compressed in several formats; the most popular format is probably Adobe Acrobat, for which readers are generally available and freely distributed. This accessibility is both a plus and a minus. On the positive side, it makes electronic distribution a low-cost breeze. However, digital documents can be easily copied, and if your business depends on the revenue from these documents, you have to protect your investment.

Case Study: LLH Technical Publishing

LLH Technical Publishing began in 1990 as HighText Publications, packaging books for established publishers. LLH's current activities include acquiring and publishing new professional titles in engineering and computing.

LLH Technical Publishing is a relatively small press devoted to books for technology professionals. In addition to selling their hard-copy books, LLH began selling their books over the Internet, referring to them as "e-books." The books are distributed as SoftLocked Adobe Acrobat files that can be examined, but not read in full without purchasing a password. LLH passes the savings inherent in an electronic book to the customer by charging 40% less for each title. LLH highlights these key points in their marketing:

- Available instantly without any additional overnight shipping charges.

- The electronic store is open all day, all night, and year-round.

- The text can be searched for any word or phrase.

- Both the table of contents and the index are hyperlinked.

Electronic Software Distribution

Although the channel of *electronic software distribution* (ESD) has been available for many years through bulletin boards and online services such as CompuServe, it wasn't until the explosive growth of the Internet that it became economically desirable. For our purposes, ESD can be defined as the ability to transfer software for profit over the Internet. Electronic software distribution is an attractive proposition for buyers and sellers. The buyer gains the convenience of an always open Internet and the global accessibility of a product not easily distributed otherwise—often at a lower price. Furthermore, upgrades are handled in an efficient manner for both the publisher and the consumer.

The seller, on the other hand, has a distinct set of compelling reasons:

- *More money, faster.* The traditional software market requires a 40% markup with a 90 to 120-day wait for payment from resellers. With online distribution, the publisher can sell at a lower cost but retain a higher margin, and the money—debited from the customers credit card—is available almost immediately.

- *All the customer information you need.* Getting a customer to send in a warranty card has proven next to impossible—the software industry reports an average 8% return rate. With ESD, customers must register before they can buy the software. With electronic software distribution, you know 100% of your customer base.

- *Upgrade faster, less expensively.* The technological clock is racing, with innovations demanded at a breakneck pace. ESD lowers the cost of providing an upgrade path for existing users. Upgrades can be distributed electronically as patches or as entirely new programs.

- *No stock problems.* With ESD, back orders don't exist. After a network of systems has been established, no significant cost is involved in publishing the software for distribution from several *mirror,* or duplicate, sites.

- *Global market reach.* Because of the relative ease of software piracy, international software distribution has long been a difficult task. The Internet gives electronic software distribution a global stage without the risk of forging international partnerships.

- *Better target-marketing.* Penetrating the mass-market is an increasingly expensive proposition for any publisher. *PC Magazine* estimates that a new software product requires a minimum of $10 million in marketing to be successful. With online distribution, you've already narrowed your marketing significantly because everyone present has a computer, and marketing dollars can be stretched to a greater extent.

Case Study: Egghead.com, Inc.

Egghead.com, Inc. began its corporate existence as Egghead Software, Inc. and now can be found on the Web at www.egghead.com. Consolidated net sales for 1997 were $88.9 million.

The advantages for electronic software distribution are so compelling that one major reseller made the move from a chain of 80 stores and a distribution center to an online presence, shown in Figure 10.2. Egghead Software decided that the time was right to reduce overhead by selling online. The reincarnated Egghead.com sells both the traditional boxed version of software and the ESD variety. Egghead said it expects that the direct effect of the reorganization will reduce marketing and administrative costs by about $38 million per year.

Figure 10.2   Egghead.com closed 80 retail stores to take advantage of the global possibilities offered by electronic software distribution.

It's too early to tell what results this bold experiment will yield. One thing is for sure, however; the combined power of ESD and the Internet make for a promising future.

Online Store Distribution

The Internet has brought a whole new class of reseller to the forefront: the virtual store. Many Web sites, even those that are commerce-capable, serve as the online presences of "offline" stores. However, a growing number of online stores exist only on the Internet and have no real-world storefront equivalent. These types of stores must be masters of distribution to make the leap from virtual to real—in the minds of their customers, that is.

Case Study: Amazon.com
Amazon.com is widely regarded as the leading e-commerce site on the Web This publicly traded (NASDAQ: AMZN) company is based in Seattle, Washington and had net sales for the first quarter ending March 31, 1998 of $87.4 million.

One store that has definitely accomplished just such a transition is Amazon.com (www.amazon.com). Self-proclaimed as "the Earth's largest bookstore," Amazon.com boasts an amazing three million titles (now with books, CDs, audiobooks, DVDs, computer games, and more) available. Since their Web site, shown in Figure 10.3, opened in 1995, they have delivered orders to over 2.2 million customers in 160 countries. And yet, they only have one physical location with space limited to holding around 500 titles. How do they do it?

Figure 10.3   Amazon.com's key to success lies in its sophisticated distribution system.

A typical large-sized bookstore holds around 150,000 titles. Maintaining that many titles requires numerous employees to continually catalog, sort, and shelve the books. A traditional bookstore's inventory might turn over two or three times a year. However, Amazon.com's inventory is turned over in excess of 350 times a year. Amazon.com depends on its extensive distributor network, which is linked electronically to the online store. When an order comes in for a title not kept on-site, Amazon.com's database is searched for the nearest affiliated distributor who carries the item. The order is placed electronically and Amazon.com can receive the book—and turn it around—in as little as 24 hours. The less current books take a longer period of time, but no more than ordering the same item from your local bookseller.

From the customer's point of view, the ordering process is seamless and, for all intents and purposes, the perception is that Amazon.com does have all the titles it claims to have. Furthermore, Amazon.com does a superb job of keeping the customer informed. Each order placed on the Web site is automatically confirmed via email—and if there is a delay in shipment, the customer receives another email when the books are actually shipped.

Distribution Security

One method of protection has been developed by SoftLock Services, Inc. (www.softlock.com). Although useful for all manner of digital media (software, CDs, multimedia presentations), SoftLock is especially valuable when it comes to protecting documents. If your business revolves around industry-specific reports, for example, you could use SoftLock to limit document distribution only to authorized viewers. If the document is copied to another system, the user can only preview the information—until it is unlocked with a password, guided by the screen shown in Figure 10.4. Depending on your business model, SoftLock can handle the password vending, or it can be taken care of internally.

Figure 10.4 Tools such as SoftLock can be used to prevent unpaid-for copies from circulating.

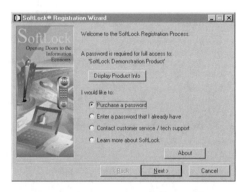

Solutions such as those from SoftLock encourage a second tier of distribution. Not only can customers download the material directly from your Web site, but users can pass the documents or other digital media on to other users—who must pay for the privilege of viewing the full product.

The main problem with electronic software distribution is the same one suffered by electronic document distribution: piracy. The SoftLock solution can also be used for software to enable a limited preview before purchasing. However, many software publishers prefer to offer software that is fully functional for a limited amount of time, usually 30 or 60 days. After the time limit has expired, trying to launch the software gives the user an opportunity to purchase it online or through a toll-free number. After the transaction is complete, the customer is given a password that "unlocks" the software to full functionality.

World Wide Importing and Exporting

The Internet is a dream come true for any company that is engaged in import/export or that is thinking about expanding its business into the global marketplace. Not only can you find contact information for customs brokers in almost every country, much of the maze of governmental regulations are online in searchable databases. Furthermore, some governments, such as the U.S., are moving swiftly toward automating their elaborate filings—all of which you can locate on the Internet.

SEE ALSO

➤ *For more about international trade, see page 335.*

Can Your Company Succeed in Another Country?
If you're thinking about exporting your products for the first time, stop by the ExporTutor (www.nemonline.org/tutor) for some insightful information. Developed by the Michigan State University International Business Centers, the ExpoTutor's site features a 10-Step Road Map to Success in Foreign Markets and various links to import/export resources.

Finding an Online Foreign Customs Broker

Looking for a customs broker in a foreign country? Follow these steps to find a broker in the country of your choosing:

1. Start your Web browser and go to your favorite search engine, such as Yahoo (www.yahoo.com) or Infoseek (www.infoseek.com).

2. In the search text box, enter the country of your choice preceded by a plus sign and the phrase "customs broker"—in quotes and also preceded by a plus sign. For example:

   ```
   +france +"customs broker"
   ```

3. The search engine will return a list of links for you to look over.

Finding English Links

Many sites on the list are represented in multiple languages. To find the English links, go to the home page of a site and select the proper link—which occasionally is represented by a U.S. or U.K. flag.

4. Click the link you think is most appropriate.

5. If the Web site doesn't meet your needs, click your browser's **Back** button to return to the search results.

What you find depends on the sophistication of the broker's Web site. Many brokers list only their contact information. Some, such as MTC-Cargo (`www.mtc-cargo.com`), enable you to fill out a shipper's letter of instructions online or download the same in English or German.

Export Regulation Compliance

Certain facilitators have brought the complex world of export regulation compliance online. ExportUSA (`www.exportusa.com`) offers valuable services in three areas through subscriptions to interactive databases:

- *License Determination.* After the customer's name, country code and ECCN (Export Control Classification Numbers) data is entered by the user, the appropriate export license type is proposed. The license type may be an exception license, an export license, or "No License Required" (NLR).

- *Denied Parties Screening.* This Web-based service checks a customer name against the latest Denied Parties List (DPL). The DPL consists of the Table of Denial Orders (Department of Commerce), the Specially Designated Nationals (Office of Foreign Assets Control), the Statutory Debarment List (Department of State), and the Entities List.

- *Export Regulations.* Use this service to search the full Export Administration Regulations (EARs) and International Traffic in Arms Regulations (ITARs) to ensure that your exports are in compliance with federal laws.

U.S. Government Regulations

The primary source for information about U.S. government regulations is the government itself. The Federal bureaucracy is alive and well on the Web. Although many departments have their own Web sites, a good jumping off place is the FedWorld Information Network (www.fedworld.gov). You can begin your customs search at the Bureau of Export Administration's Web site (www.bxa.doc.gov) for up-to-date regulations, or visit the U.S. Customs Service Web site (www.customs.ustreas.gov) for information on both importing and exporting.

The U.S. Customs Service has invested heavily in the Internet, as evidenced by their Automated Broker Interface (ABI). The ABI handles queries from importers, brokers, carriers, and port authorities. The primary benefits offered by ABI include

- A speedier clearing through customs

- Electronic payment of customs fees, duties, and taxes through the Automated Clearinghouse

- Consolidation of filings with other governmental agencies, including the Department of Transportation, the Bureau of Census, the Federal Communications Commission, the Food and Drug Administration, and the U.S. Fish and Wildlife Service

- Submission of drawback claims, protests, and queries—electronically

- Notification of liquidations, extensions, or suspensions

Contacts with Other Governments

The U.S. government is not the only one online. Many foreign governments have Web sites, and most of those have separate links to their embassies. A good centralized source for contact information is The Embassy Page (www.embpage.org), where you can search for domestic or foreign embassies.

CHAPTER 11

Outsourcing Logistics

- Outsourcing logistics overview
- Managing offline deliveries for online stores
- Coordinating warehouse management
- Enabling outsourced distribution
- Total supply chain management

Third-Party Logistics Online

Logistics planning first came to the forefront when the military needed a method to systematize the way troops were transported and supplied. Soon corporations began to establish their own logistics departments to move freight around the country. As systems became more and more integrated, logistics planning was incorporated to tie the various processes together. A high degree of logistics planning became essential for companies to make their Just in Time manufacturing goals.

Increasingly companies are turning to trusted third-parties to handle the logistics of moving goods all along the supply chain all the way to the customer. The science of logistics—especially with the advent of Internet technology—has become increasingly complex. Many corporations are discovering that outsourcing logistics enables a company to do what they do best without focusing on the mechanics of supply and distribution.

Logistics is big business. The North American Logistics Association puts the current industry size at $800 billion, which represents more than 10 percent of U.S. gross product revenue. Much of logistics planning is still taking place in-house, but outsourced logistics is growing rapidly. Third-party logistics is figured to be a $25 billion industry, which is growing at 25 percent to 30 percent per year and is expected to double early in the next century. The growth of outsourced logistics is most evident in the biggest manufacturers. Of the 600 largest manufacturers, 60 percent are currently employing outsourced logistic firms, whereas 15 percent are considering the option.

Outsourcing logistics not only enables companies to pursue their core competencies, it also saves money. In a recent study conducted by University of Tennessee's Center for Logistics Research, 80 percent of the companies using third-party services for logistics believed that it offered them a key competitive advantage.

Much of an outsourced logistics strategy is made possible by the enhanced communication brought by wide spread Internet and intranet use. The four major areas for outsourced logistics today are as follows:

- *Logistics for Virtual Companies.* With the rise of the e-commerce comes a bundle of problems. Who's going to handle all those products sold online? Outsourced logistics firms, of course.

- *Real-time Warehouse Management.* The more complex inventory management becomes, the more sophisticated the tools and techniques required. Need a radio-frequency-controlled bar code scanner? Call a third-party logistics planner with the supplies and the experience.

- *Distribution Tracking.* Want to know where your goods are at any given time? Better yet, want to be able to reroute them at the last minute to save that big sale you just made? Contact a logistics planner with experience in using Global Positioning Systems to track shipments and email to provide new shipment orders.

- *Supply Chain Management.* Sometimes it takes an outside company to best handle the back-office day-to-day work. Logistics planners use system integration techniques to coordinate the workflow from supplier to manufacturer to distributor.

Real-World Logistics for Virtual Companies

The Internet stands as both a supplier and a user of third-party logistics. Online virtual stores have grown by leaps and bounds since the explosion of the World Wide Web and there's no end in site. Although a good portion of these cybershops is based on real-world stores, many exist only to sell product over the Internet. Only the smallest of these companies can handle the logistics of getting parts and distributing product by themselves. Many opt to go the outsourcing route.

The USPS alternative

Don't rule out the U.S. Postal Service for outsourcing your distribution. In recent years, the government has gotten very aggressive both in its pricing and with its services. The USPS Web site's Business section (www.usps.gov) is a good place to start for an overview of the possibilities.

If the company is still in an early growth stage, the commercial shipping agents can be used for outsourced logistics. FedEX, UPS, Airborne Express, and many others have programs aimed at filling the distribution needs for many small to mid-sized companies. You can even generate electronic manifests, call tags, and proofs of delivery.

SEE ALSO

➤ *For more about using commercial shipping agents, see page 125.*

Case Study: Ensemble, Inc.

Although Ensemble is wholly owned by Hallmark Cards, it is independently operated. Ensemble is a small company with 50 employees. It is based in Lenaxa, Kansas and operates a Web site displaying its wares at www.brushstrokesgallery.com.

The concept of virtual companies is not limited to the Internet. Any company that focuses exclusively on product design and creation, but contracts with other companies to provide the services from manufacturing to distributing can be considered a virtual company. One such company is Ensemble, a developer of mugs, gift bags, stationary, cards, and other products intended for Hallmark stores. Ensemble develops a product idea and then presents it to the Hallmark retailers before moving into production; in this manner, the company has a clear idea of what will sell and what won't as well as number of interested vendors.

Although Ensemble works with many suppliers from around the world, it is currently only using one external distribution company: USCO Distribution Services. USCO handles all the shipments to and from Ensemble. USCO's computer system coordinates the delivery of products made for Ensemble from trucking and ocean- and air-freight containers.

Like many small businesses, Ensemble can receive orders through a variety of traditional means including fax or telephone. However, Ensemble also has an EDI (Electronic Data Interchange) system in place for accounts with its larger customers. The EDI data, along with the other input orders, is transmitted electronically from Ensemble to USCO for fulfillment.

On average, about 100 orders per day are sent by USCO on Ensemble's behalf. The turn-around from the USCO's receipt of the order to its shipping out is contractually set at 24 hours. This requires a tight coordination between the two companies—a coordination that takes advantage of a constant flow of electronic information. Ensemble feels that this relationship is the best method of leveraging its own assets and letting the logistics experts take care of their side of the business.

Outsourcing Warehouse Management

A warehouse is not a store. It sounds obvious, but it's a key concept that can free your organization to focus on its core competencies by letting someone else handle the warehousing of your goods. After most products are developed and produced, one SKU is like another, and it doesn't require your company's personal attention to house them or move them from point A to point B.

Outsourcing warehouse management has grown in popularity. The communication revolution has made it possible to track stock far more closely, and the skillset required to do so has increased. Remote portable computer systems, on forklifts or handheld, must be able to communicate with the organization's primary systems, receiving and sending transportation information.

The online store is a perfect target for outsourced warehouse management. The virtual storefront handles the sales and marketing and the orders that come in can go directly to a warehouse for fulfillment. One company, InterEDI, Inc. (www.interedi.com) understands the needs of the growing business-to-business e-commerce market and is developing the Wired Warehouse. When it comes online, the Wired Warehouse will act as the distribution center for a wide range of real-world stores. Rather than having to occupy personnel with the mundane tasks of taking an order, checking the stock, and filling out the shipping manifest, the Wired Warehouse automates the entire process. The system provides order processing, order routing, secured financial transactions, full-service accounting, customer support, inventory management, and order tracking. Because such an outsourced warehouse has no real ties to a specific product line, it can be used for event promotion or for products with a relatively short life cycle without incurring the additional costs of building and maintaining warehouse space. Moreover, an Internet-savvy outsourced warehouse can open up a distribution channel within the host country for international companies.

Case Study: Nike, Inc.

With worldwide revenues a record $9.19 billion, Nike has become one of the world's best-selling sporting goods brands. Nike runs both a consumer Web site (www.nike.com) and a separate Web site for investor relations and corporate information (www.nikebiz.com), shown in Figure 11.1.

Figure 11.1 Nike, which maintains an extensive online presence, contracted with a third-party warehouse management firm to handle distribution in the United States and in Europe.

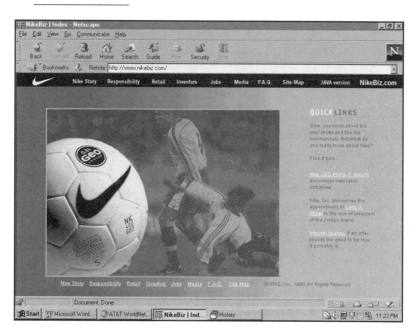

Perhaps the greatest degree of benefit in warehouse management can be gained from a tight integration of ordering and distribution. This is particularly true for a global company like Nike. Nike contracted with Menlo Logistics, the outsourcing logistics subsidiary of CNF Transportation, Inc., to manage both its domestic distribution center in Atlanta and its newly opened Pan-European distribution center in Eersel, Netherlands. By integrating order and warehouse management solutions, Menlo Logistics was able to achieve a 99.9 percent inventory accuracy rate while shipment volumes grew nearly three times faster than projected in the Atlanta facility.

Menlo's proprietary Warehouse Management System (WMS) uses computers mounted on forklifts to direct personnel through task sequences according to the latest order information. On the European side, Menlo's automated Order Management System (OMS) is electronically linked to Nike's global sales and customer service teams to manage order fulfillment and shipment prioritization. The information sharing from order desk to warehouse floor makes it possible for Nike customers to receive on-time, pan-European delivery, often within a delivery window as narrow as only a few hours.

Nike feels that its outsourced logistics strategy gives it the best of both worlds. By tracking each piece of inventory so accurately, Nike knows exactly what's on hand at any given moment, enabling it to know what to distribute, how much, when, and how. The process has been found to cut both warehousing and inventory carrying costs.

Handing Over Distribution

Of all the elements of logistics, distribution is the one most commonly outsourced. From one package to a truckload of palettes, it's often much easier—and more cost effective—to hire someone to deliver the goods than to do it yourself. The Internet connection has taken a lot of the anxiety out of handing your distribution over to a third-party. Shipments can now be tracked far more closely, from almost any point in the world.

Case Study: Zenith Electronics Corporation
With 10,000 employees and 1997 sales of $1.2 billion, Zenith is a major developer of the full range of video products, including digital HDTV.

Distribution management doesn't necessarily start on the road, tracing a shipment however. It can start closer to home, in a company's own truck yard. Zenith Electronic Corporation routinely moves 250 to 400 trucks through its Fort Worth truckyard daily. Until several years ago, the only way that management knew the status of a particular truck—where it was parked, whether it was full or empty, if it required servicing, and so on—was by manual yard checks. Each yard check would take up to 90 minutes to complete and Zenith scheduled as many as four per day. This very labor intensive, time-consuming process was replaced with an automated yard-management system, implemented by a contract logistics company, GATX Logistics.

The change was dramatic. The new system provided electronic tracking of arrivals and departures, computerized yard/trailer disposition profiles, and information about empty and full trailers. Moreover, management could produce customized reports (by carrier ID number, trailer-load ID number, or trailer number) that included trailer status, slot ID, trailer aging, location, exception reports, and shipper requirements. All reports indicated time, so the transit times, unloading times, and other measurements enabled management to gauge productivity. Productivity was shown to have improved 60 percent after the new system was fully implemented. Estimated annual savings in labor range from $50,000 to $60,000.

The actual tracking of a truck can be handled in several ways. One of the most high-tech to emerge in recent years is the use of *global positioning system* (GPS), which uses satellites to establish a vehicle's location. Cellular technology has also made it possible to combine GPS with both voice and data transmissions to ensure that the trucks on the road are in constant communication with the dispatchers in the office. Routing information can be posted to the company intranet or even a password protected Internet site and then viewed by a trucker with a laptop from anywhere. Figure 11.2 illustrates the communication links between a truck outfitted with a GPS system.

1. Log on to the Internet and go to the Web site of your global tracking system.

2. After entering your password, you're presented with a menu of your company trucks now on the road.

3. Selecting a truck displays the current position gathered from the GPS satellites and continually transmitted to the tracking station via cellular radio.

4. Both voice and data can be transmitted to the truck through the Internet connection.

5. If necessary, the controls can also be extended to lock or unlock the truck doors or even tell if the airbag has been deployed.

Figure 11.2 A Global Positioning System uses satellites circling the earth to determine your truck's location and status.

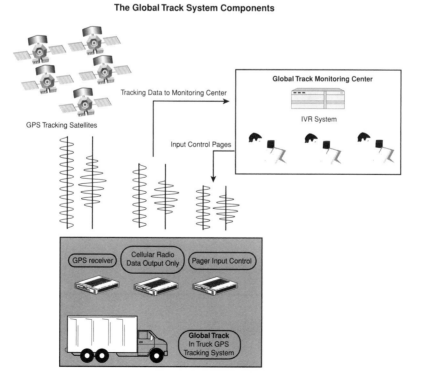

Case Study: MagneTek, Inc.
MagneTek is a manufacturer of energy engineered electrical and electronic equipment. The company had revenues of $304 million in fiscal 1997.

MagneTek found out that it wasn't a trucking company. To manage the 2,500 average monthly shipments, MagneTek management was relying on scheduling over 20 different carriers manually—and losing money on the deal. By outsourcing its distribution logistics to a company with far more expertise in the area, Menlo Logistics, MagneTek was able to concentrate on its primary business and even see some savings in the process.

Menlo has automated many of the functions previously done manually by MagneTek, with advanced systems that feed it information such as shipment status, rates, and deliveries. The arrangement has worked well for MagneTek's bottom line, saving it more than $2 million over the first 5 years of implementation.

These cost reductions, most of which are ongoing annual savings, have been realized both by Menlo's management of the dedicated fleet and its consolidation of inbound less-than-truckload shipments to full-volume truckload and multistop shipments. At the same time, increased efficiencies helped MagneTek cut out unnecessary waste from its supply chain and speed the delivery of products to the market.

Working the Supply Chain

The most complete option for a company looking to outsource its logistics is total supply chain management. Although not an ideal solution for every company or every productline, outsourcing your supply chain management is one way to ensure that systems integration receives the maximum attention. Supply chain management tries to orchestrate a fully synchronized delivery system from the ground up.

A supply chain management strategy incorporates these essential points:

- Coordinates orders to vendors.

- Assists in vendor-managed inventory.

- Monitors vendor compliance for quality control.

- Manages inbound shipments to manufacturing plants and warehouses for lowest cost and Just in Time delivery.

- Handles warehousing logistics to maximize inventory accuracy.

- Manages order receipt and scheduling.

- Schedules outbound carriers to distribution centers and resellers.

- Coordinates reverse logistics programs for returns.

Menlo Logistics offers an over-the-Internet method of tracking the various stages of your products called Supply Chain Visibility. Clients can check into the Menlo Web site, shown in Figure 11.3, to look at freight movement along the entire supply chain. Clients can track and trace products regardless of which carrier is used for any particular move. Within this carrier-anonymous tracking and tracing system, Menlo's clients are able to check inventory flow, access customized client pages, and review freight movement across the board—all over the Web. Additionally, Menlo's Web site protects client privacy by utilizing secured environments requiring user names, passwords, and specific tracking numbers, including carrier pro, booking numbers, bill of lading numbers, and customer reference numbers.

Figure 11.3   Menlo Logistics offers its clients the Supply Chain Visibility feature, which lets it check its freight status right over the Internet.

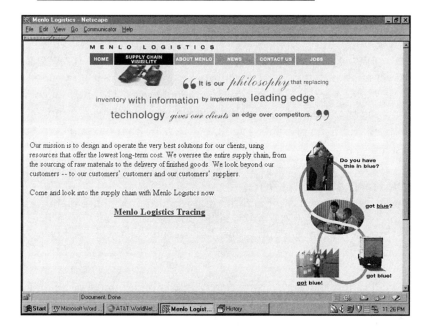

The more of an overview a supply chain management company has of your company, the better it will be able to streamline production, coordinate Just in Time supplies, and distribute goods efficiently. There are many variations of the depth to which supply chain management is outsourced. Following are two different case studies, each describing a particular scenario.

Case Study: Hewlett-Packard Company

The Hewlett-Packard Company (HP) is best known for its computer printer products, but they also produce a well-respected series of business computers. Hewlett-Packard has over 125,000 employees and had revenue of $42.9 billion in its 1997 fiscal year.

Hewlett-Packard's completion and distribution center outside of Sacramento, California is far more than a warehouse. This 800,000 square foot space handles light assembly as well as cross-docking and pick-and-pack distribution for HP's printer products. Prior to the development of this all-in-one center, managed by Menlo Logistics, HP used three different distribution centers. The new center handles parts from various domestic and Far East manufacturing plants as well as distribution to all North American delivery points.

Because Menlo can keep an eye of all the inbound shipments, it can maximize its delivery for HP. This works to ensure the best rates and service for packaged, less-than-truckload, and full truckload deliveries. Knowing when shipments are due in enables the distribution center to coordinate its warehouse efforts so that product is sent to the right place the first time and not stored in a holding bin before being redelivered.

Within the warehouse, Menlo uses computer-linked forklifts and radio-frequency bar code scanners to achieve optimum efficiency. Inventory accuracy reaches its peak because enhanced bar code scanners are used to cut down on input errors. The internal communication network among the scanners, the forklift computers, and the main computer system enable the tasks at hand to be prioritized and the material within the warehouse to be tracked consistently.

Case Study: Herman Miller, Inc.

Herman Miller, Inc., is an international firm engaged primarily in the manufacture and sale of furniture systems, products, and related services principally for offices, healthcare facilities, and residential environments. Net income for fiscal 1997 was $74.4 million.

In the corporate furniture industry, customer responsiveness is often a deciding factor. The industry standard from receipt of order to furniture shipment is six to eight weeks. Miller SQA (Simple, Quick, and Affordable), a subsidiary of Herman Miller Inc., has slashed the order/production/delivery cycle to fewer than five days using third-party supply chain management.

One technique, called production metering, is responsible for delivering Just in Time supplies needed for the tight production cycle. With production metering, deliveries are made every two hours to feed the 24 hours a day, 5 days a week production machine. After an order is received by the main office, the computer system breaks down the components necessary for the delivery and sends the list to the production metering facility. There, the components are loaded onto special point-of-use trucks. The parts list details the precise sequence for loading the trucks so that they can be unloaded in the correct order for assembly.

Obviously, such a short production cycle requires constant supervision of the inventory. The usage rate must be closely watched and vendor raw material shipping schedules must be coordinated to ensure that there are components on the shelves when the orders are ready to be produced.

PART V

Information Management

Information Archive and Access

- How Information Technology benefits your business
- Using email to its full potential
- Communicating through newsgroups
- Coordinating Human Resources online
- Publishing to the Web across the enterprise
- Outsourcing Information Technology

Information Technology Benefits

Information Technology (IT) is at the center of any Internet/intranet strategy. IT levels all boundaries and brings your entire company together so that, ideally, it is thinking and acting as one. An efficient Information Technology group can take the mounds of data generated daily by every company and make it accessible and useful.

In the age of the intranet, Information Technology is very much concerned with breaking down barriers—distance, temporal, and systemic.

- *Cut the distance.* A globally spread-out organization can be linked and knitted closer together through the common interface of an internal Web site.

- *Compress time.* Divergent teammates can collaborate on a project asynchronously at a much faster pace than ever before through listserves and Web-based team rooms.

- *Speak in a common voice.* With the common interface of an intranet, business decisions no longer depend on compatible systems. The browser becomes the universal translator for different computer systems and even different languages.

- *Empower employees.* Sharing knowledge across the board through an intranet acts as a great leveler and empowers employees to feel more like a team member than a cog in a machine.

- *Establish a corporate identity.* Perhaps most important is the manner in which IT can help to focalize a company's mission and vision. Corporate Web pages can present an identity to both the external and the internal world.

Information technology is vital to today's business. IT is usually called in to solve a basic business problem, but eventually ends up opening up new business opportunities. A recent survey of CEOs by A.T. Kearney, a management consulting firm, found that approximately 33% of those surveyed thought IT to be the number one critical success factor for their company's future. Moreover, as shown in Figure 12.1, most CEOs in the survey (58%) felt that without adequate IT investment, their company would lose its competitive edge.

Figure 12.1 When asked about the implications of not keeping up with advancements in information techonology, CEOs were primarily afraid of falling behind in business.

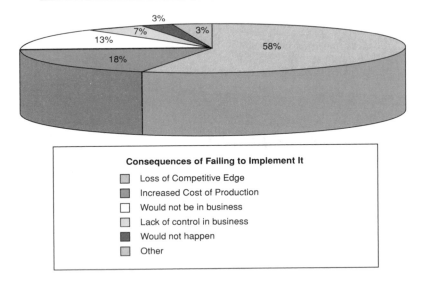

Consequences of Failing to Implement It

- ☐ Loss of Competitive Edge
- ☐ Increased Cost of Production
- ☐ Would not be in business
- ☐ Lack of control in business
- ☐ Would not happen
- ☐ Other

Intranet Acceptance

Intranets can truly have an impact only if they are accepted—and used—across the enterprise. Luckily, intranets really do seem to be living up to their promise to make information access faster and easier.

A study, *The Organizational Impact of Intranets*, conducted by Transition Management Advisors in Westerville, Ohio, bears out these claims. One thousand new intranet users at Columbia Gas, Owens Corning, and Silicon Graphics were surveyed for the study. Chief among the study's findings was that the intranet as a whole is accepted throughout the organization much more pervasively and quickly than other technology. This can be attributed both to the relative ease of use and the "grass-roots" accessibility. Furthermore, companies take to an intranet with a vengeance. Forty percent of those surveyed visit their intranet sites hourly and 44% visit daily. The remaining 16% say they accessed their intranet on a weekly, or less frequent, basis.

What pulls people into an intranet? Although the novelty of the intranet does have some impact on the high degree of use, the survey indicates that increasingly intranet usage has a mission-critical focus. The more entwined an intranet becomes in the organization the more users are found to remain connected to it throughout the day.

Like Web sites on the Internet, intranet interest is driven by a personal bias—what makes an employee's work and life better. In the study of new users, five reasons most often given for accessing the intranet were

1. Viewing the company stock price
2. Calculating retirement funds
3. Checking job openings
4. Reading current company news
5. Researching task and project implementation

Although it seems counterproductive for employees to emphasize their personal uses over their work uses, it's really not. Given the newness of the application, the more personally relevant information serves to get the employees accustomed to accessing the intranet. After the technology is familiar and perceived as friendly it is much easier for more mission-critical uses to emerge.

New intranet users also attribute their interest to the system's ease of use. Many of those surveyed came from a mainframe environment where searching for information was too daunting and time-consuming. The familiar, common interface of the browser makes the greater quantity of information now available on the intranet accessible.

A final factor in the intranet's acceptance is its ability to be universally accessible—both from a reading and writing standpoint. Formerly, all announcements had to be filtered through the IT departments for posting because only they had the technology. Today's intranet enables easy publishing from every department, which enhances the information flow as well as the sense of participation.

Implementing Information Technology in Your Intranet

Although information technology involves virtually every aspect of an Internet/intranet strategy, it's possible to categorize three main areas of focus:

- *Messaging.* Much of IT's charge is to facilitate information flow through messaging. Messaging includes all the various forms of email, listserves, and newsgroups—anything that enables an individual to distribute information directly.

- *Administration.* Information technology is responsible for transmitting the company's administrative messages to all its employees. Everything from an online human resources manual to the CEO's quarterly address can be made available across the enterprise through an IT managed intranet.

- *Document Publishing and Storage.* If messaging is a corporation's current thoughts and administration its goal, then document archive is a company's living memory. The beauty of the intranet is that the information gathered and made available is truly a collective one because it enables, and even encourages, participation from all sectors of the business.

From One-to-One to One-to-Many: Electronic Messaging

Direct communication empowers businesses on so many levels. Whether it's engineering team members' brainstorming ideas, a follow-up clarification to a point raised by a prospective client, or a vacation memo cc'd to every member of the firm, the fastest, most convenient manner of getting your point across is by electronic messaging.

The most basic form of messaging is sending email, but—as you'll see in this section—even email isn't very basic anymore. Ongoing discussions can also be held through several other electronic messaging mediums, including listserves and newsgroups.

As the case studies in this section demonstrate, a strong messaging implementation is essential to any Internet/intranet strategy. It is, in my mind, the foundation for all the other benefits that the Internet offers. Think that's overstating the case? Watch what happens the next time the email in your office goes down—or listen to the hue and cry when an international public service such as America Online has a glitch.

The Advantages of Email

Email has been called the "killer app" of the Internet, and truthfully, it does seem to have had the most impact of any new technology since fax machines, if not the telephone. Email is so much more than just a message delivered by electronic means. Each of the benefits of email can have a direct impact on your business:

- *Email is fast.* Depending on the status of the Internet, most email is delivered within 3 to 5 minutes of being sent to any point in the world.

- *Email is cheap.* Even in the worst-case scenario—a long-distance call—email can be sent for pennies. Moreover, because local phone calls are most frequently used, email doesn't have to be scheduled to take advantage of lower nighttime rates, like sending a fax does.

- *Email is global.* Need to contact your buyer in Myanmar? Get the latest figures to production in Oaxaca? Confirm a meeting in Bangladesh? Send an email.

- *Email is asynchronous.* Email in-boxes expand as you use them and will wait indefinitely for you to check them. This capability enables you to send information as soon as you'd like without waiting for the other side of the world to wake up.

- *Email is accessible.* You don't have to be in your office to check your email—in fact you don't even have to be in your own country. Most organizations are set up so that you can read and respond to your email from any Internet-capable computer.

- *Email is easy.* It takes only minutes for your staff to pick up the basics of email. Common, familiar terminology (reply, forward, cc, and so on) flattens the learning curve to almost nothing. Other, more advanced capabilities can be learned as they are needed.

- *Email is flexible.* You can cut and paste passages from and/or to documents, quote the original message, file the message into specific folders, and, of course, print a hard copy.

- *Email is forwardable.* Routing information to the necessary parties has never been easier than with email. You can forward a message to an individual or to a list of co-workers and attach your comments as well.

- *Email is multimedia.* Email isn't only words. Other files, no matter what the type (word processing document, spreadsheet, audio, or video), can be attached to an email message. Furthermore, the latest mail readers are capable of sending and reading Web pages (written in *HTML*) for a more dynamic, easier-to-read presentation.

- *Email is secure.* The latest innovation in email is the addition of security features. Using a variety of standards, email can now be encrypted, digitally signed, and authenticated through the inclusion of a digital certificate. This important feature is discussed in depth later in the chapter.

Case Study: US WEST, Inc.

US WEST provides telecommunications services to more than 25 million customers in 14 states. With more than 47,000 employees, revenue for the company reached $10.5 billion in 1997.

US WEST makes the most of its company intranet, dubbed the Global Village, in its email and other applications. One of the biggest benefits has been the cost reduction associated with publishing to the intranet rather than printing and distributing the old-fashioned way. To keep employees informed about any new developments posted to the Global Village, an email is sent to all pertinent parties. Within the email, a live *hyperlink* is included, which, when clicked, opens the corresponding Web page on the intranet in the employee's browser. This technique keeps the information centralized while making it very accessible. Moreover, emails aren't burdened with large file attachments, which can take a few moments to download. According to Patricia Hursh, manager of US WEST's intranet, the company has experienced significant time and cost reductions from this application, and it plans to use it to replace the benefits handbook, health care enrollment package, corporate policies and practices, various reference cards and information, as well as newsletters.

FAQ: How do you make a hyperlink in email?

Two methods can be used to create a "clickable" link in the body of an email message. The most widely accepted method is to include the full Internet address in the text. For example:

```
http://www.managedcaretoday.com/index.htm
```

The recipient sees the underlined link in the default link color (typically blue). The other method can be accomplished only with HTML-capable mail clients, such as the latest offerings from Netscape and Microsoft. These programs enable you to send messages scripted with HTML and insert links through a special command.

Extended Capabilities in Email

By far, most business communication is handled as straight electronic text. However, a growing trend is to take advantage of the new extended capabilities of today's email.

In much the same way as you paper clip photocopies to a message you're routing around the office, you can attach a wide variety of electronic files to your email. It's faster and easier to distribute memos or reports around the enterprise electronically than it is to use the traditional method via office mail. Moreover, the documents retain their digital character and can be easily edited and revised.

The standard that makes all this possible is called *MIME (Multipurpose Internet Mail Extensions)*. MIME is a series of file types that use file extensions to identify the kind of file attached. Each program—whether it's a word processing, spreadsheet, database, or paint program—saves files in a particular file type. The file types are most commonly seen as the extensions (such as ".doc" for Microsoft Word or ".xls" for Excel) which, since Windows 95, are no longer apparent to some users.

Email Size Limitations

Most intranets enable you to attach as many files as you like; however, some servers refuse to deliver a message greater than a particular size. The most common limitation is 1.5 megabytes. If you are having problems sending a particularly large file, check with your system administrator.

Although the process is referred to as encoding, all you do is attach the specific file, and the mail program handles all the work. The recipient of the message must have the necessary programs or *plug-ins* for reading each file sent. A plug-in is a helper program that works with your browser to decode specific file types. If you send some engineering diagrams done in AutoCad, for example, the recipient must have either a compatible version of AutoCad or the AutoCad plug-in. Most plug-ins are free and can be downloaded at the program publisher's site, or from a general site such as the Plug-in Plaza (`browserwatch.internet.com/ plug-in.html`).

Web Pages and Email

Suppose your development team is working on the new event site that must "go live" on the Web in six hours. You need a dozen people around the country to sign off on the proposed changes, and the files are too massive to send to each one—what do you do? Send each team member an email with a live, clickable link, such as this one:

`http://www.neuro.com/testsite/index.html`

and let them explore the site from their own systems.

MIME-capable email enables full Web pages or messages with HTML elements to be sent. HTML stands for HyperText Markup Language and is the computer language Web pages are written in. One of the capabilities of HTML extended messages is the ability to include images (or other media including digital video) embedded in the body of the message, as shown in Figure 12.2. This capability can help teams communicate ideas and concepts more clearly.

Figure 12.2 HTML-capable email enables the email message to include graphics directly in the message and not just as an attached file.

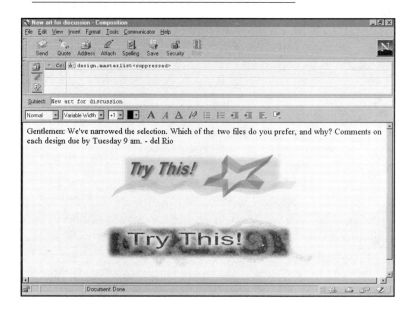

HTML mail also enables you to change the font size, type, and color for increased emphasis. You can also include a colored background or even a background image, such as a watermark. Although the layout has some limitations, you have many more options over the look and feel of your email. The most significant restriction is that the recipient must be able to read your HTML-enabled mail.

Encrypted Email

Security over the Internet is a natural concern during an e-commerce transaction when you're passing your credit card information over the Web. But aren't your internal business communications equally valuable? Although it's not child's play, your regular email messages could be intercepted and read. The same encryption and authentication methods used in electronic commerce are now available for email.

The most current versions of all major mail client software are equipped to handle email security to varying degrees. All will enable you to encrypt or code your email message so that only the recipient (who has the unlocking key) can read the message. Most programs also enable you to include a digital signature with messages that serve to authenticate your message. A digital signature is available to individuals or companies who have completed an application with a certificate authority, such as VeriSign (www.verisign.com). Security options are set through preferences, such as the one shown in Figure 12.3.

Figure 12.3 If you're routinely involved in sending sensitive information over the Internet, it's a good idea to enable your email security preferences.

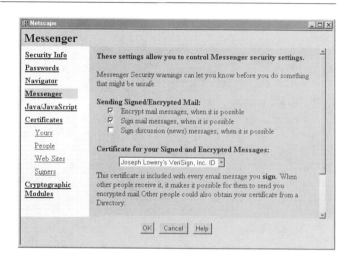

For other people to send you coded messages, they must have what's known as your *public key*. With the encryption method now in use, two keys are involved: a public key and a private key. The public key can be distributed to individuals or even to a widely accessible directory such as Four11 or BigFoot. With your public key, a message can be sent that only you, with the private key, can unlock. After it is set up, this procedure takes place behind the scenes of the program and requires no additional action from the sender or the recipient.

SEE ALSO

➤ *For more about Internet/intranet security, see page 19.*

Ten Tips for Power Email

With a few key techniques, email can improve your communication efficiency immensely. After you get in the email groove, you'll find yourself beginning to get more electronic correspondence than you know what to do with. Managing your email becomes an essential skill in today's corporate environment. The following tips can help you create more effective email and manage the responses you receive.

1. *Use filters to fight spam. Spam* is the electronic equivalent of junk mail. Just like the junk mail that gets dumped on your desk, spam is time consuming to dispose of. Most major mail programs now include a filtering option that enables you to automatically delete email that matches particular criteria. You can set the filters to look for a particular address or even text, such as "free offer," in the message header or body.

2. *Sort your messages.* With the vast, ever-increasing amount of email received daily, it's easy to get overwhelmed. Depending on how you like to work, you can structure your in-box folders to make it easy to keep up. I keep my primary in-box sort in reverse chronological order, for instance, so that the most current messages appear on top. However, I have set my newsgroup messages to be sorted by subject or *thread* so that each topic and its responses can be easily viewed.

Deleting Multiple Messages

If you find that you want to clear out a number of messages, you don't have to select each message and delete it in turn—you can erase as many as you like at one time. To delete several messages that are grouped together, select the first message, press and hold the Shift key, and then select the last message. All the messages in between will be highlighted, and you can press the Delete key or button to erase them all. To remove multiple message that aren't next to one another, press and hold the Ctrl key as you make your selections.

3. *Delete unwanted mail.* Keep only the items in your in-box that still require action. Email that has been responded to or dealt with in another manner can be deleted. Most mail programs "delete" a file by moving it to another folder called Trash or Deleted Items. In an emergency, you can always pull that file from the "trash"; in the meantime, it's not cluttering up your desk.

Reminder Messages

Some email programs (such as Outlook) enable you to flag messages for follow-up. You can even tell it when and if to issue you a reminder to do so.

4. *Use folders to manage your mail.* Just as you establish different file folders for various clients or tasks, you can set up equivalent folders for your email. Generally, you set up a new folder by choosing **New Folder** from the **File** menu and entering a name for it. Then, each piece of email that comes in can be filed in the appropriate folder—and removed from your in-box simultaneously. You can even have folders within folders, or subfolders, for a more detailed breakdown of information.

5. *CC 'em.* You don't have to send the same message repeatedly to have it reach different people. Use the CC feature to send courtesy copies to other members in your working group. Like a regular letter, everyone gets the same information, but the primary recipient is listed as such.

6. *Or BCC 'em.* Sometimes you don't want the recipients of an email message to know who else is getting the information. Mail programs include a BCC feature as well as a CC one for sending blind courtesy copies.

7. *Create a signature file.* I'm a strong believer in automating any part of my work, no matter how small. Email packages enable you to create a *signature file* that will be automatically appended to every email message you send out. Your signature file (often called a sig) can contain whatever closing you prefer, as well as your name, title, and/or phone number. Here's an example:

```
Very truly yours,
John Evermore
COO, Evermore Corp.
jevermore@evermore.com
```

8. *Use the address book.* Mail programs all contain a small address book utility. Like an electronic desk card file, the address book contains the names, email addresses, and other information of your most common contacts. Many mail programs automatically complete the names you enter in the email address line by looking up the information in the address book.

9. *Group people into lists.* If you find that you are sending to the same group of individuals repeatedly, group them into a list. Generally handled through the address book, lists are a handy method of distributing information to the same team again and again.

10. *Work offline.* You don't always have to be connected to the Internet to compose your email. If you're on the road, you can respond to any received message or create new ones. Then, select the **Send Later** option from your mail program. After you're online again, you can empty your outbox by sending the unsent mail.

Establishing Mailing Lists

Mailing lists are an email variation that enable many people to share messages. Many mailing lists, or listserves, are publicly available and aimed at facilitating communication among people with similar interests. However, a mailing list can also be a powerful collaborative tool for in-house teams. Suppose, for example, your re-engineering team is working on the latest product design. Suggestions for new features are sent from each team member to the mailing list. Everyone sees everyone else's ideas and can comment on them. A consensus can emerge without the team being in the same country, much less the same meeting room. Mailing lists work the following way:

1. Your system administrator sets up a mailing list, using a program such as listserv (for Windows) or Majordomo (for Unix systems).

2. The initial team members' names and email addresses are added to the mailing list during the set-up procedure.

3. New members can be added to the list by subscribing to it. To subscribe to a mailing list, the new member should send an email to the administrator at the mailing list address. The software then handles the actual addition. Depending on the procedure set up, the word "subscribe" should be in the header or the body of the message.

4. To remove yourself from a mailing list, send an email to the administrator with the word "unsubscribe" in the header or the body of the message.

5. All members get every message sent to the mailing list address. You can still send private messages to individuals, but you must address them separately.

Mailing List Pitfall

It's a common mistake to send a message to all members of the list when you intend to send it privately to one. Make sure that your message is addressed to the party for whom it is intended.

Depending on the number of members of a mailing list and their participation, the amount of messages flowing to your in-box can be quite daunting. Some very active mailing lists accumulate 200 to 300 messages a day. In situations such as this, some administrators elect to establish a newsgroup to hold the discussion.

Another option is to enable a digest. Digests are summaries of all the messages posted to the list on that particular day. Just how brief the summaries are depends on the setup of the digest and how many entries are involved. Lists with hundreds of messages a day often use only the message head as a summary.

Using Corporate Newsgroups

Although mailing lists are good for a short-term, highly directed topic, for more in-depth, longer-term discussions with a larger group of participants, an in-house *newsgroup* is a better solution. Newsgroups are descendants of the early computer bulletin board discussions and retain the advantages of an asynchronous discussion open to anyone around the world.

Tens of thousands of public newsgroups exist, each one centered around a particular topic. Although many individuals in your organization may subscribe to a newsgroup in a field of interest, to run a closed, private newsgroup, you have to use a type of software called a *news server*. News servers are similar to Web servers except instead of sending out Web pages, they collect and disburse newsgroup messages.

A particular newsgroup is a collection of *articles,* or messages, posted to the newsgroup. Each article posted by one person can be responded to by another person, which, in turn, can be answered by another. The articles themselves are similar to email messages with an address area, a header, and a message body. A series of articles and its responses is called a *thread*. The part of the browser that handles the newsgroups is known as the newsreader—a typical series of threads and articles is shown in Figure 12.4.

Newsgroups are excellent targets for short-term projects. Macromedia uses temporary newsgroups (and mailing lists) when it coordinates efforts during the development of a new software title. In this case, engineers, sales managers, and other individuals inside the company collaborate with advisors outside the company in a neutral environment. Another advantage to newsgroups is that the messages can be held on the server for continued reference.

Figure 12.4   Newsgroups are a perfect forum for project-centered team efforts.

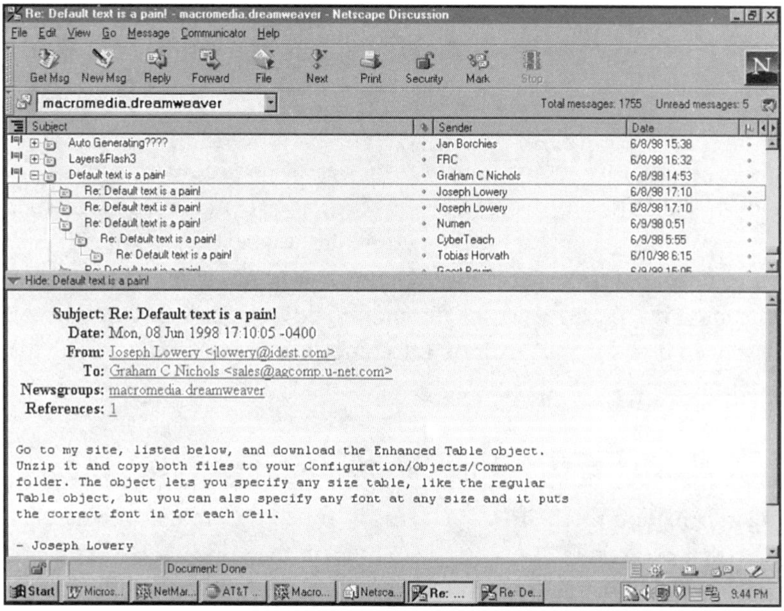

After your IT department has set up the news server and created the first newsgroup, each team member must subscribe to it to begin participating. If desired, the system administrator can secure the newsgroup and make it accessible only to those with the proper password and/or authentication code. Encrypting information sent to and received from a secure newsgroup is also possible.

Newsgroups are either moderated or unmoderated. In a moderated newsgroup, all information is passed through a designated employee, called a moderator, before being posted; whereas, in an unmoderated group, articles are posted automatically.

Case Study: Bay Networks, Inc.

Recently acquired by Northern Telecom, Bay Networks offers industry-leading LAN and ATM switches, intelligent hubs, multiprotocol routers, remote- and Internet-access solutions, and sophisticated network management applications. For the 12-month period ending March, 1998, Bay Networks had revenue of $2.34 billion.

In addition to sharing the advantages noted for email, newsgroups are distinctive in their manner for sharing information. Companies, such as Bay Networks, have come to find private news servers essential for collaborating over distance and time. Instead of restricting its benefits to one group, Bay Networks provides newsgroup discussion areas for engineering, sales, and marketing divisions. Topics covered include new software applications, competitive analysis, and product introductions. Newsgroups are especially beneficial for salespeople when complex new products are being brought to market and a wide range of issues needs to be discussed.

Bay Networks has found that adding a newsgroup server provides a structured forum for detailed one-on-one discussions that can benefit the entire company. This is especially important in Bay Networks's situation as a company that was recently formed from a merger of Synoptics Communications and Wellfleet Communications. The newsgroups serve to unite the companies' diverse populations in ongoing discussions—and now that Bay Networks itself has been bought by Northern Telecom, the need to communicate ideas and knowledge continues.

Simplifying Administration with Information Technology

Disseminating information to employees is a costly, time-consuming process. Management wants to ensure that everyone in the organization is on the same page—but that's difficult to coordinate in today's fast-paced business world. Information Technology can bring a major benefit to the administrative side of any enterprise through creative application of Internet/intranet technology.

Creative? Since when does "creative" even co-exist in the same sentence as "administrative," much less have an impact? Since the far-reaching possibilities of the Web forever changed corporate life as we know it. If you think I'm exaggerating, just look at how Sun Microsystems is reinventing its organization through an Internet/intranet strategy.

Case Study: Sun Microsystems, Inc.

Founded in 1982, Sun has become a global leader in enterprise computing solutions. Sun has more than $8 billion in revenues and offices in 150 countries.

Sun Microsystems has 12,000 employees across the world—that's a lot of photocopies to run off every time an HR manual is updated. Of course, Sun doesn't work that way anymore—the Employee Communications Group is in charge of finding the most efficient means of conveying information through its intranet, SunWeb, shown in Figure 12.5. One of the most engaging uses to emerge from Sun is a Web-based audio program called *WSUN Radio*. Employees can tune into the program on their multimedia-equipped workstations whenever they like by pointing their browser to the WSUN Web page. Sun's CEO, Scott McNealy, uses WSUN to broadcast his monthly radio program, which he uses to keep the Sun message alive.

Figure 12.5 SunWeb, Sun Microsystems's intranet, puts all aspects of the organization at every employee's fingertips.

In a more traditional vein, Sun moved its quarterly employee magazine, called *Illuminations*, to the Web. The magazine editors found the biggest savings to be time related. Because the magazine no longer has to contend with pre-press, printing, and distribution issues, more timely material is accessible—the magazine lead time is cut drastically. The monetary savings is not to be taken lightly, either. Moving *Illuminations* to the Web saved Sun two-thirds of its previous production and distribution costs.

Sun's leadership holds quarterly conferences for upper management, in which current issues are addressed and new technologies previewed. To keep the balance of the employees informed, these events, "The Leadership Conferences," are documented—in writing and photographs—and the results are posted to the internal Web. Archives of these conferences are made available for all employees.

An intranet's impact doesn't always have to be measured in terms of enterprise-wide communication. Information technology can make life easier (and more cost-effective) for specific departments with new tools that require very little training because of the common browser interface. Sun's Payroll department, for example, saved more than $100,000 a year using an automatic check-processing tool called CheckMate, which was accessible from any browser over the company intranet. CheckMate cut the estimated check-processing fees from $35 per check to $2 per check. Naturally, the time for processing a check was cut as well.

Information technology can also use intranet development to facilitate interdepartmental cooperation. As another example of Sun's intranet prowess, consider the Asset Manager's Workbench, a Web-based tool developed by Sun Information Resources to better handle asset management. In a computer-oriented company such as Sun, fixed assets such as unused computer systems abound, and three departments—Accounting, Facilities, and Information Technology—must coordinate their management. The Asset Manager's Workbench was created to enable managers to retire or transfer assets from a Web-based form, shown in Figure 12.6. The form simplifies the process, which previously required an employee knowledgeable in advanced database techniques to complete. Now, with the Asset Manager's Workbench, equipment is recycled much more expeditiously with only a minimum of managerial approval.

Directory Services

Time and again I've touted the wonders of using the company intranet to access vast pools of information. Often, such data can be as mundane as a corporate listing with contact information up and down the org chart. Information Technology is charged with maintaining such ever-changing sources—while making them as accessible as possible.

Such information is often referred to as part of directory services; however, employee directories are just the tip of the information iceberg. Depending on the depth of the IT division, directory services can pull together almost all the transactional data across the enterprise. This information management infrastructure enables managers and staff to share and access dynamically updated information in real time.

Figure 12.6   The Assets Manager's Workbench is a Web-based form that enables department
                heads to make better use of corporatewide fixed assets.

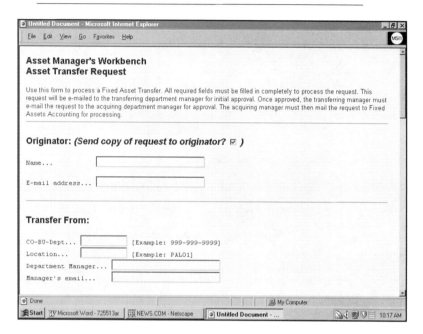

Case Study: Home Depot
With more than 600 warehouse-style stores across the U.S. and Canada, Home Depot is
North America's largest home-improvement retailer. Sales in 1997 topped $24 billion.

To better manage its rapid growth, Home Depot wanted to empower its district managers
with more across-the-board, up-to-the-minute information. Home Depot's IT department
developed a system dubbed the Virtual District Office to help in this endeavor. A constant
flow of information fills the databases on which the Virtual District Office relies. Interest-
ingly, the centralized information source enables the district managers to act more autono-
mously because they have access to a much wider range of data. However, IT has designed
the system with several degrees of control so that abuse of this power is unlikely. Training
associates can reorder stock, for example, but the database requires managerial authorization
before the transaction is completed. Similarly, VPs in the Atlanta home office can look at an
aggregate of the national sales numbers, but the district managers only have access to more
localized figures.

Human Resources

Human Resources is often cited as a key reason for implementing an intranet. Why? Because the benefits are so immediate and tangible:

- Reduction in costs for payroll and benefits administration.

- Centralization of the employee service manual, with subsequent reduction in printing and distribution costs.

- Ease of updating employee directories is greatly enhanced.

- Improved employee access to personal information, such as remaining vacation days, accrued pension benefits, and 401k status.

- Standardization of performance review and raise evaluation.

- Vastly improved access to a wider potential employee pool for hiring purposes.

- Online training applications provide asynchronous learning capability with a more contained cost than classroom learning.

- Online testing and evaluation enhance self-paced learning without involving HR personnel.

SEE ALSO

➤ *For more about online training, see page 75.*

SEE ALSO

➤ *For more on using the Internet for job recruitment, see page 89.*

One company, BC Telecom (profiled earlier in Chapter 1, "Advantages of the Cutting Edge"), established its own human resources application, named Virtual HR, on its intranet. Through Virtual HR, employees can view information on all company human resource programs, including health, safety, benefits, fitness programs, and schedules. Employees can also use the pension estimator to see what their pension will be worth upon retirement. When the Virtual HR program is completely operational, BC Telecom expects employees to be able to serve themselves, taking advantage of all HR functions online.

Case Study: Philadelphia Housing Authority
As a state-regulated agency, the Philadelphia Housing Authority must follow specific procedures in dealing with more than 2,000 employees.

Before they were "wired," the Philadelphia Housing Authority's Human Resources Department maintained all its personnel records on paper and microfilm. Requests for information took days to fill. The first phase of its intranet strategy involved entering, scanning, and storing files. Special attention had to be paid to security because Pennsylvania had recently enacted the Personnel File Act, which mandated that records are categorized either as personnel-related and accessible to all management, or confidential with a much more limited access. According to the categorization, the documents were filed in electronic folders with relevant password protection.

Document Publishing and Access

One goal of IT departments is to put themselves out of the publishing business. In earlier networking days, only a crack team of programming professionals had the savvy and the access to post documents on the system. Usually this involved employing a special set of utilities for transferring files from their native format to the lowest common denominator—losing all formatting in the process. After the files were converted, you had to speak Unix (at best) fluently in order to upload the files to the appropriate directory. Then, of course, to access the files, you had to be able to decipher the rather cryptic filenames that were system dictated, such as oct88nva.doc and the ever-popular 199811PayRecv.fs (November payroll and receivables spreadsheet—remember?).

Contrast all that rigmarole with this directive: "select File: Publish to Web." A fully implemented Internet/intranet strategy empowers all your departments—and all your employees—by enabling each segment to put out its own documentation. Sales managers can make valuable data available to on-the-road salesmen, and Human Resources can post job openings as they occur. This keeps the most current information available and eliminates time lags due to a backlog in IT. Moreover, it tightens the responsibility loophole so that if information is not forthcoming, you know exactly where to go to fix it. Finally, this policy also serves to free up your IT resources.

Case Study: Pfizer Inc.
With 40,000 employees working in 24 time zones, Pfizer is one of the world's largest health-care companies. Sales for 1997 topped $12.5 billion. Pfizer was ranked by Business Week as one of the 10 best-performing companies in the Standard & Poor's 500.

Pfizer got on the intranet bandwagon pretty early in the game, and its facilities have been extensively developed. To assist its employees in its Web publishing efforts, Pfizer established the Corporate Information Technology Division (CITD). CITD provides the resources (such as training) and establishes company standards in order to create a unified look and feel for employee- and department-published documents. One division, the Environmental Health and Safety Division, uses its publishing ability to create material safety data sheets, a regulatory requirement. The electronic process enables a much faster turnaround for updates at a much lower cost.

Pfizer's Global Research division is made up of more than 3,000 scientists in four locations around the world. The intranet publishing ability eliminates duplication of effort and speeds up the workflow by enabling researchers to share and reuse each other's work.

Standardizing Your Publishing

Even the briefest tour of the Web reveals the enormous diversity possible. Web sites look different, act different (in terms of navigation), and can even have different requirements. Although this is acceptable on the wide open Internet, it can be counterproductive to an intranet where a standard look and feel is not only "more corporate" but contributes to lessening the learning curve.

Information technology is responsible for creating the standard and supplying the toolset used in creating intranet pages. Luckily, a number of methods can be used to make publishing on the Internet straightforward and consistent.

- *Provide standard graphics.* Corporate logos and even background colors or images go a long way toward establishing a particular presence. Graphics can be kept in a central directory to be copied and used by various departments.

- *Use templates.* Current versions of office software, especially programs from Microsoft, enable documents to be built from templates. Such templates can be used for word processing, spreadsheets, or Web publishing. Templates can be modified to include company-specific language, such as copyright notices, as well as special graphics.

- *Create pages with interactive forms.* The same techniques that enable users to post answers to surveys or take tests on the Web can be used to create Web pages. A Web-based form takes the information supplied and manipulates it in whatever manner the linked program instructs. Having the form create and publish a Web page is well within the capabilities of such custom-designed programs.

- *Work with style sheets.* The current versions of both major browsers, Netscape Communicator 4.5 and Internet Explorer 5.0, both fully support *style sheets*. A style sheet is a set of instructions that gives a Web page its background color, font choice and size, and many other layout options. By using external style sheets (which are not embedded in a single Web page), entire Web sites can achieve a uniform look and feel almost effortlessly. Even more importantly, a change to a style sheet changes all the pages to which it is linked. Style sheets are structured so that divisions and departments can each have their own distinctive features, such as color coding, to make intranet navigation easier.

- *Use repeating elements.* Just as boilerplate text can save loads of time when you develop contracts, repeating elements can do the same when you create pages for the intranet. The current crop of Web authoring tools, such as Macromedia's Dreamweaver, enables the creation of a library of such elements, which can mix text and graphics. In addition to speed of creation, the other advantage of a repeating element's library is that, like style sheets, updating the primary element automatically updates those Web pages using it. This makes changing legal notices on an intranet—which could involve thousands of pages—a painless process instead of a never-ending nightmare. Changing a copyright date from 1998 to 1999, for example, becomes a matter of updating one file, not thousands.

Ensuring Easy Information Retrieval

You can make the prettiest, most informative report in the world, but if it's sitting in a box on your shelf, you may as well not have bothered. After information is published to the Web or intranet, interested (and authorized) parties have to be able to locate the document and retrieve it.

Many intranets use a *site map* to detail the layout of their internal Web and provide quick, easy access to the major departments. A site map is a graphic depiction of the intranet, generally laid out in a fashion similar to an organizational chart or workflow diagram. Each page described uses a live hyperlink, which, when clicked, is pulled up directly.

Search engines are vital on the Internet, and site-specific search engines can be just as important on an intranet. Although most search engines index every word on every document, the fastest results are tied to the title of a Web page or a special series of keywords embedded in the page's code.

It's important for all intranets and Web sites to use clear, consistent navigation techniques. The Xerox intranet, shown in Figure 12.7, is an excellent example of clarity in design. Many sites use a series of icons which—to the uninformed visitor—can be extremely puzzling. Webmasters often hold a series of focus groups, or user accessibility studies, to determine which images and icons communicate the intended message.

Outsourcing Information Technology

Although many companies handle all their Information Technology needs in-house, it's not unheard of to work with a trusted third party on IT. It's an option worth considering, especially if your company is in a startup posture, because IT expenditures can be quite burdensome. As with logistics, outsourcing IT enables your company to concentrate on its core competencies, most notably in times of a major re-engineering effort.

Figure 12.7 The Xerox intranet uses a whiteboard metaphor to make navigation intuitive for even the most novice user.

Case Study: Australian Mutual Provident Society

One of the country's oldest insurance and financial firms, Australian Mutual Provident Society (AMP), provides insurance, savings, investment, and banking services across Australia, New Zealand, and the United Kingdom.

The Australian Mutual Provident (AMP) Society has long worked with its IT outsourcing company, CSC, on its mainframe support. In 1997, as the information revolution continued to spread, CSC was contracted to extend AMP's technological reach to the desktop. CSC approached the job by consolidating various help desk services, standardizing technology solutions across the intranet, and centralizing tools to manage the desktop systems remotely. Another advantage of outsourcing IT is that consulting companies often have a wide range of experience with similar situations and have already solved many of the problems naturally encountered. CSC, for example, was able to leverage its expertise gained with other clients to benefit its ongoing relationship with AMP.

CHAPTER 13

Business-to-Business Extranets

- Extranet basics
- The ins and outs of extranets
- Extranet examples
- The largest extranet: consumers

Why Extranets?

The Internet established a global communication network that enabled anyone online to communicate with anyone else online and share posted information via Web sites. Intranets applied the Internet concept to organizations, coupling the power of enhanced communication with the impetus of working together to achieve a competitive edge. *Extranets* extend the intranet, carefully and precisely, into the realm of the Internet to encompass business partners and eventually, customers to further that competitive edge and share the benefits among all the participants.

One of the first extranets was established by FedEx when it enabled its primary customers to directly access FedEx's internal computers for tracking information. This was soon discovered to be a classic "win-win" situation. Customers got the information they needed faster and more directly by entering information in a tracking screen, such as the one shown in Figure 13.1. FedEx freed its support personnel from performing the searches over the phone. The beauty of it all is that the customers were now accessing the same databases that the FedEx people were accessing. No additional computer expenditure was incurred.

Figure 13.1   Track a package by accessing FedEx's computers through the Web—an example of a massive extranet in action.

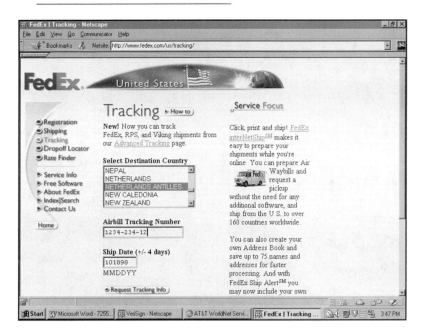

Extranets are rapidly growing in popularity. Companies have found that to maintain a competitive imperative, it is no longer enough to tighten your internal structure. To gain the most benefit, you have to open the circle of communication for your entire supply chain. It's one thing to integrate all of your in-house systems with an intranet; it's quite another to integrate your systems with those of your suppliers, shippers, distributors, and retailers. Although stumbling blocks exist along the way—and potholes must be avoided—the extranet is a road worth taking for many companies.

Extranet Advantages

The range of benefits brought by extranets depends entirely on the depth of the outreach. Simply put, the more you give, the more you get. This, naturally, is not a one-way street—it is, after all, why you consider these particular companies to be partners. To gain the fullest benefit, your business partners must open their operations as you have opened yours.

What are the gains an extranet can bring? The following overview lists the possibilities of how an extranet can be put into play:

- *Enhanced communication.* Nothing is quite as frustrating as waiting for a callback to place an order. Extranets eliminate the middleman and enable one company to talk to another directly. Furthermore, many extranets take advantage of dedicated lines and/or servers to physically speed up the transactions.

- *Increased security.* Although most of your communication can be handled over the Internet, you do so at some risk. Extranets are very security conscious, which is good not only for each company individually, but also for its transactions—whether financial or informational—as a whole.

- *Greater savings.* What's cheaper? Designing, creating, printing, and distributing catalogs (which will be out of date relatively quickly) to your retail base or creating an online catalog with instantaneous updates and worldwide circulation?

- *Quicker ordering.* In business-to-business situations, buying goods from a vendor doesn't require a trip to the store—you don't have to squeeze the AXD-4432-L2 to know what you want. You place the order; and if you can do that electronically, your day ends sooner.

- *Faster payments.* Extranets make it possible for companies to automate and speed up the payment process, whether by using electronic funds transfer or a third-party Internet payment solution, such as CyberCash.

SEE ALSO

➤ *For more about payments on the Web, see page 269.*

- *More accessible accounts.* Many times, your company needs to reconcile accounts with another of your business partners. Account balances, previous transactions, received payments—all this information can be available on an extranet. Information someone at another company retrieves in their computer can be retrieved conveniently through the extranet.

- *Easier interface.* By using a common browser interface, an extranet gleans the same benefit as an intranet—less training.

- *More complete tracking.* Not only can shipments be tracked after they leave your warehouse, but an extranet enables you to track shipments coming into your warehouse, as well. Moreover, with a fully implemented extranet, every step along the supply chain is documented and trackable.

SEE ALSO

➤ *For more about automating your shipment tracking, see page 142.*

Types of Companies Using Extranets

Although they're not yet in full bloom, extranets are popping up all over. The pattern seems to be that after one company in an industry creates a competitive advantage for itself with an extranet, other companies in the same industry want in. Try to find an overnight delivery service, for example, that *doesn't* enable you to track your shipment over the Internet—UPS, Airborne Express, RPS, DHL—they all do it. Some other industries where extranets are making notable inroads include

- *Health care providers.* The ever-increasing bond between hospitals and insurance companies has a new ally in extranet technology, which enables patient records to be shared in a secure environment.

- *Insurance firms.* Corporate employees and Human Resource departments can use extranets to enroll new employees in an insurance plan, file claims, and follow up on the claims.

- *Law firms.* Extranets enable secure document transmission—a very attractive technology to law firms and their clients who must gather and share sensitive information daily.

- *Digital production houses.* Digital media, whether photographs, 3D animation, audio, or video, means large files. An extranet connecting production houses to their service bureaus can speed transfer of the material at a far lower cost than other currently available methods. Some service bureaus, such as the one pictured in Figure 13.2, can give media companies detailed information on anticipated job completion dates.

Figure 13.2   Extranets can be used to upload and schedule digital media projects for output by a service bureau.

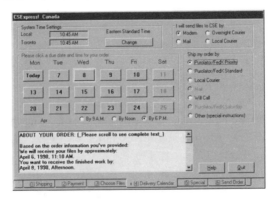

- *Technology manufacturers.* Computer supply houses and integrators have jumped on the extranet bandwagon in great number to facilitate a better ordering system and faster delivery times for electronic parts, components, and finished goods.

- *Franchise businesses.* Companies are using extranets to keep in close contact with their franchisees. Proprietary information can be transmitted securely to the outlets, and detailed status reports can flow back to the licensing company.

- *Electronic publishers.* The use of extranets in electronic publishing is a relatively new trend, but one that promises to keep growing. The incentive is money—electronic publishers have found another revenue stream by publishing strategic information directly to the customer base over the extranet.

- *Financial firms.* Larger financial service companies are using extranets to send regulatory compliance documents and to coordinate workflow with their smaller partner brokerages.

- *Energy companies.* Most energy companies must contend with a massive distributor network. Extranets cut the energy company's workload dramatically by enabling distributors to automate their ordering procedures. Distributors like it because orders are processed faster, resulting in a competitive edge.

How Extranets Work

An extranet can enable companies with different systems to share resources because it, like an intranet, is built on Internet standards. However, an extranet presents its own special challenges. How do you allow your partners into your internal network without letting your competitors in as well? Who decides which partners have access—and how much access do they have? Who monitors the system against unwanted visitors? How do you build a system that can grow in complexity and access as demand dictates? How does one company's system work closely with those belonging to potentially hundreds of partners—each with its custom configuration and setup?

Questions such as these must be discussed internally before the first extranet can go online. None of these concerns are unsolvable, and it helps to have a firm grasp of the concepts behind an extranet before tackling them. The following steps describe the process depicted in Figure 13.3.

Figure 13.3 An extranet is basically another layer of connectivity outside of a company's intranet.

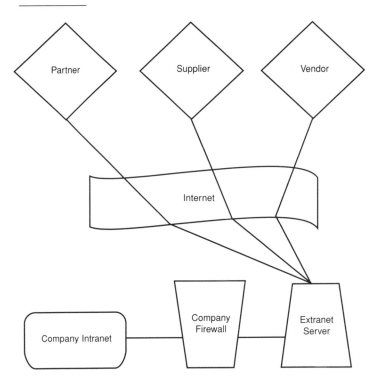

1. A business partner begins an extranet session by connecting to the Internet.

2. After the URL of the primary company is entered into the browser, the computer signal encounters an extranet server.

3. The partner is asked to supply a password (or other authentication methods used) before proceeding.

4. The password is checked within the extranet server. If a match is found, the partner's entry is noted in a log and the partner is permitted to proceed.

5. The partner passes through a second level of security, the intranet firewall. Depending on the system, a second password may be required here.

6. Inside the company intranet, the partner is restricted to viewing only files and folders for which permission is expressly granted. All other files and/or folders are off-limits.

The file permissions can range from read-only, read/write, or read/write/execute. Read-only means that the documents can only be viewed or interacted with, but not edited. Read/write enables partners to read and to alter the files for which access is granted. Read/write/execute enables extranet partners to run programs on each other's computer systems.

Initially making the extranet connection through the Internet saves the Information Technology department a great amount of work. As newer, high-speed technologies become available, IT is not responsible for upgrading partners around the globe—that's handled by the carriers. Moreover, IT does not have to maintain multiple points of entry as with the old-style *Wide Area Network* (WAN), which proved to be prohibitive from a cost and a manpower standpoint.

The Security Concern

Extranet security should be treated like Internet security on steroids. The key points of extranet security are

- *A security policy.* As with all such issues, it's best if a company develops an overall security policy.

SEE ALSO

➤ *For more on security policies, see page 18.*

Intranet Security Scanners

The very nature of the Web—information requested by a client is sent by a server—enables traffic to be monitored by security scanners. These intranet scanners watch for specific traffic patterns as a sign of attempted, or successful, break-ins. If an unauthorized visitor is trying to gain entry by sending password attempt after password attempt, for example, the scanner can intercept this behavior, log it, report it, and block any attempted entry.

- *Security audits.* Because the threat of unwanted intrusion is great and consistent with an extranet, the policy should include periodic security audits. Automated security scanning devices should be employed to look for security weaknesses and detect intrusions.

- *Established access rules.* As the benefits of the extranet become known within the company, the drive to increase its reach will increase. The administration of extranet privileges requires clear guidelines for growth.

- *Firewalls.* Firewalls are the true watchdogs of any intranet or extranet security system. Older firewalls that proved adequate for intranet protection may not be able to adapt to the needs of working with multiple partners—each of whom may have its own firewalls to contend with.

- *Monitoring and log analysis.* It's not enough to grant limited access to your partners and then look away. Visitor logs should be analyzed on a routine basis to ensure that everyone is playing by the agreed-upon rules and that no uninvited guests have intruded. Log analysis tools, such as the one shown in Figure 13.4, can give a clear picture of who is visiting the site.

Figure 13.4 Modern log analysis tools, such as this one called WebBoy from NDG Software, can give a graphic representation of intranet and extranet traffic.

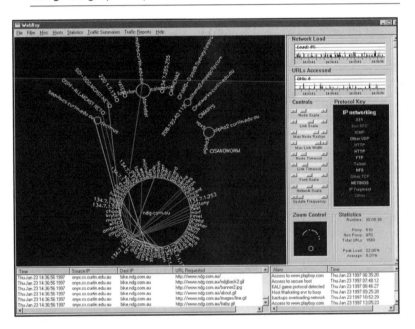

Security is such a key issue that one company specializing in extranet services, Differential, Inc., refers to the area between the extranet server and the firewall as the De-Militarized Zone. Extranet security is not just a high wall that keeps everyone out; a controlled doorway that only allows authorized partners in must be present. Moreover, after a partner is allowed into the company intranet, certain doors to internal matters must remain locked. Finally, all parties agree to keep their business private.

Security on an extranet, then, is a three-stage process. First, authenticate the visitor. At the most basic level, this is handled by a password, but more companies these days are using some form of digital certificates. Next, each visitor allowed entry is assigned a series of permissions that dictate which areas are available and which are closed. Finally, communication between the company and the extranet partners can be sent over secure Internet pathways. Although this final step slows the traffic to some degree because each bit of information must be encrypted and decrypted, it keeps the partnership as secure as each internal company.

SEE ALSO

➤ *For more on digital certificates and Internet security, see page 19.*

Case Study: @Home Network

Looking to deliver high-speed Internet access to the masses, @Home Network specializes in cable modem connections. @Home Network recently went public and closed the first quarter of 1998 with a 58% increase in revenue over the previous quarter.

The @Home Network depends on its relationship with its business partners—in fact, it would have no business without them. Because @Home (and its business-oriented spin off, @Work) delivers its high-speed Internet service through the existing cable infrastructure of such companies as Cablevision, Comcast, Cox, TCI, and others, coordination between the company and its cable industry partners is imperative.

The @Home Network's extranet is used for pass-sensitive information—such as customer account records—between @Home and their partners. A combination of password and digital certificate security ensures that each entity knows who they are sharing information with. Communication is encrypted and sent over secure Web servers. After identities are confirmed, even the email sent between the partners is automatically encrypted and authenticated using digital signatures. Best of all, this happens behind the scenes and requires no additional technical know-how from the users.

Bringing Partners In

Initially, a centralized extranet control seems like a good idea. The system administrator who handles the day-to-day operations is the logical candidate—but only for a short time. As the extranet extends to more partners, the workload of managing all the access permissions from accounts across the enterprise can quickly become unmanageable for a single individual. Moreover, account managers who work closely with business partners on a daily basis are better judges of who should be allowed access than the more technically concerned system administrator.

As your extranet reaches a certain growth stage, a more systematized approach to handling access should evolve.

1. Account executives request access for their working partners.

2. Access is considered and, if appropriate, approved by the group manager.

3. After the approval is granted, account executives detail the access permissions for specific types of content. These permissions can be part of an overall license or other agreement. The system administrator handles the actual access arrangement.

4. Account executives and group managers track the partners' activity on the extranet.

5. New files posted to the server are automatically flagged, and notices are sent to the group manager for review.

6. The system administrator must have final authority over the integrity of the system and, therefore, can override permissions if inappropriate behavior is detected.

Extranet Costs

Although it is true that deploying an extranet involves additional expenditures, the costs pale next to the benefits and the expenses of alternative methods, such as a wide area network (WAN) after a certain degree of use. The more partners networked—and the more extensive the system integration among the partners—the lower the comparative costs. Both hardware and access expenses contribute to the cost differential.

If your plans for involving your partners is limited in scope, you might want to stick with a WAN. Table 14.1, calculated with the help of Bay Networks online ROI calculator (www.baynetworks.com/products/Switches/roi_calculator/), shows the costs involved with a beginning extranet with minor usage. With only 50 potential partners, 5 of whom are on-line simultaneously and each user connecting only three hours on average per month, extranets are less cost-effective than a wide area network.

Table 14.1 Minimum Usage Comparison

	Wide Area Network	Extranet
T1 Access	500	2,850
User Access	540	1,000
Hardware	30,000	20,000

	Wide Area Network	Extranet
Equipment Management	500	200
User Support	1,250	625
Total Monthly Costs	**$2,790**	**$4,675**
Total Monthly Savings (without equipment costs)		**($1,885)**
Annual Savings (with equipment costs)		**($12,620)**

However, with extended use, the cost benefit of the extranet becomes apparent. The hardware costs on the WAN start to mount up because every site requires a dedicated system; whereas, with an extranet, any computer with Internet access will do. At the same time, the user access fees begin to climb. You will incur some costs on the support side under both scenarios; however, it's considerably less with an extranet because of the ease-of-use factor. Table 14.2 shows a moderate extranet use with a partner-base of 1,000—of whom 100 are online at any given time, with an average of 20 hours of use per month.

Table 14.2   Moderate Usage Comparison

	Wide Area Network	Extranet
T1 Access	2,500	2,850
User Access	36,000	20,000
Hardware	100,000	20,000
Equipment Management	2,500	200
User Support	25,000	12,500
Total Monthly Costs	**$66,000**	**$33,550**
Total Monthly Savings (without equipment costs)		**$30,450**
Annual Savings (with equipment costs)		**$445,400**

Under a high-usage projection, the extranet savings really take off. Certain costs, such as hardware, are fixed in the extranet scenario (the dedicated extranet servers), whereas with a WAN, hardware costs (terminals and laying of dedicated lines) goes through the roof.

The final example, Table 14.3, shows what happens with the heavier use by a 1,000 partner-base, where approximately one-third (300) are online simultaneously, and all average 50 hours per month. Quite clearly, the more the extranet extends—the lower the toll.

Table 14.3 High Usage Comparison

	Wide Area Network	Extranet
T1 Access	6,500	5,700
User Access	180,000	20,000
Hardware	260,000	20,000
Equipment Management	6,500	400
User Support	25,000	12,500
Total Monthly Costs	**$218,000**	**$38,600**
Total Monthly Savings (without equipment costs)		**$179,400**
Annual Savings (with equipment costs)		**$2,392,800**

Accounting for Scalability

When evaluating extranet systems, you want to be assured of their *scalability*. A scaleable system is one that can grow as your needs grow. While this is important in an intranet as well, it's less likely for your company to suddenly grow by a factor of five than for you to extend your extranet that much. If a system is not scaleable, you'll hit a hard ceiling sooner rather than later, and you'll have to replace the entire investment. On the other hand, a scaleable system enables you to increase only those aspects of a system, such as memory or storage, that are required by increased usage.

Case Study: VeriSign, Inc.

VeriSign is the leading provider of digital certificate solutions and infrastructure for organizations, government agencies, trading partners, and individuals wanting to conduct trusted, secure communications and commerce over the Internet.

VeriSign's business depends on gaining and keeping the trust of its customer base. The company considers that every client is a partner and, as such, must be treated in the secure manner provided by an extranet. Moreover, the digital certificates provided by VeriSign for their clients need to be accessed by others so that secure communication can be engaged. Therefore, VeriSign needed to provide a directory service through which customers could easily look up the certificates of others.

VeriSign has issued more than 45,000 digital certificates to businesses and more than two million to individuals. Although impressive, this is just the tip of the e-commerce iceberg as far as digital certificates are concerned. When evaluating an extranet, VeriSign looked primarily at performance and scalability when dealing with very large numbers. As the one million customers benchmark was approaching, VeriSign simply upgraded the memory of its system (from 256 to 384 megabytes of RAM) to ease any performance delays. VeriSign receives approximately 40,000 hits per day; stress tests showed no dips in response when the volume was increased to 100,000 hits per day during testing.

Extranets in Use

There are probably as many different uses for extranets as the companies using them. However, the primary use seems to be to automate the communication between a company and its partners, whether they are vendors or buyers.

Liz Clairborne Inc.

The name Liz Clairborne is well known in both the worlds of fashion and retail. Previous year sales reached $2.4 billion for this global company.

To better achieve its CEO-mandated, year-2000 goal to focus on design and technology as core competencies, Liz Clairborne established its extranet, dubbed LizLink. LizLink is currently being used by 25 major retailers who represent 25% of the company's sales volume. Registered retailers can log on to LizLink and check the status of their orders as well as review information on the latest product lines. The Information Services department estimates that since the extranet was established, it has replaced more than 8,000 customer service phone calls.

Case Study: Countrywide, Inc.

Countrywide, together with its subsidiaries, is a nationwide financial services company with headquarters in Calabasas, California. With 8,800 employees, Countrywide's first quarter revenue for 1998 was reported at $450 million.

For some companies, such as Countrywide, Inc., information is a product in and of itself. Countrywide is the nation's largest independent mortgage lender, and it maintains close relationships with its 330 national branch offices. In the mortgage business, lending rates fluctuate daily and the variety of product offerings is mind-boggling. To coordinate the efforts of its lending partners and brokers, Countrywide established an extranet named Platinum Lender Access. This system enables all parties to share account and transaction status as well as loan status information. Of the 500 registered partners in the extranet, 300 regularly log on several times daily for account updates. Platinum Lender Access not only maintains the password and access permissions for each lender, it also provides them with their own customized information on premium rates, discounts, and special arrangements.

Case Study: The Boeing Company

Boeing is the world's largest manufacturer of commercial jetliners and military aircraft, and it is the nation's largest NASA contractor. In 1996, company revenues were $22.7 billion; revenues for 1997 were $45.8 billion.

Boeing is a prime example of a company making life easier for itself and its customers—and making money at the same time. In the first six months after Boeing opened its extranet to its primary airline and aviation repair customers, Boeing sold more than $25 million in spare jet parts through the system. More than a third of its customer base has registered and regularly uses the extranet to scan Boeing's catalog of 410,000 airline parts. Here's how the Boeing system works:

1. A registered online partner logs onto the Boeing extranet.

2. The partner enters his password and if accepted, is allowed access.

3. Using the browser, the partner searches Boeing's online database-driven parts catalog.

   In addition to double-checking descriptions and costs, the Boeing extranet also shows availability.

4. After selecting the desired parts, the partner submits his order—much like the checkout process of an online store.

5. The order is submitted to Boeing for approval.

6. After approval, a confirmation of the order is sent via email from Boeing to the partner.

7. Shipping is guaranteed within 24 hours.

8. The shipping information is entered into the order database, and the partner can log onto the extranet to track the order.

Boeing has found that this use of the extranet deepens the relationship with its customers and significantly cuts costs while hastening delivery. Certain customers, such as Seattle-based Alaska Airlines, are so impressed with the system, they now order all their spare parts through the extranet.

Screening Vendors via the Web

Suppliers are a key component for every major corporation—and vendors know money can be made by landing ongoing contracts. Many organizations face a never-ending barrage of queries from vendors looking to do business. Cold calls are the bane of every receptionist on the planet—but how else are you supposed to get your foot in the door? Some companies have a better idea. Rather than using the Web to provide unnecessary marketing, why don't we use it to screen potential vendors?

Case Study: Columbia/HCA Healthcare Corp.

Columbia/HCA owns and operates more than 330 hospitals and other health care facilities with approximately 60,000 licensed beds in 36 states and in England and Switzerland. The company's revenue in 1997 totaled $18.82 billion.

Columbia/HCA uses its extranet in a novel manner; it maintains an open, secure channel to any prospective vendor. Then, if approved, the vendor is granted additional access privileges. This process enables Columbia/HCA to lay out its requirements in extensive detail without utilizing any of its own personnel's time. The required form helps to prequalify any interested vendor. In addition to the usual name, address, and telephone information, the Columbia/HCA vendor questionnaire looks for the following:

- The legal structure of the company and how long it has been in business

- Whether the vendor qualifies as a minority or small-business concern, which enables it to participate in Columbia/HCA's Minority Supplier Program

- The range of the vendor's service area: international, national, or regional

- Details about the company itself, such as key personnel and their length of time with the company, sales volume for the last two years, the number of employees, the square footage of the company's primary facility, and its location

- Descriptions of the vendor's products rated according to price and sales sensitivity

- The intellectual property rights claimed for the vendor's products, such as patent, copyright, or trademark

- A description of how marketing is generally handled: employee sales reps, independent sales reps, distributors, direct mail, or telemarketing

- Delivery details, such as freight terms, average lead times, and distributors

- A description of the sales organization

- Current FDA registration

- Federal censures in place from the EPA, FDA, or OSHA

As you can see, the list of qualifications is quite extensive and would require many person-nel-hours for Columbia employees to solicit the same information. Not only does the vendor preregistration give enough information for Columbia to consider the contact, it also gives enough data—in digital form—to open up an account.

EDI Extranet Applications

In some ways, extranets are the next evolutionary step of Electronic Data Interchange (EDI). EDI traditionally links businesses through Value-Added Networks (VANs) to exchange highly structured business information, orders, and payments. Companies are beginning to realize that you can replace the VAN with a modern extranet and reach the same functionality without the additional VAN charges—and with a less complex system.

Case Study: OppenheimerFunds, Inc.
Established in 1959, OppenheimerFunds is one of the nation's largest mutual fund companies in the U.S. OppenheimerFunds manages more than $85 billion in assets, including funds with more than four million shareholder accounts.

For a time, EDI was the only game in the mutual funds market. If you wanted to exchange regulatory compliance documents and transmit orders, you had to use EDI. However, EDI was initially mainframe-oriented, and using Value-Added Networks proved to be too expensive for most smaller brokerages. Mutual funds company OppenheimerFunds found that these limitations were locking out a good portion of its client base. By investing in an extranet strategy, OppenheimerFunds could work collaboratively with all its clients. OppenheimerFunds found that older EDI systems were inflexible compared to the user-oriented Web-based systems that could be deployed on the extranet. In a sense, OppenheimerFunds has brought groupware techniques to an extranet environment where access permissions can be modified as the need arises.

In a typical session, OppenheimerFunds partners log on to the secure extranet, access the compliance document, and transmit orders. After completion, the extranet software transmits the information through OppenheimerFunds' main firewall and updates the appropriate databases. If necessary, an alert is automatically sent to an account manager. This enhanced workflow gives the smaller brokerages increased flexibility and ties them closer to OppenheimerFunds.

Case Study: Mobil Corporation
Mobil is the third-largest major oil company and a global energy company with 43,000 employees working in 125 countries. Its fiscal 1997 report shows operating earnings of more than $3.4 billion and revenues of $65 billion.

Mobil Corporation got a wake-up call when it totaled its previous year's VAN charges—$100,000 plus. Mobil had been using the traditional Electronic Data Interchange method to do business with its 300 lube distributors. On closer investigation, they discovered that in addition to the excessive fees, the older software was considerably lacking in features and relatively high-maintenance.

Mobil turned to Proxicom, a system integration consulting firm, for relief. In response, Proxicom developed a secure extranet, which featured an integrated database in a more flexible system. The custom program developed validated entries to ensure that orders met specific weight, load, and order type requirements. This cut follow-up communication drastically. The lube distributors found that if the order specs were not met, feedback was immediate. The distributors could also review their order history and purchase-order status. If necessary, partial orders could be put on hold right over the extranet.

From Mobil's perspective, this was a simpler method of sending invoices or accepting purchase orders and buybacks. All these transactions were translated into EDI-compatible forms for backward compatibility with the legacy data. Best of all, this new and improved system eliminated the VAN expenses, with a minimal investment of hardware and almost no software from the distributor's viewpoint.

Widening the Extranet to Customers

As extranets gain in popularity in business-to-business circles, companies are beginning to look at the much larger pool of partners—the consumer. The more that customer communication can be moved from telephone operators to a secure extranet connection, the more savings businesses can enjoy.

The key word in the sentence above is "secure." Until consumers are convinced that the Web is secure enough for the transmission of their credit card numbers and other sensitive information, little mass-market e-commerce will occur. Luckily, the anxiety of Internet spending seems to be fading. The 1997 Christmas season was the first to see major online buying, and that caused predictions for e-commerce to double. As more consumers have successful online buying sessions—and their credit card numbers *don't* get stolen—the good news spreads to a wider audience, whose comfort level is raised and fears banished.

The same concepts of a business-to-business extranet are now beginning to be applied to the consumer market—sensitive information, transmitted over a secure network in a manner more convenient for both business and consumer. The potential for benefits on the business side are enormous, especially in the face of the rising cost of customer support.

Addressing Consumer Account Maintenance

Bill paying is an ugly fact of life for both consumers and businesses; consumers don't like to do it and businesses spend a lot of time and resources processing the payments. It's also an area that is a perfect candidate for an extranet strategy.

In addition to individual companies traveling this road, several services have emerged in the electronic bill-paying market. Chief among them is CheckFree (`www.checkfree.com`), whose EBill service has attracted numerous companies—primarily utilities—to its bill-presentment service. The benefits to companies for electronic bill presentment and paying are immediately apparent:

- No delay in payment due to mail deliveries.

- No staff dedicated to stuffing or opening envelopes.

- No payment information to record.

- No checks to record, endorse, or deposit.

- No theft or loss of checks.

- Electronic funds transferred are immediately available.

The savings can be quite substantial. One utility using the EBill system, GPU Energy, found that previously its traditional bill-presentment process was costing them one dollar per bill. The electronic method cost worked out to be under two cents per bill. With more than two million customers, GPU could save just under $2 million per month.

In addition to the increase in cash flow and reduced overhead, yet another advantage exists in electronic bill presentment and paying—electronic marketing. Electronic marketing is more cost efficient than print marketing (usually included in mailed bills); moreover, it can be targeted more effectively. A typical electronic bill presentment scenario follows:

1. The customer logs on to the company's Web site and selects the **Customer Accounts** button.

2. The system switches to a secure server for all account information and transactions.

   Security is paramount for these types of transactions, and EBill is very security conscious. Its system requires that the customer use a browser capable of 128-bit encryption. The normal browser uses 40-bit encryption.

3. From the accounts screen, the customer enters his or her account number and password.

4. When the customer's account information comes up, he or she can elect to pay the current balance as displayed, pay a different amount, or review past payments.

5. Paying the current balance requires that the customer select one of several payment options, much like pulling out a specific credit card.

    The payment options can include the customer's checking account, credit card numbers, or electronic payment method.

SEE ALSO

➤ *For more on electronic payment methods, see page 269.*

The electronic funds transfer takes effect, and the customer is emailed a confirmation letter.

Case Study: Aetna U.S. Healthcare

Aetna U.S. Healthcare is a division of Aetna, Inc. and is the first nationally managed health care company. Aetna, Inc. showed revenue of $18.54 billion for 1997, with Aetna U.S. Healthcare membership reaching 4.7 million.

Faced with more than 123,000 claims filed per day, Aetna U.S. Healthcare knew it had to find a better way. In June, 1998, the health care giant began its deployment of E-Pay, a collection of electronic-processing services for its health-care providers that promised to cut billing and payment cycles in half and eliminate paperwork.

According to Aetna, E-Pay, combined with Aetna software that automatically rules on the eligibility of claims, will deliver payment within 15 business days or less for the 90% of claims that don't have errors. The cost savings are so substantial for Aetna that the company is footing the bill for both software and training for its providers. The process is also attractive to consumers because the insurance submission process is handled by the physician's office and not the patient.

Franchise Extranet Opportunities

Franchising flourishes when a strong relationship—and a steady information flow—exists between the franchiser and the franchisee. Extranets can help build and maintain that relationship. Not only does the primary company benefit from closer contact with its licensees, but one franchisee can learn from the experiences of other, non-competing franchisees. As any franchisee can tell you, the more the overall components of the company are successful, the more benefits each individual member reaps.

The key advantages an extranet can bring to a franchiser-franchisee relationship include

- *Lower communication costs.* As with an intranet, an extranet can be used to significantly lower communication costs across the organization. Printing and distribution costs are eliminated, and up-to-date information is more readily available from anywhere in the world.

- *Shared information and tactics.* One franchisee often faces the same problem as many other franchisees—and comes up with a solution. Numerous extranets are using online chat rooms, secure mailing lists, and other network methods of sharing details of a day-to-day operation.

- *Easier ordering.* Much of a franchisee's time is spent ordering supplies from the home company. An extranet streamlines the process by enabling the franchisee to place the order online. After the order is placed, a quick check of the extranet can give a status check or answer a tracking query.

- *Advertising previews.* Communication is a two-way street with a franchise business. The better the home office informs each franchisee, the higher the degree of retention, and the better the franchisee can perform. The extranet enables the home office to share advertising details—in full color and not "fax black-and-white"—with each and every franchisee, without incurring printing and distribution costs.

The anchise extranet movement is relatively new, but some major players are already jumping in:

- RE/MAX International, Inc. is a real estate franchise organization with 3,000 sales offices worldwide. The extranet, named RE/MAX Mainstreet, is expected to provide real-time, secure information to its franchisees and real estate agents globally.

- Marriot International, Inc. is looking to leverage its information resource among the franchisees for its hotel chain.

- Mail Boxes Etc., with more than 3,300 centers worldwide, is the world's largest franchiser of neighborhood retail service centers. The company is looking toward enabling licensees to easily communicate with others in the franchise network, as well as have real-time access to the information needed to run their businesses more efficiently.

PART VI

Marketing

CHAPTER **14**

Web Site Marketing

- Generating traffic with search engines
- Using public relations to tell your story
- Links from other sites
- Email campaign
- Promotions
- Co-branding
- Email newsletter
- Advertising

Setting Realistic Objectives

When the Web first started attracting people, it was easy to get people to come to your Web site because everyone visited every new site. Of course it didn't generate much revenue because so few people were on the Web, and the purpose was largely for information and entertainment.

Now it seems as if the whole country is surfing the Web. Of course, the trick is to get a few of those millions of Web surfers to come surf your Web site!

This chapter covers several of the most effective ways to promote your Web site and your company's products. As you use these Web marketing techniques, track the results of each activity so you can compare different activities and different creative approaches; then you can set realistic, measurable objectives for your company.

Generating Traffic with Search Engines

One of the most powerful ways to generate traffic at a Web site is by being listed in all the major search engines. However, more is involved in generating traffic from the search engines than just being listed.

Finding the Top Search Engines

If you have used only one or two search engines to find sites that you are interested in, then you cannot be familiar with the top seven search engines. The search engines you should be sure to submit to initially include

- InfoSeek (`www.infoseek.com`)

- AltaVista (`altavista.digital.com`)

- Lycos (`www.lycos.com`)

- WebCrawler (`www.webcrawler.com`)

- Excite (`www.excite.com`)

- HotBot (`www.hotbot.com`)

After your pages have been submitted to these search engines, you will want to locate additional search engines. The Yahoo! index can help locate a list of links to hundreds of other search engines and directories.

Preparing to Submit to the Search Engines

Some of the directories and search engines require submission only of the URL to index. For online directories, you will probably need to provide a short description of your products or services, as well as contact information so visitors can locate you.

Directories versus search engines

Two methods are used to create the Web sites used to locate other Web sites of interest. Search engines, such as Excite, use special software to analyze the text on a Web page and automatically add it to a master index of all words used on the Web. Directories, such as Yahoo!, have a staff of people who manually evaluate Web sites and decide whether to include the submission on its Web site.

You will find it helpful to prepare as much of this information as possible beforehand so that you can paste the text into fields provided in the submission forms. In general, you should prepare a word processing or text document that you can refer to while you submit your Web site. The information that you should have handy includes

- Company name

- Address

- Telephone and fax numbers

- URL

- Contact person

- Email address

- List of keywords

In addition to these items, it is also helpful to prepare several descriptions of your Web site. Different directories require different descriptive text lengths, so you will need one description that is 15 words long, another that is 25 words long, and a third that is 50 words long. If you have prepared individual home pages for each product or category, be sure to use the URL and description that matches the product line you are submitting.

Submitting Your Site to the Search Engines

The process of submitting your Web site to the search engines can be somewhat laborious, so many people look to the automated search engine submission agents to help save time. Unfortunately, many of the submission engines just don't get the job done. Although the Web-based submission agent SubmitIt (www.submitit.com) is one of the best automated systems available, many others are listed at Yahoo! (www.yahoo.com). You may want to start by submitting your home page manually to the top search engines and then test some of the automated submission agents on individual Web pages within your site, tracking to see which ones work best for you. Keep in mind that some of the search engines take from several days to several weeks to list new Web pages.

Although the search engines say that they follow links on the pages and index the linked pages, the search engines have been so overwhelmed with submissions recently that they seldom find the new pages, so be sure to submit every page in your Web site to the search agents. This will ensure that the search engines index each page in your site.

Improving Your Ranking

After you have submitted your site to these search engines, be sure to check each search engine to confirm that your site was indexed and to see how each engine ranks your site. Because each search engine uses its own private formulas for calculating rankings, each search engine will produce different results.

Optimizing a Web site greatly improves search rankings when prospects search for companies and products. Sometimes optimization can be done by adjusting text on the home page, but at times, content pages need to be modified. Occasionally, the differences between search engines make it necessary to have at least one page designed for a particular search engine.

Before we get into how to optimize a Web site for the search engines, let's cover how the search engines, in general, rank Web sites. The objective of the developers at search engines is to deliver a list of Web site links, sorted by how well each link matches the user's search criteria. The way search engines assign scores to Web pages is often confusing, and the developers do not publish their exact formulas. However, several rules of thumb will help you achieve a high ranking in search engines.

Basically, the search engines use three parts of a Web page to determine a ranking for that page. The three sections of the page are

- *Title tags.* These include the text displayed at the very top of the browser's window and stored in the Bookmark or Favorites file.

- *META tags.* These tags are hidden text used by search engines to describe and index a site.

- *Content.* This includes visible and hidden text in the body of the Web page.

Within each of these three areas, the search engines look at the proximity of the words used in the search query. In other words, if you search using the phrase "root beer," most search engines will give a higher ranking to pages with those two words adjacent to each other than pages with just one of those two words. Of course, the search engines will find matches for pages with just one of the words, too, such as pages about "roots" (for example, gardening) and pages about "beer" (the beverage).

With these rules in mind, let's get right to key concepts for optimizing a Web page for the search engines.

Long, descriptive phrases in the Title bar improve results. This doesn't mean you need to include hundreds of words in the title, but just the phrase "Home Page" is certainly not effective. A title was designed for the DocAllen Web site, for example, to help attract the search engines when the user includes the words "health" or "health information" in a search:

```
<TITLE>
DocAllen — Health Information Center Home Page
</TITLE>
```

META tags include keywords and a description. These two tags are not seen by the person viewing the Web site, but they are used by the search engines to index your page and help rank it accurately. A description META tag for the DocAllen Web site is

```
<META NAME="description" CONTENT="The DocAllen Web site features an interactive
database of information to help normally healthy individuals with life's minor
health needs. It was created by Allen T. Schwartz, M.D., LLC to help people
decide how serious it is...when to go to the doctor, and when to treat the symp-
toms or concerns themselves. ">
```

Keywords for locating a Web site

The search engines compare the search words supplied by the Web user to their master indexes to identify the Web sites that are most appropriate. Web pages that rely on graphical images instead of text don't appear in the index of search engines. This means that words important in describing the content on the page need to be added to the hidden keyword area so the search engines will know how to index and rank the Web page.

The keyword META tag is a little more challenging to create because the writer needs to think of all the words and phrases that people might use when you want to be found by them. You need to think about keywords that describe your Web site and keywords that might be used by people you want to attract. A Web site selling writing instruments, for example, would obviously want to use keywords such as "pens" and "pencils," but it also might use "notebook" and "stationery." Because several of the search engines read up to 1000 characters, better results can be created by identifying about 200 commonly used words. The keyword META tag for the DocAllen Web site is

```
<META NAME="keywords" content=" fever , chills , weight loss(involuntary) ,
weight gain(involuntary) , fatigue , weakness , feel sick , headache , face pain
, face swelling , itchy, red eye(s) , dry eyes , eye pain , eye redness , black
eye , swollen eyelid(s) , eye discharge , bulging eyeball(s) , blood in pupil(s)
, puffy eyelids , drooping eyelid , light bothers eyes , blurry vision , sudden
loss of vision , cataract , sty , blepharitis , floaters , foreign body in eye ,
earache , ringing in the ears , dizziness , hearing loss , earwax problem ,
swimmer's ear problem , sea sickness problem , sinus congestion , runny nose ,
postnasal drip , sneezing , nose bleeds , bleeding gums , sore tongue ">
```

The third part of optimizing a Web page is to ensure that the text and tags include as many of the descriptive words and phrases used by prospects to describe your products and company. If you provide certification training, for example, you will want to include in your list of keywords several variations of the word "certify" that might be used by prospects. This could include the words "certify," "certification," and "certified."

The same holds true for phrases that use the same word. If you provide certification for computer repair, include phrases such as "LAN certification," "PC certification," and "Microsoft certification."

Companies that sell multiple types of products have a problem with the search engines when their home pages cover all the product categories. If you have four distinct product lines, for example, and each is described with a paragraph or two on your home page, then none of the products will represent more than 20% of the total words on the Web page. Therefore, the search engines will give each product no higher than a 20% ranking.

To help ensure that each of the four product lines has a chance to receive a very high ranking, create four copies of your home page, lengthen the text for the featured product and shorten the text for the other products. In addition to modifying the text to focus on only one product line in the text, adjust the META tags and the title for each of the four pages to focus on the featured product for that page.

Using Submission Services

People use a variety of sources to locate Web sites, but the most popular source is search engines. In fact, the majority of a Web site's traffic will come from the popular search engines. Although the popular search engines drive a high portion of the traffic a Web site receives, much of that traffic is from people who have little or no interest in what you offer.

Traffic from specialized search engines and directories is usually more valuable because people stay on the Web site longer, see more pages, and, therefore, are likely to be more interested in making a purchase. The challenge is finding those specialized search engines and directories.

One approach is to use a search engine submission service, such as WebPromote (www.webpromote.com), that has a staff who are constantly looking for new search engines and online directories. For less than $700, they will submit your home page to 200 search engines and directories, using the information you provide to them on a Web form. This enables you to ensure that your description and keywords are the ones you want to use, but frees you from having to research the different places to submit your pages.

Paying for Placement

Recently, several general directories and search engines have started charging for higher placement in searches. Although some people on the Internet responded very negatively to companies charging for what other search engines had been giving away for free, the excessive, irrelevant hits from the broad search engines makes the idea of finding more relevant links attractive.

Using keywords that are appropriate for you, check out these search engines and directories to see if any of your competitors are already listed. If you find your competitors listed, then you might want to participate as well. Two sites that charge are

- GoTo (www.goto.com)
- DidIt (www.did-it.com)

Follow up on submission requests
As your site is submitted to search engines and directories and a link back to your site is requested, it is good planning to log each submission and request to follow up later to make sure the request was processed. It takes several weeks for listings to show up, so you'll want to give resources enough time to process the first request before you make a second submission or request.

Locating directories
Finding directories appropriate to list your company is sometimes difficult because they may be part of another site, such as a publication or a specialized Web site; so it's easier to start with a central directory of directories, such as

- DirectoryGuide (www.directoryguide.com)
- I-Sleuth (www.isleuth.com)
- Beaucoup (www.beaucoup.com)

Using Public Relations to Tell Your Story

One of the best marketing strategies is an effective public relations program. What better pathway to attract prospects than to have a respected authority on a subject write positive comments about you and your products. For some reason, people are more likely to believe something they read in a publication than what they hear on the radio or see on television for the first time. We can take advantage of this phenomenon by helping editors and reporters at print publications write about our products and the resources we make available on our Web sites.

Obtaining news coverage in publications to drive traffic to a Web site that supports a traditional business is very different from obtaining traditional product coverage because the editor may not understand the significance of your Web site to your industry. Editors and reporters need to be courted by helping them do their job in reporting about how your Web site can help their readers.

An example of a stand-alone Web site that supports the corporate Web site is the Dole 5 A Day Web site (`www.dole5aday.com`) from Dole Food Co. (`www.dole.com`).

Dole has invested considerably in its stand-alone nutrition Web site and promotes it with public relations activities aimed at publications read by teachers. This site has generic information about fruits and vegetables, information on the National 5 A Day for Better Health Program, and information about how to order nutrition education materials for children. Because the Web site educates readers more than it promotes Dole's products, editors give the Web site the publicity it needs so that it can be helpful to its target audience.

Talking to Editors

To create an effective public relations program, one of the first things you need to do is create a list of targeted media contacts at each selected publication.

Although large corporations develop media lists with hundreds of editors, companies serving niche industries might have only two or three key publications that need attention. No matter how many editors and reporters are on your key media list, it is important to maintain contact with each of them individually.

If you are about to come out with a new product, call or email the publication and ask which editor should receive the news release. If your company has an important announcement affecting your customers or the industry, a call to the editor of the publication to explain the upcoming story lets them know you have experts available to provide quotes and insights about how their readers will be affected.

Keeping editors happy
Most surveys of editors show that they do not want to be called after you send them a news release—they will call you if they need additional information.

Distributing Press Releases

When you have something to tell the media, you will frequently be asked for a press release—that well-written piece of journalism that tells your whole story in under two pages.

The purpose of a press release is to communicate your story to editors in a format that they work with daily. What an editor does with a press release sometimes amazes many people because even the most well-crafted press release is seldom published as it was written. So why go to all the effort of crafting a press release? Before the Internet became popular, only two good reasons justified spending time developing a quality press release: to show editors you understood their format and needs, and to tell the whole story, on the off-chance that a publication would run your story as you wrote it.

Today, there is another use for press releases—distribution directly to your target market via the Web. Traditionally, two press-release distribution companies handled the bulk of the wire service distribution of company press releases. These companies are BusinessWire (www.businesswire.com) and PR Newswire (www.prnewswire.com). Over the past few years, email has become a valuable way to distribute press releases to the media, and several new companies have sprung up that distribute press releases via email. These companies include

- Internet Wire (www.internetwire.com)

- Internet News Bureau (www.newsbureau.com)

- Xpress Press News Service (www.xpresspress.com)

You may wonder which press-release distribution company is best. Because each of these companies has unique strengths, it is helpful to do a little research to see which one would be best for your needs. The next time you are chatting with an editor of one of your targeted publications, ask if they use press releases received from these distribution sources.

Creating a Media List

In addition to using a press release distribution service, you should also distribute your press releases directly to your media contacts in the format that they have told you to use. Some editors like to receive press releases via fax, but other editors simply put a trash can under the fax machine. Some editors prefer to receive releases via email so they can keep a copy after they send it along to others at the publication, but other editors refuse to use emailed press releases. And some editors still want press releases sent by mail (fortunately that is becoming a thing of the past).

As you can see, it is critical to really understand the needs of each editor so that you can help the publication give you media coverage.

You can add to your own media list the following Web sites, which provide information on publications in many fields:

- MediaFinder by Oxbridge Communications (www.mediafinder.com)

- All Media E-Mail Directory Publicity (www.owt.com/dircon)

- Gebbie Press (www.gebbieinc.com)

- MediaPost (www.mediapost.com)

- Media Directory List (www.media-list.com)

- Press Access (www.pressaccess.com)

In addition to traditional media, it is now common to include on your media list the new type of publications called *zines*. The category of zines takes its name from traditional magazines that are distributed electronically, either through email or on Web sites. These publications usually have rather small circulations but are targeted to people with strong interest in the topic covered. Because many of these publications are distributed only via email, it can be difficult to locate them. Fortunately, Web-based directories of zines can assist in identifying those of interest. A few online directories include

- ZineRack (www.zinerack.com)

- eZines Database (www.dominis.com/Zines)

- John Labovitz's e-zine-list (www.meer.net/~johnl/e-zine-list)

After you've compiled a list of publications you would like to contact, what comes next? Although directories such as Press Access tell you a great deal about individual editors and their preferences, you may decide to research the editors' preferences yourself. In that case, a call or email to each publication can identify which editor covers your industry segment. Then, ask that editor a few questions about his or her needs and preferences for being contacted.

In addition to distributing press releases to the media, you should also put press releases on your Web site in the company information area. Although press releases are sometimes the driest content on a Web site, they are a source of factual information about the company and its products.

Writing a Press Release Promoting a Web Site

When you are looking for media coverage for your Web site, you need to have your public relations tools sharp and ready to cut through the clutter that editors face every day. The traditional press release is one of those tools used to convey your story to editors. Following is a short press release that describes a new Web-based service that the company is providing to its industry.

PRESS RELEASE

For Immediate Release

Bob Roberts - (555) 765-4321

bob@mycompany.com

MyCompany Provides Free Enhanced Ball Bearing Locator

Los Angeles, CA—September 1, 1998—A new computerized service to help engineers locate hard to find ball bearings has been made available on the World Wide Web by MyCompany, Inc. The Web-based service, called "Get My Bearings," is a free service of MyCompany, a leader in the manufacture of custom-designed ball bearings.

Engineers who design materials-handling equipment for special manufacturing environments have frequently had difficulty locating certain sizes and shapes of ball bearings that help reduce friction in conveyers and other equipment. This online source of manufacturers and distributors uses the specifications provided by the design engineer to determine which supplier is likely to have specialty ball bearings.

"We had so many requests for the information that we use when a customer is in a hurry for ball bearings that we decided to share this information with the industry," said Jim Johnson, President, MyCompany, Inc. "We felt this Web service could serve the design engineers during those times when they just can't wait for custom-designed products from our plant."

The Web site is located at www.GetMyBearings.com, and also has links to the corporate design information for MyCompany. For more information about the Get My Bearings Web site or custom-designed ball bearings, contact:

Jim Johnson

MyCompany, Inc.

12345 E. 67th St.

Los Angeles, CA 90000

(555) 765-4321

# # #

Getting Links to Your Business from Other Sites

Surfing the Web takes us from Web site to Web site—clicking links that lead us to other material that interests us. From a marketer's point of view, the question is how to get other Web sites to link to your business's site.

The process of obtaining links from other sites requires a combination of research, tact, tenacity, and perseverance. A few years ago, Webmasters added a page of links to their sites to help their viewers and to provide additional reasons for people to come back to their sites. Recently, however, Web marketers have realized that it can be counterproductive to enable a viewer to link to another Web site—leaving their site behind. As Web-based publications (also called "content providers") searched for additional sources of revenue, they started selling links from their Web sites. Now it is harder to find Web sites that will link to other Web sites for free.

To obtain free links to your Web site, surf the Web looking for lists of links at Web sites that are compatible with yours, then send an email requesting that they link to you. Many times you will be asked by someone at the other Web site to link back to them—a reciprocal link.

Although it is usually best to not have a list of links to other sites on your Web site, one strategy benefits your Web audience and the other Web sites on your link list, as well. If you have an inquiry form on your Web site, then you can easily allow people who fill out your form to see a page of links to other Web sites. By that time, they have probably read all the material that interests them on your Web site, and you have a lead to follow up, so it doesn't hurt your sales potential by enabling Web visitors to surf other Web sites. Just be sure that all the links you provide are working and that they don't link to your competitors!

Eric Ward, publisher of the URLwire, a private, email-based news service, is a long-time master at obtaining links for his clients. One of the tips he frequently gives people who ask his advice is to look beyond the basics. "Everyone wants a quick fix, but if you spent six months planning and building your site, why would you think you could promote it in one day?" Eric is right. Web site promotion is time consuming and requires tracking many details.

Tara Calishain, author of the *Official Netscape Guide to Internet Research,* once described the process of requesting media coverage as "asking the editor to make a purchase—not with money, but with the space they control." Whether you are asking an editor to devote editorial space to your company, or asking another Web site to link to your Web site, you are asking them to give valuable space to you. This means the value that you provide to their audience needs to be significant to their readers in order to be considered for inclusion on their Web site.

When you treat obtaining media coverage and links as "making a purchase," you'll see how important it is to track each contact you have with those people. You may want to use a traditional, sales lead-tracking database product, or you might just create a spreadsheet with columns for each item of information you track.

What should you track? The items tracked by many professional, online promotion consultants include

- Web site name
- URL
- Target audience
- Corporate site or content provider
- Contact person
- Title
- Telephone
- Email address

Each time these people are called or emailed, an entry of the date, the subject of the conversation or email, the commitment of providing a link, and what you commit to doing in return is tracked. When you surf the Web and run through your list of expected links, you'll know what you should be receiving in links from each site. You should also check your site to make sure you are providing the link exposure to the other sites that you agreed to provide in return for the link you received.

Using an Email Marketing Campaign

When a close friend or relative sends you email, you are sure to open it quickly and enjoy the feeling of having received a personal note that builds the relationship between you and the sender of the email. That's the way email has traditionally been seen—as a personal message from someone with whom you want to communicate.

When you receive an email from a company that advertises a product—especially a product you don't want—it is irritating. Some people feel this technique is offensive, and they become outraged to the point of retaliating against the sender of the email. If you have had an Internet email account for any length of time, then you are probably familiar with the term *spam* that refers to, well, unwanted email.

The problem of unsolicited email has become so large that the state and federal governments have been reviewing legislation to ban or restrict the sending of spam email. Will the legislation stop spam? Not entirely. But the real question for you is whether spam email actually works. Ask yourself if you have ever received an unsolicited email from a major company. Probably not. The main reason is the bad image that companies project when they use spamming techniques.

Does this mean your company shouldn't send unsolicited email? Well, not entirely. The technique that does seem to work to some extent is the use of *opt-in lists*, where people have entered their preferences on a Web-based form and have requested that they receive promotional email about selected topics.

One of the best-known companies that provides opt-in lists is NetCreations, which provides email addresses under the name PostMasterDirect (`www.postmasterdirect.com`). This company has developed a philosophy about sending email advertising that appears to be accepted by the Internet community. Not only do you have to sign up to receive their email, each email has a header that reminds the receiver that they signed up to receive email on this particular subject. They also make it easy to unsubscribe from an individual mailing list.

Of course, no matter how well the list is created, the question remains of how effective unsolicited email is in terms of generating positive awareness, inquiries, and sales. Although many of us have purchased items on Web sites, and we know others who have, too, it is hard to find people who have made an inquiry or purchase as a result of receiving an unsolicited email advertisement.

The results obtained from rented mailing lists, even the opt-in lists, is mixed because of the negative reaction from the people receiving these emails. Because large companies are very sensitive to any negative reactions to their promotions, especially promotions that appear to invade peoples' privacy, well-recognized companies rarely use email promotions.

In addition, the current wave of proposed legislation at the federal level—and in several states—prohibiting unsolicited email promotions is making established companies hesitant to use this form of promotion.

However, ways to use email exist that produce positive results without the negative reaction of spam.

Sending Follow-up Emails

It is becoming a well-accepted technique to send follow-up emails to people who have inquired at a Web site. You can expect people who have already indicated an interest in the particular product being promoted at the Web site to be interested in receiving additional information via email.

The difference between this technique and renting email lists to send unsolicited email advertisements is that an in-house generated list of email addresses contains people who are more likely to appreciate periodically receiving the follow-up material; with the rented lists, you send messages to people about things they have not expressed interest in. It is becoming extremely clear that the Web audience wants to be in control of the material that they see and receive via email.

You first should experiment by sending email advertisements to your in-house list and tracking the results to get a feel for how well your audience receives this type of message. Then, when you are comfortable that your messages are being well received, consider renting a small number of email addresses of people who have requested unsolicited email, and compare the results to your other forms of marketing communications. Also, track the number of complaints that you receive with the rented mailing list so you can determine whether the benefit outweighs the potential damage to your company's reputation.

Email Content to Include

When you are sending email messages to your in-house list, you need to keep in mind several things that can enhance the results. Knowing that most people don't want to wade through long email messages, for instance, you should keep the length of your promotional emails to about two screens.

Because you have a limited amount of space in a promotional email, you will want to include hot links back to your Web site. Because today's email programs recognize well-formed URLs, you can lead a prospect directly from an email to a Web page that builds on the email. By having people link back to your Web site, you can display the graphically pleasing pages with appropriate interactivity—instead of the text-only message of email.

In addition, you can quickly measure the results of your email promotion by comparing the number of times the Web page is accessed to the number of emails sent.

Formatting URLs
Keep in mind that you need to properly format URLs so the receiver's email program turns them into links. This means the "http://" must be included in the URL.

If you are using one of the personalized email database systems, such as the one from Revnet Systems (www.revnet.com), you can add a unique code to these URLs that can be tracked back to the Web site. You can then send promotional messages to an in-house list of email addresses and know which one of those people responded by clicking the link and coming to it.

Promoting Your Business on the Web

When you're promoting a business by using the Web, you can attract a great deal of attention by running a promotion that is fun while it also promotes your product. Keep in mind that the promotion can be fun for both your marketing team and your prospects and customers. It can also be fun for those finance folks when they take those extra revenue checks to the bank because of the extra sales it generates. In addition, special promotions can increase awareness of your company—and generate word-of-mouth awareness.

The key to a successful Web promotion is to have a meaningful tie-in between the fun part and a marketing message that helps people understand why they should buy your products. This sounds easier than it actually is, which means you'll need to spend an extra amount of time brainstorming the concept for your promotion. Although it's fun to sit around and brainstorm promotional concepts, to make your brainstorming time productive you'll want to have a few objectives for everyone on the brainstorming team to keep in mind.

Suppose, for instance, you came up with a Web-based contest that required Web visitors to name a new product. Your contest should accept entries from anyone who wants to enter, but this is also an opportunity for you to explain the attributes of the product that should be named. By using this fun and lighthearted approach, you can communicate with an open-minded audience about why they might want to buy the product.

Co-branding

One of the advantages of using the Web is the ability to include material on a page from multiple servers and to link pages from multiple Web servers to give the appearance of one comprehensive, larger site. With the high cost of creating original content, this technique enables a Web site to provide quality material supplied by another source while keeping the look and feel of its own site.

Case Study: Los Angeles Times
The *Los Angeles Times* began publishing an online version of its daily newspaper in 1994, then moved to the Web in 1996. Today, the complete newspaper is available on its Web site, and it integrates content from other companies.

Web-site content providers, such as the business section of the online version of the *Los Angeles Times* (www.latimes.com/HOME/BUSINESS/), have links to material created by other companies but that carry the *L.A. Times* logo (See Figure 14.1). They provide pages of material from such companies as Hoovers (www.hoovers.com), Business Wire (www.businesswire.com), and the Motley Fool (www.fool.com) that display the brands of the company providing the content as well as the *Los Angeles Times'* logo. This enables the *Times* to use quality content that it doesn't have to create, while maintaining its own brand identity as it provides access to those content sources.

Figure 14.1 The Los Angeles Times is one of the early leaders in providing online access to a major daily newspaper. By integrating content from other companies, it increases the value of its Web site without incurring the expense of creating that content.

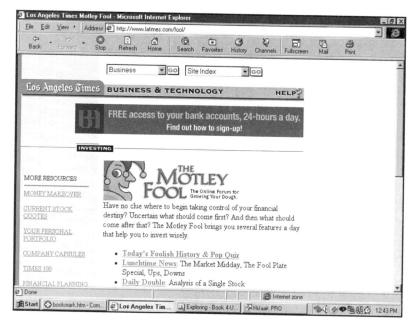

This technique works best when a logical and natural connection exists between the two sets of material. Although it's easy to see how this technique can work for content sites, it also works well for manufacturers that sell through a distribution channel.

One of the easiest ways to implement this is to create pages for dealers with their logo, contact, and descriptive material.

The benefit of providing each dealer with a Web page is that they don't have to go to the expense of creating a Web page and locating a Web hosting service. You can also ensure that each dealer maintains your corporate identity standards.

One example of a company that handles dealer Web pages well is Culligan Water Technologies. Their dealer locator (www.culligandealer.com) (see Figure 14.2) makes it easy for consumers to find a dealer near them, and it's easy for the dealers to display their marketing materials.

Figure 14.2 Culligan Water Treatment makes it easy for consumers to locate a dealer by entering their ZIP Code.

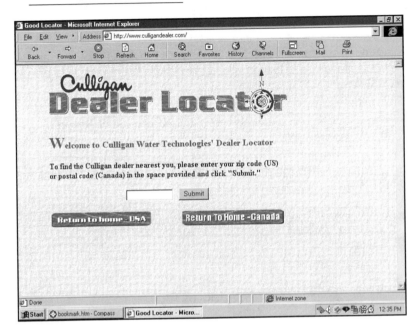

Sending Email Newsletters

One of the challenges that many Web marketers have faced is how to attract prospects and customers back to their Web sites. One way to do this is to send an email newsletter to people who have visited your Web site and have indicated an interest in your products.

Email newsletters versus email campaigns

Using an email newsletter is different from sending an email promotional message; a newsletter is mostly educational and is sent at a regular interval, but a promotional message is shorter and has a message aimed at driving sales.

The best way to create an email newsletter is to provide the headline and brief summary of each article with a link to the full-length article on your Web site or at a news publication. This approach keeps the newsletter short—which your recipients will like—and having links back to your Web site will make it easy for your readers to find the specific Web pages with articles of interest to them.

Customizing Your Newsletters

One of the hottest marketing trends is the use of one-to-one Web marketing techniques to customize information based on the profile of each person in a database. You can distribute targeted marketing messages with email newsletters in a number of ways. Some methods are easy to implement, but others require programmers to install special software and to help coordinate the use of those programs.

One-to-one marketing

Marketers have known for a long time that customers have multiple buying motives and that a marketing program should be tailored to needs, wants, and desires of each person. The Internet now allows marketers to use a database of profile and interest information to personalize the message to each person using commercial Web personalization or email personalization products.

If you have several target markets, for instance, and you have collected the email addresses from people in each of those target markets, then you should consider sending a different newsletter to each market. Even if you sell the same products to different markets, you can probably develop headlines and summaries for your newsletter that appeal to each target market—with links pointing to the same articles on your Web site.

If you have a large number of products and customers who would be interested in only a few of the articles you publish on your Web site, then you could use a personalized email service, such as the one from Revnet Systems (`www.revnet.com`). Revnet's suite of email list management products includes UnityMail for personalized, targeted direct marketing. By using personalized email, you can automatically tailor the content of your newsletters to match the needs and interests of each prospect without having to develop multiple versions of your newsletters.

One of the advantages of using a personalized email system is that you can attach unique codes, or what direct mail people call "keys," to the links back to your Web site. By assigning a unique code to each person, you can track exactly which person reading your newsletter clicked a link and saw that material.

Tying Email Newsletters to the Web

Now that you know how to customize email newsletters with links to stories on your Web site, be sure to provide easy access to the Web-based newsletter for visitors to your Web site. In addition, be sure to let Web visitors know how to subscribe—and unsubscribe—to your newsletter.

You will want to provide information in each issue of your newsletter about how to unsubscribe so that people can quickly remove themselves from your mailing list as their needs and interests change. Be sure to tell people how to subscribe to your newsletter, as well. It may sound strange to tell a subscriber how to subscribe, but many people forward particularly interesting issues of email newsletters to friends and associates, so you will want those potential prospects to be able to find your Web site and subscribe.

A newsletter published by ZD Net contains the following information in the footer:

- - - - -

AnchorDesk comes to you free of charge as a service of ZDNet.

On its companion Web site, AnchorDesk includes full details on the stories you see above, plus late-breaking news, links to in-depth information, and much more. Visit:

`http://www.anchordesk.com`

To subscribe or unsubscribe go to:

`http://www.anchordesk.com/whoiswe/subscribe.html`

To make comments or suggestions, go to:

`http://www.anchordesk.com/whoiswe/talkbackform.html`

- - - -

Advertising on the Internet

When technology creates a new form of communication, marketing people will soon find ways to use it as an advertising medium—and that happened quickly with the Internet.

Advertisements promoting a product—whether in print or on the Internet—are designed to accomplish two general marketing objectives:

- Generate awareness for the product and its brand
- Generate inquiries for salespeople to follow up

Of course, the more you can say about your product in an advertisement, the more goals you can accomplish. But on the Web, the space available for a banner ad is so limited that it can't tell your whole story. Fortunately, you can buy a number of types of advertisement to promote your products, such as

- *Banner ads.* These ads contain highly graphical pieces of art, sometimes animated, and usually appear at the top of Web pages on content sites.

- *Microsites.* A step up in size and content from banner ads, these are a few pages that provide more details than available in just a banner ad.

- *Sponsorships.* Almost anything can be sponsored on the Internet, from specific groups of pages within a section of a Web site to email messages, newsletters, chat sessions, and games—practically anything you can do on the Internet.

- *Adveratorials.* These articles are generally prepared by the advertising company and portray the company's products as the best product to choose for a need.

- *Email newsletters.* These are short pieces of promotional text included in the body of an email newsletter that emphasize the benefits of a product and include a URL to the Web site.

Buying Ads

Web advertising can generate a tremendous amount of exposure for a company, but every element of the advertising campaign must work together to reach the right audience with the right message at the right time.

Since the time when the Web became a graphical communications tool, online advertising has been moving from static Web banners to animated banners to a wide range of interactive communications. Today, banners have search forms within them, games, and full-motion video. As the available bandwidth increases, we will see online advertising that appears similar to today's TV commercials.

These new forms of banner ads are confirming the predictions by Jupiter Communications (www.jup.com) that when bandwidth increases the speed of downloading material, we will see online advertising take on a different look and feel. Advertising will move from an awareness device to an action instigator as customers move beyond clicking to see a different Web site to clicking to interact with the ad. However, until increased bandwidth is readily available, these interactive forms of advertising will be used only when they can significantly increase response.

Before we get into how ads are bought, you need to understand the terms used by media buyers so you'll know how ads are measured, and priced. You'll also learn some of the ways to make economical advertising purchases.

When media salespeople talk about their advertising opportunities, you will frequently hear terms such as page views, clickthrough, CPM, and eyeballs.

The first two things you'll want to know when you are considering purchasing ads on a content site are the type of people you'll be reaching and just how many people you will reach. As you can imagine, even if someone gave you 100,000 exposures of your ad that reached an audience that was almost guaranteed not to be interested in your product, then it would not only be a waste, but the miscellaneous traffic that would be generated on your Web site could get in the way of interested prospects trying to view your material.

So, the first thing to look at when considering an ad campaign is the quality of the audience.

Next, you'll want to know the number of times your ad will be seen, or how many page views will occur.

Now, if a Web site has a quality audience (for you), and if it will reach a significant number of people, then you can start your comparative analysis of the Web sites under consideration.

Most ads are priced in terms of a cost per thousand (CPM). In other words, a CPM of $35 means you will pay $35 for each 1,000 times your ad is displayed. Within a group of Web sites that all reach your target audience, you will typically want to buy ads with the lowest CPM.

After you start running your ad campaign, you will want to track how many of those page views result in people clicking the ad to come to a page on your Web site—the rate at which people click an ad is called *clickthrough*. Many advertisers rate the quality of an audience based on the clickthrough rate, with the assumption that a high clickthrough rate means they have a more efficient ad campaign. In reality, a number of factors work together to help you tell if you have an effective ad campaign.

Suppose, for example, you want to reach an audience that makes up only a small portion of any Web site's traffic. Because you know that only a small portion of the audience will even be interested in your product—and, therefore, an even smaller percentage will click your ad—does that mean that you shouldn't advertise? No. It just means that you need to measure your advertising on how well it works for you, and not on how well ads on that Web site work for other advertisers.

Link Exchange Services

Even though the cost of banner advertising is relatively modest as compared to more traditional forms of advertising, the costs can still be prohibitive for some companies. In those cases, another way to obtain banner advertising exists—usually at no cost.

A number of companies have come online in the past few years that provide a service to distribute an ad which will run on other Web sites in exchange for running ads for their other Web site clients. The leader in this area of exchanging ads is, as you might guess, Link Exchange (See Figure 14.3).

Figure 14.3 The Link Exchange enables companies to receive advertising on other Web sites in return for placing banner ads on their Web site.

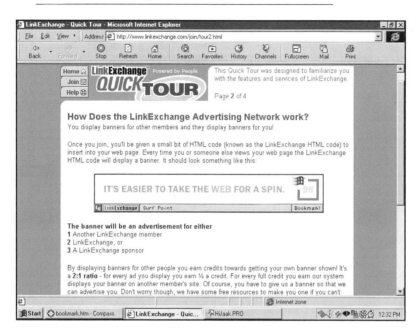

The way that most banner ad exchanges work is that you place special HTML tags on one or more pages within your Web site that cause ads to be served by the Web server at the ad exchange company. Then, as your Web site causes ads to be delivered by the ad exchange company's Web server, you receive credits. If the exchange company has a two-to-one ratio (2:1), then for every two ads you display, your ad will be run once on some Web site in the group of participating Web sites. Some ad exchange companies use 3:2 and some even give 1:1. This means you can receive free advertising on other Web sites just for displaying ads to people coming to your site.

You might be wondering if it's good to work at bringing people to your Web site and then give them an ad that will take them to another Web site. The answer as to whether it is a good deal for you depends, as many of the questions about online marketing do, on a variety of factors.

If your Web traffic analysis shows, for instance, that many people come to your site, see a page or two, then move on to other sites, then you might receive an overall benefit from being in a link exchange service. Why? Because most of the traffic to your Web site is by people who are not interested in what you are offering.

On the other hand, suppose your traffic analysis indicates that many people coming to your site spend a great deal of time viewing many of the pages on your Web site. In that case, you may not want to give people a link to go elsewhere.

Another factor that can help you determine if a banner ad exchange is right for you is image. For some companies, image is a big part of their marketing activities, so they might not be interested in being associated with a service that is typically used by companies that don't have the money to advertise.

CHAPTER **15**

Maximizing Direct Response Analysis

- Setting realistic objectives
- Analyzing Web advertising
- Analyzing Web traffic
- Analyzing email response
- Analyzing customer data

Setting Realistic Objectives

Marketing on the Web, like all other marketing activities, operates in an atmosphere of uncertainty because of the nature of consumer behavior. This makes it important to track prospects and customers from the first contact through the sale and repeat purchases. Tracking enables marketers to learn about buyer needs, wants, and desires, and then refine how to satisfy customers.

The Web offers marketers a unique opportunity to gather data about individuals in a way that no other media has ever afforded. At the same time, you can quickly become overloaded with data that doesn't improve the return on the investment of your marketing budget.

To maximize the effectiveness of your direct response efforts on the Internet, you need to look at a number of types of data from multiple sources, including

- Awareness
- Inquiries
- Number of customers

- Sales volume
- Number of repeat customers

Awareness

One of the first results of marketing activities is an increased awareness of your company and its products. Because this is the beginning of the marketing process (as far as your customers are concerned), this is an appropriate place to begin your tracking and analysis efforts.

Because awareness on the Web is generated in several ways, you need a variety of ways to track and analyze changes in awareness levels. Table 15.1 shows a number of ways that awareness is generated on the Web and ways to measure that awareness. The AltaVista (www.altavista.digital.com) and InfoSeek (www.infoseek.com) search engines have advanced search features that enable you to search only inside your Web site (to count the pages it has in the index) or search which Web sites link to you (to count links to your site) (see Figure 15.1).

Because changes in awareness occur over time, it is best to create a spreadsheet in which you can record these different values monthly or quarterly. By tracking changes in these measurements, you can project awareness—and the resulting changes in other marketing activities.

Figure 15.1 The AltaVista search engine can be used to count how many pages on the Web link to your Web site.

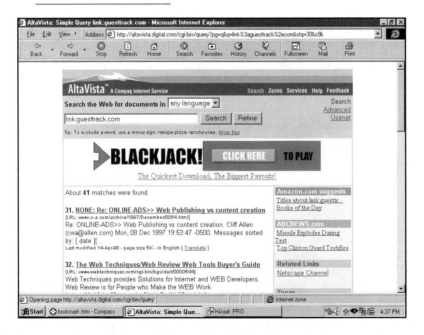

Table 15.1   Sources of Awareness Measurement on the Web

Source	Analysis Activity
Search engine links	Count the number of times your Web site is included in each of the major search engines. On AltaVista enter **host:** and your domain (for example, **host:guesttrack.com**).
Links to your Web site	Use the major search engines to count the number of links from other Web sites to your Web site. On AltaVista enter **link:** and your domain (for example, **link:guesttrack.com**).
Media coverage	Monitor online news publications for mentions of your company or products. Use the search feature at the online publications covering your industry.
Discussion mentions	Monitor appropriate discussion mailing lists and newsgroups for mentions of your company or products. On AltaVista use the Usenet search screen and enter a company or product name.

Inquiries

One of the most accurate predictors of future sales is the number of inquiries from prospective customers. The number of inquiries is normally a good overall indication both of the effectiveness of a marketing campaign and the interest that your target market has in your products. In other words, the number of inquiries per month will increase or decrease depending on how well your marketing communications is doing—and how interested the market is in buying your products.

By watching this key indicator, you can quickly spot the need to make changes in your marketing or product offerings before you experience a significant downturn in revenues.

If you already track the number of inquiries from your advertising, direct mail, and public relations activities, it is easy to add a section to track inquiries from your Web site.

Customers

Another key indicator of revenues is the number of customers served each month. Although it may seem obvious that the number of customers is a good predictor of revenues, companies sometimes overlook this key measurement, especially when existing customers are increasing their orders, which results in continual increases in revenues.

By tracking the number and types of customers over time, you can spot trends that you can take advantage of early.

Sales Volume

The most obvious measurement to track is the total dollar volume of sales each month to see how a company is doing. What is not so obvious—but very important—is the need to track the revenue generated via the Web as a percentage of total revenue.

If the percentage of Web revenue is increasing, then it's time to see if a shift in marketing activities from traditional to online methods can increase this trend. On the other hand, if your percent of revenues from the Web is decreasing, it's time for a complete marketing analysis because several things could be occurring that need attention. Your competitors could be conducting online activities, for example, that are taking potential customers away from you.

Repeat Customers and Order Size

As customers find that your products are helpful, they start ordering more and additional products. This increase in customer loyalty results in higher order size, higher revenues, and decreased marketing expenses—all of which increase profitability.

Tracking the number of repeat customers and order size are good indicators of future revenues, as well as indicators of the need to shift allocation of additional resources to customer service activities.

Analyzing Web Advertising

One of the most studied aspects of Web marketing is the effectiveness of advertising on Web sites.

Many Web advertisers link their banner ads to a unique page on their Web site that supports the message in the banner advertisement. This enables comparison of the number of times the ad was displayed to the number of times the linked page was displayed, enabling you to calculate a clickthrough rate. You can also attach codes to the links from banner ads so that the same Web page can be used for all banner ads; however, special software is required to identify and tabulate the codes.

Whether you link to individual Web pages or add codes to the links to one page, you can calculate the clickthrough rate for each ad. Although it's nice to have a high clickthrough rate, it is more important to have qualified prospects clicking your banner ad.

How do we know if a particular ad or media is working? Unlike most other media, Web marketers can track prospects from the initial clickthrough on the banner ad through to a final sale on the Web site or through offline sales methods.

Case Study: Marketwave, Inc.

Marketwave is a privately held software company in Seattle, WA, that provides Web site managers and marketers with software products to tabulate activity on Web sites using the log files. Its Web site is located at www.marketwave.com.

The software company, Marketwave, uses its own Web traffic analysis product, Hit List, to track and analyze the effectiveness of banner ad placement. Because it runs a variety of ads at multiple Web sites, it codes both the ad and the source in its ad links. Marketwave uses the "custom calculations" feature of Hit List to create a report on the cost of each ad campaign. These figures are compared to its database of sales to calculate a total return on each advertising campaign. This allows shifting in promotional budgets toward ad campaigns that perform best in terms of revenue generated in comparison to the total number of visitors brought to its Web site.

After a cost-per-thousand analysis is used to place initial advertising, you can move toward calculating a cost per sale to strengthen your media placements.

Analyzing Web Traffic

The traffic coming to your Web site generates a substantial amount of data in the Web server log files. This data can give you a great deal of insight into the people who see your Web pages. Commercial Web log analysis programs do a good job of tabulating the number of times each page is seen, along with related information, such as the most common paths people take through your Web site.

This is information you can use to discern how people feel about the information you are presenting and the product benefits you are offering. As you can imagine, if people are not viewing the page on your Web site describing your products, then they surely can't buy them. It is important to review log analysis reports periodically to ensure that your Web audience is seeing your most important information.

Some of the Web traffic analysis products you will want to consider are shown in Table 15.2.

Table 15.2 Web Traffic Analysis Programs

Company	Product	Web Site
Marketwave	Hit List	www.marketwave.com
WebTrends	WebTrends	www.webtrends.com
net.Genesis	net.Analysis	www.netgen.com

If you are not meeting revenue objectives for your Web site, you need to know why. Is it because of the information you are presenting or because fewer people are viewing your pages?

Tracking interest level

An easy way to track the number of people who have a sincere interest in a topic presented on your Web site is to break the content into two or more pages that are linked from the first page through the last page. The number of times the first page of an article is displayed shows how many people thought they had an interest, but the number of times successive pages are displayed shows how many people really had an interest in the topic.

Web Visitors

After you have analyzed the traffic on your Web site, you'll probably want to learn more about the individual people coming to your site. This requires asking individuals for information about themselves.

Basically, three approaches are used to gather specific information about visitors and their interests. One approach is simply to have people fill out what is sometimes called a "guest book," which is a one-page form that the Web server converts into an email message that is sent to you. Simple guest book information can be helpful; however, it suffers from some of the problems that many surveys suffer from—mainly, that the respondents control not only whether they respond, but also the accuracy of information they provide. When a guest book is not tied directly to the viewership of valuable content on a Web site, the quality of the data is usually low.

Another approach is to require Web users to provide information about themselves before they can gain access to certain valuable information that you provide. By giving them an incentive to provide information, you are able to obtain more responses than if you had simply used a guest book. Of course, if the information that they gain access to is not dependent upon answers that they provide, then the quality of the data they provide can still be suspect.

The best way to ensure that data is provided by members of your Web audience is to make the material they see dependent upon the answers they provide. If you describe products differently to people in different states, for example, then you can emphasize the need for the user to specify the state in which they are located in order to receive the right information. By using a Web personalization system that customizes Web pages "on the fly," you are requiring that they provide accurate information about themselves in order to benefit from your Web site. This improves the quantity and quality of the data you gather.

The Family Success Web site (`www.intelli-source.com`), for example, uses a database of more than 150 data items to customize reports based on answers to questions about family life (see Figure 15.2).

Figure 15.2 The Family Success Web site uses a Web personalization program to create pages "on-the-fly" that are tailored to the person's profile using forms such as the one shown here.

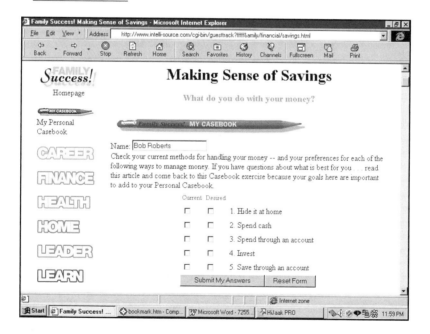

Privacy

Just as the Web can gather a great deal of specific information from your Web audience, you have a responsibility to maintain the privacy of your clients by not divulging their information to others.

In fact, the Federal Trade Commission (www.ftc.gov) has taken a strong interest in requiring that Web sites have a publicly stated privacy policy and that Web marketers honor the commitment to maintain privacy according to their privacy statement.

One of the difficulties in maintaining privacy of information collected on a Web site in this day and age is that multiple services—provided by multiple companies—are put together to create what appears to be one Web site. Data is collected, for example, at a credit card processing provider's Web site that is different from the merchant's Web site. It is hard for the merchant to guarantee that the data collected on its Web site will not be shared with any other company because at least one other company already has the data.

To accurately describe who has access to customer data, you may wind up with a long and detailed privacy statement, but that is better than misleading your audience.

Analyzing Email Response

Email is the most popular Internet activity, which makes contacting prospects and customers via email one of the most effective forms of marketing available. Email can reach into people's computers and deliver not only a compelling and timely marketing message, but also provide a link to a page on your Web site.

The value of email in Web marketing really took off when the popular email programs included a feature that recognizes URLs and automatically converts them into live links. When people click hyperlinks in their email program, their browser is automatically opened and they are taken to the Web page you have provided.

A feature found in many of the newer email programs is the ability to display HTML content, graphics, and hyperlinks within the email program. This combines the attractive layout ability of Web pages with the delivery capabilities of email.

Projected email usage

Michael Tchong has reported in his *ICONOCAST* email newsletter that more than 60 million people around the world now use email. Forrester Research has predicted that more than 135 million people in the United States will be using email by the year 2001.

Because marketing via email enables you to broadcast messages to many people very easily, you need to track the results so that you can use this technique most effectively.

One way to track the results of email marketing is to include hyperlinks that take the reader directly to a page on your Web site that is accessed only from the email message. By using a traditional Web server log analysis program, you can count the number of times people responded to your email message. By tabulating the percentage of responses for each email campaign, you can determine the effectiveness of each email marketing activity.

Because response to any direct marketing promotion can vary from one mailing to the next, it is best to tabulate the response for each mailing and notice whether an overall trend exists, either upward or downward. If you notice a downward trend or a sharp falloff, that is an indication that your market has become tired of that promotion or that you have achieved the maximum response possible for that promotion, and it's time for a change.

The difficult part of analyzing simple hit count data for Web pages is that you don't have data on individual people. This can be overcome by using one of the new personalized email products, such as UnityMail from Revnet (www.revnet.com), which assigns unique identification codes to each person receiving your promotional email messages. Because each person's ID is in the URLs, you can identify exactly which person clicks links in your email messages by examining your Web server's logs.

Of course, by using both a personalized email system and a Web personalization system, you can track response to your promotions from the very first contact, such as a direct email message, through a sale and any follow-up customer service.

Case Study: Internet Travel Network
The Internet Travel Network is headquartered in Palo Alto, CA, where it provides Web-based airline, car rental, and hotel reservations free to users of the Internet. Its Web site is located at www.itn.com.

One company that uses automated email messages effectively is the Internet Travel Network, which sells airline and other travel reservations on its Web site. They enable customers to sign up to receive email messages when the computer finds special prices on travel that meet the profile provided by the customer. By providing specific information about a special price on travel, the company invites back to its Web site customers who have indicated a specific interest in purchasing a ticket.

Advertising in Email Newsletters

Another method of using email to bring people to a Web site is advertising in email newsletters. A number of high-quality newsletters accept sponsorship and include links to the advertiser's Web site. As with including links in your own email, you can bring people to specific pages on your Web site and monitor the number of clickthroughs by tracking the number of hits to the unique Web page. By using a different page for each ad, you can measure the effectiveness of each advertising campaign.

Because each newsletter has a different number of subscribers, you will need a way to compare the effectiveness of each newsletter. By calculating the response rate and comparing it to the cost of each ad placement, you can calculate effectiveness measurements.

Renting Email Lists

Several sources exist for obtaining email addresses, similar to traditional list brokering for physical mailing labels. Some email list companies rent lists that they have harvested from Web sites and public discussion groups. These lists consist of people who have not requested that advertising information be sent to them—and who will probably be offended by receiving promotional emailings. Sending email to people on lists like this is typically referred to as *spamming*, and generally, it has not been effective.

Other companies provide what is called opt-in mailing lists, where people have identified certain topics about which they are interested in receiving information; they have selected the option to be included in the mailing list. The PostMaster Direct service from NetCreations (www.netcreations.com) rents highly targeted email lists for between $.10 and $.20 per name. The company provides not only the list rental, but also the email distribution for its customers.

Analyzing Customer Data

Whether you use your Web site for marketing communications or take prospects all the way through purchasing your products, you can collect a tremendous amount of data about these people. For years catalog marketers have used a variety of analytical techniques to optimize their response rates and revenues. It has been essential for catalogers to get the most out of their marketing efforts because the cost of postage and printing consumes such a large part of their revenue.

Although the expenses of marketing on the Web are not as high as for a cataloger, Web marketers need to apply the same analytical tools for similar reasons—to maximize profit while gaining market share and growing revenues.

Qualifying Prospects

Salespeople have known for decades that it is important to quickly identify the likelihood of a prospect making a purchase so that the amount of time spent on the sale is kept to a minimum. The process of qualifying prospects usually includes gathering four types of information:

- Does the prospect have a true need for the product?
- Does the prospect have an approved budget sufficient to purchase the product?
- Will the prospect obtain final approval in an acceptable time frame?
- Is the prospect prohibited from purchasing from the company (for example, a competitor sits on their board of directors)?

Each company needs to customize these criteria according to the purchase behavior in its own markets. An acceptable time frame for one product, for example, might be completely unacceptable for another product. Many corporate purchases are made within a six-month window of time from the beginning of the evaluation or the start of a project. Consumers at home, on the other hand, frequently make major purchases within a month from beginning their evaluation.

After you obtain positive information about the four qualification criteria, you can begin to optimize your sales efforts on that prospect based on specific criteria related to the people involved in the purchase:

- Each person's role in making the purchase
- The time frame for making the purchase

Generally, two types of people are involved in making a purchase—whether you're talking about consumers at home or a more complex purchase by a company. Although Approvers (people who can approve the purchase) are the final decision makers, Recommenders play an important function in the evaluation process, so their needs must also be taken into consideration.

Recommenders are generally looking for projects that will help them "shine" and advance within their organizations, so they are looking for the most positive benefits possible for their organizations. Approvers, on the other hand, are already in a more senior-level position within their organizations than Recommenders, so they are usually more concerned about potential problems with new products.

Experienced salespeople gather this information either by asking specific questions or by inferring the answers from conversations with the prospect. So how do you obtain this information in the more impersonal environment of the Web? The best way to quickly obtain this information is to carefully construct an inquiry form that motivates the prospect to provide this information in return for receiving the information they are seeking.

By knowing both the time frame and the person's role in the purchase process, you can respond to inquiries more efficiently by spending time with prospects most likely to make a purchase from you.

If prospects indicate they are just starting to review products, then it is not likely that they will make a decision in the near future, so you can schedule them to receive information periodically and ask if they are nearing a purchase. Leads like this from companies are generally worth following up for approximately one to two years because an actual purchase may be made within that time frame. After that time, many people have changed positions, so they are no longer interested in your product.

If they indicate that a purchase is expected to be made within 6 to 12 months, it can be a sign that a purchase will eventually be made but that the time frame is uncertain. If a Recommender says that a purchase will occur within 6 to 12 months, that indicates that he or she is *hopeful* that a purchase will be made. However, if an Approver says the purchase will be made within 6 to 12 months, that probably indicates that the purchase *will* eventually be made.

If either the Recommender or the Approver says that a purchase will occur within the next 6 months, a strong likelihood exists that there will be a purchase, and your salespeople should contact the prospect frequently to ensure that your product will be considered.

It is important to identify both the time frame and the responsibility of each person involved in the sale.

Case Study: Pall Corporation

Pall Corporation is the broadest-based filtration and separations company in the world, both in terms of technology and markets served. Pall products are used in such applications as blood collection, oil refining, power generation, drug development and manufacture, jet engine lubrication, and semiconductor and chemical production. Its Web site is located at www.pall.com.

One company that benefits tremendously from having a good inquiry form on its Web site is Pall Corporation, a manufacturer of specialized filtration devices.

When an engineer is searching for a filtration product, the Pall Web site gathers a variety of qualification information on its server (see Figure 15.3). Because Pall's Web site provides information about products that are used in many industries, its inquiry form enables prospects to provide information about their needs. New sales leads generated by the Web site are automatically stored in a Lotus Notes database, where Pall's interactive marketing staff reviews each lead and forwards it to the appropriate salesperson within a few hours.

Because they sell many products that are needed immediately, such as blood filtration products, it is important for salespeople to know quickly how much time to spend with each prospect.

Pall benefits by having both an inquiry form for people looking for product information and a Customer Satisfaction Survey form where prospects and customers can provide a great deal of detailed information about their needs, evaluation criteria, the reasons they chose Pall products, and their role in the purchase process; they can also rank the various criteria normally used to purchase their products.

Figure 15.3   This form used on the Pall Corporation Web site asks about a number of criteria used to decide whether to purchase its products. By knowing about the prospect's needs and the importance of each criteria, the marketing message can be modified to increase the appeal of the company's products.

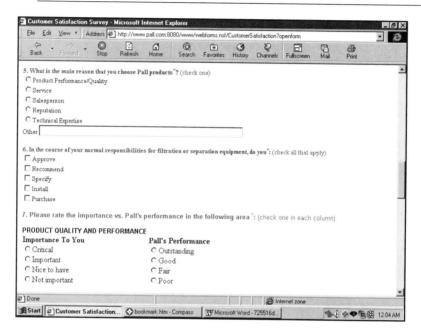

Another indicator of a prospect's quality is the method of contact requested by the prospect. Your inquiry form should enable prospects to request being contacted by email, postal mail, fax, or telephone.

People who request a telephone call are generally more eager to make a purchase, and they should receive immediate attention. In general, prospects that want to receive information by postal mail are not in a hurry to make a buying decision.

People who request an email response are a little harder to qualify because of two qualities of email: immediacy and anonymity. Some people are simply curious about a product and know that an email response can be ignored. However, many people request a response via email because they anticipate receiving a specific answer to their questions very quickly.

A well-crafted inquiry form can tell your salespeople a lot about a prospect and give them a good indication of how to respond.

RFM Analysis

Direct marketers have used a technique for many years that segments their customer base into groups of people who range from very low priority to groups that are likely to provide significantly high revenue.

The process takes into account three factors: the recency of purchases, the frequency of purchases over the past year, and the monetary size (total revenue) of purchases. This technique, called RFM Analysis, divides customers into five equal groups for each of the three factors, resulting in 125 groupings, or cells.

After your customer database has RFM codes for each customer, you can test their predictive value by running a test promotion on a sub-set of your whole customer list.

Select a portion of your whole customer database and send those people a promotional mailing (for example, an email or a postcard). After the test customers have had an opportunity to respond, calculate the response rate for each RFM cell. You can then use various analytical techniques to determine which particular cells of customers to contact in the future and which cells are not profitable.

Because this technique doesn't use any advanced statistical calculations, it can be implemented easily with simple database updating procedures and can provide a great deal of predictive ability for very little investment.

Test, Test, Test

Direct marketers know that to increase sales they need to test all the variables of their marketing to identify the combination of attributes that works the best.

Each type of marketing communications on the Internet has its own set of attributes that can be modified, thereby increasing—or decreasing—response rates.

Establishing a Control

Every marketing communications campaign can be affected by outside factors that are not under your control. Seasonality, major news events, or the weather, for instance, can affect all your marketing efforts at the same time. For this reason, direct marketers compare test campaigns to the results of a known, or control, promotion at the same time.

Suppose, for example, you want to test a new banner ad on a Web publication that you have used for some time. It's best to run both an existing banner and the new test banner ad at the same time, alternating between the two for the duration of the test, in order to compare the results of the new ad to the results of your control ad at the same time. Be sure to have each of the two ads linked to different pages on your Web site so that you can track the clickthrough rate of each ad.

Testing Banner Ads

When developing a set of test banner ads, you should try to modify only one or two attributes in each ad. You may try changing a word or two in the headline, for instance, to see if you can improve response that way. Or, you may try changing the background and keeping the rest of the ad the same.

Another test might involve changing the offer. In this case, you might add a free trial period, or bundle a free gift with the product offered.

A number of factors can be tested in your banner ads. By linking each ad at each different Web media to a different Web page, you can gather a great deal of data that can help you analyze which factors improve response.

Table 15.3 shows an example of a typical tabulation of four ads running on three Web-based publications. In this example Ad #1 is the control ad that has been running on all three sites. On the BigWeb site, the control ad outperformed the other ads, but on SmallWeb, Ad #2 and Ad #3 both did better than the control ad. On FarWeb, Ad #3 showed a tremendous improvement over the control ad. If only one ad is to be run during the campaign, then this analysis would suggest that Ad #3 be used.

Table 15.3   Example Tabulation of the Clickthrough Rates for Multiple Banner Ads Running on Three Web Sites

	BigWeb	SmallWeb	FarWeb
Ad #1	2.4%	2.4%	0.2%
Ad #2	1.1%	2.5%	0.2%
Ad #3	2.2%	2.6%	1.1%
Ad #4	1.9%	1.1%	0.4%

Testing Email Promotions

Email promotional campaigns provide a wide range of variables to test as you look for ways to maximize response.

The first variables to test against your control email are headline, descriptive copy, and length of email. After you are comfortable that those factors are doing a good job, a few other factors to test are

- *Subject field*. Obvious promotional messages might be seen as spam, and subject lines that look too personal can turn off your prospects.

- *From field.* If your prospects don't recognize who sent the message, they may not open the mail.

- *Reason they received the email.* It is becoming accepted to include a short message at the top of a promotional email telling the recipient why they are on the list; however, that uses a highly visible place on the screen that could be used for a selling message.

These are only a few of the factors that affect the response rate of promotional emails, so keep samples of each email with your log of response rates so you can adjust your testing to take advantage of what you learn from each test.

Testing Home Pages

Testing the audience reaction to Web pages is easier than almost any other promotional medium because changes can be made instantly, and the Web server log provides an instant source of data to analyze.

One of the best places to start testing a Web site is with the home page. If your company sells several lines of products to different target markets, it is likely that prospects coming to your home page will find it hard to figure out how to find the product information they are seeking. You can test this by creating multiple home pages for your company, each highlighting a different product line or customer type. After the search engines have had time to index the new pages, look for these things in your Web server log reports:

- Are more people coming to the individual home pages?

- Are people staying on your site longer?

- Are visitors viewing more Web pages?

- Has the percentage of Web visitors who complete an inquiry form changed?

Each of these Internet promotional campaigns, from banner advertising and emails to the actual Web pages, provides tremendous opportunity for testing—and analysis of the response—so you can continually improve the effectiveness of your online marketing activities.

16

Coordinating Brand Recognition

- Branding online

- Combining branding efforts

- Branding options

- Using community to build brands

The Marketing Call of the Internet

With the Internet's multifaceted capabilities, one of the strongest and most valuable roles it can play in a business is as a marketing tool. Yes, it can also be an effective sales tool, customer support tool, communications vehicle, even a human resource device, but marketing is its most established use.

Because of its broad technical functionality, the Internet can touch almost every aspect of a company. It can also affect how customers interact with the business, providing numerous opportunities for communication and feedback that never before existed. Given the increased number and frequency of interaction between a company and its customers, the issue of consistency of message becomes a big one.

It's long been a staple of marketing philosophy that the stronger the brand, the more loyal the customer. However, branding is not an easy matter on the Web. One market research firm, Cyber Dialogue, has found that 82% of online consumers look first in the category, but only 18% search for a specific brand. If the average online shopper is looking for a crystal goblet, for example, he or she is more likely to enter "crystal goblet" into a search engine than to look for the Waterford Web site. In addition, Cyber Dialogue found that even when consumers look for a specific product, only 38% initially go to a branded site; 62% still begin their search through a generic category. Companies must apply special efforts to reap the full benefits of branding on the Web.

Consistency Builds Brand Awareness

Consistency is a phrase heard often in marketing circles. Essentially, it refers to the importance of repeating the same information about your company so that potential customers begin to understand what the company does, what products it sells, and why they (customers) should buy from your company instead of the company down the street.

Advertising gurus suggest that an individual advertisement must be seen or heard repeatedly before it registers in the mind of a potential customer.

Thus, it makes sense that each ad or promotional message should be similar to—if not the same as—the one preceding it. If each ad or message varies slightly, customers will have difficulty linking the advertiser to the message the company is trying to communicate. By developing a consistent marketing look and positioning statement, a business will achieve marketing results faster and more efficiently than businesses trying to be all things to all people.

Consistency is built through every promotional tactic a company uses. In many cases, these include

- Company name

- Logo design

- Corporate colors

- Slogan or tag line

- Illustration or graphic style

- Photos

- Models used

- Spokesperson quoted

All these tools can work together to achieve heightened consumer awareness and familiarity for a company that uses them in concert—that is, a company that makes sure they complement one another. This is the essence of co-branding.

SEE ALSO

➤ *For more about co-branding, see page 210.*

In addition to repeating the same message for consistency's sake, a company also needs to ensure that each marketing tool supports and complements the others. If one does not match the look or feel of the other promotional methods, the company is losing the consistency battle.

To be consistent, a company should routinely use the same colors in all its materials, from brochures to newsletters to advertisements to Web sites. It should also use the same slogan, the same logo, and the same illustration style or photograph in its many marketing tools.

If possible, designs should be built with the Internet in mind. Not all logos transfer well to the Web. If you're using a simple line-drawing logo, for instance, the image will probably be saved in a format known as GIF. GIF files can display only 256 colors simultaneously—and only 216 of those colors look the same in the major browsers. If your logo uses a shade that does not correspond to one of these colors, the GIF file will be displayed with the nearest approximation through a process known as dithering, shown in Figure 16.1. The more your ad agency can keep the Internet in mind while your entire image is being crafted, the fewer the compromises.

FAQ: What is dithering?

Dithering, mingling dots of existing colors to create new colors, often sacrifices resolution; the colors tend to be mingled in patterns rather than smoothly blended.

Figure 16.1 The top logo didn't use acceptable Web colors, so the results are dithered; the bottom example uses Web safe colors and avoids dithering.

Integrated Marketing Creates Synergy

One important fact of marketing is that some is better than none, and more is best of all—assuming, of course, that the marketing tools being used are generating results.

What some companies understand better than others is that each marketing method, or tool, should never be expected to stand on its own. Companies that approach marketing with this mindset never achieve the results they set.

In contrast, companies that use several marketing methods at once, linking each to the others, often obtain results greater than the sum of each individual method. This phenomenon is referred to as synergy. And a marketing program that uses multiple, complementary methods will almost always result in valuable synergy, adding to an increased brand recognition.

Macromedia, profiled earlier in the book, is a master of synergy and, if no cooperative venture exists that would support a product, they'll create one. The company recently launched a new Web development tool called Dreamweaver, for example, which makes special use of a new programming technique called Dynamic HTML or DHTML. To build the support base for Dreamweaver, Macromedia set up an additional Web site called the DHTML Zone (www.dhtmlzone.com). Other than standard banner ads, no Dreamweaver-exclusive advertising is visible on the DHTML Zone site. However, the site attracts those interested in learning more about DHMTL, and they are potential targets for Dreamweaver marketing.

FAQ: What's Dynamic HTML?

The fourth generation of the major browsers incorporated a new technology called Dynamic HTML. Dynamic HTML, an enhancement on the standard HTML language used to create Web pages, is notable because of the increased freedom it offers Web designers. Dynamic HTML elements can be stacked on top of one another, fly across the screen, or disappear at the click of a button.

Offline Versus Online Brands

It's difficult to create new online brands to represent known offline brands. Time-Warner initially tried to promote all its various publications, such as *Time*, *Fortune*, *Life*, and *People*, with a single umbrella Web site called Pathfinder (www.pathfinder.com). Unfortunately, the name-brand quality already established by Time-Warner hindered the effort to launch a general-interest venue. Today, if a consumer enters "www.time.com" into his or her browser, the Time section of Pathfinder comes up, but you only know that if you are watching the address box on the browser. There is little indication of Pathfinder's existence.

Marketing Tools

Tactics used to promote a company's products and services vary greatly in presentation. In almost every case, the online market presence can be bolstered through a connection to the traditional marketing venues. Moreover, the collective use of these approaches helps to establish the brand.

- *Collateral materials.* These include brochures, direct-mail pieces, sell sheets, and line cards. The Web site address should be displayed along with all the other contact information.

- *Advertising.* This includes promotional space purchased in newspapers, magazines, on TV and radio, as well as in newsletters, on billboards, and on buses. Adding your URL in every advertisement gives the public another method to look for more information—and often a direct sell.

- *Public relations.* This includes press releases, press kits, articles, public speaking, and special events. Offering links to specific online press releases enables you to use multimedia via the Internet for more compelling presentations.

- *Trade shows and conferences.* These include industry trade shows, business conferences, and seminars. Link your Web site to an industry event for global impact—you can either post updates as they are announced or go all out and broadcast live to the Internet.

- *Direct mail.* This includes flyers, brochures, postcards, coupons, and invitations. Your traditional direct mail can direct users to visit your Web site as part of a promotion or for additional information.

- *Telemarketing.* This includes outbound phone calls, inbound call centers, technical help lines, and customer service. Informing your callers of a Web site's availability can shift customer-support calls from live operators to a more cost-effective Internet solution.

The answer to the question of which marketing tools to use varies according to the size of your budget and the composition of your target market—those customers you would most like to call your own. Certainly, the greater variety of methods you use, the greater your chance of making contact with your primary prospects.

SEE ALSO

➤ *For more about marketing your Web site, see page 195.*

Choosing to invest all your marketing dollars in one tool is unwise, like putting all your eggs in one basket. Some prospects respond well to direct mail, others to business articles generated by publicity, and others to trade show discussions. Limiting your company's marketing methods to any single tool will also limit the number of prospects you make contact with, and potentially win as customers.

One of the most talked-about marketing methods of the last decade is the Internet. In and of itself, the Internet is not a marketing method. But on the Internet, many opportunities exist for a company to market its products and services to potential customers. The key concept to keep in mind is to use all your marketing tools to funnel potential customers to your Web site.

Case Study: Dell Computer Corporation

Dell Computer Corporation, headquartered in Round Rock, Texas, near Austin, is the world's leading direct computer-systems company. With 17,800 employees around the world, revenue in fiscal 1998 reached $12.3 billion, an increase of $4.6 billion over the previous year's revenue.

One company that almost always gets mentioned in online success stories is Dell. With both consumer and business-to-business sales, Dell pulls in more than $3 million per day in orders from its Web site, shown in Figure 16.2. Recently, Dell computer announced a major branding campaign to bolster its direct-to-consumer computer sales. With a $70 million campaign, Dell hopes to sustain its phenomenal growth and to add value to the brand so that it can expand even more.

Formerly, Dell advertisements have stressed what Dell sells—the computer models with all the relevant specifications. The branding campaign focuses on how Dell sells—the essence of the company, in other words.

Each element of the campaign features the Web site address or a direct link to the site. The Dell campaign, although consumer-oriented, is targeted to its primary market—businesses—and includes

- Print ads in *Time, Newsweek, U.S. News & World Report, Fast Company, Wired, Forbes,* and in major newspapers.

- An Internet ad campaign with 10 banner ads, adopted from the print ads but modified to include animation. The ads will be placed on high-profile Web sites, such as those for *CNET, Wired,* and *CNN.*

- A television spot to be aired nationally. The spot uses a voice-over rather than dialogue so that it can be repurposed internationally.

Figure 16.2 Dell's marketing campaign ties together its online service as well as price benefits.

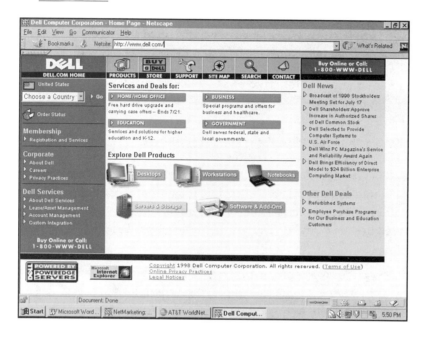

Building Communities

One technique for increasing brand-awareness seems especially suited to the Internet age: building communities. An online community is not (necessarily) linked by a common geographic boundary, but rather, by common interests. When a community emerges around a particular product, it provides a valuable marketing tool for the manufacturer—but it must be used carefully or the benefit could reverse itself.

Online communities are successors to the user groups that were established to explore the intricacies of specific computer models, and later, of specific software. Although user groups are still around, much of their *raison d'etre* has been supplanted by the newsgroups. Newsgroups share common problems—and usually, solutions—and act as a rallying point for users of a particular product. Companies can approach a newsgroup either from an official hosting capacity or from a supportive, participatory angle. Either way, the company must understand that it now has a vehicle for monitoring its consumer base—and it has to pay attention.

SEE ALSO

➤ *For more about newsgroups, see page 94.*

Case Study: DigiTech, a Harmon International Company

DigiTech is the largest manufacturer in the world of guitar equipment. DigiTech is also a leader in modernizing products for vocal harmonies and studio processors. Revenue for Harmon International was reported as $1.47 billion in 1997.

Perhaps the best circumstance for an organization is to encounter a genuine groundswell of interest developed completely outside the company. Although this may not be possible with a newsgroup, which requires access to hardware known as a server, almost anyone can begin an email discussion group, also called a *listserv*. The GSP (Guitar Signal Processor) listserv was started by enthusiasts who wanted to explore the various uses of signal processors made by DigiTech. Everyone sees everyone else's messages on a listserv, and the participants of the GSP list used this capability to share tips and how-to-avoid problems.

After DigiTech discovered the existence of the listserv, several employees signed on. Not only do engineers get to answer problems directly, but marketing representatives have access to what is essentially an ongoing focus group. A mechanism for suggesting feature improvements was established, as well as a way to report problems encountered while using the products.

DigiTech maintained a presence on the listserv while it took the next evolutionary step and began to host newsgroups. Currently, DigiTech hosts seven mailing-list discussion groups dedicated to different product series from the company.

PART VII

Sales

17

Sales Force Automation

- Advantages of sales force automation
- Choosing SFA components
- Managing sales-specific hardware
- Increasing sales effectiveness through SFA
- Sales training and support

Automating Your Sales Force

If I had to pick only one component of an Internet/intranet strategy to implement enterprisewide, I'd choose sales force automation. Actually, that's a bit of a trick answer because, done correctly, sales force automation (SFA) extends the "automation" aspect to virtually every segment of a growing business. And with SFA, you do it right or you don't do it at all.

Sales force automation began to take shape with the introduction of *contact managers*. These software tools became the automated organizers that enabled sales to manage prospects and clients much more closely. SFA figuratively hit the road with the widespread availability of laptops and—more recently—notebooks. With built-in modems (and a briefcase full of telephone adapters), the virtual office was just a phone call away. However, for a remote sales force to be truly effective, the back office has to be as wired as the front office—and they have to be fully integrated.

With a fully integrated sales force automation system, your business reaps the following benefits:

- *A central depository as information emerges.* As sales are made and orders are placed, the data goes into a pool accessible to marketing, sales managers, other sales representatives, and executives. Moreover, the information flows in from every source as well as out, and it feeds the remote sales force with the most up-to-date information possible on everything from inventory to what's selling where.

- *Sales becomes more of a science.* As early as 1993, SFA was recognized as a technology that could "transform selling from a black art into a thoroughly engineered business process" (*Business Week*, Oct. 25, 1993). It costs thousands of dollars to keep even one sales rep on the road for a week—and anything that can improve the odds of getting a return on that investment is well worth investigating. Software vendors are beginning to incorporate sales methodology in their products. This trend toward objectifying sales techniques greatly benefits training new sales agents. Furthermore, managers can better analyze the sales process and target their resources to bolster specific segments of the sales cycle.

- *Everyone in the sales force has greater opportunity.* As communication lines grow, the success of one sales territory has more opportunity to spread to others. The more sales problems are shared, the faster solutions can be found. Online, ongoing sales conferences among a company's entire sales force can lift the entire organization to the same "horizontal" plateau.

- *Forecasts can be based on current, ongoing data.* Without hard data, any sales forecast is reduced to two hunches and a half-dozen best guesses. In an disparate, unwired office, sales data would be accumulated throughout the quarter, analyzed several weeks after its end, and a report distributed about midway through the next quarter. In an SFA-enabled office, the data is always there and trends can be spotted much quicker. And recommendation distribution? It's available at the click of a **Send Mail** button.

Costs of SFA

You don't hear many horror stories about implementing an intranet or enhancing warehouse logistics—most digital-age advances, although not without pitfalls, are fairly straightforward. Unfortunately, that's not the case with sales force automation. Many companies never make it past the SFA study phase because so many choices are available and the paths to take are so varied. Other companies implement it partially and then abandon the project, feeling perhaps that SFA is too costly, time-consuming, or difficult.

Well, they're right. Implementing a sales force automation program is expensive, long term, and extremely detailed. However, the benefits are so substantial that the investment of money, time, and resources is well worth it.

The cost of SFA is largely based in the direct hardware costs of equipping your sales force and the subsequent costs involved in training and supporting them. The expense of automating a single sales person is estimated to fall between $10,000 and $12,000, according to the Sales Automation Association, whose Web site is shown in Figure 17.1. The more spread out your sales force—and consequently, the more difficult it is to support—the higher the figures.

Figure 17.1 When you research an SFA proposal, you can find a storehouse of valuable information and resources at the Sales Automation Association Web site (http://sales.supersites.net/ssnn2/saa/home.htm).

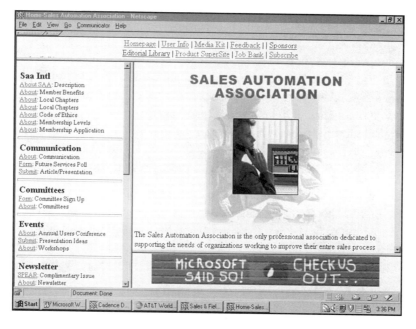

To move from planning an SFA initiative through the rollout phase all the way to benefit realization can take anywhere from 6 to 18 months, depending on the size of the organization and the infrastructure already in place. Furthermore, the SFA system needs to be set up so that new advances and developments can be incorporated into the existing system. If a new voice recognition system revolutionizes the way orders are taken, for example, an ongoing training and support mechanism must be in place to take advantage of it.

One of the reasons that setting up an SFA system is so difficult is that you have to get the buy-in from so many segments of your organization: management, marketing, accounting, Information Technology, and, of course, the sales force itself. Coordinating efforts among that many divisions and individuals is very demanding. Nonetheless, to get the maximum benefit from an SFA system, across-the-board participation is advised. The selling point, of course, is that not only will the numbers for the sales force go up, but enhancements will emerge enterprisewide.

Calculating an SFA ROI

So, what's the bottom line? How much can your organization benefit overall from an SFA investment? Most importantly, what's the payback period for implementing a sales force automation program? If you've cast your net wide enough and plan on setting up an SFA program that impacts on various areas (such as marketing, accounting, and management), you can factor in numerous cost benefits in your analysis—and your payback period drops dramatically.

However, the return on investment (ROI) for an SFA system, strictly from a sales perspective, is not at all discouraging. Typically, two criteria are used for gauging success in an SFA program: an increase in the average revenue per sales representative and a decrease in the average sales cycle time. Although it's obvious that making more per rep is a plus, the impact of a shortened sales cycle may not be so clear. Sales can be an effort- and time-intensive endeavor. Closing a big sale in the business-to-business world can take six months or more and involve six to eight sales calls. The tighter the sales cycle, the less outlay invested.

Sales force automation can shorten a sales cycle by offering more complete information targeted to the specific client. On the business-to-business level, much of a client's focus is on finding the solution to fit the perceived need, and then presenting that solution in a formal manner for approval. The more complete the presentation that the sales representative can offer, the fewer steps the client will have to take in the decision-making process; thus, the shorter the sales cycle.

Suppose, for example, that a warehouse manager has identified a need for a radio-frequency capable bar-code scanning system. The typical steps in the buying process are

1. Research potential solutions.

2. Develop a cost/benefit analysis and return on investment scenarios to present to management.

3. Create a needs requirement document and send out a request for proposals (RFP).

4. Field the responding RFPs and begin considering vendors.

5. Narrow the choices to a few vendors and hammer out a rough contract.

6. Select a vendor.

7. Complete negotiations on the contract.

8. Send out the purchase order.

9. Accept delivery of the goods and install them.

10. Train personnel on the system.

11. Request additional support, if necessary.

12. Purchase additional units.

From an SFA viewpoint, several areas in the customer buying process are vulnerable and can be addressed advantageously. One key area is the buyer's internal administrative process. The more completely a solution speaks to the client's needs, the easier the acceptance. An SFA system that includes full access to product specifications enables proposals to be tailored to a request much more efficiently. It's even possible—and desirable in many cases—to include competitive information in the proposal. This data and more should be at the fingertips of any automated sales force.

With an ROI calculation, you have to be sure to include the training and the implementation costs as well as the actual equipment costs. Table 17.1 shows an ROI scenario based on a medium-size sales force with a moderate productivity gain.

Table 17.1 ROI Scenario for a Sales Force Automation Implementation

Income	
Number of Sales Reps	400
Monthly Gross	1,000,000
Average Monthly Sales (Per Rep)	2,500
Average Gross Profit (%)	15%
Gross Profit Per Rep Per Month	375
SFA Productivity Increase	25%
Gross Profit after SFA	469
Gross Profit Increase	$94

continues

Table 17.1 Continued

Expenses	
System Cost Per User	$3,500
Training and Implementation Costs Per User	$6,500
Total Cost of System	$4,000,000
×	
Total Group Profit Increase Monthly	$187,500
Number of Months for Payback	21

Factoring in a shortened sales cycle as outlined previously will further reduce the payback period.

Choosing a Contact Manager

Most members of a sales force regard the contact manager as the heart of any automation system. Because it's the primary software that they work with day in and day out, from their perspective, they're probably right. Today's contact manager (or personal information manager, abbreviated as PIM) is extraordinarily full-featured. Almost all the off-the-shelf software, such as Act!, GoldMine, or TeleMagic, contain features that enable your sales force to

- Maintain a flexible database of contacts.

- Instantly connect with contacts via letter, phone, or email by selecting the appropriate button in the database.

- Keep notes on each call, automatically time- and date-stamped.

- Print reports on all notes with one contact or a range of contacts.

- Schedule one-time and recurring appointments with alarms through a daily, weekly, monthly, or annual calendar interface, as shown in Figure 17.2.

- Set up to-do lists, which can roll over daily if not completed.

- Mail-merge letters, labels, or email messages from the contact database.

One of the biggest problems in putting an SFA plan into motion is deciding upon a contact manager to be employed universally across the sales force. In addition to the commercially available software, such as GoldMine, whose Web site (www.goldminesw.com) is shown in Figure 17.3, numerous industry-specific and custom-written applications are available on the market. It's somewhat of an embarrassment of riches, and a carefully considered step-by-step method helps to narrow down the choices.

Figure 17.2   Scheduling to-do lists, meetings, and appointments are key to a sales rep's work and a prime feature of contact managers such as this one.

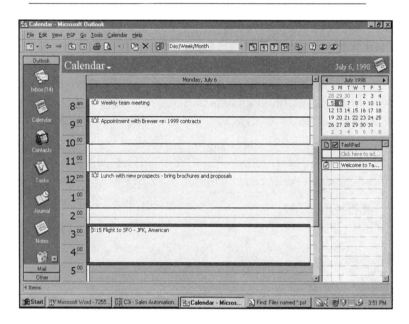

Figure 17.3   GoldMine is a commercially available contact manager that boasts a rich feature set and extensive customizability.

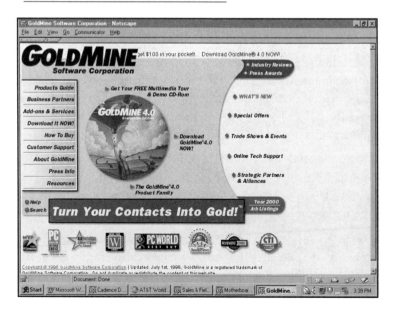

1. List specific sales objectives, including the type of information to be accessed.

2. Define your current non-automated sales process. Could any areas be improved?

3. Survey various software packages to determine each one's ease of use, feature set, customizability, and extensibility, particularly in regard to the Internet or your company intranet, as well as your legacy databases.

4. Examine the training and support options for the software. Are third-party tutorials or classes available? Is a round-the-clock help line up and running? What is a typical response time? Are other online help systems available, such as a Web site or knowledge base?

5. If the proposed product has not been on the market for long, be sure to check the vendor's bona fides. Support is a major issue with contact managers, and if the company is a fly-by-night, you could be left without any help when you most need it.

6. Ascertain the necessary hardware requirements for the software—and exceed them in processor speed, memory, and storage to better allow for easy expansion.

7. Establish a test period with a real-world basis. Track the results against the number of calls for support and the support system responses, as well as against subjective reports from your sales force.

Obviously, any assessment of a tool must take into account the opinions of the primary users. The more the contact manager you choose fits the needs of your sales force, the more assured you can be that your investment will pay off—and your sales reps will actually use the software.

Selecting an SFA Strategy

Just as choosing a core component such as a contacts manager should be handled as a detailed process, so should the entire enterprisewide SFA strategy be. It's possible to run both implementation plans simultaneously, but it's probably a better choice to focus on a contact manager first as your central element and build the enterprisewide system around it. This sequence maximizes the sales force's use of the system and prevents incompatibilities down the road that could arise from working with unknown software.

1. Establish a team to handle the evaluation project. At a minimum, the team should include members from sales, marketing, accounting, and information systems (IS). The team and its designated head should be charged with following through on the SFA implementation and gauging its effectiveness.

2. Detail your sales process. If you performed this type of survey during a contact manager evaluation, do it again after the software has been in effect for some time. You will gain a clearer picture of how your sales force operates and where automation can better serve the entire organization.

3. Enlist the sales force's support. In addition to gathering important information about your sales team's needs, keeping them involved is the best way to ensure their use of the system. This involvement should be an ongoing effort. After a system is selected, it has to be pitched to the sales force in the same way that they pitch a new product—by emphasizing how the SFA system is going to make their work more productive and their lives easier.

4. Establish objectives and priorities. It's pretty easy to just say, "Automate it all, now." It's also usually a mistake—an expensive mistake. Find the areas that would benefit most and designate these as priorities. This process creates an implementation plan that can be phased in and absorbed by the enterprise.

Hasten payback with new training options
If you implement your SFA program carefully, you can use one part of the system to train other parts. Put online training and distance-learning methods high on the priority list. After those technologies are in place, you can use them to train and support your sales force (and others) in other SFA elements. This will cut the number of training hours per employee and contribute to a shorter payback period.

SEE ALSO

➤ *For more about Internet training techniques, see page 84.*

5. Figure the return on investment. In addition to adding justification for the project to upper management, calculating the ROI helps to identify specific targets for improvement, such as a shorter sales cycle, a higher close rate, and more selling with less administrative time.

6. Make sure upper management is informed. Executives need to understand that an enterprisewide SFA program not only bolsters the sales department, but should have an impact across the organization.

The benefits of an external expert
In a 1994 study from International Data Group on sales force automation, companies with notable ROIs tended to choose to have their systems custom designed by outside consultants. Companies depending on internal systems created from scratch or customized from off-the-shelf software by their IS department didn't fare as well.

7. Choose a development route. Is your IS department going to put together your SFA system? Should you customize an off-the-shelf package? Or should you opt for a custom-designed system? The answer to these questions lies primarily in the strength of your IS department as well as its workload. Unless IS is particularly robust in internal development—along with documentation and training solutions—you almost certainly will be better off with a custom-designed system from an outside source.

8. Evaluate the software. Keep these factors in mind when comparing systems:

    • In the long run, value is more important than cost.

    • Customizability contributes to the life span of a system.

    • Keep it Simple, Sales. If a system is too difficult to use, people won't work with it; the ease-of-use factor is a major concern.

    • Extended training and support are as important as existing features.

    • Uncover the developer's upgrade path. What are the anticipated enhancements and associated costs?

    • It's better to buy from a reliable vendor with a proven track record than one that promises the moon.

9. Outline and distribute an RFP. In addition to features, the request for proposal should include the size of the sales force, the number of sales managers, the implementation schedule, and the existing hardware infrastructure.

10. Start the implementation with a pilot program. Beginning with a small rollout allows companies to work out the kinks of a program and to generate some internal excitement. The pilot program should be composed of a small group of typical users from every department involved.

11. Track the results. As part of the rollout, be sure to watch various measuring sticks throughout the organization. In addition to basic sales figures, keep an eye on the number of sales calls per day, sales administrative costs, and training costs.

Case Study: Cadence, Inc.

Cadence is the largest supplier of software tools and professional services used to accelerate and manage the design of semiconductors, computer systems, networking and telecommunications equipment, consumer electronics, and a variety of other electronic-based products. For 1997, Cadence reported revenue totaling $915.9 million, an increase of 33% over the prior year.

Cadence's business was growing. Initially, the company sold electronic design automation software systems to electronics companies, but recently, it decided to offer more complete solutions. As it broadened its services, the amount of information its sales force had to keep up with rose dramatically. Not only did the reps have to know about the solutions available, they also had to fully understand the business challenges that could arise. To keep its sales force up-to-speed at all times, Cadence developed an SFA system called OnTrack.

OnTrack centers around a Web site available on the company intranet. On the Web site, any sales team member can find a direct daily news feed about Cadence, the industry, their customers, and their competitors. The site has links to Cadence's competitors' Web sites that include current information about rival products and services. OnTrack provides a single location for reps to find all sales resources, such as product information, training materials, forms, success stories, press releases, legal agreements, and templates for customer presentations, proposals, and letters.

Key to Cadence's marketing encyclopedia strategy is the ability for each sales rep to pull the information off the site when it is needed. Previously, Cadence would send out volumes of material that was not immediately relevant across the board. However, because at some point the information could be necessary, all the data had to be stored for possible future retrieval. Each sales rep had, in essence, a distinct marketing encyclopedia that might be different from the one every other sales rep had. With OnTrack, the company is assured of a consistent availability of information controlled from a central source.

Cadence implemented OnTrack and achieved an impressive ROI of 1,766% with a payback period of under two months. Much of the savings occurred because Cadence leveraged the existing infrastructure when deploying its SFA program. However, the company also attributes a great deal of savings from the relative ease of use of a browser based system. According to one sales rep, "I learned in two days from OnTrack what it took months to learn at my previous company." As Cadence continues to expand, this shortened learning curve becomes even more significant. With 40 new reps hired in the first year and plans in place for 40 more to be hired in each of the next two years, the training savings are substantial. Furthermore, time not spent in the classroom is time spent on the road, pushing the company products.

Managing Hardware

Most of the strategies learned in selecting software systems are applicable to choosing hardware for your road warriors. In short:

- *Establish objectives first.* Look toward what your sales force needs to accomplish, and then choose components to help them meet these goals. If your sales reps use in-person presentations in conference rooms, for example, you might opt for a larger monitor screen instead of a battery with a longer life. On the other hand, if your sales force tends to work in more impromptu situations, emphasis should be placed on a more powerful battery.

- *Plan your configuration.* It's best to work from a base configuration for all the systems rolled-out. A single configuration makes repair and maintenance much simpler. The master formation must be carefully considered to include every element, even those often taken for granted, such as audio/video connectors or power strips.

- *Test your hardware.* Establishing a quality control procedure for configuring hardware systems in-house helps to eliminate on-the-road errors. During the testing phase, systems should be examined both in the office and in real-life situations. If intranet access is only tested in the office, for example, unexpected problems may occur when logging on from the outside.

- *Establish a pilot program.* As with the software systems, a hardware pilot program not only uncovers glitches before the rollout, but it also helps build enthusiasm for the project.

However, additional concerns need to be addressed for hardware support and maintenance. Chief among those concerns are system upkeep and asset management.

Implementing a Hardware Exchange Program

Unlike software, laptops and other hardware systems can be stolen, lost, or physically broken. The primary goal within an SFA program is a minimum of downtime for the sales force. One component of a successful hardware management system is a hot swap program, in which defective or lost units are replaced as soon as possible. An aggressive hot swap program can strive for a 24-hour period from discovery of a hardware problem to the arrival of a fully configured replacement as a realistic target.

For any hot swap program to work, two elements have to be in place. First, a ready inventory of equipment, outfitted to the current standard, needs to be on hand. C3i, the SFA training consultants, recommend that 5-10% of inventory be available for the hot swap program. The second requirement is the systematized backup of personal files by the sales force. Anyone who has ever had to reinstall system software—effectively wiping out all personal additions—knows what an impact a loss of data can have. In this case, personal files also means correspondence with clients, reports, charts, and other business-related documents. If the sales force has backed up its own data to an external drive, the hot swapped system can be restored to full usability in no time.

Asset Tracking

One of the main problems with portable computing is that it's—well, portable. Hardware is an expensive investment for any organization, and systems must be initiated to keep track of these assets. Moreover, leasing equipment is a very real, often-used option these days and redoubles the importance of asset tracking.

A central database, managed by IS but accessible by the sales help desk, can help keep an eye on the goods. Giving the sales help desk access to the information enables them to more accurately gauge turnaround times for out-of-service equipment and record systems as they come in for repair. Be sure that employees know that the particular equipment they are issued (right down to the serial number) is their responsibility and that unauthorized loans are unacceptable.

Maximizing Sales Effectiveness

With sales force automation, heaven—as well as the devil—is in the details. After your enterprise is working with your SFA system, it is exactly how it is used that increases sales effectiveness and bolsters the overall bottom line. Conversely, if the systems are used inappropriately—or, worst case, not at all—your SFA investment will be for naught and your organization could suffer.

What specific areas can a sales force automation system assist? An ideal system can have a positive impact on almost every step of the sales force journey:

- *Prospect gathering.* Sales force automation enables you to maximize the Web as a sales lead generator in addition to more traditional sources of leads.

- *Client research.* The more you know about your prospects, the more you can tailor your presentations to their needs—and SFA tools on the Internet can help.

- *Presentation pitches.* Presentations have been one of the primary uses for laptops in sales situations for some time. SFA technology allows for more enhanced customized presentations.

- *Query responses.* An SFA-enabled sales force has full access to an online marketing encyclopedia with all the answers necessary to turn a prospect into a client.

- *Quote generation.* To close a sale, the quote has to be immediate, detailed, and accurate. Sales force automation connections help keep the quote letter-perfect.

- *Order placement.* A front office tightly integrated with a back office can make sure that every order is placed against inventory in stock, or that the client knows when the order will be available.

Opportunity Management Systems

Much of a sales rep's day is spent amassing prospects and identifying likely targets prior to soliciting them. SFA methods, through forms such as the one shown in Figure 17.4, can help manage a much larger pool of prospects than possible before the Information Age. The Internet can also be used as a tremendous source of interested parties—and the proper SFA software can automate the mining of those prospects.

Mining Web forms

The Web is another great source for potential clients. Unfortunately, your sales force has to find a way to winnow down the overwhelming response that can come from a Web-based contact form. One company, Pentech International, has extended a traditional contact manager, TeleMagic, to handle contacts generated from a Web-based form. Once harvested, the prospects can be automatically emailed.

Figure 17.4   Registration forms such as this one are used on the Internet to gather
information on potential customers and to help qualify sales prospects.

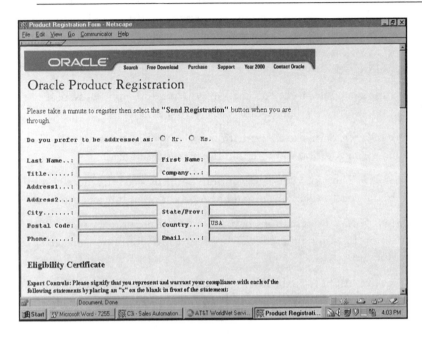

When a sales force works a region cooperatively, SFA coordination is essential. A common
database of prospects, accessible across the enterprise, enables the sales force to approach a
much larger volume of prospects without fear of duplicating efforts. Moreover, through the
use of database concepts such as keyfields—where an entry can be identified by specific
parameters such as zip code, company revenue, or primary business—prospects can be
targeted more effectively.

Case Study: CoreStates Financial Corporation

CoreStates is one of the leading banking services companies dedicated to the mid-
Atlantic states. Headquartered in Philadelphia, CoreStates has more than 19,000 employees in the U.S. and around the world.

CoreStates specializes in volume prospecting within the business-to-business sector. In one
state alone, CoreStates maintains relationships with 42,000 customers and keeps an ongoing
list of approximately 32,000 potential clients. This high degree of volume would not be
even remotely feasible were it not for its SFA program.

Using GoldMine as its contact manager, CoreStates routinely pulls contact information from its online connection at Dun & Bradstreet and integrates the data with its central database. As with any sort of data-importing operation like this, new records must be checked for duplications with existing ones. As more detailed information is gathered on a prospect, it is entered into the memo area of the record, where it can be called up later. CoreStates gathers a lot of information and requires a contact manager that is flexible enough to handle several pages of notes. The extensive databasing of prospects enables the CoreStates sales force to review up to 600 potential clients a month.

Templates are set up within CoreStates to allow for easy mass-mailing of contact letters and promotions through standard word processing programs, such as Word and WordPerfect. The combination of high-volume contacts with detailed, personalized attention has its advantages; CoreStates leads its market with the number of yields from its potential-client database.

Client and Competitive Research

When preparing for a presentation, sales reps need all the information they can get. Although your intranet can be expected to provide all the product background needed, details gathered on both the potential client and definitive competitors can make or break the sale. Identifying a client's needs is the first step to addressing them directly, and the awareness of your competitors' strengths enables your sales rep to better develop the case for your company's goods.

An Internet connection is a fabulous research tool for both client and competitor information. The first place to look for information is the client or competitor's own Web site. Not only can you glean an enormous amount of factual data, but—almost as importantly—you can discover how your target prefers to be presented. Understanding what the client or competitor values and emphasizes gives your sales force powerful ammunition for delivering its presentations on target.

Some companies develop internal jump stations for continually accessed competitive information. A jump station is a page of links to frequently visited Web sites. Although some sales reps can accumulate their own links by using the *Bookmark* or *Favorites* feature of their browser, a jump station is generally accessible across the enterprise through the intranet. A jump station doesn't have to be internally developed to be valuable. Many associations create jump stations or link pages that list the major players in an industry. The International Association of Amusement Parks and Attractions, for example, runs a Web site (www.iaapa.org) that offers links to all their members's Web pages, as well as a profile of detailed information, shown in Figure 17.5, such as names of upper management and a demographic breakdown of their customer base.

Figure 17.5 Many associations and organizations make detailed information readily available, such as this profile from the International Association of Amusement Parks and Attractions' Web site.

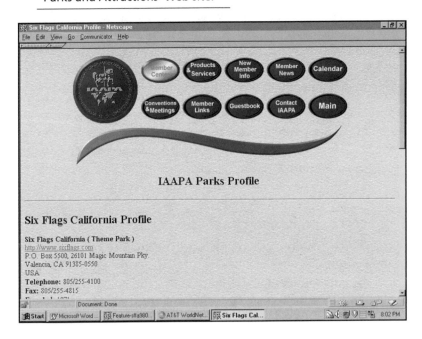

SEE ALSO

➤ *For more about amassing competitive information over the Internet, see page 54.*

Online Presentations

When multimedia laptops with large color screens and CD-quality sound began to emerge, a whole new generation of sales reps took the show on the road. Stand alone, point-of-sale presentations displaying preconfigured PowerPoint slides or Excel charts and spreadsheets can be fairly persuasive—until the client asks an unanticipated question. Then it's a round of "I'll have to get back to you," and "Let me check with the office on that." The sales presentation loses its heat, and closure is delayed, if not gone forever.

An automated sales force with Internet/intranet capabilities doesn't have to wait to check with the office because the office is online. Presentations can be designed to connect with a live database that has all the current product data, so if the client asks about a novel configuration, the sales rep can present the solution immediately. Need to know current or projected availability? Check it while you're online with the client. For a new product rollout, a presentation can be put on a password-protected area of the intranet and be accessible simultaneously to the sales force around the world.

As technology advances, so must the skill set of your sales force. According to Dave Hanaman of C3i, a consultancy firm specializing in sales force automation training,

> Sales people will need to continually improve their technology skills, especially their fundamental comfort level with automation. The sales person must have the confidence and competence to use the technology in an already pressure-charged environment. Second, sales people will need to take their core inter-personal and sales skills to the next level. These 'core skills' will be even more important as sales people add a new element—point of influence applica-tions—into their sales calls. This will require them to manage a more complex environment while remaining focused on the person in front of them. Finally, sales people who can improvise with this technology allowing the customer to lead the way will thrive in this just-in-time environment.

Technology is beginning to outpace the conventional laptop, however. Several new, small-er devices, called subnotebooks, are beginning to be used at the point-of-influence for a sale. One company, MobilePoint Corporation, is combining pen-based technology with subnotebooks to allow for a more natural style of sales presentation with an online con-nection. These tools, such as the one shown in Figure 17.6, can go all the way from quali-fying the prospect to signing off on the order—and relay the information to the home office for immediate processing.

Case Study: McKesson

McKesson General Medical is the leading medical-surgical supplier to physicians, clinics, long-term care, and home-care sites, and it is the third-largest distributor of medical-surgical supplies to hospitals. With 3,120 employees and 41 service centers in the U.S., McKesson General Medical is a business unit of McKesson Corp. of San Francisco, the world's largest health care supply management company.

McKesson General Medical is a distributor for 500 medical product suppliers and represents more than 30,000 products. Its sales force must call on every account in its respective terri-tories every two weeks. Typically, this involves calling on nurses, office managers, and doc-tors while walking through exam rooms, offices, or stock rooms. Under these conditions, even the most portable laptop is a hindrance.

Figure 17.6 The SalesPoint device from MobilePoint Corporation acts as an SFA tool for situations in which a laptop isn't portable enough.

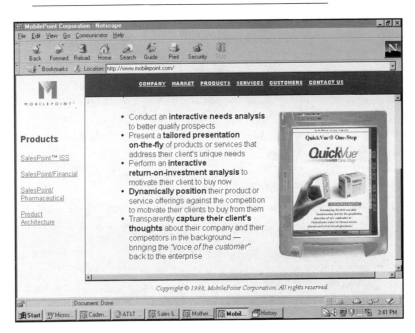

With MobilePoint's Internet connectivity, dubbed MobileGram, the sales rep can gather the latest information on products, availability, and clients. MobilePoint also enables digital capture of the order signature and includes a form-driven spreadsheet for performing ROI calculations and "what if" scenarios. Since McKesson's General Medical sales reps have begun using MobilePoint's SalesPoint devices, revenue has increased by 40%, margins have gone up 2%, and new product conversions has improved 100%.

Online Marketing Encyclopedia

Sales reps refer to the full range of product information as their marketing encyclopedia. Like the conventional sets of old, a marketing encyclopedia is an exhaustive reference that could easily overflow several shelves. A traditional marketing encyclopedia generally consists of numerous 3-ring binders with ad slicks, spec sheets, backgrounders, inventory printouts, and everything else related to the product, including competitive intelligence. It's great to have as a reference, but it's not very portable and it can be difficult to use under pressure; clients tend to get impatient after two or three minutes of "I know it's in here somewhere."

An online marketing encyclopedia is a central database of information available to every sales rep in the field or in the office. When the information is online, a rep can dial in to the intranet for the latest information on product availability, shipping schedules or pricing updates. Most marketing encyclopedias are indexed, categorized, and searchable for information retrieval. Today's multimedia systems can offer full-color, full-sound presentations that no fax to the hotel room can match. Internet publishing makes updating a product brochure a one-step process, with no additional 4-color printing or overnight shipping charges.

Case Study: Fujitsu Computer Products of America, Inc.

Fujitsu Computer Products of America (FCPA) is a wholly-owned subsidiary of Fujitsu Ltd., a global computer and telecommunications company with more than $36 billion in annual sales. FCPA markets a wide range of data-storage and imaging products to serve users ranging in size from small or home office to Fortune 500 firms.

The verdict from Fujitsu's sales force was unanimous; their information channel wasn't working. When surveyed to determine why market share was lacking, the reps responded that they couldn't sell the product if they didn't have up-to-date, accurate information all the time. In response to these needs, Fujitsu put together a marketing encyclopedia program called GamePlan. GamePlan gives Fujitsu's sales force instant online access to company presentations, competitor information, company directories, backlog information, product descriptions, inventory, and shipping data. In the opinion of Doug May, Vice President of Marketing and Distribution at Fujitsu, "GamePlan was immediately adopted by our sales force because they helped to design it."

GamePlan wasn't a static solution, either. As it became obvious that the sales force often learned of important industry news from its customers—an embarrassing situation, at best—a new segment was added to GamePlan. Info Blitz Monday, posted to the marketing encyclopedia area every Monday at noon, offers an updated product road map, the latest product information, shipping updates, and most significantly, competitor information gleaned from newspapers, magazines, and the Web. Moreover, a running news ticker, generally updated twice weekly, scrolls across the bottom of the screen to keep Fujitsu's sales force up to speed on mission-critical developments.

Since the introduction of the GamePlan (and an extranet component called The Force), Fujitsu has doubled its revenue—without doubling its sales force. May says that sales force automation played a key role in the company's growth.

Front and Back Office Integration

If you want to continue to make sales to a customer, you need to provide ongoing service after the initial sale and keep in touch with the customer to be aware of future needs. The easiest way to manage this balancing act is to integrate your front and back offices. Generally, sales and marketing are on one side of the fence, and service and fulfillment are on the other. Although this compartmentalization works for some functions each area must accomplish, without some sort of pipeline between the front and back offices, companies encounter a great deal of duplication of effort and less reliable forecasts. Some of the ways that the front and back offices can assist one another include

- Sales information shared with manufacturing, supply-chain management, and finance enables more precise forecasts which, in turn, open up just-in-time management possibilities and lowered inventory.

- The faster and more accurately the back office fulfills the sales order, the better the customer retention.

- Coordination of production schedules with the sales force allows for enhanced sales opportunities to move older stock or launch new lines.

- Giving the sales force access to order status information, as well as outstanding receivables, presents the sales rep as a true representative of your company—one whom the customer can trust.

- With total record access, including such items as the bill of materials, customer service personnel can better serve the client and make everyone in the organization look good.

- Marketing can review customer profiles to determine trends and identify emerging needs. An integration of common databases eliminates errors and redundancy among several departments.

Case Study: American General Life and Accident
American General Life and Accident is a Nashville-based subsidiary of American General Corporation. Headquartered in Houston, Texas, American General Corporation reports $79 billion in assets and $7.3 billion in equity.

American General Life and Accident (AGLA) is working to bring its old-fashioned methods up to date. As one of a handful of insurance companies that collects premiums door-to-door on a monthly—or even weekly—basis, AGLA has a tremendous amount of customer interaction. Until recently, much of its work was accomplished by hand. Quotes were prepared by hand using rate manuals, and they were often inaccurate. These inaccuracies had to be corrected by in-house underwriters and resubmitted to the client. When a policy was sold, the information had to be entered by a clerk at the central office before any of the data could be accessed. The process was slow, error prone, and inefficient.

AGLA management thought that if the front and back offices could be integrated, then they could maximize their potential. The home office would have increased control over collections, and sales representatives could capture customer data, access records and information, generate receipts, and quote prices—all during a customer call. After working with KPMG Consulting, AGLA decided to deploy an SFA system that used pen-based systems called SmartPads. Armed with SmartPads, the sales force could

- Provide customers with accurate quotes and verified receipts at the time of customer visits.

- Access the most current customer information without having to travel to the district office.

- Pull up customer records, pricing, and product information immediately.

One unexpected plus is that the cutting-edge SmartPad device helps to recruit technology-savvy college students who constitute an increasing percentage of AGLA's workforce.

Implementing Configurators

When a sales force is representing a manufacturer whose products can be ordered in many configurations, manual order-taking is quite error prone. Leave a necessary component off an order and the customer—and ultimately, the company—suffers. And if a customer is burned too many times, you can bet alternative options are going to be explored.

The problem has become so acute that a new class of software has emerged: configurators. A configurator works in conjunction with your sales force automation program to make custom ordering efficient, straightforward, and as error-free as possible. The key advantage of a configurator is that it is integrated into the supply chain, so that your complete bill of materials is coordinated —not just the primary components.

Configurators are generally presented as form-based interfaces, such as the one shown in Figure 17.7. After all the desired options are chosen, the form is submitted with the click of an onscreen button and processed by the central server. This is a flexible format that enables the user—whether the salesman or the customer—to try out various configurations to check pricing and availability. Configurators can be structured so that certain options cannot be chosen unless a particular base model is selected. Component inventory can also be a factor. Configurators improve a sales force order-completion rate noticeably and should be a part of every SFA program where custom ordering is essential.

Figure 17.7 This example of a configurator is from Innomat, Inc., a Finnish company specializing in sales force automation enhancement.

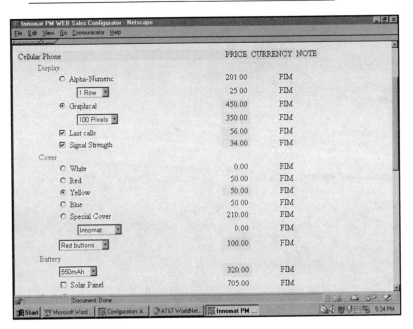

Web-based Training and Support

Sales reps need a special kind of training and support. Although many new applications (and their associated upgrades) require training of some sort, companies need to keep classroom training time to a minimum, primarily because such training is expensive—both directly and indirectly. Direct costs include conference rooms, travel and entertainment expenses, and trainer fees. Indirect costs, such as the loss of selling time, can have an equally significant impact.

As more SFA programs are placed in motion, many companies are turning to alternatives to classroom training for their sales force. One such alternative combines the sales help desk with an online training guide accessible through the company intranet. This combination, called remote-based learning, enables sales reps to schedule training in a more appropriate manner without losing time in the field.

SEE ALSO

➤ *For more on remote-based learning, see page 81.*

Other training channels that could be considered for getting your sales staff up to speed include

- *Printed manuals.* Generally useful as a supplementary guide, manuals initially tend to go unread by many sales reps.

- *Videos.* When used to reinforce an earlier training session, videos are particularly successful. They are also good for conveying overall concepts in a pre-training situation.

- *Computer Presentations.* Although computer slide shows alone don't have tremendous impact, combining them with other media elements, such as sound or digital video, can be effective. Distributing such files, however, can be troublesome because of their large file size. Two possible methods are custom CD-ROM and streaming media over the Internet.

SEE ALSO

➤ *For more on streaming media, see page 79.*

- *Computer-based Training (CBT).* Interactivity is the main draw with CBT programs—study after study has shown that retention is much higher when training includes interactive elements. Many computer-based training applications also incorporate evaluations and other self-tests.

- *Online help.* Context-sensitive help is gaining momentum in many computer applications, although to be used effectively, many implementations require training. The depth of online help (included with the computer program and locally accessible) can be enhanced greatly with an intranet-based help system.

- *SFA Newsletters.* Newsletters are particularly useful during an initial rollout of a new system. Quick tips and tricks can be incorporated into a format more user-friendly than overwhelming computer manuals.

- *Sales force trainers.* In every organization, some sales reps prove more technologically adept than others—in other words, they "get it." Where possible, it's a good idea to take advantage of this expertise enhanced with a working knowledge of the day-to-day activities of the sales force by promoting these individuals as field trainers.

On the support front, sales reps typically need help on an ongoing basis, not just during training sessions. If your organization runs a help desk to support the general staff, you should look into a special desk dedicated only to aiding the sales force. Sales reps on the road have very particular, often mission-critical needs. When a modem is not functioning properly one-half an hour before a vital presentation, the sales rep needs answers immediately or the sale could be affected. To assist in its diagnosis, a special sales help desk should have access to the same configuration of equipment and software that the sales force is using in the field.

SEE ALSO

➤ *For more about online help desk solutions, see page 269.*

CHAPTER **18**

Online Financial Transfers

- Financial transfer primer

- Offering your customers online options

- Making online retail transactions

- Conducting business-to-business transfers

Advantages of Online Financial Transfers

The exchange of money for goods, services, or information is the essence of business. Consumers in the market place have several forms of money to exchange for goods. Cash, credit cards, and checks are all acceptable means of payment.

In today's competitive business world, money is often exchanged electronically in the form of an *online financial transfer*. As the Internet continues to blossom as a business marketplace, the new, electronic versions of cash, credit cards, and checks are taking shape.

If you want to maximize the full potential of the Internet for business, at some point you will need to conduct safe, secure online financial transfers. The following examples show how online financial transfers can enhance your business:

- Direct online retail transactions can create new distribution channels for your goods and services.

- Online transactions with your bank can streamline payroll and accounting procedures.

- Secure, online communication between you and your business partners can decrease order response time and cut administration costs.

Many companies are currently competing with their products to be the industry standard for online funds transfers. To select the company and product that most fits the needs of your business, you should know a few basic concepts of online transfers.

How Online Transfers Work

Online financial transfers are defined in modern business as electronic financial transfers that require connection to a remote, third-party computer.

The third party, usually a bank or credit clearinghouse, observes and authenticates the transaction. The third party then sends confirmation to one or both of the other parties.

The transaction is not fully completed, however, until the merchant's bank credits the merchant's account for the credit card sale and the debit is posted to the consumer's bankcard account—a process known as settlement.

Establishing Goals and Limits

Business is a constant balance of supply and demand. Although all business involves money, the purposes and expectations of every business transaction are different. Your IPO, for example, may have been offered at $6.50 and closed at $70 per share the first day and may not be concerned that the dry cleaners is charging you $45.00 to starch your shirt. Or, in contrast, you may be an automobile dealer facing a large inventory tax if you don't reduce your stock of luxury sports cars. In both situations, you come to the table with specific goals and limits for the exchange.

When you are involved in online transactions, your company will need to define specific goals and limits, which are discussed in the following sections.

Breaking the Technological Barrier

If technology is hard to understand, the average consumer rarely uses it. Ease of use appears to be the largest demand of the online buying community. And the average user is often your projected customer.

Some companies have found ways to overcome the average user technology barrier. The following selling points have been proven to be incentives for customers to learn how to complete online transactions:

- *Quality*. High-quality items are not always available in every location. If you can get black caviar online and the local supermarket only carries the red, you'll have an incentive to shop the Web.

- *Availability*. It's much harder for a small boutique to make it in Anytown, U.S.A—the customer base just isn't there. An online boutique, on the other hand, has the whole world as its marketplace. And folks can shop from around the globe.

- *Selection*. It's truly amazing what you can find online. Not only is almost every type of product available, but a huge selection of brands is available as well.

- *Price*. Without the fiscal demands of a real-world storefront—property taxes, utility bills, and rent, to name a few—cybershops can afford to cut their prices to the bones and still make money. From the consumer's point of view, the low prices can usually offset any shipping charges.

Providing Secure, Simple Transactions

Offering your customers an easy, quick, safe way to buy things from you is priority number one. Many companies are positioned to help you reach that goal with products that create secure online credit card transactions.

Surprisingly, security is considered less important to consumers than had been previously estimated before online commerce. This is due to the popularity of secure online credit card payments.

Credit card companies have attempted to reduce credit card theft and identity fraud for many years. Some of the lessons gained from their efforts have helped in establishing online credit card use as the standard payment method of Internet business transactions.

Many consumers have gained a sense of security with credit cards. Customers have been using credit card numbers to pay for purchases made over the telephone since the days of the slice-o-matic infomercial. Today, online credit card transactions are more secure than both mail and telephone credit card transactions.

The Federal Government has created laws that protect and promote the use of credit cards in mail, telephone, and online transactions, as well.

Keep up with consumer protection

You can find more information about credit card laws, consumer protection, and the Fair Credit Reporting Act at the United States Federal Trade Commission Web site (http:/ /www.ftc.gov/ftc/consumer.htm).

These Federal laws effectively limit consumer liability of fraudulent charges to $50.00. They also establish a system of due process for the settlement of billing errors.

Meanwhile, the credit card companies have determined that it is still a profitable venture to offer quick, easy, credit card transactions.

Specialized payment options, such as micropayments and electronic checking payments, and online bill payments using electronic financial transfers are also beginning to find new consumer market interest. These are discussed in greater detail later in this chapter.

As customers become more aware and comfortable with paying bills and buying goods and services, your company should become more aware of how to get your goods and services in the hands of the consumer.

Security Options to Consider

Many security options are available for online transactions. Options range from no security to highly encrypted, authenticated transactions.

Choosing the amount of security that is right for your transaction is a matter of common sense and mutual agreement between you and your customers or business partners. The following sections discuss some of the methods of security frequently used in Internet commerce.

Choosing a Secure Channel

Secure Sockets Layer (SSL) is an effective server-level encryption protocol that maintains a secure connection—referred to as a *channel*—between your Web server and your customer's Web browser.

In Internet commerce, a secure (SSL) channel can be opened to ensure that all communication between your Web server and your customer's Web browser remains confidential.

SEE ALSO

➤ *For more about SSL security, see page 19.*

Verifying Customer Identity

Although ensuring secure communications is important, other security issues are factors in online transactions. For instance, how can you verify that the customer to whom you are selling really is who he says he is? The two most common solutions you can use are

- *A Digital Signature.* This is an authentication method that utilizes public-key encryption to confirm identity.

- *A Digital Certificate.* This is a detailed business identification statement issued by a trusted third-party known as a certificate authority.

SEE ALSO

➤ *For more about Digital Signatures, see page 23.*

➤ *For more about Digital Certificates, see page 23.*

Protocols

Predetermined protocols also have been tested and designed to create safer, more efficient online financial transfers.

The *Secured Electronic Transaction* (SET) protocol is a collection of encryption and security specifications that were developed by the leading credit card companies. The SET protocol requires use of high-grade encryption, digital signatures, and digital certificates combined.

Case Study: Smart Commerce Japan

Smart Commerce Japan is a consortium of Visa International and other companies sponsored by the Japanese government established to try SET procedures with the latest in Smart Card technology. Managed by Visa and Toshiba Corporation, Smart Commerce Japan included additional Visa partners Visa Sumitomo Credit Service Co., Ltd., Daiei OMC, Inc., Nippon Shinpan Co., Ltd., Visa Japan Association, and Million Card Service Co., Ltd.

SET hasn't been fully adopted yet, but some extremely interesting trials are being conducted around the world. Smart Commerce Japan was developed as a way of testing SET methodology in combination with Smart Cards. A Smart Card is a credit card with an embedded microchip that can be used in a number of payment situations. Smart Commerce Japan distributed 30,000 such Smart Cards to citizens of Kobe, Japan to gauge their effectiveness.

One aspect of the trial involved Internet purchases. The Smart Cards were "reloadable," which means that funds could be electronically transferred to and stored on the actual card. Visa cardholders can now use special Internet kiosks, which have been placed in high-traffic department stores and train stations in Kobe, to make online credit card purchases. Cardholders have also been provided with home-based options for Internet shopping. At home, these cardholders can shop at an Internet mall and pay for their purchases by inserting a Visa chip card into a special Toshiba card reader attached to their personal computer. All purchases are protected using the Secure Electronic Transaction protocol.

Another protocol used primarily for business-to-business financial communication is *Electronic Data Interchange* (EDI). EDI is a system for conducting electronic transfers that has been around since before online financial transfers. I'll discuss EDI and the new OpenEDI standard later in this chapter.

Any, all, or none of the security options listed previously may be incorporated into your online financial transfers security policy.

Offering Your Customers Online Options

At present, there's no clear winner in the online financial transaction sweepstakes. Until the dust settles and one standard emerges, it's best to offer your customer a wide variety of payment options. After all, you want to make it as easy as possible for them to part with their money.

The following services are the leading contenders in the world of online transactions. Each has its particular strengths and weaknesses; each will appeal to its own range of customers.

CyberCash Services

In 1995, an electronic commerce company named CyberCash began providing secure Internet credit card services. The service soon became a popular online payment option for online merchants and consumers. CyberCash has grown steadily ever since. Millions of online transactions per month are currently processed using CyberCash secure Internet credit card services.

CyberCash, Inc.
CyberCash, Inc., headquartered in Reston, VA, was founded in August, 1994 by Bill Melton, founder of Verifone and Transaction Network Services; Dan Lynch, founder of Interop; and Steve Crocker; and Bruce Wilson.

CyberCash credit card services offer all the tools needed for your company to accept secure credit card transactions over the Internet, including

- Real-time authorization
- Voids
- Returns
- Account settlement

Now, before you sign up for an account, you should know a few things about CyberCash.

First, CyberCash does not use standard, export-grade 40-bit SSL encryption technology. (You can equate the number of bits to the degree of security; the more encryption bits, the higher the security.) Actually, CyberCash uses a much tougher 768-bit encryption technology. How do they do it? Well, the United States government has determined that Cyber-Cash's use of the encryption technology is safe and cannot be used to exchange secrets. CyberCash supports both standard SSL and SET transactions.

Second, CyberCash credit card services are only part of a complete product for merchants that the company calls The CashRegister 3. The CashRegister 3 system offers three payment collection options that you, as a merchant, can offer to your customers:

- Secure Online Credit Card Services is the current industry standard.

- CyberCoin enables cash payments in increments as small as $0.25. Although intended for electronic delivery of information, products, and services, it is useful for companies dealing with micropayments.

- PayNow Electronic Check enables consumers to pay their bills directly via the Web.

CyberCash secure online credit card services are the industry standard for online consumer purchases.

CyberCoin is the CyberCash answer to the micropayment problem. It supports small payments over the Internet for mostly digital goods. CyberCoin payments can also be used to purchase actual products with values of $10.00 or less.

FAQ: What is a "wallet" in an online retail transaction?

Wallet is the term used in online retail transactions to describe the customer's central repository of financial information. It is basically a graphical user interface that enables the customer to select what credit card information to enter with a point and a click.

Remember ease of use?

The CyberCoin is kept, along with customer credit card information, in the customer's *wallet*. Actually, funds always remain in bank accounts until settlement. No funds are kept within the customer's wallet software, your merchant server, or CyberCash's gateway servers.

You can even offer online "pay-per-view" services that can charge a customer $.25 or more per page. Basically, your company creates a "payment URL" on an HTML page that explains the product and displays the price, and the user clicks the payment URL to purchase the goods or service. The wallet enables you to keep spending for each view without asking you to go through the entire payment procedure.

As an added feature of the wallet, the customer has the capability to create and maintain spending rules known as confirmation threshold amounts. These rules enable the customer to automatically accept nominal "pay-per-view" charges. Purchases above the threshold amount will alert the customer and ask for confirmation, but those below the threshold amount are automatically accepted.

To round out its services, CyberCash offers an electronic checking and billing service known as PayNow electronic check service.

The PayNow service offers you, the merchant, the capability to collect bills electronically. It also encrypts consumer checking account information and offers it up in much the same way as credit card services. PayNow is available for business-to-business and business-to-consumer transactions.

First Virtual Services

First Virtual Holdings Incorporated, based in San Diego, CA, was—and still is—a pioneer in the offering of online payment services. First Virtual is the creator of one of the first online financial transfer systems ever used on the Internet.

First Virtual Holdings Incorporated

Founded in 1994, First Virtual Holdings Incorporated (NASDAQ: FVHI), is a leader in advanced communications and marketing systems for Internet commerce. The company pioneered secure online payment systems and now focuses on supplying an integrated system for relationship-based transactive messaging using standard email. First Virtual maintains its headquarters in San Diego, as well as a data center in Dallas. The company has strategic relationships with First Data Corporation, Paymentech, Inc., and GE Capital Corporation.

The First Virtual Internet Payment System is a safe, simple and secure way to sell on the Internet. But I still haven't told you how it is safe and secure.

The secret is in the mail—the email. First Virtual's Internet Payment System and Virtual-PIN service is an email-based financial transfer system. What's the difference? Time. And it is a big difference. The difference is in the processing of the customer's order and the time required for settlement of the transaction. We'll talk more about this in a moment.

For starters, both you and your customer are required to have a First Virtual account. First Virtual offers two types of merchant accounts:

- *Pioneer Seller account.* For small businesses, First Virtual offers the Pioneer Seller account. To get started, you need a secure email account, a bank account for collecting all the money, and a check drawn on the bank account. The account activation fee is $390.00. The Pioneer Seller account is designed to make it easy for new merchants to get going online.

- *Express account.* For larger, more established firms, First Virtual created the Express account, which requires that you possess a solid financial history, an excellent credit record, and an existing credit card merchant account at a bank. The account activation fee of $640.00 includes a check of your excellent credit record.

First Virtual offers one type of account for consumers. Consumers can register for a First Virtual Internet Payment System account online at its Web site (`www.firstvirtual.com`).

After receiving a customer's online registration, First Virtual calls the customer on the telephone and gathers the important financial information (credit card number). This is an important safeguard in the First Virtual system.

First Virtual then links the customer's information to a VirtualPIN without ever having to place sensitive credit card numbers online. An activation fee of $10.00 is charged for consumer VirtualPIN accounts.

Think that's it? Not quite. That's only the registration. Next comes the easy part. You get a customer who has money to spend. Let's take a look at the actual business transaction.

1. After you and your customer agree to a fair price for your product, the customer gives you a copy of his or her VirtualPIN.

2. You send a transfer request via email to First Virtual that includes your account code, the buyer's account code, and the price agreed upon.

3. First Virtual receives your transfer request and sends an email confirmation request to the customer's email account. This is another safeguard to assure that the buyer has approved the transaction.

4. The buyer sends back a Yes, No, or Check For Fraud response to First Virtual. If it is a yes response, First Virtual, at the appropriate time, deposits the money into your merchant account.

If you are an Express account holder, the funds are held for four business days to ensure that payment is received from the customer's credit card company (this is similar to standard credit card settlement terms).

If you are a Pioneer account holder, however, that last step can be a doozy. Pioneer account holders, because they are small-time operators, are required to wait a full 91 days for account settlement. The wait is to ensure that the purchaser pays the bill and that you deliver the goods or service. Credit card fraud by disreputable merchants is a growing problem, and a 91-day wait is the First Virtual solution.

That, then, is a First Virtual Internet Payment System transaction. Instead of relying on high-grade encryption, First Virtual has created a secure procedure that keeps confidential information confidential by never actually sending it over the Internet.

Security for a First Virtual transaction is as secure as your email account. Security could be compromised if a rogue hacker could manipulate an email server to send phony email and simultaneously filter Internet email to reroute First Virtual's confirmation request. With the current consumer interest in free email accounts, this scenario is difficult, but not out of the question.

Anonymity is probably the biggest question facing First Virtual's Internet Payment System. In the First Virtual transaction model, everyone knows who everyone else is—especially First Virtual. This knowledge, not surprisingly, is already being targeted by First Virtual for use as a sellable marketing tool known as the Interactive Messaging Platform.

For consumers, this means if someone buys a few golf balls with a First Virtual account, he shouldn't be surprised if he gets an email next week about the latest titanium driver offered at an unbelievably low, low price.

Your company can get access to detailed marketing and contact information about people who have already bought goods or services from you or someone like you, and you can contact the people inexpensively through email.

This marketing capability can be good or bad, depending on your perspective.

MilliCent

Digital Equipment Company's MilliCent microcommerce system enables you to quickly and easily sell information, magazine articles, cartoons, music, video clips, online games, and software to online consumers without a subscription.

Micropayments on trial

Currently, MilliCent is being offered on a trial basis as Digital expands the network of scrip vendors.

MilliCent was started as a solution to the electronic commerce problem of micropayments. MilliCent is primarily concerned with the capability of a merchant to offer Web content for a price, but as with all micropayment systems, it offers the capability to sell anything small.

Suppose, for example, you have content on your Web site that you believe is valuable. Usually this information is pulled from a database and presented to the consumer in a "search our database" format. The consumer searches the database, obtains results, and, voilà... you have a customer.

The traditional method of collecting for pay-per-view Web content has been subscription based. Basically, you convince your customers that the content is of such value that they should pay for a year's worth today.

MilliCent offers you the capability to charge your customers for the online content one page at a time. Instead of making your customer buy a year, you allow them to buy a penny's worth (or less—MilliCent even offers payments in the fraction of a cent range). This is impulse buying at its finest.

How does the micropayments system work? MilliCent is a complex conceptual system that differs from most other online payment options. MilliCent requires you to embrace two new ideas:

- Scrip is a form of micropayment (digital coin).

- A broker is a trusted third party that authenticates transactions and regulates the use of scrip.

As a merchant, you can contract with a broker to sell MilliCent scrip to your customers at face value. Real money flows outside of the MilliCent system from consumers through brokers and on to merchants like you.

Meanwhile, all online purchasing is completed using MilliCent scrip. Consumers do not give their credit card numbers to Web sites or maintain accounts and passwords with hundreds of merchants. Instead, they purchase scrip in advance from their favorite broker. Then they shop online and use the scrip as the method of payment.

Unlike most public key encryption-based security systems, the MilliCent microcommerce system uses secure hash functions as security. The functions are faster to compute and less restricted for exportation than public key signatures.

Case Study: Technological University of Munich

Founded in 1833, the Technische Universität München, or Technological University of Munich, serves as a polytechnic institute for research and learning. The University has approximately 21,000 students, 240 full professors, and 9,315 full-time employees.

A trial program using MilliCent has been set up as part of the digital library initiative at the Technological University of Munich. MilliCent is being used as the digital payment system for its online library, MeDoc, which specializes in high-quality multimedia computer science research. The primary use of the MilliCent trial is to make a new MeDoc feature available: pay-per-view sale of digital content. Journal articles typically cost $2 to $3, and individual pages are sold at $.02 to $.05. Encyclopedia and dictionary entries or the use of full-text indices fall into sub-cent pricing. If regular credit card purchasing were used instead of MilliCent, MeDoc would have to charge substantially more for its services just to offset the financial services fees.

MeDoc has found that substantially more users are attracted to the site since the MilliCent system was implemented. Previously, MeDoc used a subscription method, which was offputting to the consumer and meant more work for the staff; before MilliCent was implemented, each new user had to registered and authenticated and the subscription invoices had to be collected. Because MilliCent scrip is purchased through a broker, almost all the paperwork is eliminated.

Making Online Retail Transactions Happen

Everyone has heard of the big name online retailers that have made large profits from electronic commerce. Most of these retailers have one thing in common when it comes to exchanging money on the Internet—secure online credit card payment options for customers.

Online credit card transfers are quick and easy. All your customers need to do is type, click, and relax. And it is done in the privacy of their own homes, 24 hours a day, seven days a week. Consumers are highlighting the quality of convenience as a driving force in electronic commerce.

Merchants can enjoy the ease of secure online credit card services, as well. If words such as capture and settlement don't make you smile, then you should probably take a look at the next section.

Getting Paid in Online Retail

Running a business, in its simplest form, is a two-step process. The first step is selling a product. The second step is collecting the money. And the steps do not necessarily follow in that order.

Getting paid in online retail is much like getting paid in traditional storefront retail, except for one thing. Your customer is at home and is communicating with your secure Web server through a dial-up modem connection to the Internet. Simple, right?

1. To begin, you will need an account at an acquiring financial institution if you don't already have one. The acquiring financial institution deposits daily credit card totals into your account, minus the applicable fees. Generally, these arrangements are made with your merchant account bank.

2. Next comes the easy part. You get a paying customer. So, you agree to terms and the customer sends her financial data (credit card number) to your Web server.

3. Your Web server bundles the customer information with your own financial information and sends it together as an authorization request to the customer's credit card company requesting approval and authorization for the transaction.

4. The customer's credit card company returns an authorization response back to your server, telling it yes, no, or maybe. If the transaction is approved, the response will normally include a digital receipt called an authorization code. The authorization code serves as proof of authorization.

5. The next to the last step is called capture. It is the act of submitting the accounts involved for settlement.

6. Settlement, the actual change to account status to reflect the transaction, is often performed at night with other transactions in a bulk process at the bank.

Dealing with Micropayments

At this time, the standard online consumer transaction is a credit card purchase via the World Wide Web. Sometimes, however, this is not the most efficient method when dealing with small transactions.

The answer to the question, "Is it profitable to buy a pack of gum for $.25 with a credit card?" is usually no. The cost the merchant pays for each transaction makes it hard to strike a deal. Although a secure, online credit card payment is a popular choice for medium to large purchases, it is not cost efficient for purchases from $.25 to $10.00. A *micropayment* is this type of small payment.

FAQ: What is a micropayment?

A *micropayment* is an electronic transaction that is so small (usually $10.00 or less) that it is cost effective for merchants and banks to process electronically.

Micropayments will enable merchants to offer small, "pay-per-view" online transactions and inexpensive, downloadable products.

Micropayments present a challenge to the small, online entrepreneur who wants to offer electronic delivery of low-cost programs, digital images, sound clips, and other pay-per-view entertainment services.

Online commerce is expected to grow quickly as processing costs are reduced to levels that enable online retailers to make money from micropayments.

All the current industry leaders in online payment services are aggressively pursuing methods of obtaining the lowest processing cost per transaction possible.

Minimizing Retail Loss and Liability (Security Concerns)

What happens if you wake up tomorrow and learn that last month's profits evaporated because of credit card fraud, and, to make matters worse, you already shipped the product? You learn a valuable lesson.

As a business, your profitability can be maximized by reducing the opportunity for loss—loss prevention—and limiting your liability if loss does occur.

Security issues on the Internet have created a wide range of encryption technologies that vary in the amount of knowledge that is necessary for buyers and sellers to understand.

Creating a balance of consumer convenience and consumer protection should be at the top of your list of strategies for online financial transactions.

It is also important to note that you should always enable a third party to authenticate the transaction and offer some form of authorization code. This will ensure that you are not held liable for credit fraud.

Creating Online Business-to-Business Relationships

With this chapter's information concerning online retail, it might appear that secure, online business-to-business transactions may not play an important role in today's business world. Nothing could be further from the truth.

Quick, clear, concise communication can enhance any business relationship. When you couple that communication with reduced overhead and increased response time, you have a business tool that can quickly become the most valuable one in your arsenal.

Business-to-business communication is about relationships—relationships that you have with your suppliers, your financial institutions, your customers, your phone company, and the Internal Revenue Service (we can't leave them out!).

Actually, business-to-business transactions have been around for quite some time. Many companies have complex groups of networks that can span many miles, ensure secure communication, exchange financial information, and cost a large amount of money.

The Internet offers new opportunities for companies that want the maximum benefit of online communication for the least amount of capital.

There's Something Familiar About You

The most important difference between online retail transactions and online business-to-business transactions is that you and your partner are not strangers.

To quote an old phrase, "You know where they live."

Because you and your business partners have more than likely already agreed to the specifics of your transactions, you have a shared awareness of the goals and limits of your financial transfers.

Security levels, time of transaction, required confirmation, and many other transaction issues can be predetermined by you and your business partners. Your perspective in the transaction has changed significantly.

Instead of using a "lowest common denominator" policy for consumer transactions, for instance, you may determine that it is more sensible to hire a full-time information technology person to administer your business-to-business transactions.

What is left for you and your partners to determine is which protocols and security measures you would like to implement. Many companies have agreed to abide by a protocol of electronic transfer that was created before electronic commerce.

EDI and You

The protocol is known as Electronic Data Interchange (EDI). It was designed in the 1960s as a series of protocols to aid large business suppliers in communicating over private networks called Value Added Networks (VAN). VANs are still in use today, but are employed mainly by large corporations because of the high maintenance costs of the private networks.

Many exciting things have happened to EDI since the beginning of the Internet and electronic commerce.

Instead of using large private networks, most EDI service providers now give businesses the option of using the Internet to access EDI services remotely. Businesses that take advantage of this Internet EDI save money by reducing hardware and software costs because the work is performed at the EDI service provider location.

A new implementation of EDI known as *OpenEDI* has made the implementation of EDI between two business partners easier to initiate over the Internet.

Most of the time-saving secrets of OpenEDI are in the use of templates. The templates are predefined transaction specifications. OpenEDI templates have been created for all types of transactions, even transactions that bridge the gap between business sectors.

So now you know what EDI is and how it has changed, but what you really want to know is how it can help your business.

It is necessary to outline the scope of EDI to understand the benefits of EDI. EDI is not just a payment service. More than that, it is a data exchange service that can transfer data about any facet of your business. And when that happens, the process of doing business is running like a fine-tuned German luxury car engine.

FAQ: I have heard of both EDI and FEDI. What is the difference?

Electronic Data Interchange (EDI) is a broad scope of protocols that can be used to exchange data of all kinds.

Financial Electronic Data Interchange (FEDI) is the part of EDI that concerns financial transactions. It is used only in business-to-business transactions.

Shipping, receiving, sales, marketing, financial, and inventory information can all be streamlined via EDI within your internal network, increasing overall efficiency and ensuring clear, quick, concise company communications.

Coming to Grips with Anonymity

The knowledge of consumer spending habits can sometimes be sensitive, inside information. Many online consumers are concerned that by using the Web, someone, somewhere is tracking their buying habits. It may very well be true. Will electronic commerce lead to an Orwellian future?

On the other hand, law enforcement and intelligence agencies are concerned that total anonymity online will protect criminals and hide illegal activity. This is the reason that top-grade encryption technology cannot be exported from the United States.

Consumers and merchants alike are debating the concept of anonymity in online financial transfers. All companies and products for use in online transactions must consider the issue of anonymity.

Many of the questions concerning anonymity are being answered by the consumer's willingness to purchase goods online. So far, the rule has been if consumers are willing to risk it, merchants are willing to track customer purchases as a source of marketing information.

CHAPTER 19

Building the Virtual Storefront

- The "big picture" as it pertains to e-commerce

- The requirements for a successful virtual storefront

- When to build it with internal resources or employ external resources

- How to choose the right site host for your needs

- Tips for a profitable online catalog

Components of E-commerce

A virtual storefront is but one part of a bigger picture, electronic commerce. To build your e-commerce solution, you may need several basic products and services to create a virtual storefront. Depending on your particular needs, all the components listed below may not be required, but it is always good to know your options.

- Software to build an online catalog, preferably one with a shopping cart feature

- A Web hosting company (unless you are hosting it internally)

- A payment-processing service for real-time credit card transactions

- A merchant account to transfer funds

Real-time payments

A merchant account provider coordinates the transfer of funds between your bank, a payment processing service, and a customer's bank. It is this service which facilitates real-time payment processing.

SEE ALSO

➤ *For more on protecting your virtual storefront from being hacked, see page 19.*

➤ *For more on evaluating the total cost of software ownership, see page 29.*

➤ *For information on business to business e-commerce, see page 177.*

E-commerce Varieties

As any good businessperson knows, before you can sell anything, you need to know who it is you are selling to. This rule applies to a virtual storefront, as well. When considering your target audience, also consider the following:

- *Employees.* Consider how to enable them to act as better sales tools.

- *Existing customers.* Consider how your site will enable you to "upgrade" your existing business and customer service.

- *The press.* Targeting the press can help generate positive publicity.

- *Consultants.* Consultants can help you generate positive "word of mouth" as they use your site as a reference to generate new business for themselves.

In general, two main types of electronic commerce exist. You are selling a product or service either directly to a consumer or to another business. Fundamentally, the e-commerce process you go through for each type is similar, with the variations discussed in the following sections.

Online Sales to Other Businesses

Business-to-business commerce can be referred to as an *extranet*. When setting up a virtual storefront to sell to other businesses, you should familiarize yourself with some special considerations that are not a normal part of online sales to the general public.

SEE ALSO

➤ *For more about extranets, see page 195.*

- *Electronic Data Interchange.* EDI is a term applied to the exchange of data between businesses, such as inventory quantity and backorder status. But it is more than that. Each type of EDI transaction has a standard specifying the transport protocols and specific data formats. It's important to follow the specific standard used in your industry. The book industry, for example, uses EDI 823 X12 standard for transmitting title status and bibliographic information between publishers and resellers.

- *Custom logins.* You may wish to have a secure site to enable only selected businesses access to sensitive information. After you know who your users are and what preferences they require, you can tailor their experience to fit their needs. This is also called *personalization*, which is covered later in this chapter.

- *Custom catalogs.* After you identify who the business is (as with the above login), it is possible, and most likely preferable, to customize your product selection, whether it is soft-goods or hard-goods, to the needs of your customer. This applies to predetermined discounts as well as payment options. The example in Figure 19.1 is a site set up by Macmillan Computer Publishing for use by Amazon.com and other online resellers.

Case Study: Macmillan Computer Publishing, Inc.
Macmillan Computer Publishing (MCP) is the largest publisher of computer reference materials in the world.

Macmillan Computer Publishing (the publisher of this book) sells a lot of titles through the major online booksellers, including Amazon.com. Therefore, MCP makes sure Amazon.com has the most accurate information on its titles, including the best descriptions, book cover images, and even the stock status. MCP keeps Amazon.com and other online booksellers up to speed through a process over the Internet. By providing Amazon.com with the sales tools it needs to present a clear, accurate picture to the consumer, MCP ultimately sells more books.

MCP and Amazon.com established a standard format in which they exchange standard title information. This is a simple file format to which MCP writes its title data. The file is then stored on a secure area on its site for Amazon.com to pick up once a month. This file contains changes to existing titles carried by Amazon.com, as well as new title information for books soon to be published.

Financial transactions are accomplished through a separate process via a more standardized EDI format, which does not take place over the Internet but over a Value Added Network (as covered in Chapter 10, "Enabling Direct Distribution").

Figure 19.1 A business-to-business catalog will contain quite different information than one intended for consumers.

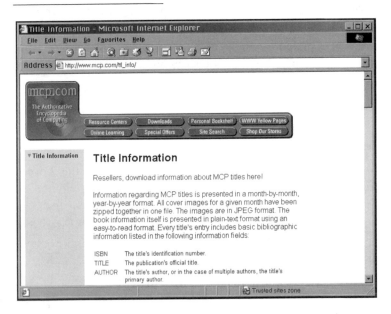

Direct Consumer Sales

In selling your product to the general consumer, you'll need to consider additional requirements over and above those in business-to-business sales..

- *Distribution.* Consider whether your current warehouse/distribution system is tasked. Can your current distribution system take on the added burden of a successful virtual store? Although the Internet can quickly and efficiently supply you with an additional revenue stream, it can also place your company under a very uncomfortable microscope. Internet shoppers expect quick turnaround.

SEE ALSO

➤ *For more on analyzing your distribution system for e-commerce see page 123.*

- *Customer support.* Your support team will require additional training on the possible problems that may arise as a result of doing business on the Web. Problems that may not have anything to do with your virtual storefront can and will be attributed to you by uninformed consumers.

- *Web site aesthetics.* This is a delicate balance. Consumers want graphically rich sites, yet do not want to wait for heavily graphic Web pages to download over their 28.8K modems. Studies indicate that the sites consumers find easiest to navigate—and therefore, where they find and purchase the item they are seeking— are simple, text-linked sites. Yet, when they are asked which sites they like the best, they picked the graphic-oriented sites. So you need to ask yourself whether you are looking to impress or to sell product. With careful Web design, you can do both.

- *Cross-selling.* Consumers may not be aware of all the different, but related, products/services you offer. Your virtual store can be designed to present the user with suggestions for related items, based on previous purchases. A great example of this is Amazon.com. In Figure 19.2, I've selected a title on designing Web sites, and Amazon.com is suggesting other books that I might care to read.

Figure 19.2 Amazon.com uses cross-selling to increase sales.

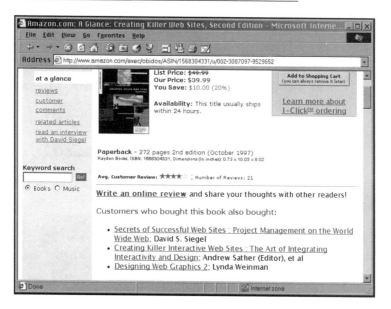

The Successful Online Storefront

Designing a virtual storefront is not unlike designing a real-world store. You have to consider traffic patterns throughout the store, establish colorful displays to attract customers, and—above all—make it easy for customers to give you their money.

The main part of your virtual storefront is the online catalog. The successful online catalog must offer shoppers everything a traditional catalog offers, such as clearly written product descriptions, color photos, and so on. It also must allow shoppers to easily navigate through-out the virtual store, with clear directions so they can navigate between sections or depart-ments. Stores such as the KillerApp Computer Channel, shown in Figure 19.3, offer links to various departments as well as the most commonly selected items in particular categories.

Figure 19.3 KillerApp Computer Channel (`www.killerapp.com`) is a good example of an easily navigable site that is visually appealing while completely dynamic.

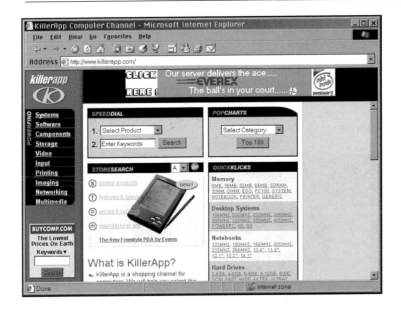

Below, I've listed some basic pointers that all effective virtual storefronts share and that you can apply to your virtual storefront design.

- A corporate mission or philosophy statement.

- Product statistics regarding sales trends, such as "top 10 best sellers."

- A home page that conveys a clear, consistent message regarding the company, its mer-chandise, and its "in-store" activities.

- Ease of navigation, making it simple for customers to shop the store and find the items they want.

- Sharp pricing.

- Regular sales promotions.

- Invest in displays of impulse merchandise and change them as often as budgets will permit.

- Incorporate value-added services, such as gift reminders and address finders to stimulate repeat purchases.

- Minimize the number of clicks required to purchase your product. Try to keep the clicks to two, if possible.

- Provide superior customer service that exceeds the customers' expectations.

- Make "need to know" information readily accessible.

- Clearly articulate return policies and other product guarantees.

- Facilitate rapid checkout through storing of customer profiles and buying histories.

- Drive traffic to the site through online advertising, testing the placement of embedded products within banner advertising on targeted sites that drive shoppers directly to the product rather than to the homepage.

The ability to create customized products may also be a requirement for some virtual storefronts, such as a merchant selling PCs or network routers. The sheer magnitude of options these merchants offer prohibits successful merchants from publishing static online catalogs.

In addition, an online catalog must be an engaging experience for customers. Hire professional graphic designers or involve your company's design department in the design of your catalog. This will give your site the professional look it needs to distinguish itself from the "Mom & Pop" stores that can be readily found with the same search terms used to find you.

Just what is the potential?

Odyssey, a market research firm, reports that 7 million households made an online purchase during the last six months of 1997, compared to 3.2 million a year earlier. Forrester Research reports that shoppers spent $2.4 billion on the Net in 1997, compared to $600 million in 1996. They predict that figure will double in 1998.

Forrester Research predicts that by 2001, the amount of purchases made online will jump to $17 billion, up from $2.4 billion in 1997. The Consumer Direct Cooperative predicts that 200,000 U.S. households will be buying food and household goods and services online in 1998. By the year 2007, that number is estimated to reach as much as 15 to 20 million.

At this point, you may be wondering whether a virtual store is something you can tackle in-house, or whether you should seek an expert(s) to build one for you. You have many options here, as well as combinations of internal/external development. But to make an informed decision, you should start by researching Web sites that offer products or services similar to yours. As with any programming task, the more functionality you wish to include in your site, the more difficult (and expensive) it will be to develop. Assessing the competition may help in deciding what functionality your site will need to compete effectively. The bottom line is maximizing your profit, not just your sales.

Researching Similar Sites

Before you begin making decisions on how to build your storefront, you should research existing, successful sites. Good places to start are the Internet search engines such as AltaVista, Yahoo!, Infoseek, Excite, and even Netscape's Netcenter (http://excite.netscape.com/shopping/). One quick way to search eight of the top search engines simultaneously is to use a tool that searches the search engines. A few good ones are available and will return results with various degrees of usefulness. One of the easiest to use is also free. WebFerret©, by FerretSoft LLC, shown in Figure 19.4, can be downloaded from the company's Web site at www.ferretsoft.com.

Figure 19.4 WebFerret can search multiple search engines simultaneously.

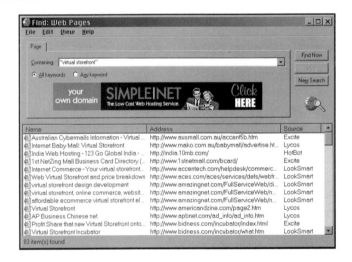

This exercise will also show you how hard it really is to find things on the Internet. The saying, "if you build it, they will come" is not necessarily true on the Internet. Increasing your visibility in search engines is a black art—and a topic for another book.

SEE ALSO

➤ *For more on increasing your visibility in search engines, see page 196.*

Another great way to find sites is through online magazine reviews. Sites such as Zdnet (www.zdnet.com) include online versions of their magazines, such as *PCWeek*, *Sm@rtReseller*, and *PC Magazine*. These trade magazines regularly review Web sites and offer tips on how to improve them. A recent review by *PCWeek* of 500 top corporate users of Web technologies can be found at www.fasttrack98.pcweek.com.

After assessing your competition and your internal resources, you're ready to look at the software tools available and decide whether to outsource your virtual storefront or build it internally.

Choosing the Right Software

One can go about building an online catalog in myriad ways, some of which are more difficult to build but more flexible to modify than "off the shelf" solutions. An online catalog can be built from scratch with standard programming tools such as C++ or Visual Basic. If you are using internal resources for your online catalog, then there's not much a typical businessperson needs to read about here. Those tools and software components will be chosen by your IT staff. However, if you don't have the internal resources or programming talent for in-house development, then I can point you in a few directions. Wading through the available choices of online catalog products to find the right one for your situation is the first step in producing a successful online catalog.

Many factors influence which product to use, ranging from the cost of the software to its flexibility, ease of installation and maintenance, and report-generation capabilities. iCat's (www.icat.com) entry-level, standard edition of Commerce Suite, for instance, costs $1,495, and a Professional version aimed at resellers costs $3,995. Microsoft's Site Server Commerce Edition costs as much as $5,599, depending on user licenses required, but it will provide more flexibility than iCat's product, although at the cost of ease of initial setup. Still another e-commerce product, called Transact 4, is from Open Market (www.openmarket.com), who won't even put a price on its Web site. I guess if you have to ask.... The point is that it really depends on what you want to do and how much you are willing to pay to get it.

Make sure your software is secure

A Lucent Technologies scientist recently discovered a way to crack the encryption code used in secure Web sites. This is the Secure Sockets Layer or SSL, a key element in online commerce. The good news is many companies, including Netscape Communications, Microsoft, and Security Dynamics Technologies' RSA Data Security unit, have already issued a patch to fix this. When you shop for software, security is a key concern.

One key factor that is a must for any good online catalog product is tight integration with a *Relational Database Management System*, or RDBMS. Most will support *Open Database Connectivity* (ODBC) compliant databases. Although this is acceptable, even tighter integration, such as pass-through user authentication can be found in products such as Microsoft's Site Server, Commerce Edition. This product is tightly woven into the company's SQL Server RDBMS. These are things the shopper may never know, but your Webmaster or online catalog manager will surely appreciate.

FAQ: RDBMS versus ODBC?

A relational database management system is a type of database that is robust enough to handle e-commerce transactions. Companies such as Oracle, Sybase, Microsoft, and Computer Associates make one. ODBC or open database connectivity is one standard way some software will interact with an RDBMS.

Internal Development

Although many companies today use a mix of internal and external resources for their Internet projects, most are now leaning heavily toward in-house development. Probably, as many reasons for this exist as the number of companies, but the bottom line is that no one knows better what a company's needs are than those who work there. IT departments are also finding that there is no mystery to Web development. It follows the same project cycle as more familiar software development. Also, the tools used to build and maintain a Web site are more mature now, and more of them are available from which you can choose.

Most internal IT organizations already have standards that must be met for any development project. If your company has standardized on Windows NT as its networking software of choice, for example, you may be required to use Internet Information Server (IIS) as your Web server. IIS comes with every version of NT Server sold today. If you are using IIS as your Web server, you will most likely want to use FrontPage to design and manage your site. Again, FrontPage is included with NT Server. However, if your company relies on UNIX as its backbone, then Netscape SuiteSpot may be required because IIS only runs on NT. You get the picture. Building a consensus is a good rule for all projects and, in the case of internal Web projects and your IT department, a must.

If your internal standard is UNIX, ICentral's ShopSite may be the quickest and least painful way to build your first online catalog. ShopSite software is an online store creation system that enables merchants to build and maintain catalogs of products to sell on the Internet. It includes tools for site creation and management, sales and traffic statistics, secure encrypted transactions, and online order fulfillment.

ShopSite Manager is for the small- to medium-sized business manager who wants to begin marketing and selling products on the Internet, or who currently has a Web site but wants to take the next step of selling products online. The product features easy data-entry screens, product-layout templates, shopping baskets, secure credit card handling, site statistics, email notification of orders, online order tracking, and customizable payment, shipping, and tax options.

ShopSite Pro is a secure, online store creation and management application designed to meet the needs of site developers and merchants who are seeking to build a professional storefront. ShopSite Pro, shown in Figure 19.5, includes real-time credit card authorization, a site search engine, detailed sales and traffic statistics, and features that make handling larger product databases (2000 products and higher) easier and more efficient.

Figure 19.5 An example of an online catalog built with ShopSite.

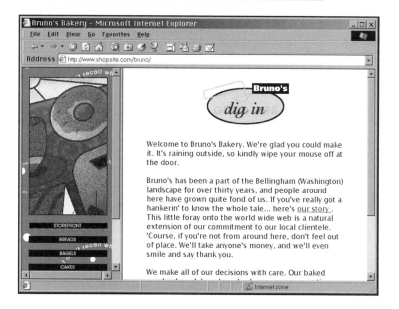

For the experienced Internet developer, Netscape Commerce Server is an industrial-strength set of e-commerce application servers that can arguably be called the best solution for UNIX environments with world-class Web sites.

Netscape's electronic commerce software product offerings come in three basic groups: what Netscape calls its Commerce Platform, its Commercial Applications suite, and the Netscape SuiteTools application-development tools. These tools are not for the fainthearted. They use Netscape's own proprietary programming language called LiveWire. The good news is that it is much like JavaScript, which has been the de facto standard for browser scripting for the past few years; so experienced Web developers will already be familiar with the code.

Netscape's solutions require much more building of your own applications, and it is up to you to glue them together—in contrast to products such as ShopSite.

I know that some people out there would say Linux, a free UNIX derivative, and its Apache Server are superior to Netscape's offerings, and from a purely technical standpoint, they may have a valid point; however, I can't recommend a server solution with no real support solution. No one person has accountability for Linux, and no one group exists to go to reliably for answers to your questions. You get what you pay for.

If your internal networking is provided via Windows NT, then a good out-of-box, comprehensive solution might be iCat Commerce Publisher. This software provides everything you need to easily collect and organize product information into a database, as well as preview, publish, and manage catalogs from one place.

With Commerce Publisher Standard, you can create a database of your products, organize information into unlimited category sections, choose the design for your catalog from a variety of predefined iCat Layout Templates, preview staging catalogs locally on any desktop computer (even without an Internet Web server), and receive, process, and track orders electronically 24 hours a day. The downside is loss of flexibility. If you don't like the predefined templates, you need the Pro version.

The Commerce Publisher Professional is for technically savvy users who need advanced features and the ability to customize catalogs, including a syntax checker for HTML pages and the ICL (iCat Carbo Command Language) wizard to create new commands. The Professional Edition also includes support for a multi-user client/server Data Entry Manager, and it comes with additional plug-ins for advanced indexing, searching, user tracking, sale pricing, implementing member discounts, and more.

iCat also has the ability for small merchants, strapped for cash, to build their own store, completely online, free of charge. Figure 19.6 shows the start of a new online catalog. Figure 19.7 shows the iCat mall you become part of after you have completed your catalog.

Microsoft's Site Server Commerce Edition is the better choice for those NT merchants that have greater requirements. Site Server is the product used by companies such as Dell Computer (www.dell.com), Barnes & Noble (www.barnesandnoble.com) (see Figure 19.8), and The Gap (www.gap.com) to conduct commerce, analyze usage, and track the thousands of visitors they receive each week. If your in-house programming standard is Visual Basic, then Site Server is the only way to go. It was designed with the VB programmer in mind and is easily extensible to that language.

Figure 19.6 Small merchants can create an online catalog free online.

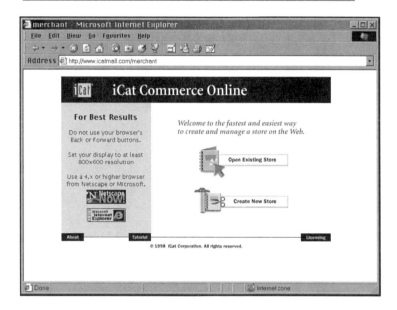

Figure 19.7 After you complete your free, online catalog, you become part of the iCat mall.

Figure 19.8 Barnes & Noble is a relative late comer to the online arena, no doubt due to the enormous success of Amazon.com.

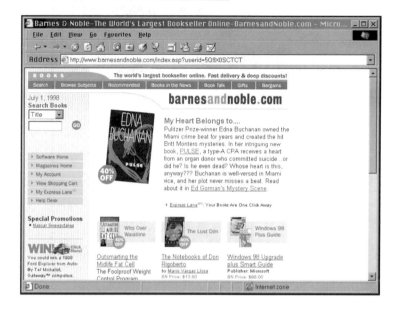

An online checklist

IBM provides a valuable resource on its Web site called the IBM Commerce Assistant (http://advisor.internet.ibm.com/inet.nsf/eye?OpenForm). It's free, and it will help you evaluate the issues involved (as IBM sees them) in trying to market a product or service on the Internet.

External Development

Many companies, large and small, have opted to farm out the development of their Web site to companies who specialize in professional e-commerce Web development. For the company new to the Internet, this is the fastest—and possibly the best— way to go. It's not always an issue of money, either. Fry Multimedia (www.frymulti.com) designed 1-800-FLOWERS and Eddie Bauer's e-commerce sites, among others. Ford Motor Company's customer care site (see Figure 19.9) was built by Sigma6 (www.sigma6.com).

Figure 19.9 Ford contracted with Sigma6 to develop its customer care site.

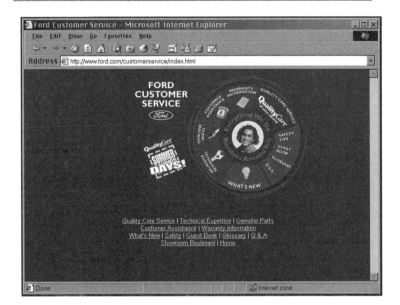

The bottom line here is that some of the best e-commerce sites today are contract sites. If you are new to e-commerce or the Internet, then one of these design firms may be just the ticket. You can always take over the site after it's developed. External development also provides you with a "proof of concept" for your online product. If your product or service doesn't take off online, you can't blame it on naive Web site design. The downside is that you will not be developing the skill set internally that you will need one day.

Internet World Magazine published a listing of the top 124 design firms. You can get that listing at this Web address:

```
http://www.internetworld.com/print/1997/12/01/undercon/19971201-webdesign.html
```

I know it's long, but it's a good place to start if you don't already have a firm in mind.

SEE ALSO

➤ *For outsourcing information technology, see page 151.*

Choosing Your Site's Host

With more than 3,000 Internet Service Providers offer hosting platforms for electronic commerce, you could say you have your pick. Some focus on a particular technology, such as Windows NT hosting. Most will offer both UNIX and NT.

If you have picked out a tool set you wish to publish or maintain your online catalog with, that may be a criteria to use to weed out vendors that don't support it. FrontPage 98, for example, is a widely popular site building/editing tool from Microsoft. It requires server extensions for it to work to its fullest ability. Therefore, a potential site host must support FrontPage 98 server extensions, and not just enable you to use the FrontPage Editor to design your HTML.

Other factors to look for include, but are not limited to:

- *High bandwidth access to the Internet.* The greater the ISP connection to the Internet, the less chance the user will experience a slowdown to purchasing your product.

- *High availability.* This must be 24 hours a day, 7 days a week, with an uptime in the 99% range. If the site is not functioning, you can't sell your product.

- *Firewall security.* As mentioned in Chapter 2, "Risk Assessment," firewalls help keep out the hackers.

- *Email accounts.* One or more email accounts should be provided for you to answer questions, customer complaints, suggestions for improvements, or merely to communicate with your customer base.

- *Unlimited email forwarding.* If you were to switch ISPs, email forwarding enables you to still receive email sent to your old address from customers, who didn't get the notice or just don't know how to change their address books.

- *Anonymous File Transfer (FTP).* A standard way of transferring large numbers of files over the internet, FTP can utilize a user ID and password-authentication scheme. Anonymous is used when you want to enable everyone to access a file or directory on your server.

- *Web site statistics.* You will need to know how many people visit your site each day, week, and month; how many pages were viewed; which pages were viewed the most; what was the best referring URL; from what page the users leave your site the most, and so on.

- *Additional disk space.* As with any computer, the more disk space, the better.

- *Custom CGI programming.* Common Gateway Interface is one of the most used programming methods to perform actions on a Web page.

- *Audio and video streaming.* Audio and video streaming enables the user to start the playback of large audio or video files before the entire file has been downloaded to his or her PC. This helps prevent lag time, where the user is just sitting and waiting for something to happen.

Pricing for the electronic commerce service should include installation of the Web server (if you are not renting one from the site host), transfer of content to the service, registration of your URL and domain, support of certificates, and firewall configurations. The hosting agreement should enable companies to provide content on an ongoing basis, and also allow for advertising agencies and business trading partners to be given access to create content for the hosted site.

New players are showing up in this area every day. This means more competition for your business. IBM has recently thrown its hat into this arena, and that's no surprise. According to a recent study by Forrester Research, revenues for hosting complex business sites were $213 million in 1997, and are projected to increase more than tenfold over the next two years, reaching an estimated $2.8 billion in 2000.

Check with your local ISP (Internet Service Provider) as well. Many times they also offer site hosting in addition to Internet Access. Macmillan Computer Publishing uses a local ISP primarily for its bandwidth. For MCP to get the kind of Internet bandwidth that the ISP already has, it would require network connections that would increase the cost of business by ten times what they are now.

Some of the top providers in this market are GTE Internetworking, Digex, ANS Communications (America Online), and PSINet. A comprehensive listing of Web hosts can be found, of course, online at `www.webhostlist.com/`.

Collecting Product Information

After you've settled on an online catalog product (or even decided to develop your own from scratch), the next logical step in building an online catalog is collecting the catalog information. This includes the names, prices, descriptions and the location of any supporting files (such as GIFs, PICs, or scanning existing images), and sound and video, that you want to use to represent the products or services you plan to market in your online catalog.

Intergration with Standard Databases

After you have all that product information, it should be integrated into a *relational database management system* or RDBMS, which offers your business the following benefits:

- The RDBMS enables customers to search for products in a variety of ways.
- Site managers can take advantage of the reporting tools within the RDBMS.
- RDBMS can handle catalog scalability as your site (and product line) grows.

With flat files, such as FileMaker, Excel, or Word documents, customers are limited to a static view of the catalog. Database-driven Web pages are created dynamically, with the HTML generated on-the-fly. Moreover, database-driven catalogs such as the ones in Figures 19.10 and 19.11, enable online businesses to create customer-specific or *personalized* views of the catalog. This is a particularly crucial capability in the business-to-business end of e-commerce.

FAQ: What's a flat file?

A flat file is simply a list of information. There is no way to relate, for example, a customer number with the customer's name or email address without a manual lookup. A RDBMS will relate these items.

Figure 19.10   KillerApp Computer Channel uses Microsoft's ASP to enable dynamic menu reconfiguration based on items selected from the list on the left.

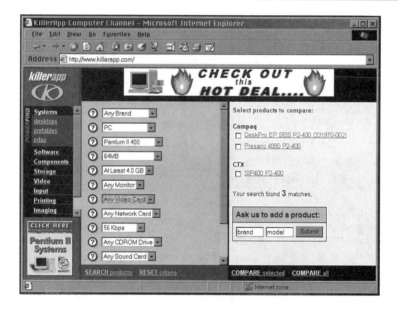

In the consumer world, you may have only one price for a product, but in business-to-business commerce, pricing is often different for each customer, and that increases the complexity and cost of any online transaction. Database-driven catalogs can reduce this complexity by producing customized Web pages for each customer.

Database-driven Web catalogs also enable close tracking of customer shopping habits. When shoppers visit the site, they can peruse a RDBMS of thousands to tens of thousands of products or services.

Figure 19.11   After narrowing down your choices, killerapp presents you with a table for product comparison.

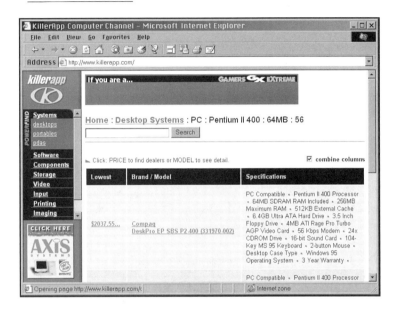

The RDBMS can also be used to track site statistics: who's coming into the site, where they come from, where they go to. This is important to companies who wish to sell advertising space on their site. Advertisers will want to know how many people visited you, in what time frame, and how long they spent looking at which page, so they can target the page that will maximize their return. It's a much more personal and targeted approach than any kind of hard copy catalog can provide.

Navigation and Organization

After you've collected that information and stored it in a database, you'll want to organize your catalog and determine its hierarchy, its sections and subsections, and where each item falls in the catalog.

With Web catalogs, the most important thing with design is navigation and organization. With a paper catalog, people can flip from page to page. With the Web, however, they have to navigate, so online commerce developers have to spend time thinking about how people are likely to search on the site.

In designing the catalog itself, it's also important to pay attention to cross-sell relationships that generally are not part of standard hierarchy.

When developing an online site's organization, it's important to realize that the Web is a different medium, and you have to design for the medium. Merely putting up a static Web site won't work. You have to offer more than the hard copy catalog to generate orders, such as enabling the user to search by keyword, category, or in natural language for exactly the product or service they require. Enable the user to "configure" his own product, like Dell does with its PCs, or offer the user more than any hard copy catalog could ever physically hold, like Amazon.com does with its book listings.

Designing the "Look and Feel"

One underlying thing to keep in mind when designing your virtual storefront is that the reason it exists is to sell product/service, not to wow the shopper with your technical savvy. Don't get me wrong; I don't mean you should simply have a page with a 1-800 number saying, "Call to place your order," but don't let yourself get sidetracked on technology that doesn't help sell a thing. Ask yourself, will this animated logo help me sell my product?

Content is king

Research conducted by the Gartner Group in 1996 suggests that 90% of business Web sites are not delivering content and services that meet their customers' requirements. As a result of this, Gartner predicts that 75% of Web sites will need to be rewritten or re-architected within the first 12 months of operation. The study suggests that users do not want content such as corporate descriptions and press releases. They want useful applications, such as advanced interactive technical support and the ability to query databases to get answers to their questions. They want to be able to access product information that specifically meets the needs they define.

Use navigational toolbars along the top or left side of the page. Offer a table of contents or index for your site. Site maps help user find things you didn't think of; they're kind of a catchall.

Remember not to use technologies that will not work in all browsers. Dynamic HTML (DHTML), for example, is a slick way of creating animated "layers" on a page that gracefully degrade if the browser doesn't support DHTML. Unfortunately, Netscape and Microsoft are in disagreement on how this should be implemented. Netscape still holds the edge over Microsoft in sheer number of users, but not by much. Therefore, if you choose Netscape's DHTML implementation over Microsoft's, you are cutting out almost half of your potential shoppers. For extranets, this is less of an issue.

With Web sites, design can have a significant impact on who can visit your site. Consider which versions of the browsers are out there. A lot of 3.0 version browsers are still surfing the wires and doing just fine. Those users may or may not ever upgrade to the latest version of their favorite browser. This is where you can run into version incompatibility, and implementing a technology that is available in a new browser may have negative repercussions in older versions. In this case, implementing JavaScript, for example, works predictably for Netscape 3 versions, but not Internet Explorer 3. The following table shows you the JavaScript version and the corresponding browser with which it works best.

JavaScript version	Browser needed to run:
JavaScript 1.1	Nav3+, IE4+
JavaScript 1.2	Nav4+, IE4+

With all that said, it is still possible to have cross-browser compatibility if careful consideration is given to your storefront design. Netscape has released documentation on its Web site that explains how. You can view it online at `http://developer.netscape.com/program/devedge_news/index.html?content=current.html#1`.

Less Is More

In general, a good storefront will employ a minimum of graphics and clutter. This also speeds download time for modem shoppers. The goal is to keep the number of mouse clicks someone needs to perform to purchase any product to a minimum—two, if possible. Good examples of this are Amazon.com (`www.amazon.com`) (see Figure 19.12) and Eddie Bauer (`www.eddiebauer.com`).

Figure 19.12 Amazon.com likes to keep the path to purchasing as uncluttered as possible.

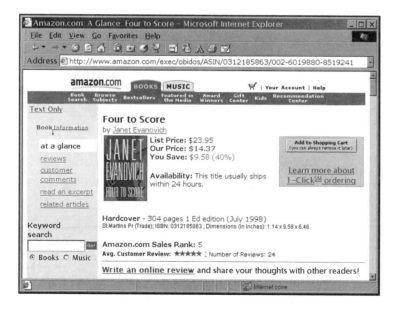

Make Merchandise Easy to Find

Shoppers can't buy what they can't find. All too often, it amazes me that I'm able to find anything on some sites.

Amazon.com's home page presents the shopper with a keyword search and subject search in the left hand column, as shown in Figure 19.13, and a best seller book I can click and get to a buy screen in two clicks of the mouse.

Figure 19.13 Amazon.com does a good job of streamlining the purchase process.

Eddie Bauer's "shop" screen follows the same concept, as shown in Figure 19.14. All the searching and navigation tools are located on the left, and browsing and quick purchases occur in the main portion of the screen.

Personalization

Organizations with hundreds or thousands of products, or those with products that are complex or offer dozens or hundreds of configurations, face even greater challenges in developing online catalogs.

Gateway2000, for instance, uses a self-developed "configurator," as shown in Figure 19.15, that enables a customer to pick a standard PC system online, then select a variety of different hardware configurations, such as the size of a hard disk drive or the amount of RAM, from drop-down lists. The customer can then see what the price differentials for different configurations are—and then the customer can hit the order button.

Figure 19.14 The customer has no need to guess how to find a product here.

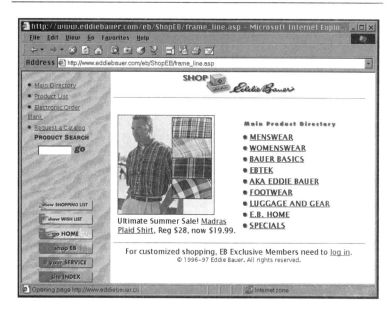

Figure 19.15 Gateway's custom PC configurator enables the customer to pick and choose PC options.

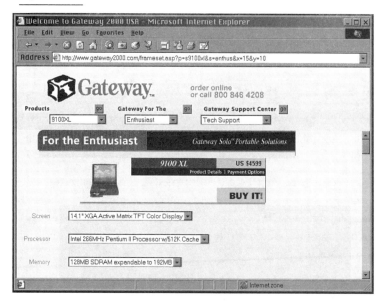

Figure 19.16 shows how Microsoft uses the Personalization capabilities of its Site Server Commerce Edition to provide a *portal* to the Internet for millions of Windows users.

FAQ: What is a portal?

A portal is a term used to describe the home page or service a user would use to start exploration of the Internet.

Figure 19.16   With *personalization*, Microsoft enables users to "configure" its home page to user preferences.

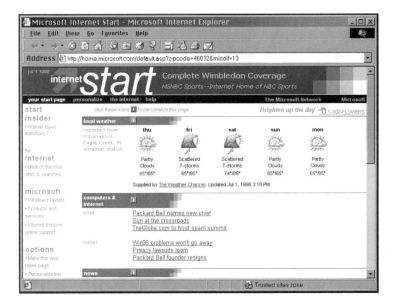

Netscape uses its Publishing System Server in combination with Verity Index Server to provide similar results. Macmillan Computer Publishing uses parts of each, along with a lot of custom CGI scripting to build its Personal Bookshelf, as seen in Figure 19.17.

Other commercial products require Web developers to build specialized product catalogs, or databases, then publish them with vendor-specific server applications. Calico Technology's Concinity product configurator, for example, enables organizations to use its Workbench development environment to build a product model as well as the end-user screens that describe the products or services.

SAQQARA Systems's Step Search Enterprise products enable online customers to search for specific configurations from among thousands of products available, but not to configure a custom product. They give users so-called parametric search capabilities, which enable shoppers to search for products based on a variety of product features, or parameters.

Figure 19.17   The MCP Personal Bookshelf enables users to "check out" up to 5 online books
from about 200.

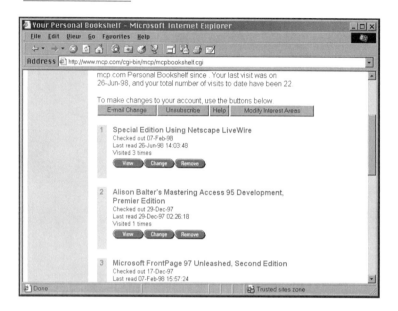

These products naturally add to the cost of doing business on the Web. Concinity, for instance, typically costs several hundreds of thousands of dollars, depending on configuration and number of users. SAQQARA's parametric search engine, Step Search Enterprise, starts at $20,000 per CPU.

CHAPTER 20

Entrepreneurial Business Models

- Web entrepreneurship overview
- Types of Web businesses
- Revenue sources for Web sites
- Evaluating Web business opportunities
- Financing the venture

Deciding to Become a Web Entrepreneur

Many of us have sat at our desks, wishing we owned the company so we could change things and make them better not only for ourselves, but for our employees.

Sometimes the situation is so bad that several people in a company become dissatisfied, and they start talking about quitting and forming a partnership and doing things "their way."

What's wrong with this picture?

Several things stand out as examples of the way many entrepreneurial ventures (or adventures) start out—and also why so many of these businesses fail.

Entrepreneurship is a very attractive way of life. Notice we said attractive—not easy. Entrepreneurship is actually very difficult for several reasons:

- Long lead time from start up to success
- Tremendous amount of resources required
- Uncertainty the business model will work

So what is the right approach to entrepreneurship on the Web? Several steps lead to becoming a successful entrepreneur. Some of the steps that successful entrepreneurs have used as they plan to start a new business include

- Inventory your strengths, contacts, and resources

- Determine the business model that best fits your strengths and resources

- For new businesses, write a complete business plan

- For companies adding a Web component to an existing business, develop a business case

- For both startup and existing businesses, prepare an implementation plan

Many entrepreneurs have succeeded beyond their wildest dreams. These executives have worked 60 to 80 hour weeks for several years to reap the benefits of entrepreneurship:

- Control over how their business is run

- Become an expert in their industry

- Receive tremendous financial rewards

Many steps are taken to becoming a successful entrepreneur, but the journey generally starts by developing an effective business model and writing a business plan that describes the venture to investors and others who will become part of the team.

E-commerce Opportunities

Entrepreneurs who are still wondering about the potential for generating revenue on the Web just need to take a quick look at the research reports.

The *1998 eCommerce Report* from eMarketer (www.emarketer.com), which looks at the consumer and business segments of sales over the Web, projects e-commerce will increase dramatically. It projects that business-to-business e-commerce will increase to $268 billion in 2002, up from $5.6 billion in 1997 and $16 billion in 1998; and consumer e-commerce will reach $26 billion by 2002, up from $1.8 billion in 1997.

Other forecasts show e-commerce at even higher levels in the years to come, so doing business on the Web will no doubt continue to grow for a long time. Now is a good time for entrepreneurs with a good business model to start building their businesses.

According to NetNames Ltd. (www.netnames.com), more than 3.6 million domains have been registered worldwide on the Internet—and 56,000 are being added every day; it's clear that businesses are flocking to the Web.

Although it seems like every business in the world is on the Web, millions of entrepreneurial businesses have yet to create a presence on the Web. The Entrepreneurial Research Consortium found that at least one person in 6 million U.S. households is involved in a new start-up. What's more, in approximately 22 million households, someone is already involved in a business startup or owns an existing business.

Types of Web Businesses

With millions of businesses on the Web trying to attract customers, it can be a challenge to select the business model that is best for the entrepreneur and that will ultimately lead to success. Over the past few years, we've seen many businesses on the Web, and to help you evaluate and select an appropriate business model, we've categorized businesses by several criteria. By helping you look at the attributes of several narrow categories, we hope you can select attributes from each category that will lead you to your successful Web business model and aid you in developing your Web business plan.

As we look at the different attributes of Web businesses, the key factor used to describe these business models will be their sources of revenue—which also help describe the product or service they provide.

It's great to provide real value to your customer, but it's just as important to generate revenue—or you can't have a profitable business with long-term staying power. Of course, most entrepreneurial businesses have expenses greater than revenues for the first year or two. After the initial startup period, though, investors will be looking for the business to have the momentum necessary to generate a profit.

In general, businesses on the Web fall into one of these categories:

- Traditional businesses adding Web marketing and sales to their existing operations
- Traditional business concepts used to create a Web-based business
- New Web-based business concepts

Traditional Businesses Adding a Web Site

Many existing businesses have found that the Web is a fast way to publish existing product information for prospects. In many of these cases, the Web is seen as an extension of their traditional marketing communications activities. In fact, many businesses simply convert their existing corporate and product brochures to the Web—leading to the descriptive word *brochureware*.

Unfortunately, brochureware does little more than provide information quickly because it doesn't take advantage of the power of interaction on the Web. In fact, relying on a Web site of static, non-interactive pages may lead a company to be compared unfavorably to its competition that is making full use of the Web's capabilities.

A number of companies have taken their Web sites beyond simple brochureware and have integrated their entire catalog, ordering, and tracking processes into their Web sites. Many of the popular companies on the Web in this group are the traditional mail-order catalog companies, such as Land's End (www.landsend.com), Spiegel (www.spiegel.com), Sharper Image (www.sharperimage.com), and Hello Direct (www.hellodirect.com).

The benefit to an existing company is that they don't have to develop a complete infrastructure for marketing, obtaining product inventory, and processing orders. The challenge for an existing company with a well-known brand image is that its Web site needs to be as impressive and complete as its other marketing activities. In other words, the Web audience expects these companies to have as many products in their Web catalogs as they have in their print catalogs and to make ordering as easy as calling toll free to their call center.

Unfortunately, the process of integrating a Web site with an existing call center order-processing system can be expensive and time consuming. That's why some companies forgo the complete integration for a more modest approach of only accepting inquiries, which are followed up by a telemarketing person, or only receiving orders, without offering confirmation, tracking, and the other services of full integration.

If your company is considering integrating your Web site with your order-processing system, you will need to create a number of committees to plan the development process because practically every department in the company will need to be involved from the beginning. It may seem counterproductive to have multiple groups of people working on the various aspects of Web integration, but you'll quickly find many places within the existing processes. The best way to make sure that everything needed for integrating a total e-commerce system into the existing system is to have several small groups working on their piece of the puzzle. Of course, each team needs to be in close communication with all the other teams, and with the project leader.

If it sounds like a big project, be assured that it is a big project. With the cooperation of each team working together, however, the project is as manageable as most other new data-processing development projects.

Traditional Business Concepts Brought to the Web

Many new entrepreneurs have taken what they know about running a traditional business and have started similar businesses that exist only on the Web.

By starting a new Web business based on traditional business concepts, they have been able to start quickly and eliminate much of the risk associated with startup businesses. The challenge, of course, is that the entire company has to be created from scratch. In addition, the interactivity of the Web enables—and almost demands—a higher level of interactivity than would be expected of traditional businesses.

Case Study: CareerWeb

A corporation's need to improve its competitive position in the Web market led Landmark Publishing to create an intrapreneuring group within the company to create CareerWeb. This Web site, designed to help match job seekers with employers, has grown into a family of Web sites servicing several specific career needs.

CareerWeb (www.careerweb.com), shown in Figure 20.1, is a Web-based business that helps people find job openings at companies looking for people like them. In a traditional job placement company, the candidate provides the career counselor with a resume, then the counselor sifts through a stack of orders they've received from their client companies. This means that the job seeker has minimal interactivity with the open job orders—and usually is prohibited from seeing those open orders—so he or she is dependent on the counselor to evaluate skills and match them with a good company. The job seeker is also dependent on the job placement company to have a large inventory of open job orders—which the job seeker is also prohibited from seeing.

With CareerWeb, most of these problems are overcome through the use of its extensive database of job openings that every job seeker can look through to locate appropriate openings. By investing in a customized Web database software system, CareerWeb enables job seekers to search for jobs that meet their criteria, post and update their resumes in a special database for employers, and review openings at participating companies. In addition, CareerWeb has an automated email system that sends notices to job seekers when new jobs are added to the database that meet their individual criteria.

Like other Web-based companies, CareerWeb has multiple sources of revenue, which include advertising fees and a comprehensive online bookstore. Because they have job seekers and employers visiting their site, they have included books to help the job seeker and books on career development and multimedia materials for human resource professionals.

The CareerWeb family of sites also include "content sites"—providing interesting and helpful articles to aid job seekers in the difficult transition between jobs.

After demonstrating that a Web site for professional, managerial, and technical people could succeed, they established a family of similar Web sites, including HealthCareerWeb.com, CarolinasCareerWeb.com (for North and South Carolina), and two Web sites focusing on helping people make the transition from government to the private sector (BlueToGray.com and GreenToGray.com).

As you can see, many of the services provided by CareerWeb cannot be offered by a traditional career counseling service because they are made possible by the interactivity of the Web.

The challenges faced by a company such as CareerWeb include the startup costs associated with developing the Web database software, the marketing costs necessary to attract attention and Web traffic, and the cost of sales necessary to sell companies on placing job openings on CareerWeb.

Starting Web-based businesses, even though they use many of the same principles of their counterparts in the traditional business environment, requires a great deal of work to be done before business can begin.

Figure 20.1 CareerWeb was created by intrapreneurs who spotted a way to use their database publishing knowledge to help job seekers and help their company compete in the fast-growing Web market.

New Web-based Business Concepts

Perhaps the most challenging—and most risky—category of businesses on the Web includes companies that provide a completely new product or service only through the Web. Of course, the ones that first come to mind are the companies that enable us to use the Web— the search engines, such as Infoseek (www.infoseek.com), shown in Figure 20.2.

Figure 20.2 Infoseek has grown from an entrepreneur's dream of creating a better way to index online data to a leading search engine. Its original subscription-based business model quickly changed into the advertising-based business used today.

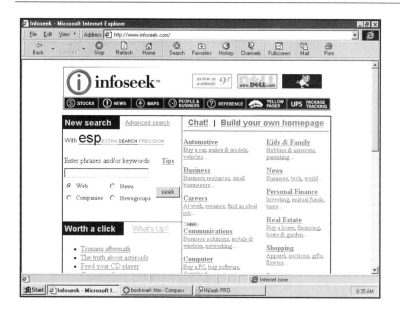

Case Study: Infoseek

An entrepreneur's vision to help people find information on the Web led to the creation of a starting point used by millions of people. Infoseek was founded in 1994 by Steven Kirsch as a subscription-based, personal newswire service providing an index to electronic versions of news and other articles.

Because Steven Kirsch had experience with high-tech startups—he had founded Mouse Systems and Frame Technology—he knew he needed quality people, adequate funding, and plenty of lead time to create what is today one of the leading Web-based companies.

Early relationships with Microsoft and NYNEX gave Infoseek's search engine exposure to key Internet users.

In 1997, the company launched Infoseek Spotlight, which gives users a shortcut to a number of popular Web sites, including Sports Illustrated, National Geographic, Women's Wire, and Dow Jones. That year, it extended an agreement with Netscape whereby Infoseek appeared as one of five primary Net search providers on the Netscape site.

With all search engines appearing to provide similar services, Infoseek has been striving to create a distinct brand identity for its services. Part of its strategy to differentiate its service has been to introduce a new format for links by subject matter, new formulas for ranking the appropriateness of sites, and links to topical current news and related articles.

The success of Infoseek is demonstrated by the more than 100 percent growth in revenues the company has experienced, taking it to $34.6 million in 1997. However its loss of $24.6 million in the same year shows that it is expensive to generate revenue quickly—a fact of life in the entrepreneurial world.

Other companies in this category are the news and information Web sites that provide an integrated and interactive environment. One example is CNET (www.cnet.com) with its wide range of branded Web sites, including Builder.com (www.builder.com) for Web developers; News.com (www.news.com) for up-to-date news about the Internet; and Radio.com (www.radio.com), which provides audio Webcasts of news and interviews throughout the day.

Case Study: CNET

Halsey Minor founded CNET in 1992 to create cable programming on computers and technology. CNET went from a television show with a Web site into a full range of Web-based publishing sites, all linked to form a large family of Web sites, each serving a distinct target market.

CNET is an example of how entrepreneurs need to be flexible and adapt to the needs of the Web audience.

Halsey Minor's earlier work in producing multimedia business-training products gave him a sound understanding of television, and an early agreement with USA Network helped launch the *CNET Central* series in 1995.

Then, the company added Web publishing with its CNET.com site, later followed by eight additional sites attracting more than one million people. CNET went public in mid 1996 and has become one of the most visited places on the Web, generating revenues of $33.6 million in 1997 with a loss of $24.7 million.

In addition to what are referred to as "content sites," such as CNET, other companies in this category are computer software and hardware companies that enable us to connect to the Internet and to use the Internet safely and securely.

Revenue Sources for Web Sites

The primary sources of revenue for most Web sites are

- Product sales
- Services

- Content access/subscriptions

- Advertising

- Sponsorships/partnerships

- Sub-licensing

Product Sales

Selling products to customers is undoubtedly the most valuable way to generate revenue with a Web site, but Web entrepreneurs face special challenges in selecting, marketing, and selling products. In addition to the traditional questions about which products to sell, as well as pricing and fulfillment issues, the big question is whether the Web audience will be interested in buying the products.

Some Web merchants manufacture their own products, but a larger proportion of Web merchants are resellers of products manufactured by others.

Case Study: CDnow

What happens when a music enthusiast becomes frustrated with service in a retail store? The leading music retail store on the Web is created.

As with many other entrepreneurial startups, Jason Olim was frustrated about the service he received in local music stores and decided he could do a better job on the Web. With the help of his parents and twin brother, Matthew, they launched the company in 1994, at the time when the Web was experiencing tremendous growth. CDnow had $2.2 million in sales in 1995, $6 million in 1996, and $17.4 million in 1997.

CDnow (www.cdnow.com), shown in Figure 20.3, sells music CDs the same as a traditional retailer does, but it provides several services that are not available from a traditional retailer. Some of these additional services include audio clips, album information, and reviews from a number of music magazines. In addition, CDnow has an operation that enables customers to create their own CDs from a library of available songs.

Over time, CDnow may face competition from both traditional retailers who provide additional services, and from the music companies as they sell directly to consumers on their Web sites, but for now, CDnow is recognized as a leader in online music sales.

Several factors differentiate CDnow from traditional retailers. It keeps no inventory but has a distributor that drop-ships customers' orders. In addition, CDnow also provides easy access to more than 70,000 reviews and 275,000 audio samples, all of which make it easy for the customer to order.

Profits, on the other hand, are hard for any startup to generate, and it is especially difficult for Web-based startup companies. Although in 1997, CDnow generated revenues of $17.4 million, they lost $10.7 million doing it!

Figure 20.3 CDnow is an example of how far two brothers can take an entrepreneurial concept on the Web. This music retailer is a leader in its market, providing a large catalog of products, competitive pricing, online listening to samples, and convenient ordering.

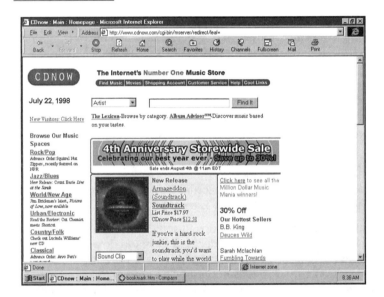

Providing Services

Providing services to customers attracted to your Web site is a growing area for Web entrepreneurs because of the ease of marketing services and the potential for lower costs.

Case Study: Peapod

One recipe for success on the Web is to start with years of experience in an industry, add seasoned relatives and financing, then cook well until the IPO is done.

Peapod—an online grocery shopping service (www.peapod.com)—is the brainchild of two brothers, Andrew and John Parkinson, who worked in the packaged goods industry prior to forming Peapod. Andrew Parkinson had been an executive at Kraft and Procter & Gamble, and Thomas had worked for those two companies and Furton. They tested their concept and developed online software starting in 1990; then when the Internet became popular, they moved to providing Web access.

Peapod.com is a rather unusual Web-based service company because they actually sell products to the consumer. Peapod has more than 250 employees, most of whom are professional grocery shoppers at key grocery stores in the markets they serve; they push carts down the aisles, select produce, and then deliver groceries to their customers.

Although it's important to have shoppers who know how to select the right produce, meats, and groceries, their challenge was in developing the complex software that makes it all possible. While consumers are shopping on the Peapod.com Web site, for instance, their previous grocery list is available to them, as well as a listing of their favorite brands. In addition, their current purchases are being monitored so that coupons and specials can be presented on the fly to help build brand loyalty, or help move consumers from one brand to another.

By tracking the purchase behaviors of shoppers, it can offer manufacturers the opportunity to test a wide variety of promotional activities, including

- Promotions aimed at consumers loyal to another brand, without targeting their own brand for deals

- Comparing the effectiveness of ads versus samples

- Promoting a product when a complementary product is being purchased

Although Peapod has attracted competitors in the online grocery shopping segment, its experience in the grocery industry has made them one of the more successful Web-based businesses. With revenues in 1997 of $59.6 million and one of the smallest losses for Internet companies its size—$13.0 million—it is poised for significant growth and profitability as the company goes nationwide.

The area for providing this type of service for other kinds of products is wide open, and the growing interest in convenient shopping is attractive to entrepreneurs looking for a Web-based business.

Content Access/Subscriptions

The content providers that publish magazines, newspapers, and similar types of information on the Web have received a great deal of attention, but very few of these businesses derive any significant amount of their revenues from subscriptions. The reason is that most consumers feel that information should be free, so they don't support most information providers through subscriptions. Because television and radio are free to the audience, and daily newspapers cost a small fraction of the total cost to produce the publication, it is no surprise that it is difficult for content providers to generate subscription revenue.

Some information, however, is valuable enough to consumers that they are willing to pay for it.

One of the first national publications to be successful in selling subscriptions to its Web site was the *Wall Street Journal* (www.wsj.com). They began by offering free access to the Web version of the daily financial newspaper, then converted to a paid subscription service. Many initial subscribers converted to the paid version of the online edition. The *Journal* charges $49 per year for the online version alone, or $29 for those with a print subscription.

Another Web subscription service is the health information Web site DocAllen (www.docallen.com), a database of thousands of symptoms and recommendations for professional medical treatment. Monthly subscriptions of $9.95 enable families to have immediate access to personalized recommendations on a wide range of medical problems that many people experience. This Web-only service asks the subscriber a number of questions about the ailment, then uses a complex logic analysis to recommend the best action. This type of analysis and recommendation is not available through other media, so promotion of this Web site is one of the larger challenges facing this company.

Serving Free and Paid Subscribers

Newspapers and magazines that cover areas other than financial news have tried to convert their free subscribers to paid subscribers and have either given up and reverted to a free service, or have gone out of business. One of the recent daily newspapers that tried to charge a subscription fee is the San Jose *Mercury News* (www.sjmercury.com), a daily newspaper for the Silicon Valley area of California.

So, if a daily newspaper can't charge a subscription fee, where is the revenue for content sites? Fortunately, many opportunities exist to generate revenue by charging for advertising, access to specialized databases, and subscription access to detailed articles that go into more depth than the free versions of the same articles. But keep in mind that the value has to be very high.

One Web subscription service that added the Web to its line of print products is Hoover's, Inc. (www.hoovers.com), a company that publishes information about thousands of companies. The information in the Hoover database includes summary and detailed descriptions of a company, its top officers and their salaries, financial data, and access to its recent government filings.

Hoover's has found what many other content providers have found, that the Web consumers want a significant amount of information for free, but will pay for a relatively small amount of information with extraordinary value. In the case of Hoover's, it provides summary information on more than 20,000 companies for free, but subscribers have access to detailed information on about 5,000 companies for a monthly subscription fee of $12.95.

An advantage that Hoover's had when it began publishing its information on the Web was that it was relatively well known for its printed directories with the same information. Of course, with printed directories, readers can't do the searching on multiple criteria that is possible with the Web site, or use the other services that are easier to provide on the Web than in a print format. Hoover's customers also benefit because they can generally obtain the specific information they need at a lower total cost than if they had bought the printed directories. Of course, Hoover's counts on subscriptions that are continued month to month by people who anticipate needing to use the service again in the near future.

News or Database Format?

Entrepreneurs who are considering starting a Web-based subscription service need to evaluate what information they can provide, what the monetary value is to the audience, and how large of an audience will subscribe to the service. With this information at hand, it's possible to develop revenue forecasts that can be compared to the expense budgets of creating, gathering, publishing, and marketing the information.

One other consideration in planning to start a Web-based information service is whether the information is more appropriate for a news format, or whether the information is in a consistent format that can be published using a database publishing format. This is an important area to consider because the expense of a news format is much higher than a database format due to the manual labor required in the news business. This is the primary reason that news-oriented Web sites have had a difficult time generating a profit—despite having a tremendous amount of Web traffic—whereas the database-oriented Web sites have required fewer employees to generate a similar level of revenue.

Advertising

Many Web marketers are attracted to the idea of selling advertising on their sites to either generate the dominant share of their revenue or to supplement their revenue from other sources.

The reason is not only the availability of space on many Web sites, but also the current growth in advertising revenue for Web sites. The Internet Advertising Bureau (`www.iab.com`) projects that in 1998, Internet advertising will surpass $1 billion in revenue for the first time.

At this point, advertising on the Web is undergoing a series of changes that will likely result in rates for banner advertising on many content Web sites stabilizing at around $10 cost per thousand (CPM) views, although some sites are still able to charge higher CPMs.

Because revenue projections are so important to evaluating a business model and developing a business plan, you can use the $10 CPM as a rule of thumb, along with the projected number of page views, to project revenue. If you expect to have 100,000 page views per month, for example, then advertising revenue at $10 CPM will generate $10,000 per month in advertising revenue.

For a new Web site without existing traffic, it is difficult to convince media buyers at advertising agencies to buy ads for their clients. You will need to show that you will be running banner ads, obtaining links on compatible Web sites, and will have an effective public relations program—and that all are likely to generate the projected traffic.

Another commonly used approach is to give early advertisers special pricing and free advertising to "jump start" the site. After Web traffic reports are available, other advertisers see the early advertisers and subsequent traffic reports, and then are inclined to buy ads.

Some Web sites that sell advertising are also finding additional revenue through participation in the actual sale of products by their advertisers. By agreeing to accept part of the risk of advertising on their site through revenue participation, Web sites are finding a greater reception with advertisers who are unsure of the results they would receive from a particular Web site.

In addition to receiving revenue from actual sales of products, another source of ad revenue is based on the number of times an ad is clicked, called *clickthrough*.

Sponsorships/Partnerships

You've probably heard announcers for television shows say those profitable words, "and now a word from our sponsor." Sponsorships of media have been with us since the original soap operas on radio—which were sponsored, of course, by a major soap company.

Sponsorship revenue for Web sites can work well for many companies to provide long-term, consistent revenue in return for continuous, high-profile placement of an ad. Examples of sponsorship ads can be seen at a number of search engines, such as Infoseek, with links to UPS, Auto-By-Tel, and Borders.

Another source of revenue is to form a partnership with another company to jointly sponsor a Web site. ESPN Ventures is a joint venture between ESPN and Starwave that includes such Web sites as ESPN SportsZone, NBA.com, and NFL.com. Although ESPN provided access to sports information, Starwave had experience creating and managing news, sports, and entertainment Web sites. By combining their skills and resources, the two companies were able to develop a Web site that generates tremendous traffic.

Sub-licensing

Just when you thought you'd found every possible way to generate revenue on your Web site, keep in mind that other Web sites will pay you to use your content on their Web sites. If your Web site provides content to your Web audience, then it's possible that it would be suitable as part of other Web sites, too. By combining your content with the brand image of other Web sites, you can generate additional revenue while you keep other Web sites from having to create the same content—and, therefore, you reduce your competition.

The *Los Angeles Times* (`www.latimes.com`) incorporates links within news stories to sites such as Hoover's (`www.hoovers.com`) and Quote.com (`www.quote.com`) to provide readers with easy access to additional information and keep the cost of content down. By including information from the Hoover's database in Web pages designed to look like the L.A. Times Web site, Hoover's has created an additional source of revenue without reducing its existing customer base.

Another way to connect different Web sites is through an affiliate program that compensates a Web site for referring Web customers to the Web site selling products. The early users of this concept were the online book resellers, such as Amazon.com (`www.amazon.com`) and Books.com (`www.books.com`), which have thousands of affiliates that link to their sites in return for a small commission on the sales they generate.

The flexibility of programming behind the scenes allows for practically any form of compensation based on activities of the Web users. Amazon.com, for example, pays a commission when a customer follows a link to a particular book and makes a purchase. Books.com, on the other hand, tracks a customer's interest in a book from one Web session to another and pays a commission on all books the customer was interested in, no matter when the customer eventually makes the purchase.

Evaluating Web Business Opportunities

Now that you know the various sources of revenue you can expect, the next step in preparing your business plan is to create some preliminary revenue forecasts and expense budgets.

This part of creating a business plan is normally a time-consuming process, changing the spreadsheet here, then altering assumptions there, until you have the right combination of revenue and expenses. We're not going to try to give you an exact set of data or formulas tailored to your Web business, but we are going to give you a head start by setting up the basic framework of the spreadsheet you will be developing.

In the following examples we'll use two types of Web businesses—a product reseller and a content provider.

Product Company's Assumptions and Forecast

Startup companies don't have any historical operating data, so the basis for the financial projections comes from assumptions about how the business will operate and the economic impact of those operations.

The assumptions we'll use for the product reseller are

- Average product cost is $5.00 per unit.

- Average shipping, handling, and administrative cost is $4.00 per unit.

- Average product price is $15.00 per unit.

- Web site development cost is $50,000.

- Web site operating cost is $10,000 per year.

- Marketing cost is $50,000 per year.

- Web site traffic is 100,000 people per year.

- Close rate of sales is 10 percent.

Even though this is a simplified set of assumptions, we can project revenues and expenses for a preliminary income statement, as shown in Table 20.1.

Table 20.1 Basic Income Statement for the First Year of Operation for a Web-based Product Reseller.

Revenue:	
Traffic	100,000
Close rate	0.10
Sales	10,000
Order size	$15.00
Revenue	$150,000
Expenses:	
Cost of product	$5.00
Cost of shipping & administration	$4.00
Total cost of product & overhead	$9.00
Number of orders	10,000
Cost of Goods Sold	$90,000
Web site development cost	$50,000

Expenses
_____

Web site operating cost	$10,000
Marketing cost	$50,000
Expenses	$200,000
Net Profit (Loss)	**($50,000)**

In this example, the first year's revenue and expense forecast shows the company would spend about $50,000 more than it would bring in, which is also the budgeted amount for the one-time Web development costs. Additional revenue in the second year from the momentum of the marketing would make this a profitable business in the second year if the marketing budget and other costs remain the same. As you've seen with the publicly held Web-based businesses profiled in this chapter, they tend to spend more than they bring in for the first few years as they try to gain a leadership position in market share.

Content Provider's Assumptions and Forecast

A startup content provider has a challenge in developing a business plan and financial projections because of the uncertainty of its reception by its Web audience, but every business plan needs the projections—no matter how much uncertainty (that is, risk) you have when you develop the plan.

The assumptions we'll use for the content provider are

- Average advertising revenue is $10 CPM.

- Average production cost is $500,000 per year.

- Web site development cost is $50,000.

- Web site operating cost is $20,000 per year.

- Marketing cost is $50,000 per year.

- Web site traffic is 100,000 people per year.

- Average number of pages viewed per subscriber is 150 per year.

These assumptions enable us to calculate revenue and expense forecasts for this content provider. Like the product reseller, this is a simplified set of assumptions, but the projected revenues and expenses show how profit—or loss—can be estimated prior to spending a single dollar.

Table 20.2 Basic Income Statement for the First Year of Operation for a Web-based Content Provider.

Revenue:

Traffic	100,000
Page views	15,000,000
Average ad rate per thousand views	$10.00
Ad revenue	$150,000
Directory ad revenue	$100,000
Sponsorship & licensing revenue	$200,000
Total revenue	$450,000

Expenses:

Production cost	$500,000
Web site development cost	$50,000
Web site operating cost	$10,000
Marketing cost	$50,000
Expenses	$610,000
Net Profit (Loss)	**($160,000)**

As with the product reseller, the first year of operation will cost more than the revenues, which is typical of most startup businesses. In this example, the costs are substantially greater than the product company; however, more sources for revenue exist than with the product company. This means that the sales staff will need to be creative and persistent in order to maximize revenues.

For this content provider, the repeat viewership provides an opportunity to grow the number of page views, which translates directly into higher revenues from advertising.

Financing the Venture

Of course, economic projections of profitability are not the only criteria for deciding to start a particular Web-based venture. Most startup ventures that eventually succeed depend upon having a viable "exit strategy," in which the entrepreneur and investors are able either to take the company public or sell the company to a larger company. In both cases, additional capital is brought into the company, which can help take the company to a higher level of promotion, revenue, and profitability.

Earlier, we touched on the entrepreneur who becomes frustrated and starts a company—what might be called an "accidental entrepreneur." Most of the time these ventures do not succeed, partly due to poor planning, but more often because of lack of working capital.

Because most entrepreneurial startups don't qualify for bank loans on their own, entrepreneurs need to consider using some of the typical sources of startup capital:

- Personal resources
- Private investors
- Customer financing

Although some entrepreneurs have the personal wealth to finance a startup business, most do not. This means you should be prepared to present your business plan to private investors, called *angels*, who help entrepreneurs by providing that much-needed initial startup capital.

The challenge that most entrepreneurs face is how to approach angels and professional venture capitalists (VCs). The answer is relatively simple—you don't, your accountant or attorney makes the initial contact on your behalf. As unusual as it may sound, about 90 to 95 percent of the investments made by private investors and VCs start by a referral from someone they have worked with on previous investments.

Investors work this way for many reasons, such as wanting to avoid public exposure and being overwhelmed with business plans, but the biggest reason is trust. Whether it's an angel investing $250,000 of his or her own money or a VC investing $2 million of clients' money, they must trust the entrepreneur to spend their money wisely. Who knows the entrepreneur better than the accountant who has probably known the entrepreneur for some time.

Unfortunately, not every accountant or CPA has experience in helping an entrepreneur raise funds for the new venture, so even if you have had a long relationship with an accountant, it may be time to switch to a firm with extensive experience with entrepreneurs. All the major accounting firms have special Entrepreneurial Services groups that help entrepreneurs through the fundraising process—and have special compensation schedules that help avoid the typical, high hourly fees until the business has been established.

Firms such as PricewaterhouseCoopers (www.pwcglobal.com) and KPMG Price Waterhouse (www.kpmg.com) have helped entrepreneurs in every industry obtain the funds needed to launch ventures and help through the IPO process. Another source of funding that some entrepreneurs take advantage of is to rely on early customers to provide needed funding. One way this can be done is to secure contracts from potential customers prior to starting the business.

Occasionally, you can obtain a commitment from your existing employer to become your customer when you start your business. Obviously, this requires that you leave your present employer on good terms—which is why quitting your present job without proper planning can cut off a potential customer and source of funding.

PART VIII

Globalization

International Partners

- Applying global strategies
- Researching intercultural differences
- Worldwide intranets
- Linking international extranets

Moving in International Circles

Doing business in another country—whether opening up a remote office, buying from overseas suppliers, or selling to a foreign concern—is a major step for any organization. Language differences, cultural variances, import/export regulations, and time-zone changes make working in multiple countries extraordinarily challenging. However, the rewards, which range from a less expensive labor pool to the opening of new markets, are so tempting that the challenges need to be met.

The pervasiveness of the Internet and worldwide intranet systems have brought the challenges—and the costs—of international dealings down a notch. Previously, international expansion could be considered only by the most liquid of companies. Now, much smaller companies can consider branching out beyond their national borders without the fear that the communication costs alone would be more than their projected income.

Three major arenas exist in which a company can expand internationally:

- *Internally.* Companies split across borders for many reasons. One division in another country may have been recently acquired, or a plant may have been opened in a foreign country to be closer to raw materials. Whatever the reason, a company divided can benefit greatly from the enhanced communication opportunities offered by an Internet/intranet strategy.

- *Through business partners.* As supply chain and distribution management increasingly become the focus of competitive advantages, it is imperative that partners work together as closely as possible. Disparate business partners can use the Internet to leverage their particular territorial values and offset the disadvantages of geographic differences.

- *With business-to-business commerce.* When you get up at 3:00 a.m. to check the status of a purchase order, you have to know there's a better way. Internet commerce opens up many new possibilities for business-to-business dealings, without requiring a major investment in travel or long-distance calls.

SEE ALSO

➤ *For information about expanding your customer base internationally, see page 359.*

Governmental Support

Global commerce does not consist of just a few companies taking advantage of the Internet. Many international governments, the U.S. chief among them, have realized the potential of worldwide electronic commerce. President Clinton's administration has issued guidelines for pursuing international business over the Web. In a presidential directive outlining these guidelines, President Clinton states,

> According to several estimates, commerce on the Internet will total tens of billions of dollars by the turn of the century and could expand rapidly after that, helping fuel economic growth well into the 21st century. For this potential to be realized, governments must adopt a market-oriented approach to electronic commerce, one that facilitates the emergence of a global, transparent, and predictable environment to support business and commerce. Government officials must respect the unique nature of the medium and recognize that widespread competition and increased consumer choice should be the defining features of the new digital marketplace.

The Clinton administration has issued a report, *The Emerging Digital Economy*, to support this view. Furthermore, President Clinton has issued specific directives to the heads of numerous federal departments and agencies to facilitate the electronic commerce initiative. The most important directives, from a global commerce perspective, are

- U.S. trade representatives are directed to work with foreign governments to prevent goods and services sold over the Internet from being subject to any tariffs.

- The secretary of commerce is directed to protect the intellectual property rights of digitally transmitted material by supporting the World Intellectual Property Organization (WIPO) Copyright Treaty and the WIPO Performances and Phonograms Treaty.

- The secretary of the treasury is directed to facilitate standard methods of electronic payment with foreign governments and to work to assure that no new taxes are imposed that discriminate against electronic commerce, either domestically or internationally.

- The administrator of general services is directed to expand the GSA Advantage, its online shopping service, to include four million items.

For international Internet commerce to become globally acceptable, many governments and private sector parties will have to agree to proposals similar to those outlined by President Clinton. Luckily, the benefits of electronic commerce are readily apparent, and an international consensus seems to be building.

Intercultural Communication

Even as trade barriers fall, other, more deeply-rooted barriers must be addressed. Different languages, local traditions, and business customs provide hurdles to be cleared in the electronic commerce race. The Internet, through its extensive knowledge base, can provide an informative window into other cultures. You can even get a few pointers in your pronunciation, whether you're trying to say, "We have a deal!" in Icelandic or "What's the margin?" in Afrikaans.

The view from the World Bank

Looking for detailed economic indicators for a particular country? Visit the World Bank's Web site (www.worldbank.org). Not only does the World Bank keep track of traditional indicators, such as gross domestic product, it also follows Internet age figures, such as the per capita density of telephone lines in a given country. What gives the World Bank the true inside scoop is that it is known to invest in information infrastructure for many developing nations, such as Zambia.

Even if you're lucky enough to transcend the language barrier, you're still faced with understanding the many cultural differences that exist between countries. The Web is filled with numerous sources detailing everything from the customs to the political climate. One such site, shown in Figure 21.1, is the Global Emerging Markets Database (www3.pitt.edu/~ibc-mod/gem/) sponsored by the International Business Center of the Katz Graduate School of Business and University Center for International Studies at the University of Pittsburgh. The site contains information about each of the countries profiled, including

- Economic indicators, such as Gross National Product and U.S. export growth, as well as a list of the country's leading imports and exports

- Descriptions of the emerging markets within the country: health care, transportation, aerospace, infrastructure, and so on

- Market access information, such as tariff and import barriers, government procurement policies, foreign investment potential, intellectual property rights status, and current competition

- Export information, including rules and regulations, suggested "best prospects," and a listing of trade events

- Key contacts information for the country, including name, mailing address, and phone and fax numbers

- Email contacts for a full range of public and private sector trade export experts specific to the country

Figure 21.1 Sites such as the Global Emerging Market Database offer precise details on the cultural, legal, and market differences of many countries.

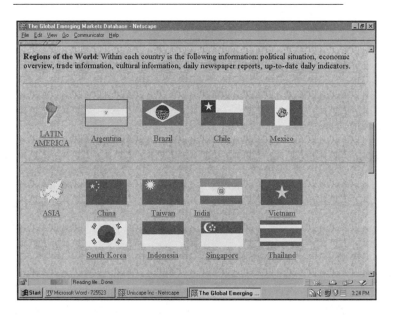

You may have thought I was exaggerating when I mentioned the language-learning possibilities of the Web. If so, take a look at the Travel Language site (www.travlang.com), shown in Figure 21.2. In addition to offering online language dictionaries, a worldwide hotel database, and a currency exchange rate utility, you can also have key phrases translated into 60 languages.

Figure 21.2 Want to pick up a phrase or two of Azerbaijani before traveling? Visit the Travel Language site to hear translations from a native speaker via downloaded audio files.

FAQ: What do I need to hear audio over the Internet?

Most recent versions of browsers come set up to download and play common sound or music files. Typically, these are called wave or MIDI files and have the file extensions of .wav or .midi, respectively. Other file types, particularly those known as *streaming* music files, such as RealAudio, require special plug-ins. A streaming file doesn't have to be completely downloaded before it can begin to play. After a few bars have been transferred to your system, the streaming player plays the music while continuing to download the balance of the clip. The most popular streaming format (for prerecorded or live audio and video or animation) is from RealNetworks and available as a free download from its Web site (www.real.com).

On the site, after you've picked your language and the language you want to speak, you can choose from a wide range of phrases. An audio file of the spoken phrase is then downloaded to your computer, where it can be saved and replayed as often as necessary. Any foreign business expert will tell you that even attempting to speak a foreign business prospect's native language can be very advantageous.

Cultural Resources

Before you expend precious resources to begin doing business in another country, it pays to understand the local culture as well as the language. A few examples show mistakes made by companies that didn't do their homework:

- Parker Pen attempted to market a new ballpoint pen in Mexico with the tag line, "It won't leak in your pocket and embarrass you." Unfortunately, the slang for "embarazar" translated the slogan into "It won't leak in your pocket and make you pregnant."

- Colgate saw no pharmaceutical challengers for its new toothpaste, Cue, to be introduced in France. However, no one thought to check the newsstands for an adult men's magazine—also named *Cue*.

- Scandinavian vacuum manufacturer Electrolux wanted a memorable slogan for its new American campaign. They got more than they bargained for by first using, "Nothing sucks like an Electrolux."

- Looking for a close phonetic equivalent when introducing Coca-Cola to the Chinese market, the company initially decided on the ideogram "Ke-kou-ke-la." After thousands of signs had been printed, it was discovered that the phrase means "bite the wax tadpole" or "female horse stuffed with wax" depending on the dialect.

Thousands of missteps are possible when cultures clash—and the more research completed prior to investing resources, the better. Luckily, the Internet offers a wide range of sites designed to introduce you to the cultural specialties of various countries—everything from gestures to cuisine. One of the most expansive sites is the Web of Culture (www.worldculture.com), shown in Figure 21.3. Created as a project of the American Graduate School of International Management, the Web of Culture site offers comprehensive links to consultants, consulates, embassies, languages, and religions for hundreds of countries around the world.

For more in-depth information, it's best to visit a site dedicated to a specific region or country. An excellent example is the Latin America Network Information Center (www.lanic.utexas.edu), hosted by the University of Texas. This site covers 45 topics for more than 30 Latin American and Caribbean countries, with sections devoted to management, labor, finance, and business in general.

Figure 21.3 Get the inside picture of a country—without costly airfare—by visiting a site such as the Web of Culture.

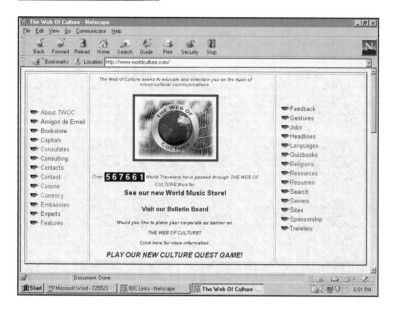

International Intranets

Throughout this book, I've extolled the virtues of enterprisewide intranets in bringing departments and the entire company together. Nowhere is the positive effect of an intranet more profound than when it is applied to an international company with divisions in many countries. However, international intranets are not problem-free and can have their own special challenges to overcome.

In an international situation, an intranet's primary advantages are in overcoming geographical and temporal boundaries. Communicating via the intranet—whether it involves accessing information on an internal Web page, sending email, or joining in a private newsgroup discussion—can take place around the clock, and around the globe. The availability of the Internet to act as a connecting superhighway is what makes this an everyday reality instead of an exorbitantly priced, one-company-in-ten-thousand dream.

Security limitations on exports

If you're deploying an international intranet, your legal department may need to investigate a gray area. The U.S. has set stiff export restrictions for the use of encryption software in many intranet Web servers; nothing higher than 40-bit encryption can be sold outside of the U.S. Depending on the legal standing of your company and each of its offices located in different countries, you may have to investigate your legal alternatives.

Because so many intranets are interconnected via the Web, security deserves a special focus. At the very least, sensitive information should be encrypted by using a secure server. Additionally, digital signatures and digital certificates may be used to ensure the authenticity of the parties. Finally, because so much traffic goes from local intranet to Internet and back to a remote intranet, the firewall systems that protect intranets from unauthorized visitors must be scrupulously maintained and audited.

SEE ALSO

➤ *For more about Internet security, see page 19.*

Another problem associated with international intranets is information bloat. With disparate divisions, material can be posted to the intranet from many sources. If not monitored, multiple divisions can publish the self-proclaimed "definitive" data on the same topic—and each could be different. Depending on the size of the organization, a single indexing authority or different regional servers—each with a clearly outlined area of responsibility—might be the answer.

Case Study: Eli Lilly and Company

Eli Lilly is one of the world's largest pharmaceutical companies, with offices in 156 countries. Based in Indianapolis, Lilly employs more than 30,000 people worldwide and had net sales in 1997 of $8.5 billion.

Lilly has approximately 16,000 desktop computers scattered throughout North America, South America, Central America, Europe, Africa, Asia, and the Middle East, all connected to 20 different servers. The intranet servers are located in the large data centers as well as in small offices in the United States, the United Kingdom, Germany, Italy, Austria, and Ireland; all servers are integrated into the company's wide area network. Each server-based location is responsible for the content published on its section of the Web. Because the servers aren't based in different divisions, but in different locales, conflicts can arise in what is published to the intranet.

John Swartzendruber, an information consultant for Lilly, described a situation in which four individuals (in different locations but in the same division) each proposed to post the Web page for their department. The conflict was resolved among the parties by consensus. Lilly is looking toward centralizing intranet servers and maintaining a single index to resolve problems like this one in the future.

International Extranets

The farther your company can extend its extranet to incorporate supply or distribution chain partners, the more efficiently the entire organization can move product. From just-in-time manufacturing techniques to tightly integrated shipping logistics, extranets gain tremendous power when you take advantage of a particular region's cost effectiveness. It does an enterprise little good to use a low-cost labor source if too little or too much product is produced due to insufficient communication. Similarly, you can work with the least expensive distribution agent anywhere, but if the goods are sitting on your dock for weeks at a time waiting for shipment, time is wasted.

As an example, take a look at the diagram explaining JapanLink's services in Figure 21.4. JapanLink (www.japanlink.com) acts as an intermediary to connect U.S. and Japanese companies via the Internet. Its service is useful for companies that do not have the expertise or the resources to manage an extranet between the two countries themselves. Databases located in each organization's extranets can be written to and read by the other company, to a limited degree. The degree of access is controlled by the extranet server.

Figure 21.4 Extranets can work with two primary partners, as shown in this diagram from JapanLink, or with a host of supply chain and distribution partners.

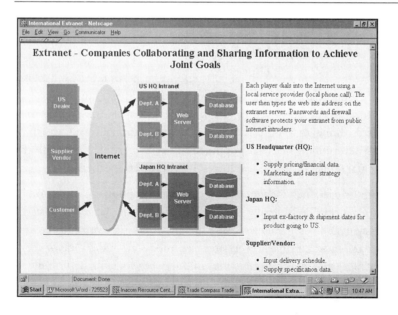

Distance Issues with International Extranets

In this age of digital transmissions, probably the last problem you would expect to emerge would be one of speed. I've often had the experience where, after working with a new, super-fast computer, even the quickest access times seem lengthy because I've become acclimated to the system. Over an extended extranet, the problem becomes magnified until it is quite noticeable. Local access for any participating country may seem almost instantaneous. However, a transmission from Company A's intranet to its extranet to the Internet and then to Company's B's extranet to its intranet can seem to take forever, relatively. Although usually not noticeable on an extranet within one country (or even neighboring countries for that matter), distance can be a factor with global extranets. Some companies have reduced the lag on the partner side by physically housing their extranets in the same country as their partner. This has one primary advantage—the distance/speed problem is eradicated. Of course, this doesn't cut the overall time of transmission—the loop is still the same and only the servers are in different locations—but it is faster for the extranet partner.

This solution is not without its associated potholes, however. Maintenance and security issues must be addressed. You are, after all, installing an extension of your network in another country, away from your home base. Although all manner of electronic protections can—and should—be put into place, you want to be sure to physically protect the Web server and ensure its continued functionality should problems arise.

Finding an International Partner

Extending your extranet to international partners is a fairly straightforward task, but what if you don't have a partner in an emerging country? In the past, hunting down potential business opportunities abroad meant time and money spent on phone calls to government agencies, on international market research, and on international travel, which could be considerable—all to determine whether an opportunity even existed. Now, with the Internet, much of that initial research can be conducted online, at little expense.

The Internet can be extremely beneficial in locating international partners on both the supply and the distribution side. Literally hundreds of sites are dedicated to assisting you in finding business partners. Generally, the sites are either country or industry specific, although some of the most expansive Web sites encompass all trade. One of these, Trade Compass (www.tradecompass.com), offers multiple services to facilitate finding and working with international trading partners. Sample services include:

- *National Export Offer Service (NEOS)*. With more than 1,000 companies marketing under 135 categories, NEOS is one of the Internet's largest databases of U.S. export services and products. Listings include links to Web sites and email addresses for direct contact.

- *Trade Broker.* Use Trade Compass' Trade Broker automated search facility to scour 100,000 listings for targeted sales information. Trade Broker indexes between 10,000-14,000 trade leads each week in dozens of product or service categories.

- *Global Tradesearch.* Looking for a U.S. export partner? Try Trade Compass' Global Tradesearch online database, shown in Figure 21.5. You can search by product, Standard Industrial Classification (SIC) Code, company or region—or combine filters to narrow your search.

Figure 21.5 Trade Compass' Global Tradesearch enables you to find U.S. export partners right online.

- *Projects and Prospects.* Opportunities in government procurement, including those from Japan, Central Europe, the U.S., and state and local government, are found under this heading.

Avoiding "denied persons"

A *denied person*, according to the Bureau of Export Administration (www.bxa.doc.gov) is a person or company forbidden to export from the U.S. The Bureau of Export Administration keeps close tabs on the activities of individuals and businesses shipping outside the country. In addition to following its host country's rules, a company must also adhere to the destination country's import regulations. To misstep can mean fines, penalties, and even arrest. Companies and individuals that fall into this category can be easily identified by visiting the BXA Web site and reviewing the list of denied persons.

The federal government also maintains an extensive listing of potential trade partners in many industries. For the best results, visit the U.S. Trade and Development Agency's Web site (www.tda.gov). Although small in terms of federal bureaucracy, the Trade and Development Agency works with large-scale projects in the following areas: agriculture, energy, environment, health care, manufacturing, mining and minerals development, telecommunications, transportation, and water resources. Its primary focus is to enable American businesses to become involved in the planning stage of infrastructure and industrial projects in middle-income and developing regions, such as Africa/Middle East; Asia/Pacific; Central and Eastern Europe; and Latin America and the Caribbean.

CHAPTER **22**

Multinational Customer Outreach

- Approaching the global marketplace
- Handling multilingual customerbases
- Marketing to multinational groups

The International Market

Everyone (myself included) talks about the phenomenal growth of the Internet and the global markets now available. But who exactly is on the Internet—and how can your company get its slice of the worldwide pie? One of the first steps by a marketer is to study the marketplace; the Internet should not be approached any differently.

The first question that should be asked about international Internet marketing is: is it worth it? My answer now is a qualified yes —and a resounding "Absolutely!" in the foreseeable future. Currently, the larger Web sites, such as CNet, Disney, and ESPN estimate that about 30% of their traffic comes from non-U.S. sources. Moreover, online stores such as CDNow.com, Cyberian Outpost, and L.L. Bean indicate that about a third of their sales are foreign-based.

The primary factors that are driving international consumers to Web sites for U.S.-based companies are selection, convenience, and price. Unlike the rest of the world, America has long been home to huge shopping malls across the land, but the range of goods available in these superstores pales next to what's for sale on the Internet. And this range of selection is up for grabs to almost anyone who logs on to the Web from anywhere in the world.

Convenience cannot be underestimated as a factor. I live in New York City, where four all-night deli/fruit stands are located within two blocks of my residence, so I'm used to convenience shopping. Many international shoppers aren't so lucky. Ever try to buy anything in England after 6:30 p.m.? Unless you're living in the heart of London, you won't have much luck. On the Internet, shopping can be handled anytime of the day, any day of the week.

Because of the high volume and lack of a middleman, many Web products are offered at terrific discounts. Books and music are two good examples. Generally sold at a premium in stores outside the U.S. (with a 30% or greater markup), these products can be found on the Web for 30-40% off the U.S. price. This makes it possible for a customer in Germany to order a book published in the U.S. from an online bookseller, such as Amazon.com or Barnes and Noble Online, pay the overseas shipping, and still get it cheaper than if it were bought locally.

International Internet Demographics

A recent study by online marketing consultants, eMarketer (www.emarketer.com), sheds some much needed light on the true demographic nature of the Web as it stands today and offers some projections for the future. According to eMarketer's research, approximately 60 million people are Web users in over 150 countries. A lot of bodies, you say—but from a truly global market perspective, it's really just a drop in the bucket. Why? Because currently, the user base is heavily concentrated in North America. The U.S. has approximately 37 million of those users, and with Canada contributing another 4 million, North America accounts for 68% of the Internet citizenry. Moreover, 90% of the Internet users speak English. However, this market concentration is about to change.

The eMarketer report predicts that the Internet will widen its present size nine times within the next five years to 225 million people. As exciting as that may be, from an international perspective, it's not the good news. The best news is that the bulk of this expansion is going to come from outside of the U.S. As shown in Figure 22.1, the non-U.S. Internet population will soon equal the U.S. market penetration and begin to exceed it.

The explosive growth in the world market comes from a confluence of five factors:

- *Internet saturation in the U.S.* Internet use is already at a fairly high concentration among computer owners in the U.S. Before too long, the Web will have no further markets that it can be expected to penetrate.

- *Lower PC costs.* Aside from WebTV, you need a PC to go online. Luckily, the cost of PCs continues to drop—a less-than $500 PC, complete with modem, has already been announced.

- *More PCs globally.* As prices drop and Internet connections spread, more PCs are snapped up around the world. Furthermore, the increased number of users encourages additional PC owners to join the market.

- *Worldwide deregulation of telephone companies.* More and more, countries are seeing that a free marketplace for telephone companies spurs business. The move to deregulate is gaining strong support in the newly unified European Union countries.

Figure 22.1 Not only is Internet growth predicted to continue to happen at an astounding rate, but non-U.S. users will soon be in the majority.

	1996	1997	1998	1999	2000	2001	2002
U.S. Users	12.5	28	47	54	62	68	82
Non-U.S. Users	6.5	16.4	29	54	67	68	143
Total Users	19	44.4	76	108	129	156	225

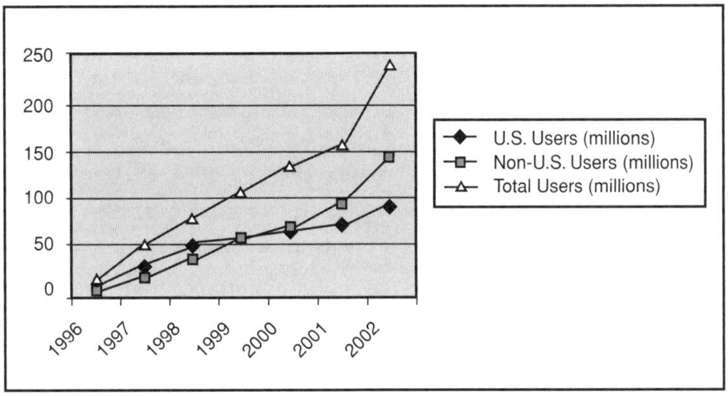

- *Alternative Internet delivery systems.* Newer, faster Internet connection methods are emerging almost daily. Curiously enough, the less-developed nations, such as those in Africa, may be able to benefit from this new technology at a much faster pace. It's far easier to implement a digital infrastructure in a country that has none than to convert an existing analog telephone system.

As rosy as the near future looks for international sales, where can you market your products globally today? From several indicators, the strongest three markets, after the U.S., are Japan, Germany, and the United Kingdom. A branch of eMarketer, called eStats, researched the global PC concentration, shown in Figure 22.2. You'll notice that the top four countries have a strong English-speaking contingent; this factor is both a cause and effect of the prevalence of English-oriented software.

Although Japan has fewer PCs per 100 people than many countries, it actually ranks second in global share of the Internet because a significantly higher proportion of its computers are used to access the Internet, as shown in Figure 22.3.

Figure 22.2 One indicator of current and potential Internet markets is the number of computers per 100 people, as shown here (courtesy of eMarketer).

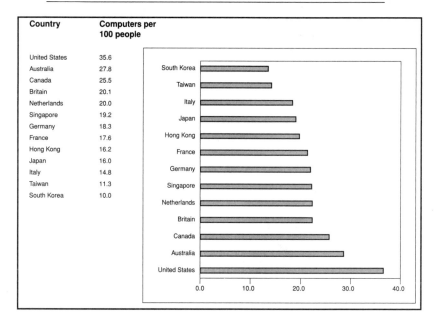

Country	Computers per 100 people
United States	35.6
Australia	27.8
Canada	25.5
Britain	20.1
Netherlands	20.0
Singapore	19.2
Germany	18.3
France	17.6
Hong Kong	16.2
Japan	16.0
Italy	14.8
Taiwan	11.3
South Korea	10.0

Internationalizing a Web Site

Marketing to an international arena is a complex and difficult process. While trying to balance product quality and delivery on one hand, you've got to juggle multicultural promotions with the other. Suzan Nolan, President of Bluesky International (www.blueskyinc.com),
advises companies how best to internationalize their sites. She offers 10 pointers to companies looking to expand globally:

- *Include proper telephone numbers.* It's a good habit to always list your country code as
  well as your area code. The generally recognized format is a plus sign in front of the
  country code, like this: +1 (212) 555-1212. Remember to include other appropriate
  contact numbers as well, especially fax numbers for those who may want to contact
  you the "old-fashioned" way.

Figure 22.3 Japan leads the world in the percentage of households with PCs that are used to access the Internet (courtesy of eMarketer).

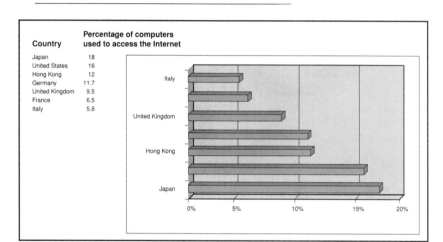

Country	Percentage of computers used to access the Internet
Japan	18
United States	16
Hong Kong	12
Germany	11.7
United Kingdom	9.5
France	6.5
Italy	5.8

- *Encourage email.* As noted in earlier chapters, email is a tremendous time and money saver for your organization. It can also perform the same service for your customers. Unlike a fax machine, no long-distance phone call charges are incurred, and delivery is almost instantaneous. Not all browsers have a built-in program to handle email, so be sure to offer a form-based method for customer contact as well as an email link.

- *Specify your customer support hours.* Not every clock in the world reads the same as those in the U.S. Some countries use a 24-hour clock, where 3:30 p.m. is written 15H30. To cover all your bases, include your time zone with reference to the international standard, Greenwich mean time (GMT). For instance, regular customer support hours might be expressed as "8:00 a.m. to 6:00 p.m. EST (8H00-18H00 GMT –5)."

- *Watch your dates.* Did you ever receive an invoice due date such as 13-3-99 from an overseas supplier and have to stop and stare at it for a moment? Then you remember that outside the U.S., many countries use a Day-Month-Year format, in contrast to the U.S. standard Month-Day-Year format. It's best to spell out either the entire date (March 13, 1999) or, at the very least, abbreviate the month (13-Mar-99) to sidestep any problems.

- *Think metric.* When it comes to measurement systems, the U.S. is pretty much on its own. The rest of the world has gone metric, and if you want to sell to them, you need to use metric measurements, as well. The best approach is to always specify both types of measurements. A small package, for example, might be listed as having the dimensions of 51mm x 25mm x 76 mm (2" x 1" x 3").

- *Remember other cultural differences.* Size isn't the only difference. Any ad copy specifying temperature should be expressed in both Fahrenheit and Celsius. Electrical devices should always specify the megahertz and voltage, as well as the plug type. If possible, stationary goods should be offered both in standard U.S. sizes, such as 8.5" x 11", and European sizes, such as A4.

- *Offer multiple payment options.* The more types of payment possibilities you can offer, the more business you'll get. Aside from various online payment options, such as CyberCash or credit cards, be sure to allow those who aren't yet comfortable with Internet security a chance to buy your goods through more traditional methods, such as a wire transfer or a money order. Because the U.S. has been so protective of its encryption software, secure transactions have been slow to emerge in other countries.

- *Mind the address forms.* When I was running trade shows in Germany and Switzerland, our manager continued to use U.S.-generated forms to gather names for our database. Because European addresses differ significantly from U.S. ones, we had to toss out a good percentage of incomplete forms; I'm sure it was equally frustrating for our visitors. Generally, you'll need to offer more space and additional fields to handle non-U.S. addresses.

- *Follow local tax guidelines.* Many countries impose their own set of value-added taxes or tariffs. Protect yourself from extended liability by making it clear to your foreign visitors that such additional fees are their responsibility.

- *Avoid casual Americanisms.* Although I think this is quickly changing in the age of MTV and other cultural exports, you need to be a bit more formal when addressing Web site visitors from another country. Keep an eye out, too, for slang that might obscure your meaning in areas such as shipping information pages.

SEE ALSO

➤ *For more on online payment options, see page 269.*

Accounting for Language and Cultural Differences

As tempting as a global Internet market is—it's hard to resist a market made up of 225 million people who can visit your store 24-hours a day, 365 days a year— significant issues must be addressed. Chief among these difficulties is the question of *localization*. For a marketing plan to be localized, a country's language, as well as its culture, must be considered. Although language is the primary concern, a localized Web site must also take measurements and currency into account.

As noted earlier, English is the predominant language on the Web, and it is especially prevalent in business-to-business communications. However, when you're attempting to reach new international mass-market customers, it's best to speak their language. Anyone who has ever had advertisements, business documents, or marketing materials translated into another language knows that translation is an intensive, costly—often time-consuming—process. Translating materials for the Internet presents an ongoing problem because of the constant updating that a Web site undergoes. Any company considering Web site marketing to a multinational customer base must make translation costs a budget priority.

Speaking global English

One basic technique that U.S. companies publishing to an international market can use to cut down translation costs is to create the Web marketing materials in global, or controlled, English. Global English avoids U.S. slang and "Americanisms" that might be misunderstood. Creating the materials in global English circumvents the costly step of translating material from a U.S. to a U.K. perspective. Furthermore, it gives many foreign customers for whom English is a second language a much better chance to understand your meaning.

If your company is working with an OEM (Original Equipment Manufacturer), or other resellers within various countries or regions, it's a good idea to bring them into the translation process. Not only are they more likely to translate the information correctly—using the correct vernacular and proper grammar—but they also have much to gain by presenting the proper "national" face to their customer base.

Case Study: AMP, Incorporated

AMP Incorporated is the world's leading supplier of electrical and electronic connectors and interconnection systems. Headquartered in the United States, AMP boasts 45,000 employees in 50 countries. In 1997, AMP reported record sales revenue of $5.75 billion.

Some companies with established Web sites are finding that entering a multilingual international market online can be a daunting and expensive task. AMP understood its international mandate from the beginning and designed its Web site with multilingual capabilities from the ground up. Currently, AMP's Web site, shown in Figure 22.4 supports eight languages: English, French, German, Spanish, Italian, Chinese, Korean, and Japanese. Plans are in motion to add Russian next.

Figure 22.4 The AMP Online Catalog is available in 8 languages: English, French, German, Spanish, Italian, Chinese, Korean, and Japanese.

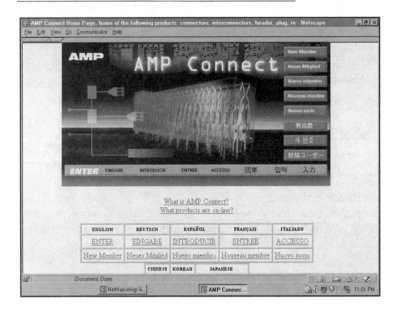

From the user's perspective, AMP's approach appears to be extremely localized. To gain access to the catalog, users must register and, in doing so, specify their home country and language preference. At their next log in, users are greeted with a site in their own language.

AMP's Web site features its extensive catalog with more than 500,000 electronic parts, as well as test data and design drawings. Initial bids to translate each page of the catalog were exorbitant—more than $1.5 million, a figure greater than the entire Web site budget. But AMP had a better idea. Rather than translate each page literally, AMP translated the term for each part just once and put the results in a database. The information from the database is then used to construct the catalog pages on-the-fly, as requested by the user. Suppose, for example, that a Web page visitor asks to see resistors matching a particular set of specifications. After the request is submitted, a page is built from the database based on the results of the query. Basic elements, such as a logo and ordering information, are added to each page. However, even these are translated only once. This database-driven technique is extremely cost-efficient and brought the bids down to less than $100,000.

Although a multilingual online catalog is not an inexpensive endeavor, the savings can be substantial. Prior to the launch of its Web site, AMP was budgeting $15 million annually for worldwide catalog printing and distribution. The electronic online catalog has enabled AMP to cut that figure by 40%. Additionally, the Internet connection has trimmed another 20% from a yearly $800,000 fax bill.

To maintain high customer-service levels, AMP has adopted a slow rollout method for all elements of its Web site project. Initially, only English, French, German, Italian, and Spanish were supported. This allowed the company to establish the level of traffic and usage on the Web site. After AMP was assured that sufficient bandwidth was available, it entered the expansive Asian market with its Chinese, Japanese, and Korean language support.

A similar, slow rollout tactic is planned as AMP unveils its online ordering capability. To maintain the compartmentalization of its database technique, each part will be given one unit price, which can be supplemented in each country by specific tariffs, value-added tax, or other additional charges.

International Online Marketing

Now that you've invested heavily to get your international Web site off the ground, how are you going to get those potential international customers—with their Eurodollars and other currency—to visit? Like any other marketing effort, you have to "keep up the volume" for a considerable period of time before you can expect to see any payoff. Many of your U.S. Internet marketing techniques—cross-advertising on other marketing materials, seeding search engines, and arranging for cooperative links, among others—can be duplicated with some measure of success in international waters. However, additional marketing opportunities—and pitfalls— come with the more expansive global territory.

Strategies

As far as marketing on the Internet is concerned, the primary difference between U.S. and non-U.S. markets is the relative newness of the experience in foreign countries. This allows you to adopt certain strategies to gain an edge when you enter an international market. These strategies involve

- Banner ads
- Local advertising
- Cybercafe advertising

Although other countries will catch up to the U.S. and this difference won't last long, it's still true that many of the marketing approaches that were so successful in the early days of the U.S. Web can be recycled for international efforts. Specifically, I'm referring to the use of banner advertising. In the U.S., banner ads have become an established part of the Web page background and, as such, they don't generate as much response as they did in the early days when the Web was young. However, in many of the emerging nations, banner advertisements—particularly those rendered in a country's native language—are not that plentiful.

Early advertisers in this medium can expect around the same 80-90% clickthrough rate for Web visitors that was evident in the U.S. initially.

SEE ALSO

➤ *For more about banners, see page 214.*

International Web browsers may have seen numerous banner advertisements already. However, the key difference is language. Banner advertising is increasingly sophisticated, and new systems are now capable of selecting an appropriate ad for a visitor to see based on different criteria. That criteria could be the page just visited, the keywords typed in a search, or the host country of the ISP in use. Serving a language-appropriate advertisement to an international visitor is a major enticement.

Local Web ads

One of the major Internet advertising firms, DoubleClick, recently announced the formation of DoubleClick Local, a service that enables local advertisers to reach Web users from their own communities. This same technology could be used for localizing international advertising. Internet analysts, Jupiter Communications, predict that localized Internet ads will account for $1.5 billion in spending by the year 2002.

In addition to advertising your Web site in standard venues such as foreign language magazines or at trade shows, you should also consider one other venue: cybercafes. Although cybercafes, with their combination of coffee-house atmosphere and online access, never really took off in the U.S., they are much more popular where computers are not so prevalent—that is, in the rest of the world. The Cybercafe Search Engine (cybercaptive.com) listing, shown in Figure 22.5, holds more than 1,800 cafes in 150 countries, as well as 1,600 public Internet access points and kiosks. Many cybercafes are open to advertising possibilities—you can market your Web site via mouse pads and screen savers and achieve a high degree of customer contact.

Using Portals

One of the biggest buzz words in the Internet marketing game today is *portal*. As the name implies, a portal is a doorway—in this case, the door is the primary entrance for millions of Internet users. Every browser, when it first logs on to the Internet, seeks out its home page. Generally, the home page is initially set to that of the computer manufacturer, the Internet Service Provider, or the browser developer. Any user can change his or her home page fairly easily and set it to any other page available on the Internet.

Figure 22.5 Cybercafes make terrific point-of-sale advertising opportunities—and you can use the Cybercafe Search Engine to find these opportunities by city, state, or country.

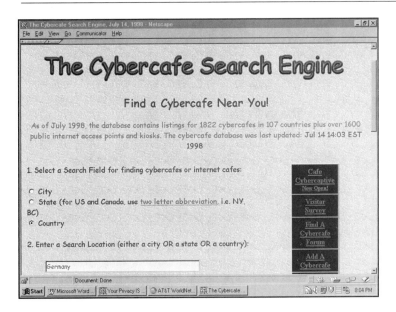

One of the most popular choices for designating your home page is the group of sites known as search engines, notably Yahoo!, InfoSeek, and Excite. As it became obvious that these sites were seeing millions of visitors daily—even if it is to log on and immediately jump to another Web site—their importance in terms of advertising increased. These portals began to enhance their sites with additional content, such as news stories, special shopping sections, and other areas, to entice Web visitors to stay. Consequently, these portals get enough visitors to charge some of the highest advertising rates on the Web.

Although these portals are very useful on the U.S. Internet scene, they are extremely valuable in the international market. Most of the successful portals have launched other national sites, with some language-specific variations. These portals include:

- InfoSeek (www.infoseek.com) has eight variations for the European market, including Germany, the U.K., Ireland, Holland, Spain, Sweden, Denmark, and France. They also maintain Brazilian and Japanese portals.

- Yahoo! (www.yahoo.com) has twelve portals worldwide: France, Germany, the U.K. and Ireland, Sweden, Denmark, Norway, Canada, Australia and New Zealand, Japan (shown in Figure 22.6), Korea, Southeast Asia, and, of course, the U.S.

Figure 22.6 Many portals build language-specific sites for their international clientele, such as this site for Yahoo! Japan.

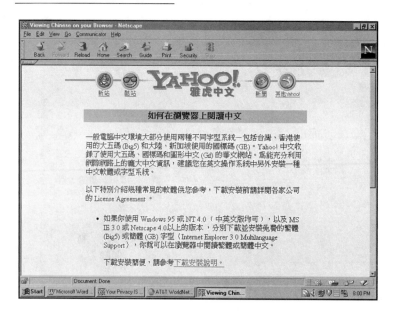

- America Online isn't just for Americans. AOL offers additional sites in Sweden, Japan, Canada, and Australia.

In planning a global marketing strategy, international portals deserve a measure of consideration. In addition to their reach, they simplify the marketing process by offering a single contact for placing a multinational buy.

CHAPTER 23

Business Expansion via the Internet

- Internet expansion enhancements

- Raising capital on the Web

- Looking for companies to buy

- Improving valuation

Expanding the Possibilities

In the minds of many, a company that does not grow is a company that is doomed to failure. Growth can come from acquiring other companies, merging with former competitors, or transitioning from a privately held organization to a public one—all these options open up new worlds of challenges. As you might expect, the interconnected global network known as the Internet can help you meet many of these challenges.

The Internet can be used to assist your expansion efforts in three main areas:

- *Undertaking Research.* Whether you're performing due diligence on a company under consideration for acquisition or need to clarify SEC regulations, the Internet is an excellent research tool.

- *Making Contacts.* Negotiations for any merger and acquisitions arrangement or expansion endeavor requires close, ongoing communication. Although the Internet can't really help in this regard (beyond the use of email), it can help you make initial contacts with brokerage houses, valuation services, or companies looking to buy or sell.

- *Raising Capital.* The Internet has, quite literally, opened up an entirely new front for revenue generation; since 1996, companies have been going public right over the Web. And if a direct IPO is not your cup of tea, a multitude of venture capital firms are approachable through cyberspace. Just type "venture capital" into any search engine and take your pick.

Pursuing Public Offerings over the Web

All the evaluations, planning, and considerations to take a privately held company public usually boils down to one overarching need: cash. For many types of expansion, only the degree of equity capital obtainable by going public will do. The Internet gives you access to the entire realm of lawyers, consultants, government officials, brokers, and even, in a recent development, investors necessary for conducting an initial public offering (IPO).

Rules and Regulations

The process for taking a private company public is a slow and tortuous one. One key advantage that the Internet can bring to that process is information. The better armed you are with pertinent knowledge, the smoother the journey.

The EDGAR connection

The SEC Web site is an extremely valuable resource both for information on companies in the public sector and for fulfilling your regulatory requirements as a public company. EDGAR, short for Electronic Data Gathering, Analysis, and Retrieval, is the SEC's automated filing system. To manage the information flow, most SEC filings are handled through EDGAR. Moreover, because it is public information, it is accessible by anyone—also through EDGAR.

The Securities and Exchange Commission (SEC) offers an excellent resource—a kind of FAQ—for companies considering raising funds in the public sector. Although it can be found under the Small Business section of the SEC site (www.sec.gov), shown in Figure 23.1, the questions asked are important to any size organization. On the Small Business Q&A page (www.sec.gov/smbus/qasbsec.htm), you'll find answers to questions such as

- What are the Federal Securities laws?
- Should my company go public?
- How does my business register a public offering?
- If my company becomes public, what disclosures must be made?
- Are there state law requirements in addition to federal ones?
- Are there legal ways to offer and sell securities without registering with the SEC?

Figure 23.1 The Securities and Exchange Commission, overseers of all public companies, maintains an extremely informative Web site.

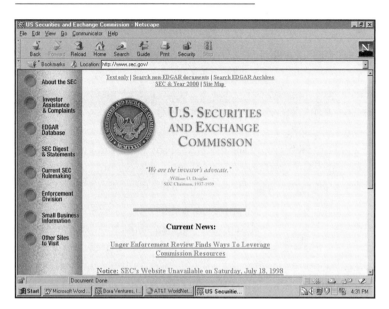

The answer to the final question is a resounding yes, and it opens the door to raising public funds over the Internet, as discussed next.

Going Public on the Internet

A minor revolution took place in March, 1996. For the first time, a company went public using the Internet as a primary means of raising capital. The company, Spring Street Brewery, Inc., raised $1.6 million by selling 870,000 shares at $1.85 each. The maneuver proved so successful that Spring Street established a company, Wit Capital, to facilitate other companies wanting to raise money in the same fashion— over the general Internet and through its newly founded online brokerage.

Direct online solicitation, often called a Direct Public Offering (DPO), became possible when the SEC passed what is known as Regulation A. Regulation A allows the short form of registration, which requires simpler financial statements and does not require periodic reporting. However, the amount of money that can be raised under Regulation A is capped at $5 million. The other major difference between an IPO and a DPO is that an IPO requires the use of an underwriter or investment bank and the involvement of registered brokers/dealers for handling the securities.

Three basic steps give a simplified overview of the online DPO process:

1. The company posts a description of the potential stock offering on a Web site to gauge the level of investor interest. The description includes a summary of the offering and a response form.

2. If the company feels that there is sufficient interest (received through the response form), it files the required offering statement with the SEC. This starts the official waiting period, generally 60 days, during which the company may make no public announcements that may affect the sale of the stock.

3. If the offering statement is accepted by the SEC, the SEC notifies the company that sales can begin. Emailed announcements are sent to all the interested parties to view or download. Sales can be charged to the investor's credit card. The only physical document required by the SEC is a confirmation letter to the investor.

Like the traditional offering memorandum, the online version contains background information about the principals, a description of the risk factors, and an outline of the company's intended business and strategy, as well as other financial information. Unlike the traditional offering, the online counterpart can include multimedia elements, such as digitized video or slide show presentations with voiceovers and sound tracks. Wit Capital refers to these presentations as a virtual roadshow.

As you might suspect, one of the leading advantages of an online versus a standard IPO is cost—you can go public over the Internet for a lot less money. Part of the cost savings, those in documentation and distribution, you can probably guess from similar savings identified throughout this book. However, a major savings comes from the lack of any broker's commissions or underwriter's fees, which can range anywhere from 7-15% of the gross amount raised. Table 23.1 breaks down the relative costs for an offering that brings in $1.6 million.

Table 23.1 Cost Comparison Between a Standard IPO and an Online IPO

Activity	Standard IPO	Online IPO
Broker's commissions (10%)	160,000	0
Underwriter's Fees (10%)	160,000	0
Legal Fees	110,000	110,000
Prospectus	80,000	5,000
Accounting Fees	60,000	60,000
Roadshow Expense	62,000	5,000
Public Relations	5,000	5,000
Registration Filing Fee	320	320
Total Costs	**637,320**	**185,320**
Net Proceeds	**$963,680**	**$1,414,680**
(from $1.6 million)		

Merging and Acquiring

Should your company be more interested in acquiring (or being acquired) than in going public, you'll find a generous supply of resources on the Internet to assist you. Business brokerages—whose focus is on facilitating the buying and selling of companies—have taken to the Web in great numbers. The Yahoo! search engine lists more than 50 brokerages, many with multiple offices located around the country.

One of the most useful sites for either a buyer or a seller is M&A Online (`www.maol.com`). Here you can search for companies in many subcategories, such as Agriculture, Mining, Manufacturing, Finance, Retail, Services, Transportation, or Wholesale. You can also limit your search to a specific region of the country or widen the criteria for international businesses. Finally, you can search for companies that match a particular revenue standard—from under $2 million to over $50 million. The results of your search, a sample of which is shown in Figure 23.2, briefly describe the company for sale and show its annual revenue, as well as its EBITDA (short for Earnings Before Interest, Taxes, Depreciation, and Amortization). Additional data, including contact information, is available online for a minimum charge. Any company for sale can be listed on M&A Online free of charge.

Figure 23.2 Business brokerages, such as M&A Online, are beginning to post their listings of companies for sale on the Web.

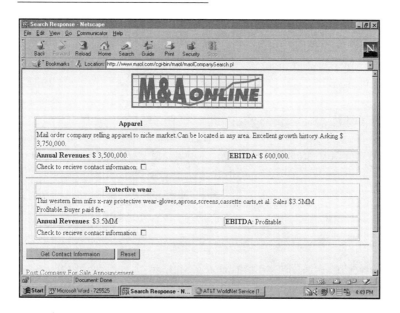

Increasing Valuation

If you're thinking of selling the business—or merging with another company—you'll need to provide any serious potential buyer with a statement detailing the worth of the business. Generally, this is known as a valuation. One of the key benefits of a fully (or even partially) realized Internet/intranet strategy is an enhanced valuation. Such a company is easier to manage and maintains higher profit margins; therefore, it is worth more to others.

Case Study: Technology Builders, Inc.

Technology Builders, Inc. is a privately held Atlanta-based software products and services company providing integrated customer solutions comprised of software products, training, and professional services. Currently, the company maintains a client base of more than 150 companies, many of which represent the Fortune 1000.

Bringing in Investors

Some companies looking for a cash infusion opt to bring in additional investors. Technology Builders, Inc. (TBI) was one such company. As it moved from being a reseller into becoming a software publisher, it realized that it needed to take on additional partners to get the needed equity. TBI contracted with an investment banking and consultant firm, Ambassador Capital Corporation, to provide valuation services necessary to complete the transactions.

As it began to perform its due diligence on TBI, Ambassador Capital discovered that the company was heavily invested in a sales force automation program. TBI's tight integration of its front and back offices offered three significant advantages in a valuation. First, Ambassador was able to increase its valuation from 14% to 28%—primarily because the SFA approach enabled TBI to forecast enhanced sales targets with great accuracy. Second, the very nature of the SFA implementation, with access to sales history and lead tracking, enabled the company to demonstrate how it had developed and met previous forecasts. Third, the SFA strategy included a full-featured customer response mechanism. This further bolstered the image of the company as one with a firm grasp on its market.

SEE ALSO

➤ *For more about Sales Force Automation, see page 269.*

A buyer or an investor looks not only at what a company has done in the past, but also what it anticipates doing in the near future. This is, after all, where the payoff lies. An Internet/intranet strategy, such as the one undertaken by TBI, strengthens the valuation of a company's past and offers validity to the predictions for its future.

Directory of Business Web Sites

This appendix is a list of business resources you can find on the Internet. Whether you're just in the planning and startup phase of your business, involved in international trade, need legal or accounting assistance, or interested in the latest trade shows and conferences, you'll find a Web site here that can help you find answers.

Advertising

Advertising Age

http://www.adage.com

Advertising Age has been providing marketing, advertising, and media news for more than 65 years in print, and it brings a substantial site to the World Wide Web. Browse news and feature articles, including Bob Garfield's "Ad Review," find marketing/advertising conferences and events, or do a search on one specific product or advertising term to find all related articles. Interact in message-board style with others on advertising issues and commentary. This is a highly interactive and graphics-intensive site, so make sure you're accessing at the highest possible speed, or be patient.

Advertising Law (University of Texas)

http://www.utexas.edu/coc/adv/research/law

This page (hosted by the University of Texas) states that it is intended to supplement, not replace, Lew Rose's popular Advertising Law Internet Page (reviewed later in this chapter), and that some of the links are to resources on that site. Whereas Lew Rose's site focuses on law, this site includes a lot of good information on ethics in advertising, including deception, subliminal appeals, and self-regulation.

AdWeek, BrandWeek, and MediaWeek

`http://www.adweek.com`

A review of general advertising resources would not be complete without a discussion of the AdWeek/BrandWeek/MediaWeek site. Although this site is geared toward big business and advertising agencies, some of the information and advice here—particularly the "Anatomy of an Ad" and "Q&A" in the Features section—can be extrapolated to smaller businesses. The best way to experience success is to model success, and you can base some of your own advertising/marketing on what the "big guys" are doing, often without investing big guy money. Skip the NewsWire section unless you're just dying to know which big name signed which big-name agency for what reason.

AGAnet Glossary

`http://www.AGAnet.com/html/glossary.html`

If you're looking for a glossary of production terms so you can speak intelligently about the subjects of collateral or advertising production with your vendors or agency, be sure to visit this page. It's provided as a service to Internet users by AGA, an advertising agency specializing in catalog and direct-marketing design and production. The glossary is alphabetized and linked so that you can select any letter of the alphabet to go immediately to that glossary location. This site is a handy resource if you're confused by discussions of "ascenders," "mortise," and "soft dot," to name a few.

IPSOS-ASI Marketing Research Center

`http://www.asiresearch.com`

The IPSOS-ASI Marketing Research Center offers a comprehensive list of links to advertising agencies with a World Wide Web presence, in case you're looking for agency assistance with Web advertising. They also provide free market research publications such as "Advertising's Role in Managing Brand Equity" and "Secrets of Related Recall—What Makes A Great Commercial" at `http://www.asiresearch.com/freepubs/pubs.htm`. Additional information is available on such diverse subjects as copyright and testing copy for children's advertising from the index page, `http://www.asiresearch.com/index/ndx.htm`. This is a substantial site for substantial advertising information.

Getting Free Publicity for Your Small Business

`http://www.kciLink.com/brc/marketing/v1n2.html`

Dheeraj Khera, principal of Khera Communications, a Web site development services company whose clients include Kodak, the Smithsonian Institution, and the U.S. Department of Agriculture, provides an article entitled "Getting Free Publicity for your Small Business." Although it's short (less than one Web page) it offers detailed information on how to create a press release.

Electronic Data Interchange (EDI)

DISA

`http://www.disa.org/`

DISA (Data Interchange Standards Association) was formed in 1987 to be the secretary for the Accredited Standards Committee X12 (ASC X12); it also administers the Pan American EDIFACT Board (PAEB). In layman's terms, DISA serves as the centralized clearinghouse for EDI standard development and discussion. Its site includes an EDI reference desk that discusses EDI in simpler terms and links to all the relevant standards and standards boards. Use the site map (`http://www.disa.org/sitemap.html`) to navigate this site.

Electronic Commerce World

`http://pwr.com/ediworld/`

Electronic Commerce World is a monthly publication covering trends and management of electronic commerce solutions. The January, 1997 feature article discussed how Elizabeth Arden jump-started its EDI programs so that within 24 months, more than 70% of its business transactions were processed using EDI. Unfortunately, archives of past articles aren't available, but an online subscription sign-up form is. Subscription rates are reasonable, and EC World also sponsors many conferences and seminars. An enormous list of EC Association links is also included.

Harbinger

`http://www.harbinger.com/resource/`

Harbinger is a developer of EDI translation software and has one of the best EDI sites on the Web. The most valuable part of the site is the EDI Standards section. Observing the standards when developing EDI applications increases the likelihood of finding a vendor who can do business with you. Harbinger's site links to all the relevant standards and papers on EDI. Also included is a mini case study on how Staples (the office supply chain) implements and manages EDI transactions. Harbinger's Resources area includes listings of EDI events and other resources, such as mailing lists, network providers, and organizations.

San Antonio Electronic Commerce Resource Center

`http://www.saecrc.org/`

The San Antonio Electronic Commerce Resource Center (SAECRC) site helps vendors deal with the transition of many government agencies to EDI. However, even if you don't sell to the government, this site can be useful. The SAECRC offers training classes and seminars, a useful FAQ, free downloads, and a list of VANs (value-added networks). One of the most useful features is a downloadable guide to EDI that is actually an interactive tutorial that walks you through EDI terms and EDI implementation. The tutorial only runs on Windows. The entire site is written in easy-to-understand terms, which makes it a great place to start.

International Business and Trade

Asian Connection—Singapore Network Services

`http://www.asianconnect.com/home.shtml`

Asian Connection is a meta site for links to Asian business resources. Although the site as a whole is slanted toward Singapore resources, its Trade & Business Opportunities section is a collection of excellent sites, divided by country, for most Asian nations. Unfortunately, no direct link is available from the home page to this great list of resources. To reach it, go to `http://www.asianconnect.com/trade/trade1.shtml`. Another area of the site, the Singapore Business Directory, is a joint venture between Singapore's Department of Statistics and Singapore Network Services. It provides links to more than 80,000 Singapore-based businesses, and invites U.S.-based organizations to use this area to search for potential business partners and to establish trading contacts with companies located in Singapore. This site also offers links to Singapore-based recruiting companies, the National Library of Singapore, the Singapore National Chamber of Commerce, and This Week Singapore.

Asia-Pacific Business Browser

`http://www.nikkei.co.jp/enews/BB`

The Asia-Pacific Business Browser is run by Nihon Keizai Shimbun, or Nikkei for short. Nihon Keizai Shimbun is the self-proclaimed primary business information source for top corporate executives and decision-makers in Japan. NikkeiNet's Business Browser site is created in English and provides information of interest to anyone doing business in the Asia-Pacific region. This site is quite extensive and is updated frequently. Links are provided here to its English language newspaper, *Nikkei Weekly*, Asia-Pacific company Web sites (divided by country), Asia News Stand, and rankings of Asia-Pacific companies. This site has a very user-friendly interface, and it includes a user guide, a search utility, and clear explanations of the information that's available in each area of the site.

Australian Trade Commission

`http://www.austrade.gov.au`

This site, created and maintained by the Australian Trade Commission, exists to promote trade between Australia and other countries around the world. Although the site is not easily navigable, a wealth of information is available, including extensive lists of Australian businesses and corporations, trade statistics, major trade events, and incentives for investment in Australia.

BizWeb

http://www.bizweb.com

This is a meta site with links to businesses in many industries, both in the United States and abroad. A keyword search feature at the site makes finding specific companies easy. Searching for "international and trade," for example, returns a list of more than 50 businesses, including trade lead generators, law firms, information brokers, and global financiers.

Business Week

http://www.businessweek.com

The offline source for U.S. and international business information is a well-stocked online information source as well. *Business Week* provides the full text of each current issue online, including international sections not available in the printed version. It also includes searchable archives from October, 1995 to the present. Go ahead and add this site to your short list; you won't regret it.

CommerceNet

http://www.commerce.net

CommerceNet is an organization that exists to promote global electronic trade via the Internet. If your company is interested in exploring the issues, opportunities, and benefits of online commerce, this site is an excellent place to start. Included is a monthly newsletter, *Buzz*, information on CommerceNet's Global Partners Program, and links to sister organizations based in other countries. It is also an information clearinghouse for issues related to electronic commerce. Follow the link to Jumpstation for a meta list of products and services related to Internet-based business in the areas of graphic resources, Internet technology, people and groups, news and information, and Internet directories. Also, spend some time at the iStore to see firsthand what technologies are being used to facilitate electronic commerce. This area is provided mainly for member evaluation and review of member-created solutions, so the selection of items is limited. However, several CommerceNet publications, logo items, and audio tapes are available.

Commercial News USA

http://www.cnewsusa.com/

Are you an exporter looking for a reliable source of current information? The Department of Commerce will help your business locate foreign trade partners and assist with direct export sales, human resources, licensees, and more. Commercial News USA boasts 140,000 screened subscribers and 2,000,000 bulletin board users in 155 countries. Although posting export information requires payment, viewing export opportunities is free.

Dow Jones Telerate

http://www.djmarkets.com/

This well-designed site is a one-stop source for monetary and financial information world-wide. Features of this site include Today's Global Market Snapshot, Global Financial Market News, and up-to-date commentary. Click Technical Data for global information specific to your international market of choice, and try out Quick Quote for daily information on your favorite stock. Telerate's Foreign Exchange Calculator is a must see, providing real-time exchange rates for 34 international currencies. Also, although Telerate's BanxQuote service provides only U.S. bank information, it is worthwhile to see—if you have the time. This service provides current interest rates for major banks, as well as links to U.S. sources for online banking services. Links to for-fee products and services are also available, as well as links to other Dow Jones sites.

Ecola Newsstand

http://www.ecola.com/news/

This site contains links to the online versions of more than 3,300 printed publications, which have been filtered by the maintainers of this site to include only those publications which allow unlimited access, are presented in English, and are frequently updated. The links are divided into three categories: newspapers, magazines, and computer publications. Navigation for each area is slightly different. Choose **Newspapers** to view a list of countries. Select **Magazines** to view topic categories, and scroll down the page to select from the list of countries. The full text of newspapers from more than 50 countries and of magazines from more than 30 countries are available for viewing online. This site is a valuable resource for anyone doing business with a foreign country.

The Electronic Embassy

http://www.embassy.org/

A product of TeleDiplomacy, Inc., the Electronic Embassy is a window to the world of foreign government, overseas businesses, trade organizations, and foreign affairs. The information provided here will arm you with both official and unofficial information on your country of interest. Especially useful is the list of all embassies located in Washington, D.C. Each listing provides contact information and a link to the embassy's Web site, if it has one. Use this site also for obtaining official government data, such as updates from the U.S. State Department's Foreign Affairs Network, the U.S. Information Agency, the CIA, and the U.S. Department of Agriculture's Foreign Agricultural Service.

EUROPA—European Commission

`http://europa.eu.int/`

Interested in doing business in Europe, but don't know where to start? You need look no further than EUROPA, the site established by the European Commission on behalf of the European Union. This site provides high-level information on the Union and the Commission, as well as links to EU offices around the world. Brush up on your foreign language skills, however, before visiting these offices, because many deal only in the local language.

ExportNet

`http://www.exporttoday.com/`

This sister site to the print publication *Export Today* is, in its own words, a "tool to help people and companies worldwide profit in the new global economy." This modest statement, however, doesn't begin to describe the variety and depth of information and services available at the site. ExportNet's intuitive interface and design make it easy to navigate throughout the site and encourage interactivity. In fact, you'll find forums and matchmaking opportunities in several areas. The Spot Market, Export/Import Services, and Matchmakers areas, for example, allow free listings of buy, sell, and barter opportunities, as well as services listings. Read the list, or post your own opportunity here. Paid listings at the site provide additional services, such as real-time lead generation and custom marketing services.

Freightworld

`http://www.freightworld.com/`

Freightworld is a transport information clearinghouse with links to airlines, logistics providers, transportation software and technologies, warehousing, postal services, railroads, seaports, and trucking services, to name a few. The site is divided into several areas, including classifieds, finance and leasing providers, laws, news and weather, and suppliers. This is a great place to find providers for shipping and related needs, thanks to frequent updates and solid links.

GlobaLink—Singapore Trade Development Board

`http://www.tdb.gov.sg/`

From Singapore import and export information to Singapore-based travel and trade associations, GlobaLink is a great place to stop. This site, which was created and is maintained by the Singapore Trade Development Board, will be useful to exporters, travelers, and organizations currently trading with Singapore-based organizations.

How Far Is It?

`http://www.indo.com/distance/`

This is a distance service provided online for cities around the world. Enter the names of two cities and have it calculate the distance. Also, the two cities are marked on maps from Xerox's PARC research center. The distances provided are as the crow flies, so it may not be the best source for actual transport mileage information. The service can also be used, however, to determine the geography of a particular location and to locate multiple cities of the same name.

International Business Network's Global Index of Chambers of Commerce and Industry

`http://www1.usa1.com/~ibnet/chamshp.html`

Looking for local commercial information in other countries? This comprehensive list offers a direct link to chambers of commerce around the world. Additionally, you can find information on GBX (The Global Business Exchange), the Consortium for Global Commerce, the Global Management Center Trade Information Network, the International Bureau of Chambers of Commerce, and more.

International Chamber of Commerce

`http://www.iccwbo.org`

ICC Business World presents news and information of interest to everyone involved in international trade. Learn about ICC's commissions, which are made up of experts from the world's major corporations and business organizations, and whose business is addressing critical multinational trade issues and making policy recommendations to governments and intergovernmental organizations. ICC's International Court of Arbitration works to resolve international commercial disputes, and it hosts seminars and other events to educate interested organizations. Use the ICC National Committees Worldwide area to contact the national committees of the International Chamber of Commerce in any of the 63 countries where the ICC is represented. Other ICC concerns include ICC Commercial Crime Services, which provides prevention counseling to companies based on internal research, as well as ICC Publishing and ATA Carnet System.

International Finance Corporation

`http://www.ifc.org/`

If your company is interested in establishing trade in a developing country, the International Finance Corporation is here to help. Whether your business is in need of financial assistance, risk management, or professional advice, this member organization of the World Bank

Group provides expert services to both governments and private sector companies. This site details the resources available, procedures for engaging with the IFC, and ongoing projects in which private organizations can participate.

International Monetary Fund

http://www.imf.org/

The role of the International Monetary Fund is, in short, to promote international monetary cooperation. A much more descriptive definition is available at the site, along with statements on the changing international economic environment, guidelines for IMF financing, surveillance initiatives, and a comparison of the IMF and the World Bank. This site is well-organized and well-maintained, making it easy to find the information you need. A search engine at the site locates all IMF references to your specified topic or issue. Great insight into U.S. trade relations with other industrial nations is also available here, including tables providing current data on trade deficits and surpluses and commodity prices. Also useful is information on U.S. lending to other countries via the IMF.

International Trade Banking Services—BankAmerica

http://www.bankamerica.com/corporate/corp_intltradeov.

BankAmerica offers convenient information and leads into its services for importers and exporters and provides an attractive range of services to its customers, including collection and credit services and government incentive programs.

International Trade Centre—United Nations

http://www.unicc.org/itc

Whether it is information on legal aspects of foreign trade, statistics on trade, market news, or trade contacts you need, stop by the International Trade Centre for the answer. This organization, built on the foundation created by GATT, operated by the World Trade Organization (WTO), and acting through the UN Conference on Trade and Development (UNCTAD), is the well-connected organization directly responsible for implementing projects for trade promotion with developing countries and economies in transition.

International Trade Law

http://ananse.irv.uit.no/trade_law/nav/trade.html

This site is a one-stop source for anything and everything you may want to know about laws relating to international trade. Winner of several awards, this is one of the most comprehensive sources on the Internet. It includes meta lists of treaties and multinational organizations, in addition to extensive information and the complete texts of customs regulations, interpretations of laws, and current news.

InterTrans

http://www.itlink.com

This Washington, D.C.-based firm specializes in translation and export management services. Whether your translation needs are for manuals, Web pages, or software, InterTrans can help. Its export management services can assist your company in research and feasibility studies to actual promotion and distribution of your products in overseas markets. And check out the Professional Trade Leads area for the Import/Export Bulletin Board, which includes links to business opportunities, success stories, and offers to buy and sell.

Irish Trade Web

http://www.itw.ie/ (Requires Shockwave plug-in.)

What are the benefits of creating operations in Ireland? Why have many American companies set up manufacturing bases in Ireland? What incentives are offered for trading in Ireland? This member country of the European Union (EU) is not only compact, but it is a gateway to all European markets. A table of trade statistics offers great insight into Ireland's economy, and Trade Web's "Best U.S. Export Prospects" takes the guesswork out of deciding what products and services are encouraged by Ireland to do business there. Get in-depth information from the sections on Irish trade shows and exhibitions, taxes, and resources for business travelers. You are also invited to participate in Business-to-Business, a forum for matching importers and exporters, which is a bulletin board for free postings of opportunities and trade requests related to Ireland.

I-TRADE—International Trade Resource and Data Exchange

http://www.i-trade.com/

Exploring international trade opportunities is interesting, but how do you really get started? Where can trading partners be found? How can a country's current events affect your company's profitability? Is electronic commerce feasible? What about marketing overseas? I-TRADE has the answers to these and other questions. Targeted toward organizations new to international commerce, I-TRADE seeks to provide a guide to businesses as they go through the process of establishing trade with other countries. Additionally, I-TRADE's Index to Free Services is a meta list with excellent descriptions and links to organizations providing free services online.

Japan External Trade Organization (JETRO)

http://www.jetro.go.jp/top/index.html

Visit the home of the Japanese organization dedicated to the promotion of mutually beneficial foreign trade and economic relations to learn about Japanese export and investment assistance programs, economic information, statistics, and the Asian Trade Promotion Forum. Important documents relating to Japanese culture, trade, and business practices will come in handy for those not familiar with the Far East region, including "Negotiating with the Japanese," "Distribution in Japan," "The Japanese Consumer," and "First Steps to Exporting in Japan." Remain abreast of current events by reading *Focus Japan* and *Tradescope* magazines, each published monthly and available in its entirety at the JETRO site.

Japan Window

`http://jw.nttam.com`

This site, originally developed jointly by Stanford University in the United States and by NTT in Japan, operates with the purpose of providing Internet-based information on Japan. Resources available at Japan Window are not limited to business, but include cultural, travel, technological, and government information and links as well. With the wealth of information available here, this is not a site that can be fully explored in a single sitting.

John R. Borchert Map Library

`http://www-map.lib.umn.edu/map_libraries.html`

Increase your geographic awareness at this meta site for maps, map libraries, and map organizations around the world. Link to political maps, atlases, topographical and natural resource maps, to name a few.

Journal of Commerce

`http://www.joc.com/jocweb/`

If you've been relying on the printed version of the *Journal of Commerce*, this site presents the opportunity for electronic delivery of this trade and transportation resource. Although a subscription is required for viewing any complete issue, the full text of JOC's front page stories and special sections are presented here. Also, current oil prices from several sources is a single mouse click away from the home page, as are comprehensive listings of industry events, such as trade shows, seminars, and conferences. Subscribers to JOC are also entitled to download Electronic ShipCard, which enables daily database updates of sailing schedules.

Maximov Online—Your Window on Russia and the New Independent States

`http://www.maximov.com/`

In addition to providing basic geographical, cultural, and economic information on the former Soviet Union, Maximov Online does an excellent job of bringing together sources of news and events for a continually current stream of information on Russia and the Independent States. Links to Interfax, World Watch Russia, and the Federal News Service, as well as

Executive Search Russia and the Adam Smith Institute, are brought together in this single interface to bring Russia to your desktop.

Mexico Information Center

http://www.mexico-trade.com/

The Mexican Information Center site is maintained by the Mexican Bank for Foreign Trade, Bancomext, the Mexican federal government's leading financial institution for channeling of credit, promotional services, and assistance in obtaining guarantees for the cultivation of foreign investment in Mexico. At this site, you will find a descriptive list of government agencies, a directory of Mexican exporters, and a comprehensive guide for U.S. importers and exporters called "Mexico Business Opportunities and Legal Framework." You can also use the Trade Center area to locate Mexican export opportunities in dozens of categories. Other points of interest at this site are links to Mexican Trade Commission offices, a calendar of Mexican trade shows, lists of legal resources, news and current event publications, and extensive sources of NAFTA information.

NAFTAnet

http://www.nafta.net/

Just about anything you may want to know about the North American Free Trade Agreement (NAFTA) is available here, including a special area devoted to electronic commerce and electronic data interchange, better known as EDI. An extensive list of trading opportunities is available in the Global Contact area, with postings arranged by SIC code. If your needs include transportation and logistics services, NAFTAnet provides a search function for private sources of trucking, brokering, warehousing, and freight-forwarding services.

National Institute of Science and Technology (NIST)—Technology Services Information System (TESIS)

http://ts.nist.gov/

Have you considered how the differences in U.S. standards and the standards of other countries can affect your company's ability to trade with them? How universal are our codes? Does U.S. accreditation in a given field have meaning in Spain? Differences in the ways countries operate, and in the practices and standards they support, can result in significant barriers to trade for U.S. companies. NIST eases the burden associated with these differences, in part through its programs, such as Standards in Trade and the Small Business Innovation Research Program. The work of TESIS also includes services—some of which have been created specifically for use by small businesses—such as the Global Standards Policy and Standards Information programs. Other services, such as technology evaluation and commercialization assistance, aid in the advancement of technological innovations.

Organization of American States (OAS) Trade Unit

http://www.sice.oas.org/Tunit/tunite.htm

The OAS is a regional organization within the United Nations, representing 35 North and South American states, which exists to promote dialog throughout the hemisphere on political, economic, and social issues. The Free Trade Area of the Americas (FTAA) section of this site, called "The Trade Unit and the FTAA," provides high-level technical support to working groups of the OAS. Browsing through the FTAA Process area provides background documents on trade relations between member countries and current initiatives. Follow the link to the Foreign Trade Information System for a compendium of practical information, including trade statistics, trade leads, and country-by-country guides on how to do business within their respective borders.

Pacific Basin Research Center—Harvard University/Soka University of America

http://www.ap.harvard.edu/

The modest home page at this site belies the wealth of information available here. Information on all Asian countries is provided by the PBRC, which is part of a Harvard University post-doctoral program. Follow the links for Asia in the World Economy and Working Papers to access country- and region-specific trade, economic, and cultural information.

Polyglot International—Translation and Localization Services

http://www.polyglot.com/

Because approximately 90% of the world's population does not speak English, language differences may create barriers to your international business goals. Polyglot International is a private firm specializing in language services, multilingual communications, and cultural consulting. Polyglot has assisted such clients as Boeing, SyQuest, and Dupont with one or more of its services, which include translation, localization, interpreting, and creative writing, in more than 100 languages, including Chinese, English, French, German, Italian, Japanese, Portuguese, Russian, and Spanish. Polyglot calls itself "an integrated language services company," and it provides language services across all industries.

Saudi Arabia Royal Embassy

http://www.saudi.net/

Looking at business opportunities in Saudi Arabia? There's no better place to start your research than the Royal Embassy of Saudi Arabia. Included in this site's offerings are a profile of Saudi Arabia and its government, details on Saudi-U.S. relations, information on travel to Saudi Arabia, monthly publications addressing current events, and local news and embassy press releases. To pre-empt a long wait for the home page to load, it may be a good idea to turn off graphics before loading this page.

Small Business Administration—Office of International Trade

http://www.sbaonline.sba.gov/OIT/

This is another excellent starting place for A to Z information on establishing trade with other countries. With its focus on small businesses, the Office of International Trade presents information on trade finance programs, export information for beginners, trade missions, and links to publications, export assistance centers, and special programs for women-owned companies. A meta list of international resource links is also available, including pointers to trade leads, periodicals, and international directories.

South Africa Online Guide

http://www.southafrica.net/

Changes in South Africa's government and economy make it an appealing place for American companies to do business. Learn about U.S.-South Africa relations and opportunities for U.S. businesses and investors. Governmental and general reference information, as well as links to news and cultural events, will help you decide if South Africa should be your next destination for international expansion.

Stat-USA

http://www.stat-usa.gov

Stat-USA, a service of the U.S. Department of Commerce, serves as an information clearinghouse for economic, trade, and business data, which is compiled from more than 50 U.S. government sources. Although a subscription is required for access to all areas of the site, such as the National Trade Data Bank and trade leads, useful information is still available to nonsubscribers. Daily Economic News, for example, provides foreign exchange rates, and is a great source for up-to-the-minute economic facts. Complete past issues of the Stat-USA newsletter are also available.

Taiwan Products, Manufacturers, and Suppliers

http://manufacture.com.tw/

Looking for import opportunities? If you are looking for something in particular and you know it is made in Taiwan, this site can probably lead you to it. This collection of hundreds of Taiwan-based manufacturers is divided by category and frequently updated, increasing your chances of finding the product you seek. Browse through the product showcase by category to see the available selection, or view this week's featured companies. You can also check out the Trade Services area for assistance in importing to or exporting from Taiwan. If your need is specific and immediate, visit the Taiwan Trade Opportunities forum, which enables posting and reading of current opportunities. Choose from the areas "Offer to

Buy," "Offer Business Service," and "Offer to Sell." No charge is made for either viewing or posting information.

TradeAccess Business Information Service

`http://www.tradeaccess.com`

TradeAccess presents a searchable index of manufacturers and trade groups via an innovative search feature for Pacific Rim countries. Search through a single country or a combination of countries using the same interface. Links are also available to the various trade sources themselves.

Trade Compass

`http://www.tradecompass.com/brief/`

This site is, by far, the most comprehensive online source of current and historical international trading information and services. Although a subscription is required for total site access, browsing through the site will lead you to accessible information in a number of areas, such as the Trade Compass Daily Brief, Trade Gateway, and Featured Companies, to name a few. A free trial is also offered for temporary access to all site areas, which include daily coverage on international trade issues, a marketplace, online chat, a search library, an air cargo tracking service, a Q&A forum with Trade Compass staff, insurance services, a logistics management system (EDI interfacing with U.S. Customs), and more. Attempting a comprehensive list of information and service areas at this site would be too long for the space allowed in this guide. Suffice it to say, if you're engaged in international trade or interested in exploring trade opportunities, this is a must-use site.

Trade Show Central

`http://www.tscentral.com`

Participation in overseas trade shows can jump start your organization's involvement in a foreign marketplace and can be a good barometer for the level of local interest in your company's products or services. If this is the approach you choose to take, your first stop should be Trade Show Central, which is constantly updated, and which provides both summaries and detailed entries on more than 30,000 trade events around the world.

TradeUS

`http://www.tradeus.com/`

This site proclaims that it provides "Everything you need to know about...importing from the U.S.A., plus information on trade leads, regulations, trade shows, transportation, trade stats, trade magazines, and much more!" More specifically, information offered includes credit checking, technical safety standards, finding a partner, and marketing. TradeUS also provides a bulletin board for U.S. company postings of trade inquiries and opportunities, and it enables viewing of foreign postings as well.

Travelocity

http://www.travelocity.com

Travelocity is an online travel service for individuals and small businesses. Use this online reservation service to directly book flights, cars, and hotels around the world. Descriptions accompany just about every listing, regardless of the category or destination city. And if you choose to create a profile, Travelocity will remember your reservations and preferences.

Union of International Organizations

http://www.uia.org/

Since 1910, the Union of International Organizations has been providing information on international organizations and their global challenges. This site provides an easily navigable interface to more than 40,000 international organizations and constituencies. This information clearinghouse, based in Brussels, Belgium, contains valuable data and tools for research and decision-making. If other international sites fall short of providing the information you seek, this one is certain to have it, or at least to provide the pointer to it.

United Arab Emirates Internet Pages

http://www.middle-east-pages.com/uae/uae.html

With a page design similar to that of Yahoo!'s, you will easily find your way around the United Arab Emirates Web site. Search throughout the site for specific information, or browse information by categories, which include business and economy, government, reference, news, regional, and society and culture. Follow the links to Compass Middle East News, the Khaleej Times Newspaper, or Gulf News for current information on business, politics, and more. Reference information at the site includes maps, libraries, and Middle East search engines. And learn about cities such as Dubai, Abu Dhabi, Sharjah, Al Ain, and Fujairah. Government information includes information on housing, women's organizations, social services, and more.

United Nations Development Programme

http://www.undp.org

If your international trade interests are balanced with charitable motives, this site provides all the information necessary to get started. With links to local and regional offices of the UN Development Programme in areas including Malaysia, China, Estonia, and Jamaica, you can find out about specific program activities and regional activities, and learn more about the locale from the UN's perspective. Mailing lists are available for delivery of current news and information by request as well. Follow the link to "Other UN and Related Organizations" for an extensive list of international organizations including the International Monetary Fund, the UN International Computing Centre, the World Symposium on Trade Efficiency, the International Labour Organization, the UN Conference on Trade and Development, and more.

United Nations Trade Point Development Centre and Network

`http://www.unicc.org/untpdc/`

Targeted at supporting international trade by small and medium-sized companies, this site is part of a larger initiative from the United National Centre for Trade and Development. Through this site, private and public sector organizations worldwide are working to eliminate barriers in six main areas: customs, banking and insurance, business information, business practices, transport, and telecommunications. UNCTAD's mission, to harmonize trade procedures worldwide, has received a boost from the proliferation of the Internet. Navigation from the home page at this site is not dependent on the graphically intensive menu, so you may want to configure your browser to read text only before visiting this site.

U.S. Chamber of Commerce

`http://www.uschamber.org/`

Need to stay up-to-date on international issues and how they are affecting your business? Browse the latest publications via an online catalog of informational books and periodicals. Link to the quarterly newsletter for the International Division Information Center (IDIC), and look through publications for purchase, including titles such as International Business Quick Reference Guide, ISO 9000: An Introduction for U.S. Business, Directory of Chambers of Commerce Abroad, and Directory of Local Chambers of Commerce Which Maintain International Trade Services. Reference materials are provided for conducting business in Europe, Latin America, Asia and the Pacific, and the Middle East. The site also provides a searchable database of news and media releases, as well as information about its broadcasting services and production facilities, a guide to available training services, and a directory of chambers of commerce and other professional associations worldwide.

U.S. Customs Service

`http://www.customs.ustreas.gov/`

The U.S. Customs Service is responsible for enforcing U.S. import/export law through regulation of goods and services entering and leaving U.S. borders. The Import/Export area details regulations, quotas, procedures, and an increasing number of automated systems for brokering, paperless cargo, manifest documentation, and more.

U.S. Department of State

http://www.state.gov

For a wealth of official information regarding current relations with other countries, treaty affairs, support for U.S. businesses, background information on various countries, travel advisories, and foreign policy, visit the Department of State site on the World Wide Web. If your company has placed U.S. employees overseas, the Department of State can help with determining the proper amount for their daily allowance, cautions to observe, areas to avoid, and how to enlist local embassy assistance in overseas transactions. In addition to a comprehensive library on issues of state, publications, including *State* magazine and *Dispatch* magazine, are available, as are links to foreign affairs mailing lists and sites.

U.S. Information Agency International Home Page

http://www.usia.gov/usis.html

A knowledge of the foreign territories where your company proposes to do business will prove essential for success. Tactical and strategic plans should be built upon keen insight into the culture, current events, and issues faced by the people who will be purchasing your company's products or services. This site, an information clearinghouse for government-produced publications, reports, initiatives, and contact information of international interest, consists of hundreds of pages of data, links, and services online. Reports on the global information infrastructure and protection of intellectual property, resources for women, and current international crime alerts are just a sampling of the information available.

U.S. International Trade Commission

http://www.usitc.gov

Charged with providing objective trade expertise to the executive and legislative branches of government, the International Trade Commission Web site offers a host of news releases, reports, *Federal Register* notices, and other publications. Petitions and complaints are also included, which offer a gauge of current trade issues involving U.S. companies and industries.

U.S. International Trade Statistics

http://www.census.gov/foreign-trade/www/

Creating the business case for your company's foray into international business? Need current and historical information to support your company's decision to trade in a particular foreign country? The U.S. Census Bureau's foreign trade site presents current and historical international trade information, including press releases and trade reports, regulation letters, a who's who of foreign trade, and the list of the United States' top trading partners. Statistics of U.S. exports, categorized by Schedule B classifications, are information you can use to support your case. Export services are also offered via the Automated Export System, and a downloadable Shipper's Export Declaration form is available, along with special reports for orders and links to other services.

The World Bank Group

`http://www.worldbank.org`

Does your organization qualify for one of the World Bank Group's 40,000 contracts won by private companies each year? The World Bank Group, established more than 50 years ago, seeks to cultivate global economic growth and social progress. This site presents the organizations existing under the World Bank Group umbrella, such as the International Bank for Reconstruction and Development (IBRD), the International Development Association (IDA), and the Multilateral Investment Guarantee Agency (MIGA), along with their associated services.

World Wide International Government Sites

`http://www.lgu.ac.uk/psa/intgovt.html`

Using an imagemap interface, link to governmental and political information about an area of the world you select. Get details on organizations and institutions within that area and link to other topics, such as equal opportunity employment and labor policies. Links are also available to multiple media sources dealing with affairs in your selected geographic region.

Intranets

Building a Corporate Intranet

`http://webcom.com/wordmark/sem_1.html`

This online seminar, written by Ryan Bernard, discusses the age-old problem of distributing information in a corporate environment and how the use of Web technologies can overcome these roadblocks. Bernard gives excellent examples of the potential applications of intranets in disseminating information. The seminar can be downloaded in its entirety or viewed section by section.

Building the Case for Your Intranet

`http://www.pcweek.com/archive/960429/pcwk0052.htm`

This article by Valerie Rice appeared in *PC Week* and profiles the intranet experience of Cargill International, the world's largest privately held corporation. Rice talks about how a small group of IT people quietly launched a small intranet page and waited to see what happened. As users raved about the application, the IT team got more management support for the concept. A more formal team was established and the intranet was officially sanctioned. Cost justification tips are also included in the article.

Complete Intranet Resource

http://www.intrack.com/intranet/

This site has a section on all things intranet-related, including FAQs, discussions, vendor lists, white papers, and firewall resources. One of the more innovative sections is called the Intranet Help Desk, where visitors post more complicated questions, which are then answered and posted to the area. The only drawback is the questions aren't indexed or sorted, so you have to scroll through them to look for your answer. The site even has a huge case study of a company that has recently implemented an intranet, covering the entire implementation process and lessons learned by that company. This site definitely earns its "Complete" title.

ComputerWorld—Intranets

http://www.computerworld.com/intranets/

The quote from its mission statement says it all: "We commit to providing the best, most objective, hype-free, user-focused coverage we humanly can." Read the great case study on Banc One's intranet project, which includes flowcharts and even a RealAudio clip. The Getting Started area gives you a few bullet points on setting up an intranet, including defining what you consider groupware.

Fortune—Building an Intranet

http://pathfinder.com/fortune/specials/intranets/index.html

This article originally appeared in a *Fortune* magazine special advertising section. The four sections are great—covering why, what, who, and how in easy-to-understand terms. The article cites a survey that indicates that 22% of U.S. companies are already using Web servers for internal applications, and another 40% are considering it.

Hummingbird Communications—The Intranet

http://www.hummingbird.com/whites/intranet.html

The official title of this document takes too long to type, but it's a fairly complete listing on the whats, whys, and hows of implementing an intranet. The introduction covers the benefits, and the remainder of the document covers the technologies, who's implementing what, user needs, the basic building blocks, and basic desktop requirements. Print this document and refer to it often.

The Intranet 100

http://techweb.cmp.com/iw/606/intranet.htm

This online special edition from CMP Media's Tech Web site evaluates what's going on with intranets, and it profiles companies that have taken the plunge. "The Revolution" article discusses the experience at 25 companies, such as Rockwell, HBO, Burlington Coat Factory, and others. Also profiled are the top 25 hardware and the top 25 software vendors for intranet applications. The top 10 opportunities for intranets are also profiled. Security issues are discussed in the Battle Scars site reviewed earlier.

The Intranet—A Corporate Revolution

http://www.intranet.co.uk/papers/intranet/intranet.html

Wow! What a paper! Written by surfCONTROL, a subsidiary of JSB Computer Systems, it makes a case for intranets. The language tends to be a bit stuffy, but the content is first-rate. Discussed is the impact of intranets on corporate efficiency and communication, along with the technologies that could help corporations. The case for intranets as a way to quickly disseminate information is bolstered by a discussion of the demands on business today: short product life cycles, evolving markets, increased cost pressures, and more. The authors discuss the differences between intranets and the Internet, as well as some of the technologies involved.

Intranet Design Magazine

http://www.innergy.com/

This is the site for Intranet Design Magazine by Innergy, Inc. If you're looking to design your own intranet or want to check up on what your intranet designer is recommending, this might be a good site for you. They've got discussions of intranet standards, events, news briefs, and samples of various Web development tools.

INTRAnet Handbook Page

http://www.ntg-inter.com/ntg/intranet/intra_in.htm

NTG International, a Canadian networking company, brings you this page on intranet issues. The entire site is no more than links to other sites, but the links are worthwhile. Take a trip to the case studies on other businesses who have implemented intranets. Find links to companies that consult on intranets and those that have products to make it work. And don't forget to link up with companies that can make your intranet more secure.

The Intranet Journal

http://www.intranetjournal.com/

The Intranet Journal is one of the best top-level sites for people interested in intranets. They've got news, opinions, links, FAQs, a toolbox, and even an area called Intranet 101 for those who want to learn more. The Toolshed area includes downloadable software to use on your intranet, such as training programs, development tools, and applications that can help you integrate some of those legacy systems into your intranet. Its Soundings message board helps keep you in touch with others involved with setting up and maintaining an intranet.

Intranet Security Roundtable

http://www.infosecnews.com/article7.htm

Infosecurity News brought together representatives from various organizations to discuss how they are dealing with intranet security issues. The discussion shown is rather free-form, but it is grouped into relevant areas, such as security needs, data ownership, intranet-to-Internet access, standards and policies, and control. Change management is also discussed. The entire discussion is excellent because it allows several experts to share their opinions as well as tell how they have handled these intranet issues.

Intranets—How the Web Is Used Within Enterprises

http://www.cio.com/WebMaster/sem3_intro.html

This online seminar from the creators of *WebMaster* magazine covers all the relevant topics related to intranets. As you move from slide to slide, you can read about the benefits of creating an intranet, some companies that are using intranets, and the challenges creators might face. The biggest drawback to this worthwhile presentation is that you have to view each slide. No top-level table of contents exists.

Intranets-IS 698: The Information Superhighway

http://sd.znet.com?~zoro/is698/index.html

Why such a strange title to this page? It was created by Craig McLaughlin, a master's-level student at Hawaii Pacific University. Skip all the links and head straight for the research paper. Four companies were studied to evaluate the before and after effects of implementing an intranet. McLaughlin's results indicated that the most benefits were derived when a company had inefficiencies to begin with. You will have to request the complete paper, but it appears to be worth it.

Intranet White Paper: INET '96

http://www.process.com/intranets/wp2.htp

This lengthy paper prepared for the INET '96 annual meeting contains a wealth of information about who is creating intranets, why they are being created, and how it's happening. They cite a survey that showed that only 34% of corporations have no plans to create an intranet, and that intranet service license sales in 1995 were 55% compared to traditional Internet servers. One of the key intranet benefits cited is reduced time to market.

Surf & Turf: Amoco's Intranet Implementation

```
http://www.cio.com/archive/webbusiness/0796_amoco_1.html
```

This article from *WebMaster* magazine shares the trials and tribulations Amoco Corporation went through when it implemented its intranet. How do you put new technologies in place without jeopardizing corporate mandates and policies? The article walks readers through the initial months, from what applications were developed first (directories and phone listings) to the real meat—document sharing.

Understanding the Intranet

```
http://www.reengineering.com/articles/mar96/mkcnct.htm
```

Intranets do more than just move information through an organization; they can contribute to process reengineering. This article by Russ Haynal appeared in Enterprise Reengineering. By changing the flow of information, intranets can give companies the chance to change business processes and eliminate inefficiencies.

WebMaster Intranet Resource Center

```
http://www.cio.com/forums/intranet/
```

Although the site might be dedicated to Webmasters in charge of running Web sites, the Intranet Case Studies section will help you better understand how a variety of companies implemented their intranets. Be sure to check out their What We Learned section to learn what is going on in the world of intranets. Don't miss the Reports section where recent seminars, case studies, and experiences are profiled. After all, it always pays to capitalize on the experiences of others so you don't make the same mistakes.

Legal and Regulatory

American Law Source Online (ALSO)

```
http://www.lawsource.com/also/
```

This site is notable because it has links to all American online legal systems, including the federal judiciary and all 50 states and territories. ALSO has equally far-reaching coverage of Canadian and Mexican law.

Business Law Site

`http://members.aol.com/bmethven/index.html`

Sponsored by Methven & Associates, the Business Law Site covers federal and state statutes, as well as legal research sites for both business and high-tech law. You can also find a full compendium of tax forms, information on international law, and a list of legal research sites.

Corporate Counselor

`http://www.counselconnect.com/corporate_counselor/`

The Corporate Counselor has resources including daily news columns and articles on employment law, securities, antitrust, and other business issues.

Department of Labor Poster Page

`http://www.dol.gov/dol/osbp/public/sbrefa/poster/main.htm`

A fixture in every American workplace finds its online equivalent: the Department of Labor mandatory notices. So far, you can download posters for the minimum wage requirements, OSHA, the Family Leave Act, and the Equal Opportunity Act. All posters are in PDF format; you'll need a PDF reader such as Adobe Acrobat (`http://www.adobe.com`).

International Trade Law

`http://itl.irv.uit.no/trade_law/`

You can search this site (sponsored by the Law Department at Norway's University of Tromsø) for virtually any subject related to international trade law. Typical topics include Dispute Resolution, Customs, Protection of Intellectual Property, GATT, and other free trade treaties.

The Legal Information Institute

`http://www.law.cornell.edu/`

Sponsored by Cornell University, the Legal Information Institute Web site houses its collection of recent and historic Supreme Court decisions, hypertext versions of the full U.S. Code, U.S. Constitution, Federal Rules of Evidence and Civil Procedure, and recent opinions of the New York Court of Appeals, complete with commentary. It's fully indexed and searchable.

QuickForms Online

`http://www.quickforms.com/`

QuickForms is an easy-to-use interactive system that drafts sophisticated agreements automatically weighted in your favor. Answer a few questions online and you have your draft agreement in 10 minutes. A wide range of contracts is available.

Marketing and Market Research

American Demographics/Marketing Tools

`http://www.marketingtools.com/`

At the American Demographics/Marketing Tools Web site, you can check out consumer trends, tactics and techniques for information marketers, or access *Forecast*, a newsletter of demographic trends and market forecasts.

American Marketing Association

`http://www.ama.org/`

AMA is a national organization of marketing professionals. Its Web site features a special section on Internet marketing ethics, as well as a calendar of events, publications, and information on regional chapters.

Business Intelligence Center

`http://future.sri.com/`

What type of person is your customer? The Values and Lifestyles (VALS) program at SRI Consulting, hosts of this site, studies consumers by asking questions about their attitudes and values. You can answer an online questionnaire to determine your VALS type—and see how you fit with other consumers.

Business Wire

`http://www.businesswire.com/`

Business Wire is a leading source of news on major U.S. corporations, including Fortune 1000 and NASDAQ companies. You can look up a company, category, keyword, or region and find all the pertinent business news. You can sign up for its service online.

Commando Guide to Unconventional Marketing and Advertising Tactics

`http://199.44.114.223/mktg/`

This online reference covers such topics as how to market survey your competition, doing your own professional marketing and business plan, referral systems, barter exchanges, print advertorials, and telemarketing.

First Steps: Marketing and Design Daily

`http://www.interbiznet.com/nomad.html`

Developed by the Internet Business Network, First Steps contains a rich source of articles on market research and industry analysis regarding business-to-business transactions. Much of the marketing and design work is Internet oriented.

International Public Relations

http://www.iprex.com/

IPREX specializes in international public relations. Its areas of expertise include business-to-business, crisis management, energy and environment, and technology. Its news section has valuable information on public relation trends.

Market Facts and Statistics

http://www.mightymall.com/sevenseas/facts.html

This 1996 survey covers the countries of the world by population, gross national product, and growth rate. Each country has a small paragraph on its economy and markets. The information is organized by major regions: Asia, Western Europe, Central Europe, Middle East, Atlantic, and West Indies.

Marketing Resource Center

http://www.marketingsource.com/

Sponsored by the Concept Marketing Group, the Marketing Resource Center maintains an articles archive with more than 250 business-related articles. Its Tools of the Trade section links to an association database and software for general business and project management.

Sales Leads USA

http://www.abii.com/

This site is run by American Business Information, Inc., which specializes in generating company profiles. Free services include searching for businesses or people by name with American Directory Assistance or searching by type of business with American Yellow Pages.

Selling.com

http://www.selling.com/

This site is dedicated to salespeople and their needs. Here you'll find a collection of selling concepts and exercises written by salespeople for salespeople.

Sharrow Advertising & Marketing Resource Center

http://www.dnai.com/~sharrow/register.html

You have to register at first to visit this site, but it's well worth it; the Advertising Parody section is worth the time by itself. The BizInfo Resource Center has an overview of database marketing, a direct-mail profit spreadsheet, and information on approaches to integrated marketing.

U.S. Census Bureau

http://www.census.gov/

The Census Bureau is a great site to gather social, demographic, and economic information. The site has more than 1,000 Census Bureau publications featuring statistical information on such topics as the nation's population, housing, business and manufacturing activity, international trade, farming, and state and local governments.

World Business Solution

http://thesolution.com/

The World Business Solution is a free marketing manual available from TheSolution.com. One section is devoted to downloadable reference.

Travel and Transportation

Airlines of the Web

http://w2.itn.net/airlines/

Where can you find a list of all the airlines, both passenger and cargo? At the Airlines of the Web site, of course. Passenger airlines are categorized by region, and you can also find airline-related information such as 800 numbers and a link to a real-time reservation service.

American Airlines

http://www.aa.com/

The American Access Web site takes a full-service approach. Here, you can plan your travel, check out Advantage frequent flier miles, take advantage of the NetSaver fares, and download Personal Access, American's Windows-based software program that brings you dedicated Advantage information, travel planning, and up-to-the-minute information and specials.

American Movers Conference

http://www.amconf.org/

The American Movers Conference is an association of 3,000 professional moving companies in the U.S. Its site has information on how to prepare your move, how much a "self-haul" might cost, and lists of movers across the country.

Continental Airlines

http://www.flycontinental.com/

Continental On-Line's main claim to fame is its C.O.O.L. Travel Assistant, which can be used to schedule and book airline travel on Continental, Continental Express, and Continental Micronesia, as well as more than 40 rental car companies and 26,000 hotels around the world.

FedEX

http://www.fedex.com/

Not only can you now track your overnight package online, but you can also use FedEx's interactive rate finder, and even ship packages via the Internet to more than 160 countries from the U.S. and Canada. A searchable database offers locations of drop-off sites and downloadable software for managing your shipping, including the airbill printing.

HomeBuyer's Fair

http://www.homefair.com/home/

Although most of this site is dedicated to helping you buy or sell your home, the HomeBuyer's Fair has some amazing interactive tools in its Popular Exhibits area. A Salary Calculator compares the cost of living in hundreds of U.S. and international cities, a Moving Calculator figures the cost of a move, and a Relocation Crime Lab compares crime statistics.

InterKnowledge Travel Network

http://www.interknowledge.com/

When your business takes you to an exotic locale—meaning you've never been there before—stop by the InterKnowledge Travel Network site first. The site includes beautiful images and full details on geography, culture, and climate.

Northwest Airlines

http://www.nwa.com/

This Northwest Airlines site has information on CyberSavers, its online low-cost tickets, as well as regular travel and frequent-flier information. A full slate of vacation packages rounds out the site.

U.S. Air

http://www.usair.com/

Tune into the U.S. Air Web site to schedule and book a flight or check your frequent flyer miles. An extensive area of the site is devoted to its U.S. Airways Cargo service, where you can use the software to track shipments with real-time information from airport drop-off to pickup.

United Parcel Service

http://www.ups.com/

Interactive functions featured at the UPS site include package tracking, cost-estimating, a drop-off locator, and pick-up scheduling. UPS also makes available free software for all these functions as well as up-to-the-minute zone and rate charts.

Trade Shows and Conferences

EventSeeker

http://www.eventseeker.com

EventSeeker's site enables you to do two things: locate trade shows and events that you can participate in, or put your advertising on the EventSeeker site. EventSeeker's site is aimed at a large audience interested in knowing what special events are happening around the world. They suggest that if you are looking for a quick, cost-effective way to target business and leisure travelers or special-events seekers, you can reach a segmented market by placing your ads at specific locations on the site. Rates for banners or linked buttons are reasonable (beginning at $750). Keep an eye on this site. Right now it's still growing (a search for trade shows and events relating to telecommunications for the year 1997 brought up no matches), but it could become a valuable resource over time.

EXPOguide

http://www.expoguide.com

The principals of EXPOguide are Jacqueline G. Labatt-Simon, President of Exposition Research, Inc., and Chris Labatt-Simon and Michael Ferioli of D&D Consulting, an established provider of Internet Integration and WWW design, implementation, and management. A powerful search engine incorporated on the site, with specific searching tips on the page, enables you to search for trade shows, conferences, and seminars either alphabetically, by date, by geographic location, or by concept. A search on "small business" netted more than 40 trade shows and seminars with a small business focus. They also provide a small number of links to trade show resources and classified ad services relating to trade show support. This site is a valuable resource for small and medium-sized businesses interested in advertising their products or services through the trade show outlet.

CD Information

http://www.cd-info.com/CDIC/Industry/TradeShows.html

Today, much of computing and information storage and retrieval revolves around the CD-ROM. This site is CD-centric and lists many upcoming exhibitions, conferences, seminars, and workshops in a month-by-month format.

Guide to Unique Meeting Facilities

http://www.theguide.com/

A terrific resource for meeting planners, the Guide to Unique Meeting Facilities covers colleges and universities, retreat centers, camps and lodges, cultural and historical venues, as well as traditional conference centers. A Hot Date/Cool Rate area highlights facilities with open, economical dates.

Trade Show Central

http://www.tscentral.com/

Sponsored by the International Association for Exhibition Management, Trade Show Central gives you easy access to information on more than 30,000 trade shows. Its searchable database links to an email notification service where you can request more information. Its AudioNet connection broadcasts and archives keynote speeches from major events.

Wall Street Directory

http://www.wsdinc.com/index.html

Wall Street Directory offers a wide range of information for traders and investors. To see its up-to-the-minute conference information, select the Seminars-Shows-Conventions category and click the Search by Category button.

EventWeb

http://www.eventweb.com/

A free mailing-list service for meeting, conference, and trade show promoters. Sample articles include "How to Exhibit at a Virtual Trade Show," "Expanding Educational Horizons in the Online World," and "Promote Your Speakers—Inexpensively!"

Tradeshow News Network

http://www.tsnn.com/

The Tradeshow News Network enables you to search for a trade show in the United States by location, date, or industry. Its Trade Show Education department offers tips both on exhibiting and attending, as well as an Ask the Expert section.

Glossary of Internet Terms

A

Access An area of an Internet security policy that determines who can retrieve what information and what they can do with it.

Active Desktop A feature of Internet Explorer 4 that controls the appearance and feel of your Windows desktop. Additionally, the Active Desktop integrates the Internet Explorer browser with the desktop.

ASCII format A format for electronic files that uses only text characters and can't be used to store text attributes or graphics images.

Authentication A process that occurs behind the scenes during an SSL transaction that makes your sure your identity matches the one shown in your digital certificate.

Autosearch A special browser feature that enables you to type a simple search query directly into the Address box.

B

Bandwidth The amount of data you can send through a network connection at one time. Bandwidth is usually measured in bits-per-second (bps).

Bidding agent A software program that automatically enters and raises bids at online auction sites.

Binary files Files that are stored in computer code so the computer can understand them quickly. Program files, graphics, and zipped files are examples of binary files.

Bookmark   A site address that's recorded within a browser so you can return to it quickly. Browsers provide a list of bookmarks to which you can add sites you want to revisit. Internet Explorer refers to bookmarks as "Favorites."

Browser   A program used to navigate the World Wide Web. The browser controls the look of the Web documents and provides tools that enable you to move from one Internet location to another. Internet Explorer and Netscape Navigator are examples of Web browsers.

Browser-based email   A way to send and receive email using a Web page instead of a standard email program.

Bug   A problem or error in a program that's typically discovered after the program has been released commercially.

C

Cache   The area on your hard drive where temporary information is stored. Web pages you've viewed are stored in your browser's cache.

Certificate Server   A host computer (or the software) on a network that handles authentication requests for information from it.

Channel   A Web site that's updated with new information. The updated information is sent to users who have subscribed to the channel.

Channel Definition Format   Microsoft developed CDF as a standard format to be used by all Internet channel content providers. Netscape does not use CDF format, but has its own Netcaster channel format.

Client   A remote computer connected to a host or server computer. It also refers to the software that makes this connection possible, which is often called a browser.

Compressed   A term that describes a file that has been compacted, significantly reducing its size. Compacted files take less time to copy and less space to store. Files you download from the Internet are often compressed. See *decompressed*.

Computer virus   A computer virus is a malicious program that is concealed inside another file or on the boot sector of your computer. When you use the file, the virus can harm your computer by destroying data and making your system inoperable.

Contact Manager   Software used to organize client information including addresses, phone numbers, schedules, and to-do lists.

Content Advisor   An Internet Explorer feature that enables parents and other adult supervisors to limit children's access to sites on the Internet based on the content of the sites.

Cookie   The exchange of information between your browser and the site you're visiting. A cookie can contain your name, your company name, your location, the type of computer you're using, your operating system, the type and version of your browser, and the Web pages you've visited. Cookies are stored on the hard drive of your computer.

Cross-posting   The practice of posting the same message simultaneously to a number of newsgroups. See *spam*.

Cybermall   A Web site that contains an online collection of merchants.

D

Decompressed   Files that are compressed in size to reduce transmission time or hard drive space on your computer must be inflated before they can be used. Programs such as WinZip are designed to decompress the files you copy from the Internet. See *compressed*.

Denied person   According to the Bureau of Export Administration, a denied person is a person or company forbidden to export from the U.S.

Digital cash   Similar to the principle of a checking account, you submit information to an electronic merchant who uses that information to get cash from your account.

Digital certificates   A personal certificate that identifies you or the vendor during secure business transactions. Because digital certificates add an extra layer of security, they are not required for most Web transactions.

Digital signature   Electronic messages can be authenticated by a digital signature. Digital signatures are another way to assure the recipient of an electronic message that the message is coming from a particular source.

Digital video camera   A camera that records the pictures on computer disks, rather than on film.

Directory server   A listing of people who are available to participate in an Internet conference.

Disintermediation   The process by which a company sells its goods directly to customers, without going through the usual retail outlets or another middleman.

Dithering   The process of mingling dots of existing colors to create new colors.

Domain   A set of network addresses that are organized in levels. The top level identifies geographic or purpose commonality (for example, the nation that the domain covers, such as "ca," or a category, such as "com"). The second level identifies a unique place within the top-level domain. Lower levels of domain may also be used.

Domain name Also known as the host name, the domain name is a unique identification for a Web site's address. Each computer on the Web has a domain name that distinguishes it from the others. Domain names are registered with a central authority, such as InterNIC.

Dot Pronounced "dot," the period character that separates portions of a URL, a newsgroup name, or an email address. The dot character also separates portions of domain names and IP addresses. For example, microsoft.com is pronounced "Microsoft dot com."

Download To copy a file from another computer (usually a server on the Web) to your computer.

Drivers Software that serves as an interface to some hardware that's connected to your computer. Printer drivers, for example, are needed by your computer so that it can successfully "talk" to the attached printer.

Dumb terminal A computer that's attached to a server and can only run programs through that server. When you attach to a Telnet server, for example, you can only use your keyboard and monitor because the program on the server is in control.

E

Electronic Data Interchange (EDI) A system used between business partners to exchange manufacturing, vendor, and sales information in a standard format over a private network or the Internet. EDI can also be used to authorize electronic fund transfers.

Electronic Software Distribution (ESD) The use of the Internet to deliver electronic goods.

Electronic wallet A software program that enables consumers to store credit card information in an encrypted form and access it when buying goods online.

Email A system in which users can send and receive messages through their computers. Users have their own "mailboxes" that store messages sent by other users. When you open an Internet account with an ISP, you're provided with an email address.

Email survey An online marketing technique that uses the email system to send and receive questionnaires.

Encryption A way of making data unreadable to everyone except the recipient. An encrypted message must be decoded before it can be read.

E-résumé An electronic version of a résumé that's designed to be stored on a computer.

Extranet An intranet to which access has been granted to users outside the company. Many companies grant business partners access to selected pages on their intranets.

Favorites   A list of marked sites in Internet Explorer to which you can return quickly.

File extension   The suffix that follows a computer file name. The file extension generally identifies the file type. Most executable files (the ones that run programs), for example, carry an .exe file extension.

Firewall   A program, usually an Internet gateway server, that protects an intranet from users from other networks. Firewalls can also limit the Internet sites accessible to users who are accessing the Internet from their company's connection.

Frames   A browser feature that enables a user to split a Web page into separate, scrollable windows.

Freeware   Software programs that you can download and use for free.

F

FTP   Short for File Transfer Protocol, a set of rules, or protocol, that controls the transfer of files between computers. Files can be transferred by other Internet protocols, including http://.

G

GIF file   Pronounced "jiff file" or "giff file," it's a graphics file format that's used in many Web pages. GIF (short for Graphics Interchange Format) was developed by CompuServe. GIF files are great for storing graphic information with a limited range of colors while maintaining a small file size.

Global Positioning System (GPS)   A means of determining the physical location of any transmitter-assisted object through orbiting satellites. Some logistics programs use GPS to track goods en route.

Gopher   An older Internet program that is based on a hierarchy of menus and submenus.

Groupware   Software designed to allow individuals to work together by sharing files and applications.

GUI   Pronounced "gooey," this is a graphical user interface that enables you to easily interact with a computer via pictures and menu-driven options for performing tasks. Typically, you use your mouse or other pointing device to make choices in a GUI program.

H

Hardware token   Authenticates remote users and allows them secured access to sensitive information.

Home page   The first page of a Web site. It usually serves as an index or table of contents for the rest of the site.

Hyperlink   A word, picture, or other element that you click to move from one Internet location to another. Hyperlinks, usually called *links*, can help you jump to a different location on the same Web page or to a different site.

Hypertext Markup Language (HTML)   A simple programming language used to create Web pages. The set of "markup" symbols or codes placed in a file that's designed for display on a Web browser program are HTML.

I

Intelligent agent   A software program that uses artificial intelligence routines to perform a specified task. Intelligent agents can "learn" from choices made by their users or the subsequent results.

IMAP   Short for Internet Message Access Protocol. IMAP is the most current standard protocol for receiving email messages from the mail server. It provides options such as viewing only the header or storing the messages you've read on the mail server.

Internet Service Provider   Often called an ISP, a company that provides individuals and other companies with access to the Internet.

Internet Society   Known as the ISOC, a nonprofit, nongovernmental organization located in Reston, VA, that brings users of the Internet community together. Visit the ISOC at www.isoc.org on the Web.

Internet telephony   The use of the Internet, rather than the traditional telephone company infrastructure and rate structure, to exchange spoken or other telephone information.

Intranet   A company's private internal Web site that lets only the people inside that company exchange and access information. An intranet usually looks much like any other site on the World Wide Web.

IP address   The unique number that's assigned to each computer connected to the Internet. IP addresses are written as a series of four numbers separated by periods.

IRC   An Internet system for live chatting that involves a set of rules and conventions and client/server software.

J

JPEG file   Pronounced "jay-peg," this file type is commonly used on Web pages for storing graphics files that contain a full range of colors. JPEG is an acronym for Joint Photographics Expert Group. The file extension .jpg is used to indicate a JPEG file.

K

Key   In a secure business transaction, the key is actually the code used to scramble and unscramble the information—your credit card number, for example—as it's sent over the Internet and received by the merchant.

Keywords   Words that highlight or describe. In a search query, the keywords describe what you're looking for. In an e-résumé, keywords are the nouns that highlight your special talents, skills, and experience.

L

Local Area Network (LAN)   A group of computers that is connected, usually at a company, school, or government branch.

LDAP   An email protocol, LDAP (Lightweight Directory Access Protocol) stores and retrieves directory information. Generally, LDAP enables you to search through Internet directories from your Personal Address Book.

Link   See *hyperlink*.

Listserv   A software program that sends posted messages to everyone on a specified list via email. Listservs are often used as collaborative tools.

Localization   The process of converting a Web site or software program to different languages local to one or more countries.

Lurking   Hanging back and reading the postings of a newsgroup without replying to or submitting any new postings.

M

Mail servers   Electronic postal agents that send, sort, and deliver email messages using special mail protocols.

Meta-search engine   A powerful search tool that looks through multiple search tools to match your search query.

Micropayment   Electronic transactions of small amounts, generally from less than one cent to $10.

MIME   *Multipurpose Internet Mail Extensions*—an extension to the traditional Internet mail protocol that allows binary, or non-text, files, (that is graphics, executables, audio files and so on) to be sent as attachments to regular email messages.

Mirror site   A server that duplicates all the files available on another Web site, usually employed in high-traffic situations.

Modem   Short for MOdulator-DEModulator. A device that enables computers to communicate over a standard telephone line. It translates digital computer information into analog format for transmission, and back again for reception.

N

Narrowcast   The act of using the Internet or intranet to transmit digital video and audio to a select group.

Netiquette   The conventions of politeness expected by Internet users. Although netiquette technically covers the use of the Internet, it's most often referred to in conjunction with newsgroups.

Network News Transfer Protocol   Often called NNTP, the server your Internet service provider uses for news.

Newsgroups   Themed Internet bulletin boards for users who share a common interest. Messages are posted to a newsgroup and can be read and replied to by all members of the group.

Newsreader   A special software program that enables you to read and reply to Internet newsgroup postings. Both the Internet Explorer and Netscape Communicator suites feature newsreaders. If neither of these suit you, you can choose from a number of third-party newsreader programs.

Notification services   Services offered by Web sites to alert subscribers of news, information or new products.

O

OCR software   Computer programs that are designed to convert scanned graphics images into text documents. OCR stands for optical character recognition.

Online auction   Web sites that allow visitors to bid for merchandise against other visitors. The merchandise can either be offered by a manufacturer, reseller or other consumer.

Online backup service   A service that enables you to have data from your hard drive backed up on another, remote computer via the Internet.

Online financial transfer   Electronic transactions using credit cards or electronic cash systems.

P

Page designer   A professional company or individual who designs Web pages for a fee.

Patch   A software program designed to correct problems or errors in an existing program or to extend the power of the initial program. A patch for Internet Explorer, for example, was designed to correct security errors in the original release of the program.

Payback period   The time it takes for the project to return enough money to cover the investment.

PICS   Platform for Internet Content Selection. A group of people from all walks of life who screen Internet sites and rate the content.

Plug-in   A program that is linked to your browser and extends its capability. Plug-ins usually open in the same window as your browser.

POP3   Short for Post Office Protocol 3, the POP3 protocol deals with the way incoming messages are handled on the mail server. After you read a message that's been stored on a POP3 server, the message is deleted from the server (although it can be stored on your computer).

Portal   A Web site used primarily as visitor's home page or entry to the Internet.

Private key   Used in secure business transactions, the private key is a random number that's known only by one party or the other   the merchant or the browser.

Profile   A file used by your browser to hold all your personal settings and preferences. Individual profiles are especially helpful if more than one person is using the same browser program on a single computer.

Protocol type   The rules that computers follow to store and transfer data over the Internet. HTTP:// is the most common protocol, but you might see GOPHER:// or FTP://.

Public key   Used in secure business transactions, the public key is a random number that's known only by your browser and the merchant, or to whomever you give it.

Push technology   A technology that delivers information to your computer at preselected times. You can read the information while your computer is still connected to the Internet, or you can disconnect and read it later.

R

Résumé bank   A Web site that stores electronic résumés. Prospective employers look through résumé banks to select candidates for positions within their companies.

RSAC   Short for Recreational Software Advisory Council, this independent, nonprofit organization based in Washington, D.C., uses a content advisory system to help parents and educators rate Web sites that may be viewed by children.

S

Scalability   The ability of hardware or software to handle a substantial increase in the amount of usage.

Scannable   A document that's ready to be fed through an electronic device. After a document is scanned, the resulting image file is read by an OCR program and converted to text. See *OCR software*.

ScreenTip   A pop-up explanation of a toolbar button's function that appears when the mouse pointer passes over the button.

Search agent   An automated process that enables specific criteria to be continually monitored and, when met, alerts the subscriber via email. Search agents are often used in online job banks to look for specific positions or candidates.

Search engine   Web sites on the Internet that enable users to search through databases of information and return hyperlinks as results.

Search query   A keyword or phrase used by the Internet search tool to find matching documents on the Web.

Secure Electronic Transactions (SET)   A newly developed standard for making secure credit card transactions on the Internet. Security is achieved by allowing merchants to verify a buyer's identity through a digital signature.

Shareware   Computer programs you can use for free on an evaluation basis, and then pay for if you decide to continue using them.

Signature file   A file that's attached to outgoing email messages and newsgroup postings. Called a *sig*, a signature file can contain address information, a funny or philosophical comment, or a picture drawn with text characters.

Site Map   An overview of all the pages on a particular Web site.

Smart Card   Smart cards look like credit cards but function differently. With the use of an internal computer memory chip, a smart card can be used to store a large amount of information with a maximum amount of security, including everything from medical records to digital cash. To access or alter the information on a smart card, you have to use a smart card reader.

SMTP   Short for Simple Mail Transfer Protocol, SMTP is the protocol that processes outgoing email messages.

SOHO business   Small office or home office business.

Source code   The underlying HTML code that instructs your browser to display a Web page.

Spam   Unsolicited junk email.

SSL   An acronym for Secure Sockets Layer, SSL was developed by Netscape to provide security to buyers and sellers during an online transaction.

Streaming media   Media files, such as video, audio, or animation, that begin playing as soon as the initial data is transferred, instead of needing to be completely downloaded first.

Subscribe   The action of adding a newsgroup name to your regular newsgroup or listserv list so the newest postings are downloaded to your computer.

T

TCP/IP   An acronym for Transmission Control Protocol/Internet Protocol, TCP/IP is the preferred way for data to be transferred over the Internet. The sending computer places the data in packets and then sends the packets out. The receiving computer removes the data from the packets and reassembles the data into its original form.

Telnet   A system that enables you to connect to a server and run programs as if you were sitting at its keyboard.

Thread   An original posting and collection of related responses in a Usenet newsgroup.

U

Unsubscribe   Removing the name of a newsgroup or listserv from your regular list. When you unsubscribe from a group, you no longer receive its postings.

Upload   The act of transmitting a file from one computer to another.

URL Pronounced either "you-are-el" or "earl," the Uniform Resource Locator is the address of a file or other resource you access on the Internet.

Usenet The collection of more than 32,000 Internet discussion groups that post messages to Internet newsgroups. Your ISP might not carry all the Usenet newsgroups.

V

Value-Added Network (VAN) A computer network used to convey electronic data interchange information.

Virtual LAN A method of networking remote users via the Internet instead of using a typical local area network.

Virus A computer virus is a malicious program that hides inside another file or the boot sector of your computer. When you use the file, the virus can cause harm to your computer by destroying data and making your system inoperable.

W

Wallet See *Electronic Wallet*.

Web-based survey An online questionnaire hosted at a specific Web site that is visited by respondents.

Web hosting A company that provides space and services for housing Web sites.

Web Server The computer that actually connects the internal network to the Internet.

Web site A related collection of Web files that includes a beginning file called a home page.

Web ring A group of Web sites that are linked so that you can visit each site, one after the other, eventually returning to the first Web site. Web rings are used to connect sites that share a similar topic (for example, Elvis sightings).

Whiteboard An application in conference software that enables participants to view and/or modify the same image.

Wide-Area Network (WAN) An expanded network of computers physically located in diverse locales.

WYSIWYG Pronounced "wiz-ee-wig," the letters stand for What You See Is What You Get. WYSIWYG Web page design programs show you how the end result will look as the page is created.

Z

Zip A compression scheme used for combining and/or reducing files. Zipped files must be "unzipped," or decompressed, before viewing. See *compressed*.

Index

Symbols

A